UNIX® System V Release 4 Administration, Second Edition

SAMS

HAYDEN BOOKS

Kochan & Wood's

Hayden Books UNIX® System Library

Programming in C, Revised Edition
Stephen G. Kochan

Programming in ANSI C
Stephen G. Kochan

Advanced C: Tips and Techniques
Paul Anderson and Gail Anderson

UNIX® System Security
Stephen G. Kochan and Patrick H. Wood

UNIX® Text Processing
Dale Dougherty and Tim O'Reilly

UNIX® Step-by-Step
Ben Smith

Exploring the UNIX® System, Second Edition
Stephen G. Kochan and Patrick H. Wood

UNIX® System V Release 4 Administration, Second Edition
David Fiedler and Bruce H. Hunter

UNIX® Shell Programming, Revised Edition
Stephen G. Kochan and Patrick H. Wood

UNIX® Networking
Stephen G. Kochan and Patrick H. Wood, Consulting Editors

Related Titles

The Waite Group's UNIX® Communications, Second Edition
Bart Anderson, Bryan Costales, and Harry Henderson

The Waite Group's UNIX® System V Primer, Revised Edition
Mitchell Waite, Donald Martin, and Stephen Prata

The Waite Group's UNIX® Primer Plus, Second Edition
Mitchell Waite, Donald Martin, and Stephen Prata

The Waite Group's UNIX® System V Bible
Stephen Prata and Donald Martin

The Waite Group's Inside XENIX®
Christopher L. Morgan

The Waite Group's Tricks of the UNIX® Masters
Russell G. Sage

UNIX® System V Release 4 Administration, Second Edition

David Fiedler and Bruce H. Hunter

Revised by Ben Smith

Consulting Editors: Stephen G. Kochan and Patrick H. Wood

SAMS
PUBLISHING

A Division of Prentice Hall Computer Publishing
201 W. 103rd Street, Indianapolis, Indiana 46290 USA

We would like to dedicate this book to our wives, Susan Fiedler and Karen Hunter. Without their encouragement, support, long hours of typing, and careful editing, we could not have finished—or even attempted—this book.

— *D. F. and B. H. H.*

The work of the revision is dedicated to Lee Burwell, without whose patience and perseverance this project might have ended differently.

— *B. S. S.*

© 1991 by SAMS

SECOND EDITION
EIGHTH PRINTING — 1994

International Standard Book Number: 0-672-22810-6
Library of Congress Catalog Card Number: 91-061657

Publisher
Richard K. Swadley

Publishing Manager
Joseph Wikert

Acquisitions and Development Editor
Linda Sanning

Managing Editor
Neweleen Trebnik

Senior Editor
Rebecca Whitney

Production Editor
Virginia Noble

Editorial Consultant
Jodi Jensen

Editorial Assistant
San Dee Phillips

Technical Reviewer
Bruce Dawson

Book Design
Scott Cook

Cover Design
Macmillan Computer Publishing

Index
Hilary Adams

Production
Jill D. Bomaster
Martin Coleman
Sandra Grieshop
Tami Hughes
Betty Kish
Bob LaRoche
Sarah Leatherman
Howard Peirce
Cindy L. Phipps
Tad Ringo
Bruce Steed
Susan Tully
Johnna VanHoose
Mary Beth Wakefield
Christine Young

Composed in Garamond and Macmillan Digital by Macmillan Computer Publishing

Printed in the United States of America

Overview

Contents

Acknowledgments

First edition: The authors would like to thank Tom Marshall of tmmnet, Ltd., and Ron and Mary Ann Lachman of Interactive Systems Corp., for their many suggestions. Thanks are also due to Hayden Book Company staffers Maureen Connelly for her great patience and intelligence, and Juliann Colvin Hudson for a great job of copyediting. Jim Joyce of The Gawain Group and Les Hancock must be acknowledged for offering their valuable editing services, even though logistics did not permit this. In addition, we would also like to acknowledge Les and Chris Hancock and Sol and Lennie Libes for warning us about how much work is involved in writing a book. We did it anyway.

— D. F. and B. H. H.

Second edition: Many hardware and software companies provided valuable information and equipment necessary for researching this revision. Special thanks go to Dick Muldoon (and others) at AT&T for System V Release 4 documentation hot off the press. Visual Technologies provided the essential X terminal on which much of the revising was done. Commodore Business Systems provided an Amiga 3000UX with an early version of its VR4 so that we could actually use it. Intel and UHC provided copies of VR4 for i386/i486 computers. The support staff of Santa Cruz Operations also provided substantial help and information. Telebit provided its T2500 modem, the most popular UNIX modem today.

Tom Yager, the pinball wizard of *BYTE* magazine, was most generous with his time in getting us out of some of the twisty little passages of networking. Linda Sanning of Macmillan Computer Publishing was as enjoyable and helpful on this project as any author could wish.

Finally, the quality of this book is due partly to the excellent technical editing of Bruce Dawson and the fine copyediting of Ginny Noble.

— B. S. S.

Trademarks

All terms mentioned in this book that are known to be trademarks or service marks are listed below. In addition, terms suspected of being trademarks or service marks have been appropriately capitalized. SAMS cannot attest to the accuracy of this information. Use of a term in this book should not be regarded as affecting the validity of any trademark or service mark.

Altos is a trademark of Altos Computer System.

Amiga is a registered trademark of Commodore-Amiga, Inc.

AUX is a trademark of Apple Computer, Inc.

Bernoulli is a registered trademark of Iomega Corporation.

BSD is a trademark of University of California at Berkeley.

Centronics is a registered trademark of Centronics Data Computer Corporation.

Coherent is a trademark of Mark Williams Company.

COMPAQ is a registered trademark of COMPAQ Computer Corporation.

CompuServe is a registered trademark of CompuServe Information Services and H&R Block Company.

CP/M, CP/M-80, DEC, Ultrix, and VAX are registered trademarks of Digital Equipment Corporation. DECstation is a trademark of Digital Equipment Corporation.

CRAY is a registered trademark of Cray Research, Inc.

dBASE IV is a trademark of Ashton-Tate Corporation.

Ethernet is a registered trademark of Xerox Corporation.

Frame is a trademark of Frame Technology Corporation.

Hayes is a registered trademark of Hayes Microcomputer Products, Inc. Hayes Smartmodem 1200 is a trademark of Hayes Microcomputer Products, Inc.

HP is a registered trademark of Hewlett-Packard Corporation. LaserJet and HPUX are trademarks of Hewlett-Packard Corporation.

IBM, OS/2, and PS/2 are registered trademarks of International Business Machines Corporation.

Idris is a registered trademark of Whitesmiths, Ltd.

Intel is a registered trademark of Intel Corporation.

Interleaf is a trademark of Interleaf, Inc.

Preface

They've just delivered your new UNIX workstation. What do you do first? How do you make that shiny workstation actually work?

Or maybe you've inherited a multiuser UNIX computer, with fifty users, a disk farm, network connections, and a couple of laser printers. How do you keep those fifty people off your neck?

Perhaps you've been running a UNIX system for years, but you now want to add Usenet news. How do you set it up? How do you keep Newszilla from devouring your disks?

In the past, you'd knock on the door of your local UNIX wizard, who'd perform the proper magic and set your system straight. Now, alas, there's a scarcity of such wizards. Or maybe there are far more UNIX boxes than before.

Here's how you can squeeze by: read this book. Fiedler, Hunter, and Smith show you how to keep your UNIX system happy. They've compiled techniques that once were only rumors and witchcraft.

Once there were standalone UNIX systems. Now, no workstation is an island . . . we're all interconnected. How do you manage your system in such a global community? This book shows you how. Since this book covers X, you'll be able to keep smiles on your workstation windows. The authors hold your hand while you set up mail and show you how to add a new printer to your system. They point out common security holes and tell you how to tighten down your system.

Someday, UNIX systems won't need administrators or wizards. Until then, keep this book near your keyboard. It won't turn you into a wizard, but then, you may not need a wizard after reading this.

Cliff Stoll

Introduction

I f you run a UNIX operating system or compatible, this book is for you.

It doesn't matter if the system is a tiny IBM PC/AT XENIX and you're the only user. Nor does it matter if the system is an IBM 760 under UNIX System V, with 20 modem lines, 15 printers, and a user population of 1,000. Every UNIX system needs someone to take care of it, look after its needs, and sometimes give it love and affection. That someone is usually called the System Administrator (or SA)—a rather formal-sounding title for such a caring position. That someone is probably you!

We'll show you how to do it all as painlessly as possible. Together, we've pulled SA duty on systems ranging from the tiny AT&T UNIX PC to giant Amdahl mainframes, including just about everything in between. We've experienced the challenge of running multiple systems simultaneously and the thrill of having them all *crash* simultaneously. Along the way, we've picked up quite a few tricks and shortcuts, as well as the realization that the job is both easier and harder than you might expect after reading the official documentation. It's easier because once you understand what the manuals are *trying* to say, your job is pretty straightforward. It's harder because no manual (or even book) can prepare you for the endless parade of unusual circumstances you will have to face in what is sometimes referred to as "the real world."

This second edition of *UNIX System Administration*, now entitled *UNIX System V Release 4 Administration*, focuses heavily on the many changes that Release 4 of System V (SVR4) has brought to system administration, even though most of the systems currently in use have not seen SVR4. But this edition is not exclusively about SVR4. As the best-selling book on UNIX system administration for all systems, this edition needs to continue offering information for a wide spectrum of systems.

If you count individual manufacturers' changes (such as Ultrix, HPUX, AUX, and AIX), literally dozens of variations of the UNIX system are available on the market today, even though only about 10 official versions exist. These include the Sixth, Seventh, and Eighth Editions (often referred to as Versions 6, 7, and 8); System III; System V; System V Release 2, Release 3, and the recent Release 4; and Berkeley 4.1, 4.2, and 4.3. This list does not include variants such as PC/IX, UniPlus+, Ultrix, VENIX, XENIX, or any of the UNIX look-alikes such as MINIX, Idris, or Coherent.

Because of the many variations in Bell Labs and commercial UNIX versions, your system may differ in its commands or locations of commands as presented in this book. Because we can't possibly cover everything, out of necessity we have limited this book to the descendants of the original AT&T Bell Labs UNIX operating system. We emphasize the AT&T UNIX System V Release 3 (currently the most popular) but also focus on the newer SVR4 whenever there are major differences. Although you will undoubtedly learn enough here to be able to keep a Berkeley (BSD) system and the related SunOS system running, enough differences between BSD and AT&T UNIX exist that you could possibly get confused. If you *are* trying to run a BSD system by using this book, start by looking at the SVR4 variation, keep an open mind, and prepare yourself for a good number of files to be in different places.

This advice applies to almost everyone. Because each implementation of UNIX is different (even when they're all "standard"), minor differences between this book's examples and your system will probably exist. We've tried to anticipate most of these, but some variations in spelling, file names, and locations are unavoidable. If you listen to the spirit of our words, and don't limit yourself to a literal rendition of each letter, you'll do fine. You learn to be flexible when using UNIX, and that will serve you well when running the system.

That brings us to the anticipated audience of this book. We assume that you already know how to use the UNIX system. But if you are still at the point where you don't know how to log in, look at files, edit them, redirect input and output, and send mail to other users, you're not quite ready to run an entire system. You wouldn't want to run a nuclear power plant if you had trouble plugging in a radio without electrocuting yourself, would you? In this case, we recommend that you read a good introductory book, such as *UNIX Step-by-Step* by Ben Smith (SAMS, 1990), before you start changing things around. (See the Bibliography for other titles.)

Maybe you got this book, though, because you've been told (or have told yourself) that a UNIX system is coming in and *you're going to run it*. Chapters 1 through 6 will help you with getting UNIX started, but we strongly recommend that you learn how to use UNIX before going any further than that. You wouldn't want to risk a meltdown, would you?

Beyond Chapter 6, this book deals with specific aspects of running a system and handling the everyday problems of system administration, such as user accounts, backups, security, terminals, printers, and remote communications. You will need this information if you are administering a system with users besides yourself or if you are connected to other systems, either through a local area network or through serial/modem connections.

You won't find long lists of UNIX commands and their options in this book. You already have such reference material in your UNIX system documentation. This book is meant to be read with your system manuals by your side and your terminal in front of you. Try things out as you read them, and make notes as to how things work differently on your own system. We think you will have fun exploring the system, once you realize that there are ways of doing it without the risk of blowing anything up.

Explore Your Own Unique Style

Don't be afraid to do things your own way once you understand what you're doing. But we recommend that you keep to the general "flavor" of UNIX command naming and use. That way, you can easily work on another UNIX system if necessary. When you write a program to put a new user on the system, whether you call it `newuser` or `adduser` isn't really important, as long as you don't call it `whiffenpoof`.

Certain UNIX traditions, such as leaving vowels out of command names, are not always for the best. Even so, using a traditional UNIX method to solve system administration problems is almost always the best approach, and the traditional method is usually easier to maintain afterward than other methods. If everyone follows UNIX traditions, UNIX systems will continue to be relatively consistent.

Imagine the fun that would develop if you went to another machine and found that the SA there had changed all the major command names and directories. Although such changes would certainly demonstrate the flexibility of the UNIX system, they would not be to anyone's benefit. Do we mean to say that UNIX is perfect as it is and can't be improved? No, but just make sure that any change you make is a real improvement.

The UNIX system furnished with your machine is called the standard distribution. The system administrator's tools are always in `/etc`, major user commands are in `/usr/bin`, and so on. The locations and names of files and commands are dictated by tradition, although UNIX, with its multiplicity of tools, is malleable enough for you to change those locations and names. Individualizing your system is one of the thrills of being a system administrator, but heed this word of warning. As you tailor your system, for the sake of consistency, keep your user areas and homegrown commands away from the standard distribution. (We recommend a directory called `/usr/local/bin`.) Tailor your system to suit your needs, but make it easier to get support from your software vendor and fellow administrators by keeping the standard distribution undisturbed. You will avoid confusion, make life easier on yourself, and have more time to enjoy the rewarding challenges of being a UNIX system administrator.

Conventions Used in This Book

To help you understand the examples throughout the chapters, certain typefaces are used. Language keywords, programs and code fragments, the names of files and directories, system prompts, and all system output appear in a `special font`. Text that the user enters at the prompt appears in a **boldface version** of the special font. On syntax and format lines, variable arguments (which the user substitutes with the appropriate words or values) appear in an *italic version* of the special font. When you see a character combination like $^\wedge D$, that means Ctrl-D—in other words, a combination of the Ctrl key and the D key.

Don't forget that UNIX is case-sensitive; that is, it sees *FOX* and *fox* as completely different words. In examples and listings in this book, when uppercase letters are used, they are special. In general, UNIX commands and arguments appear in lowercase.

1

The System

Administrator's Overview

of UNIX

UNIX is a very special operating system. It is not a manufacturer's system, steeped in hardware dependence and tied by a binary umbilical cord to the whims and fancies of one company. Neither is UNIX limited in application—it is an ideal system for writing, programming, and communications. UNIX is easily the most complete operating system in existence today.

Because UNIX is such a comprehensive system, a well-rounded approach to UNIX system administration is necessary. Remember the parable about the blind men who examined an elephant? One man felt the trunk and concluded that an elephant was shaped like a serpent. Another man felt the legs and determined that elephants were shaped like tree trunks. Both men were partly right, but neither understood the whole elephant. In this chapter, you will look at UNIX from many different angles—UNIX past to UNIX present, a user's point of view and a system administrator's perspective, UNIX internals, and hardware and software considerations. In short, you'll get an overall view of the beast.

What Is an Operating System?

The stock description of an operating system is that it is a large body of software that acts as a "traffic cop" and directs the flow of information to and from the hardware. Although this description is technically true, it brings us back to the elephant-as-serpent analogy. Any operating system, especially one as powerful as UNIX, consists of several different parts:

- *Device drivers* or programs stand at the lowest level and allow control of actual hardware devices. These drivers negotiate between the kernel and the hardware bus.

- A *scheduler* decides which user programs are to be run, when, and for how long. On a primitive operating system such as CP/M-80 or MS-DOS, there is no scheduler because only one program at a time runs under the control of the operating system.

- *Memory management* determines how much memory to allocate for each program. If enough memory is not available to run a given program, the memory manager will move other programs (or parts of them) to temporary disk storage as necessary. This is known as *swapping* or *paging*.

- The *file system* is a structure used to locate and store programs and files on disk.

- *System programs* are the software programs accessible directly by users, enabling them to manipulate files and devices in various ways for getting basic work done. These programs may include utility programs, text editors, language compilers, debuggers, and shells.

Shells

A *shell* is a command processor that is the actual interface between the UNIX kernel and the user. The shell runs commands when you type their names, expands wild-card characters such as * and ?, and takes care of redirecting input and output. Three common shells are available. The first is the *Bourne shell* (written by Stephen R. Bourne), which is the "standard" shell supplied with most UNIX systems. Bourne shell command syntax is reminiscent of the Algol language.

The *C shell* was developed by William Joy at the University of California at Berkeley. As the name implies, command programs written in the C shell resemble programs written in the C language.

More recently, AT&T began distributing the *Korn shell*. This shell combines many of the benefits of the C shell with a high degree of compatibility with the Bourne shell. Using the Korn shell (or the C shell) can offer some advantages to you, as a system administrator or a regular user. One advantage is its history mechanism, which permits the reexecution of complex commands and allows you to see the commands you executed during a login session. This last feature can save you when you get confused about what you did while working late at night. Another advantage is the capability to assign *aliases*, which permit commands to be "tailored" for the local system. The Korn shell has the added feature of a real command line editor, with which you can edit any command in the history list. The command line editor emulates the vi and emacs editors.

Even though the Korn and C shells offer advantages, we strongly recommend that all your shell programs be written in the Bourne shell. They will be portable to *any* UNIX system.

The Kernel

What is generally referred to as the UNIX *kernel* includes the scheduler, memory-management routines, and device drivers, as well as a large number of built-in system functions that are hidden from the casual user. These functions, known as *system calls*, are actually subprograms or primitive functions that are accessible to user programs. The kernel is simply a program called unix that is loaded when the system is started and runs continuously until shutdown.

Portability

Portability is a significant feature because it signals the end of machine-dependent operating systems. Digital Equipment Corporation (DEC) has its VMS, Data General (DG) has AOS, and International Business Machines (IBM) has MVS. All of these work just fine, but only on their own machines. The strengths and weaknesses of machine-dependent operating systems tend to reflect those of the hardware, not the system software itself.

3

UNIX, however, is system-independent. It is designed for portability, so it can run on many machines, from supercomputer to microcomputer. Should you need to change or upgrade machines, the cd command will still change directories on a machine of any size that runs UNIX—an AT&T 3B2/300, a VAX 11/780, an Amdahl 580, or a Cray II. Users can jump from supermicros to minis to mainframes with little retraining if they are all running versions of UNIX. Students coming right out of colleges and universities can enter industry and go to work almost immediately on UNIX because most have been exposed to UNIX at school. Portability, then, is one of the UNIX system's most important and unique features.

C—The Key to UNIX Portability

The traditional view of UNIX is that it is a set of layered spheres, each sphere representing a different level of the system. The outermost sphere represents the users, and the innermost sphere represents the system's hardware (see Figure 1.1).

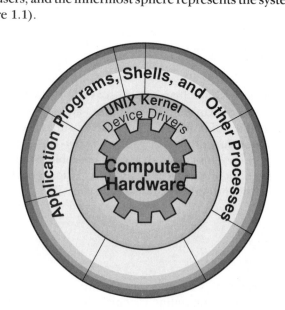

Figure 1.1. *The UNIX kernel provides a common interface between the hardware and the tasks.*

Notice that the layer surrounding the kernel consists of device drivers, which interface between the heart of UNIX (the kernel) and the hardware.

UNIX is portable because most of it is written in the high-level C language with only a small portion in native assembler code. A device driver is divided into two parts: the top end is written in C, and the bottom end is written in both C and assembler. Surprisingly, 90 percent of the UNIX kernel is written in C (and recently, in C++). Assembler sections of the kernel are kept to a minimum, each module consisting of only a few lines of code called by a larger C module. Addressing registers, saving context, and restoring context (the CPU registers and immediate stack) are done from C, not assembler. C is the key to UNIX portability.

To see how vital C is to UNIX, note that porting UNIX to a new processor (target machine) requires only three major steps. The first step is to write a C compiler in that processor's assembly language. (This is the most time-consuming part of the port, which often has been done already, because of the increasing popularity of the C language and the proliferation of C compilers.) The second step is to take an existing version of UNIX that is closest to the new processor's instruction set and to modify the assembler-level code and low-level device drivers accordingly. Once the system can read and write to disk satisfactorily, the third step is to cross-compile the C code on a development computer and then bring the code to the target machine. As more and more of the UNIX system begins running on the target machine, development can continue directly on that machine until all the necessary code has been compiled and tested.

Originally, the only version of UNIX outside of Bell Laboratories was the DEC PDP-11 port. Now many AT&T-supported commercial UNIX ports are available, including the DEC VAX machines, the Motorola 680x0 family of processors, the Intel 80x86 family of processors, and most RISC processors (such as SPARC, RS/6000, Motorola 88000, and MIPS). At the small end of the scale is the little IBM PC and its army of UNIX derivatives, look-alike and work-alike systems (such as QNX, MINIX, and Coherent).

UNIX as a Self-Sufficient Programming Environment

Some mechanical trades allow a craftsman to create his own tools, such as the blacksmith and the machinist. UNIX is like a machine shop, foundry, blacksmith shop, sawmill, and woodworking shop all in one. The variety of UNIX programming languages used with its program development tools makes it an ideal programming environment, powerful enough for developing almost any application. If a certain programming tool is not available, you have everything you need in order to create your own.

Today, most commercially viable business programs, even micro-oriented ones such as dBASE IV, are developed in C under UNIX. A program developed under UNIX takes advantage of UNIX programming tools during the product's development. The tasks of preprocessing, compiling, and linking scores of header files, macros, and programs are kept simple and effortless with make (part of PWB, The Programmer's Workbench). SCCS (also part of PWB) keeps control of the project source code and keeps its documentation manageable and traceable with a minimum of effort. The lint program shows up errors before the code passes through the C compiler. UNIX debuggers find problems that lint misses. Additional UNIX utilities profile, monitor, and trace the program to make it both fast and efficient. Tools to analyze a core dump (should the fledgling program fail), programs to examine the executable code, and programs to examine the data that the code reads and writes are available as support tools.

Once a software package has been developed under a host UNIX system, it is ready to go out to any system where the software is commercially viable. Because the software is written in C, moving it to a new processor or operating system is relatively easy.

UNIX for Writers

UNIX's capability to handle text is well documented. In fact, the first application of UNIX (outside the development lab) was as a multiuser system for Bell Labs' patent writers. For writing a simple letter or creating an entire book, UNIX gives you everything you need. UNIX formatting systems are universal. All are offshoots of a text system called roff and include nroff, sroff, troff, and ditroff. There are commercial variants as well, such as xroff, to take advantage of special hardware like laser printers and phototypesetters. Thus, with UNIX, you can write a book, typeset it, and send it to a publisher, ready for final printing. The original version of this book was produced in this way.

A set of programs is available on UNIX, known collectively as The Writer's Workbench. It includes programs that analyze text for readability, grammatical errors, and adherence to a particular style and level of writing. They can even determine whether text contains sexist words and phrases. A spelling checker is already standard on UNIX.

Now you can find popular word processing programs, such as Microsoft Word and WordPerfect, on UNIX systems. (This revision of *UNIX System Administration* was edited with Microsoft Word.) On the high end are several desktop publishing systems, such as Frame and Interleaf, which take advantage of the capabilities of UNIX graphical workstations. These products enable you to view the layout of each page (including graphics) as you write.

The Communicating System

UNIX is a chatty system. Users can `write` or send `mail` to each other internally, or communicate from machine to machine. Networking software is built into the UNIX system. Remote mail, file transfers, and remote execution require a minimum of effort to install. Someone familiar with setting up a `uucp` network can get a new UNIX machine attached to a WAN (*w*ide *a*rea *n*etwork) in an hour or two. Hooking systems together with standard phone lines can take anywhere from 15 minutes to a day or more, depending on the cooperation of the machines involved and whether you read this book! This kind of networking can be done either locally or over long distances, anywhere that phone lines or satellite communications are available.

Using standard LAN (*l*ocal *a*rea *n*etwork) connections, any UNIX system can be hooked up to another UNIX system, becoming a terminal on the remote system, allowing the remote system to become a terminal on it, or running different parts of a program on different systems. Files and mail can be transferred immediately or stored and forwarded at a more convenient time.

The capability to network machine-to-machine opens new communications possibilities to computer users. It allows expensive peripherals such as typesetters, laser printers, plotters, high-speed printers, and mass-storage devices to be shared by all machines within the network. It also minimizes the cost of software, because expensive software can reside on the machine for which it is legally purchased and still be used by all other machines and terminals within the networked system. File serving—keeping a single copy of all critical files on one machine—is a reality with networking. It cuts the cost of mass-storage devices to a small fraction of what it would be if every machine in the system had a private copy. File serving makes archiving easy and practical, as well as helps prevent data loss.

In some implementations of UNIX, the processors of individual machines can share the load of any task on the network. This is the direction of all UNIX systems.

Networked systems offer exciting opportunities. The original edition of this book was written using six different UNIX machines in different parts of the United States. Two machines with radically different architectures were closely networked by hardwire, one doing duty as an external communications machine, and the other as a file server. A mainframe 40 miles away was used for bulk spelling correction and Writer's Workbench work (the style and diction programs). A fourth machine on the other side of the country kept in constant touch with `uucp` for electronic mail and for sending the chapters back and forth during editing. The manuscript was printed with `nroff` on a dot-matrix printer and sent to the publisher for review. Another

7

pass for proofing was done with a laser printer and `troff`. After final approval, the manuscript was sent to yet another machine to be typeset, and the typeset galleys were sent to the publisher for printing. The sixth machine was used for developing and testing examples used in the original edition.

Here is the power of UNIX in a nutshell. The two linked machines were a Codata 3300 (a 68000-based machine running UNIX System III) and an AT&T 3B2/300 (a WE32000-based machine running System V Release 2). The mainframe was an Amdahl 470 V7a running UTS, System V (UNIX 5.2). The fourth machine, a Cadmus 9790, used System V Release 0 on its 68010 CPU. The fifth was an AT&T 6300 running XENIX System V, and the sixth was an 80286-based Altos also using XENIX. Without the ability to use different hardware while communicating easily and quickly, we would have taken a lot longer to write this book.

The commercial applications of networking can already be seen today. UNIX's capability to network coupled with PC DOS's growing similarity to UNIX has resulted in the inevitable networking of PCs to UNIX machines. Companies have purchased hundreds of PCs for various uses, but networked, they become part of an overall computer system.

UNIX Software

UNIX has a great deal of software built into its standard distribution, including several programming languages, program debuggers, and text manipulators. Just a few years after UNIX became a commercial product, a third-party software base emerged that fills hundreds of pages in AT&T's latest *System V Software Catalog*. Now you can have UNIX and your favorite applications software too. Many PC DOS programs have been successfully ported to UNIX, including Lotus 1-2-3, the single most significant program in the PC world.

Most UNIX software is quite sophisticated. Database managers can be tied to applications generators that in turn are joined to applications packages like accounting systems. The power of UNIX enables firms with offices across the country to tie them all together through electronic mail and `uucp` capabilities, running the same software at each local machine and updating company-wide files automatically each night.

Third-party UNIX software addresses a wide-ranging market because UNIX is ported to so many machines. Prices are usually proportional to the size of the machine. A relational database manager that costs a few hundred dollars on a popular 680x0-based machine, such as an NCR Tower, costs about $40,000 for a mainframe implementation.

UNIX Is Friendly

Controversies have raged over whether UNIX is easy to use, but the fact remains that only UNIX has the capability to be almost totally reconfigured. You can change its prompts and command names, move around its user file trees, and replace the entire user interface if you like. UNIX may not be ideal for everyone, but it does not force you to accept it "as is." Although UNIX has been criticized for its complexity when compared to personal computer operating systems, most of these PCs add UNIX-like features as they mature.

As the cost of graphical display terminals and workstations gets closer to the price of text-based terminals, the graphical user interfaces (GUIs) become more prevalent as a standard way to interact with UNIX systems. A great deal has been learned about how people work effectively with computers. These new interfaces have made it far more intuitive for users to manage their UNIX work environment and files. By combining the icon-based environment (such as that of Open Look File Manager) with the power of the UNIX command line and utilities, UNIX has moved from being a working environment scorned by all but engineers to an environment anyone can easily use and enjoy.

The Guru Is In

A user's perspective of UNIX is much different from that of a system administrator. The user sees his own environment, his immediate user area, some libraries, and a few other user group areas. To the user, UNIX seems moderate in size and complexity.

The system administrator is also a user. In fact, he frequently is his own best customer. But an administrator sees a much larger UNIX. There are hundreds of directories and thousands of files, and the administrator must know where they are and how they fit into the larger whole. Whereas the user has executable commands searched automatically by his path as defined in .profile or .login, the administrator must execute commands hidden in many strange places. He first has to acquaint himself with all the commands, and then has to remember where they are. For example, uucp commands are in one place, lp commands are in another, and standard administration commands are somewhere else.

If a user loses a file, directory, or tree, he simply goes to the system administrator, tells his sad tale of woe, and his worries are over. All the user has to do is wait for the system administrator to find the lost data from the preceding night's backup tape. Users have the luxury of being able to make mistakes, but a system administrator does not. If system backups are not done adequately and a user loses a file, the data can be irrevocably lost.

In time, users get used to relying on the system administrator for just about everything. She seems to have all the answers. (System administrators, like ordinary people, come in two sexes. Both are referred to in this book.) UNIX has traditionally been taught by word of mouth, and the teachers are usually the system administrator and fellow users. This is true probably because the most vital UNIX system administration resources are the hardest to read—the manual sets. As system administrator, you also learn to rely on (and maintain!) the online manuals (man pages), learn help, and any interactive commands available. The best way to learn is to take this book firmly in hand and prowl around your entire system. Draw yourself a map of all the important files, as well as everything that "looks interesting." (Figure 2.1 in the next chapter is only one possible configuration.) A few days spent this way pays large dividends later. And soon you'll have a reputation as a UNIX *guru*, someone who knows all about the system.

A Note about Systems

In this book, you will see references to small, medium, and large computer systems. These distinctions can easily be blurred, so they should be considered general terms.

A *small* system is one that supports 1 to 4 people. Such a machine might have a few serial ports, up to 80 MB of Winchester disk, and from 2 MB to 16 MB of RAM, with minifloppy or cartridge tape for backup. Small, single-user workstations, such as the Commodore Amiga 3000UX and the SUN IPC, fit into this category. Some workstations have no disk drive and rely entirely on another system (a *server*) to supply the operating system and all the disk storage.

A *medium* system (a "supermicro" or "small mini") generally is packaged in a system cabinet, with a backplane for plugging in expansion boards. Such a machine supports up to 16 simultaneous users or connected workstations, 600 MB of disk storage, and 64 MB of RAM. Backups are done on cartridge tape. EISA bus, Intel i486-based machines, engineering workstations, and departmental servers fit in here.

A *large* system usually has a special environment that includes its own air-conditioned room with a raised floor for cables. For simplification in this book, this category includes machines with capacities ranging from 17 to 500 users or attached workstations. Large machines may have more than 4 GB (gigabytes) of disk storage and 1 GB of RAM, and backups are done with

triple density 1/2-inch tape as well as removable disk packs and optical drive
jukeboxes. The one factor that separates this group from smaller machines
is that the large ones *always* require a full-time system administrator.

The System Administration Workload

Smaller, lightly loaded UNIX systems with built-in, menu-driven system
administration programs—such as those that use Santa Cruz Operation
UNIX/386 and Interactive Systems 386/UNIX—are easy to run and take little
administration time. At the other extreme are large UNIX machines with a
high level of user activity, loads of software coming and going, and little in
the way of dedicated system administration routines. In any case, understanding what's going on is of paramount importance once the unexpected
happens. Even if you are lucky enough to have a great set of canned menus
or shell scripts, the day will come when the pressure will be on *you*. The
administrator of an active system must be able not only to work without
simplified administration menus but also to create them if needed. Most
people going into system administration by choice or chance find their
workloads somewhere in the middle. There is time to work as system
administrator, system programmer, and user.

Help and Where to Get It

UNIX is still a maturing system, and it changes a bit with each new official
release. Because any operating system is such a large concept, few people
understand one completely. Even after trying man, the printed manuals, and
the tutorials, you are going to need outside aid from time to time. It goes
with the job.

Your primary source is the software support you purchased when you
bought the system. Sometimes software support is part of the cost of the
system, and sometimes you pay extra for it. Either way, it is invaluable.

Free help is available on the Usenet network (see Chapter 14). If you're
not in a rush, post your problem in net.unix or net.news.sa, and with
luck, someone will return an answer to you in a few days.

In the long run, the greatest help is continuing education. Organizations that teach UNIX system administration are located all across the United
States and Canada. A good course is well worth the time and money. You get
education and interactive experience as well as an opportunity to share your
problems with sympathetic souls who have been in the same position. Some

computer manufacturers also run excellent courses, such as Hewlett-Packard, Amdahl, and DEC. These courses are especially designed for their specific brand of hardware and corresponding version of the system. There are several UNIX organizations such as USENIX and UNIFORUM that have seminars with excellent tutorials for administrators at all levels of experience. Perhaps the best courses available today are from The Source itself, AT&T.

Naturally, not everyone has the time or the funds to attend courses. A number of periodicals on the market provide a consistent flow of quality information on keeping your UNIX system happy. And among the dozens of UNIX books around, we've picked out our favorites. All these invaluable sources are annotated in the Bibliography.

Finally, a good consultant who specializes in UNIX system administration is worth his weight in memory chips. If he has already done the kind of task you are looking for, especially on your hardware, he's probably worth twice what he's asking, considering the time he can save you. Good consultants rarely need to advertise. Ask around.

The Standardization of UNIX at SVR4

UNIX emerged commercially from AT&T as Version 7. It continued to develop, but other versions of UNIX quickly proliferated. Berkeley UNIX split away at Version 6. Some UNIX look-alikes stopped at System III. As a system administrator, you should be aware that there are many versions of UNIX out there at various stages of development.

At this writing, UNIX System V Release 4 (SVR4 or just UNIX V.4) is the current AT&T standard. AT&T paid for ports to all major processors and architectures and developed a standardization suite (a collection of standards compliance tests) to ensure uniformity. UNIX VR4 is noticeably better suited than previous System V releases for LAN installations. It includes the best of Berkeley UNIX and XENIX.

As of this edition of *UNIX System V Release 4 Administration*, two strong factions exist in the UNIX community. The first is UNIX International (the AT&T camp). The second is the Open Software Foundation (OSF), which consists primarily of Hewlett-Packard, Digital Equipment Corporation (DEC), and International Business Machines (IBM). This second group has publicized its own version of UNIX, but is just producing the first ports to hardware. DEC and HP processors are the first. Because of the increasing compliance with standards such as POSIX, it is unlikely that the OSF operating system will look significantly different from AT&T UNIX. The major differences will be in the design of the UNIX kernel and the programmer's libraries.

AT&T has spent millions of dollars advertising System V as the standard for the UNIX system. There are tens of thousands of older computers running the earlier versions of UNIX, and many others running Berkeley versions. Although System V is not the only force in the market, the AT&T campaign has given enough momentum to System V to convince major players like Amdahl and NCR to adopt it. It pays to know about System V, without losing sight of the techniques needed to run other systems. The OSF operating system's commands and file structure are not significantly different.

Where Do We Go from Here?

Commercial viability determines the ultimate success of an operating system, and UNIX is no exception. The push for standardization at UNIX VR4 makes UNIX more homogeneous than ever. Implementations exist on all sizes of machines, from micros to mainframes, and the huge UNIX software library is addressing a wide market. The best implementations of networking are now in the commercial UNIX market. Where does UNIX go from here?

We have already seen full implementations of UNIX on small inexpensive hardware. Now the move is toward diversity and complexity: diverse multiprocessor designs, real-time systems, and embedded systems. This is only the beginning; UNIX has a bright future.

Handy Shell Programs

Toward the end of each chapter are a number of programs you can type and use. Most of these are written in Bourne shell language, and some are in C, but all of them should work on any UNIX system.

print_all

Some sites have the `dtree` program, which draws pictures of all the files and directories. Although `print_all` is not as pretty, this command line prints out everything on your system by `finding` everything and piping it to the printer through the `pr` program:

```
# find / -print ¦ pr ¦ lp
```

Use lp if you are running pre-System V UNIX, and use pr -w132 -2 instead of pr if your printer has wide (14 7/8-inch) paper. This will print the information in two columns, which saves paper.

mkcmd

Because you frequently will be creating shell programs, here's a shell program to help you create them without even using the editor. To use it, give mkcmd the full path name of the program-to-be, type the program itself, and then press Ctrl-D:

```
# mkcmd /usr/local/print_all
find / -print ¦ pr ¦ lp
< ^D>
# ls -l /usr/local/print_all
-rwxr-xr-x   1 root    root    24 Sep 13 16:36 /usr/local/print_all
#
```

Here is the mkcmd program itself:

```
cat > $1
chmod +x $1
```

mkcmd simply takes its input from the terminal as you type it (until you end it by pressing Ctrl-D), stores the input in the file you named, and makes that file executable so that you can use its name as a command.

Summary

As a multifaceted, multiuser system with enormous quantities of built-in software, UNIX requires comprehensive administration techniques. Now that you have taken an overall look at the system, you are ready to get down to some specifics. The next chapter presents the basics of getting your UNIX system running and keeping it that way.

2

Bringing Up

the UNIX

System

E very journey starts with the first step, and the first step in dealing with UNIX is to know how to bring up the system. There are several basic steps:

1. Turn on the system peripherals.

2. Turn on the computer.

3. Start the bootstrap program that loads /unix (the kernel).

4. Set the date.

5. Go into single-user mode.

6. Check the file system.

7. Go into multiuser mode.

On many systems, all of these steps happen automatically from the point of booting or even from power up. You learn more about these steps in the following sections.

Turning It On

The first step is to turn on the console, terminals, and any other peripherals that normally are attached to the computer, such as printers, modems, and external disk and tape drives. You want these devices on so that the computer recognizes them when it comes up. The next step is to turn on the computer itself.

Booting the System

Once you have turned on the computer, you need to load the operating system. This is called "booting" the system, from the expression "pulling yourself up by your own bootstraps." The term is appropriate because the boot program reads in a very small program from disk, and its sole function is to read in *another* program from disk, which then loads and starts the kernel. (If the computer refuses to come up at all, we sometimes give it a good boot in the side. This is merely a coincidence in terminology.) Computers generally boot the system in one of two ways, either from a PROM (*p*rogrammable *r*ead-*o*nly *m*emory) program stored in a chip or from a disk. If the console is not turned on first, the PROM program is not able to send its message to the console. Computers that boot from a disk send messages to the console during the boot process.

If, for any reason, a message does not appear on the console when you bring up the system, do a manual reset. This usually involves pressing a little button on your computer's front or rear panel. Push that button, and your computer reads the bootstrap program either from the startup PROM or from disk. Don't push the power-off switch by mistake! That might damage your disk, which is no way to start your day.

Starting Up UNIX

Sometimes the primitive startup program requires something simple to load /unix into memory, such as pressing the Enter key. At other times, you have to give an entire command line to the boot loader. The command usually tells where (on which device) to find the kernel and what it's called. On most systems, the kernel is an executable file called /unix in the root file system. On VAX systems, the kernel is sometimes called /vmunix (for *v*irtual *m*emory UNIX). Or it might be named after the particular variant, such as

`/venix`, `/idris`, or `/xenix`. Loaders that accept a human-entered kernel name are more flexible because you can specify a "backup" version or test a different release:

```
BOOT: rh(0,1) /unix
Loading UNIX at 0x400000...
1,024,000 bytes of memory found.
Set the date:
```

It is always a good practice to wait 30 to 60 seconds before letting the computer start reading from the hard disk. If you try to read from a hard disk that is not yet up to speed, you can cause a disk-read error. Although such an error is generally harmless at this point, there's no sense in taking a chance. Table 2.1 lists some common boot prompts and the appropriate responses.

Table 2.1. Common boot prompts and the proper responses (manufacturer's models vary).

System	Prompt	Response
DEC	>>>	**b**
HP (automatic)		
IBM (automatic)		
MIPS	>>	**auto**<Enter>
ISC (automatic)		
SCO	boot:	<Enter>*
SUN	>	**b**

*After a one-minute wait for any special boot directives, SCO will go ahead and boot the file `/unix`.
Note: <Enter> means that you press the Enter key.

If your system boots and loads automatically, just sit back and wait for Step 4. Once `/unix` is loaded, the machine automatically starts the `sched` (process 0) and `init` processes, which are the first two processes in UNIX.

The `sched` is called `swapper` or `swap` on some systems. It is responsible for moving processes in and out of the CPU (*central* processing *unit*). `init` makes shells. Shells are spawned (created) early in UNIX, and `init` is the system's number one program, process 1, from which all other shells and processes are spawned. The shell provides the entire interaction between the user and the kernel.

The machine then contacts the outside world, the console, and asks you for the date. (We told you that UNIX was friendly.)

Setting the Date

Once UNIX is loaded into the system, the first order of business is to set the date and time. Although setting the date may seem trivial, its function within the system is not. UNIX needs an accurate date. If an erroneous date is entered, the wrong creation, access, and modification dates and times are attached to files. Several UNIX functions rely on the accurate date and time stamps.

Many modern computers have a built-in clock that functions even when the computer is off or being shipped. If you are lucky enough to have one like this, you'll know because the date will be correct when the system comes up (although the time may be set to the wrong time zone). In such cases, the date prompt will probably be omitted.

The date command has the following format in System VR4:

```
# date mmddhhmm[yy]
```

The first *mm* subargument is month, *dd* is the calendar day (number), *hh* is the hour (on a 24-hour clock), and the last *mm* subargument is minutes. (Don't enter the #; that is the "sysadmin" prompt.) The last argument, *yy*, is optional (which is why it's shown in brackets) and is used to set the year.

To enter January 4, 1991, at half past six in the evening, you type

```
# date 0104183091
```

You have the option of abbreviating it like this:

```
# date mmddhhmm
```

In this case, you can leave out the year and type

```
# date 01041830
```

Leaving out the year causes the system to default to the year that was last set in the computer. If the system crashes in a peculiar way, using the default year can cause some interesting (and wrong) results.

Note that each element of the date is entered as two numbers, no more and no less. Entering the date this way won't work:

```
# date 141830
```

After you enter the date, the system responds with

```
Fri Jan 4 18:30:00 PST 1991
```

Just so that it was different, the date command was changed starting at System III. Before System III, the format was

```
date [yy]mmddhhmm[ss]
```

On large systems that ask for GMT (*Greenwich mean time*) on startup, be sure to give the system what it asks for, not local time! This raises another peculiarity that you, as administrator, must understand. *All* UNIX systems operate internally on GMT and convert to local time only when necessary for display. When you first start the computer, you will probably be confronted with a time zone, either EST (*eastern standard time*) or PST (*Pacific standard time*), depending on where the computer was made. A shell environment variable called TZ (TIMEZONE on some systems) is used to tell the system the local time. To convert the entire system to local time, you simply set the environment variable where it will be in effect for all users. Sometimes there is actually a file called /etc/TIMEZONE or /etc/tz. If that is the way it's done on your system, change the variable there; otherwise, the best place to do this is in a file such as /etc/rc or /etc/profile. Look in these two files for references to the TZ variable.

What do you actually do? Generally, you set the TZ variable to a value in this way:

```
# TZ=EST5EDT
# export TZ
```

The EST refers to the eastern time zone, and the 5 refers to the number of hours that the eastern time zone is *west* of Greenwich mean time. The EDT signifies that daylight savings time is in effect during certain times of the year, when the time is officially EDT, or eastern daylight time. The system knows when daylight savings time goes into effect and changes itself automatically, so you have to set this only once. Therefore, in California you set TZ to PST8PDT, and in Chicago you set TZ to CST6CDT.

Coming Up in Single-User Mode

On pre-System V machines, you come up in single-user mode automatically. System V machines give you a choice, but the first few times you bring up UNIX System V, you should be in single-user mode. One way to do that is to use the init command at level s:

```
# init s
```

Other System V machines may ask you this:

```
Enter init level:
```

You simply respond with **s**. Some machines come up automatically in multiuser mode, forcing you to return the mode to single-user with **init s**.

Checking the File System

You use single-user mode to do the kind of system administration tasks that require a quiescent machine, such as checking and repairing the file system or running backups. Although running fsck to check the file system is an optional task on many implementations of UNIX, you should know that running UNIX with a bad file system can quickly spread whatever maladies exist to far reaches of the disks, causing damage that only a complete restore can repair. In such a case, there is no room for error. It takes only about five minutes to check the whole system, but a restore can require many frustrating hours, even days. The simple solution is to type **y** (for *yes*) when UNIX asks you a question such as Check file systems? The fsck program is generally easy to use, but it has been given most of a separate chapter (Chapter 3) because of its importance.

When you have no more system administration tasks to do, the final step in bringing up the system is to go multiuser.

Going Multiuser

Except for allowing the SA to log in at the console, UNIX will not accept users until it is in multiuser mode. You bring up some systems in multiuser mode with a Ctrl-D (^D), because you are literally logging out of the single-user shell. You bring up other systems in multiuser mode by going to a numeric init level, usually level 2 (or 3 if network daemons are to be started). The command line is

```
# init 2
```

When the system comes up in multiuser mode, it sends a login: message to each active terminal, including the console. In technical terms, a getty is spawned for each *tty*. At this point, UNIX is officially up.

A Quick Review: Bringing Up the UNIX System

1. Turn on the console, terminals, and other peripherals.

2. Turn on the computer. Warm up the system for 30 seconds or more to let the hard disk come up to speed.

3. Start the bootstrap program that loads /unix.

4. Set the date.

5. Type **init s** for single-user mode.

6. Check the file system.

7. Type **init 2** to go into multiuser mode.

8. Check the file system or press Ctrl-D to go into multiuser mode (SCO).

Automating System Startup with */etc/rc*

You have now seen the most general procedure possible for starting up UNIX. Don't be alarmed if your system acts a bit differently. Once you've gotten to the stage where you feel confident enough to want to run the system instead of simply accepting whatever default behavior the manufacturer has decreed, you will want to make some changes. With changes, you can do the following tasks:

- Speed up system startup
- Check the file systems
- Start system accounting and statistics
- Run driver programs for special hardware
- Recover files after a crash
- Start the printer spooler

All of these tasks, and more, can be best accomplished by automating the boot procedure. The place for this is the file /etc/rc or the files under the subdirectory /etc/rc.d. The rc file is covered in Chapter 4, "Where Everything Is and How to Find It."

Root and Superuser

Root and superuser are sometimes confused by beginning system administrators because the concepts they represent are so similar. If you don't learn the subtle differences here and now, you will miss the meaning of other differences.

Root

The UNIX system has an elaborate security system designed to let users protect their files and directories to any extent they want. However, there is one user on the system who can circumvent all this protection. The name of this user is *root*. Root has both user ID and group ID number 0 (the group ID is 1 on SVR4) and can create or destroy anything on the system—files, directories, or processes—with just a few keystrokes. A user with the power of root is needed because some things are almost impossible to do otherwise, and someone with special powers and skill is needed when things go wrong.

When the system is up in single-user mode and you are at the console, *you* are root. This shouldn't scare you too much if you use the root login wisely. That's why you do things slowly in these first few chapters! Most of the time, when operating as system administrator, you will need root privileges. Even so, it's a bad habit to operate as root all the time. The eventual result will be either weakened security or making a mistake that would have been harmless had you not been logged in as root.

In some cases, your system will not come up automatically in single-user mode without a root login. This is necessary so that the system can be protected against unauthorized personnel being able to reboot the system and thus become root, as was possible before XENIX and System III. If this is the case, you get a login: prompt at boot time, to which you should respond with **root**, followed by the root password when prompted. If this is the first time the system is being brought up, the root password is generally either nonexistent or is the word *root* itself. (SUN workstations use the host ID number, which is displayed as the system comes up.) The whole sequence looks something like this:

```
Crosswind Computer X-15 with UniCom Version 5.2
login: root
Password:                    - The password is not displayed
SINGLE-USER MODE
#
```

The special prompt # shows that you have root privileges. This prompt
will appear in examples in which you must become root. Get into the habit
of never leaving your terminal when this prompt is active, so that system
abusers won't have the chance to do sneaky things behind your back.

Superuser

The name *superuser* conjures up a mental image of some kind of superhero,
but this is not quite the case. Superuser comes from the acronym *su* for
*s*ubstitute *u*ser ID. The su command allows a user to substitute his user ID
for another user's ID as long as he knows the other user's log name and
password. If a user needs to work on John Parker's files and gets his
password (and therefore permission to do the work), she can use su to
"become" John temporarily for working purposes. John can, of course,
change his password later so that it is private once again:

```
$ whoami
emdall
$ su parker
Password:
$ whoami
parker
$
```

If su is used without an argument, however, the command takes on
another meaning. The user invoking su with the proper (root's) password
takes on the identity of root, with all of its rights and privileges. That's how
people started thinking that su stood for superuser, because root's powers
are so great!

The root password should be changed regularly. When anyone with
root privileges leaves the company, the password should be changed as
well. The number of people who know the root password should be kept
to an absolute minimum. We can guarantee that your system will become
almost unmanageable if more than five people know it. If you work for a
large company and you are the system administrator, your boss is likely to
be the head of data processing. Even your boss should not know the root
password! Instead, write it down and place it in a sealed envelope in her
desk. Then it should be used in an emergency only.

23

Keeping the UNIX File System
Healthy and Happy

The UNIX file system is a little more complex than most file systems because of its unique file tree structure. Although it's called a tree, it is an upside-down variety (see Figure 2.1). As you can see, the top of the tree is where everything else "sprouts," and for that reason, it's called the *root* directory (not to be confused with the user *root*). The root directory (written as /) is the top-level directory on the UNIX system. All second-level directories and files are located just under root, so all their names (such as /usr, /bin, and /unix) begin with a single slash.

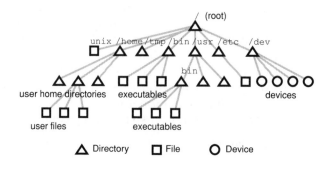

Figure 2.1. The UNIX file system.

Each directory can have a large number of other directories and files under it. At the same time, an entire new disk drive (or section of a disk drive) can have a file system created on it and "mounted" on any existing directory. This means that, theoretically at least, any UNIX file system tree can be expanded as "deep" and "wide" as you like, with the only real restriction being the amount of money you have for hardware.

It is imperative that this file system be kept in perfect order, and checking the file system frequently is the only way to ensure its health and safety. You can check the UNIX file system in several ways, but first you need to know some details about how it works.

UNIX File Theory

The file system design is one of UNIX's unique features. Understanding its structure will help you to work your way through some file system corruptions you may encounter some day.

Blocks

UNIX files are measured in a unit called a *block*. Block sizes vary. Generally, System V systems have a block size of 1024 bytes, and pre-System V systems have a block size of 512 bytes. Some UNIX systems use larger block sizes, such as UTS with its 4096-byte blocks.

The block exists because disk devices used to store files are most efficient when reading, writing, and storing large quantities of data at once. If it takes a disk drive 10 milliseconds to read 1 byte from the physical disk, it might take only 11 milliseconds to read 512 bytes, and 15 milliseconds to read 4096 bytes. Actually, the disk cannot deal with anything *less* than a block at a time, so only an integral number of blocks can be written or read at once. Block sizes on UNIX systems, then, tend to match the most common disk or hardware block sizes.

When a file is stored on the disk, the file takes up as many bytes on the disk as needed, plus whatever is necessary to fill to the end of the disk block (although nothing extra is stored there). Therefore, if UNIX is using a block size of 1024 bytes, a 1023-byte file takes up 1 block, and a 1025-byte file takes up 2 blocks. Even a 1-byte file takes up an entire block. The user never sees these details. To the user, a 1-byte file is 1 byte long, and a 1025-byte file is 1025 bytes long, because that is how the UNIX system presents those files to the user. On other operating systems, the user often has to take into account the number of blocks taken up by the file, which is unnatural and time-consuming.

The fact that files smaller than a block nevertheless take up a full block is known as *block breakage*, which may account for a large portion of disk space being totally wasted. If your file system consists mostly of many small files, a large block size wastes more space because most of the files are less than a block. However, systems with a relatively small number of large files benefit from using large blocks because the disk can read them more efficiently. In many cases, the computer manufacturer has already determined the block size to be used on your system, based on either statistical analysis of the kind of files most customers use or whatever was most convenient.

Each file in the UNIX system has a name. Some files have more than one name. For example, the mv command is used to rename files. On many systems, mv is actually the same physical program as the commands ln and cp. If the program is called by one command name, the program performs one function; if the program is called by another name, the program performs another function. This seemingly impossible feat is accomplished by links. A *link* is a connection between a file name and the pointer that actually represents the file. Therefore, a single file with more than one name has several links.

Here's a trick using links that works on many UNIX systems. The `ls` command is often used as `ls -l` to find full details of directory contents. The source code for `ls` has sometimes been fixed so that if the program is called `ll` instead of `ls`, it becomes equivalent to typing `ls -l`. To see whether this works on your system, go into the `/bin` directory as superuser, make a link to `ls`, and see if the `ll` link works differently:

```
# cd /bin
# ll
ll: not found
# ln ls ll
# ll
total 3035
-rwxr-xr-x   1 bin      sys        36928 Dec  3 1989     adb
-rwxr-xr-x   1 root     bin          566 Dec  3 1989     as
-rwxrwxr-x   1 root     bin        60922 Dec  7 1989     awk
-rwxrwxr-x   1 bin      sys          903 Aug 30 01:04    calendar
-rwxr-xr-x   1 root     bin         7304 Dec  3 1989     cat
...
-rwxr-xr-x   2 bin      bin        17418 Dec  3 1989     ll
-rwxr-xr-x   3 root     bin         8614 Dec  3 1989     ln
-rwxr-xr-x   1 root     bin        19082 Dec  3 1989     login
-rwxr-xr-x   2 bin      bin        17418 Dec  3 1989     ls
...
-rwxr-xr-x   1 bin      bin        12420 Dec  3 1989     who
-rwxr-xr-x   1 bin      bin        15594 Dec  3 1989     write
-rwxr-xr-x   1 bin      bin         7034 Dec  3 1989     xargs
-rwxr-xr-x   1 bin      bin         8256 Dec  3 1989     xd
#
```

If this works, we've found other links that may work. `l`, `lr`, `lf`, and `lx` automatically activate the `-m`, `-r`, `-F`, and `-x` options, respectively. If no change is noted, simply get rid of the new link, and the old `ls` program will remain:

```
# rm /bin/ll
#
```

Inodes

Each file in a mounted UNIX file system is identified by the system with a unique pointer called an *inode* number. (You learn more about inodes in Chapter 5.) The basic rule of thumb is "One file for each inode." The system keeps track of how many inodes are in use and how many are unused or free.

The number of inodes in use plus the number of free inodes must equal the total available number of inodes. Any inconsistency points to potential trouble.

The directory entry for a file has only two pieces of information: the file's name and the inode number. The inode itself contains the rest of the information about the file. The inode tells about the file mode (permissions), file size, whether the file is a directory, where to find the data contained in the file, and other pertinent information such as whether the file is a "special" file.

There is more to UNIX file theory, but it will keep. Armed with this rudimentary knowledge, you are now ready to examine some of the ways to keep the UNIX file system healthy and happy.

The *fsck* Program

fsck (for *file system check*) is designed specifically to test and repair the file system, pass after pass, until everything is checked. Each pass through the individual file systems is called a *phase*. The phases test blocks and sizes, path names, connectivity, reference counts, and the free block list. If inconsistencies are found or errors are detected, fsck gives you the opportunity to repair the file system. fsck is so vital to system health that it should be incorporated into the regular routine of bringing up the system. The best time to do an fsck is on a quiescent machine, and running it in single-user mode before bringing the machine up to multiuser mode is ideal.

One of the most valuable features of fsck is that it enables you to check file systems interactively. When inconsistencies are found, fsck sends diagnostics to the console along with suggestions for repair of the damage. The administrator is then free to ignore or act on the error.

fsck can be used with a variety of flags that vary from system to system. The syntax for one system is

```
fsck [-y] [-n] [-sX] [-SX] [-t filename] [-D] [filesystem] ...
```

Note that manual pages for system administration commands are most often found in a separate manual devoted to such commands. Therefore, when you do a man, the manual entry is not always (1) but often (1M). Now take a look at a few possible uses of fsck with flags.

In its simplest form

```
fsck -y
```

not only checks the file system but makes any necessary repairs automatically. It tells the system, "Check the file system and make any needed repairs without bothering to ask me whether I approve." This is convenient but dangerous. If major file system damage has occurred, you want to know about it. Intelligent human intervention is often better than that of a machine, so do not use fsck -y exclusively. Rely on it, instead, as an occasional time-saver.

To see whether there's anything wrong with the system without doing anything about it, use fsck -n. The -n option assumes a *no* response to fsck questions. It is useful for testing the file system without making any repairs.

The -sX option ignores the current free list and unconditionally makes a new one. (The free list keeps track of all the blocks in the file system that are not being used to store any data.) This option's counterpart is the -SX option (note the capital S). It does a reconstruction only if nothing is wrong.

These options can greatly speed up disk operations on busy file systems. The options work because a newly created free list is more likely to have large, contiguous chunks of free space, rather than single blocks scattered all over the disk.

The last fsck option, -t, is used on small-memory machines. It uses a scratch (temporary) file to make up for lack of memory. This file must not be located in the file system being checked, so you should use an appropriate full path name.

The -D flag performs extra consistency checks on directories. It takes only another 5 to 10 seconds per file system. Use it!

Here are two examples that show how to run fsck when you want to check a particular file system. The first example is

```
fsck -t /tmp/junk dev/hd07
```

This says, "Check the file system on hd07 and put the scratch file in /tmp/junk." The second example is

```
fsck -y -D /dev/rhd06
```

This says, "Check the file system on hd06, using the raw character device for higher speed (see Chapter 4); check the directories; and do whatever you (the program) think is best.

Other File System Consistency Programs

Because the file system is so important to the health of your system, you may want to use more than just fsck. When modern tools are not available, you can use some older ones.

ncheck

The `ncheck` program finds the name of a file when you have its inode number only. The syntax on some systems is (check your `man`) the following:

```
ncheck [-i i-numbers] [-a] [-s] [filesystem]
```

Everything is technically optional here because the default operation of `ncheck` generates a list of all file names on (usually) all file systems, which is not very useful. Most of the time, `ncheck` is used in the following way. Suppose that you are running `fsck` to check the root file system and you get a message like this:

```
BAD/DUP FILE I=564 OWNER=root MODE=755
SIZE=14839 MTIME=SAT Mar 1 17:37:23 EST 1975
CLEAR?
```

You can tell that the size of the file is not zero (so the file might be important), and the file is owned by root and executable (so it might even be a system command, especially with the date as old as it is). Because you don't want to wipe out an important file like `/bin/sh` by mistake, you answer *no* to `fsck` and eventually regain your shell prompt:

```
# ncheck -i 564 /dev/xt0a
/dev/xt0a:
564 /etc/temp.password
#
```

This way, you find that the file in question is actually a backup copy of the password file you made a long time ago. Once you make sure that the *real* `/etc/passwd` file still exists and is in good shape, you can rerun `fsck` and clear out this extra file.

Another way to find the file is to use the `find` command. This command is a syntactic anomaly; instead of single-character options, it has full words (perhaps because it has so *many* options). The syntax for finding the path to the file that corresponds to an inode number is

```
find / -inum inode-number -print
```

The first command-line parameter (/) is the point at which to start the search. In order to cut down the search, you can use any point in the file tree.

Predecessors to *fsck*

fsck is a relative newcomer to UNIX. Other commands existed before fsck, and they either tested the file system or repaired it. This section covers dcheck, clri, and icheck, although you should treat them as antiques because fsck tends to outperform them all. Use these commands only if you have a system without fsck.

dcheck reads through the directories in any specified system (defaulting to all available file systems) and tests the link count in each inode entry with the directory entries. Its syntax is

```
dcheck [-i numbers] [filesystem]
```

You use dcheck in this way:

dcheck /dev/dsk220

You can use the optional -i flag to specify one or a group of inode numbers about which you want more information.

Before fsck became available, one of the more reliable and commonly used file system repair programs was clri. It clears inodes that diagnostics like icheck uncover as damaged. Once a "bad" inode is discovered, clri is invoked to zero out the inode. The syntax for clri is

```
clri file-system i-number ...
```

You use clri like this:

clri /dev/dsk550 497 556

icheck is fsck's predecessor and is no longer found on modern UNIX machines. icheck sent forth a fair amount of diagnostics to your terminal, including the number of regular files, directories, and block and character special files; the number of blocks used as directory blocks; the number of free blocks; and the number of missing blocks. icheck was also capable of reconstructing a new free list, if asked to, with the -s flag.

The *lost+found* Directory

What happens if a file loses its link to its file name by accident? (If you rm a file, of course, it *is* gone forever.) Is the file discarded and lost forever? UNIX is far too clever for that. When fsck checks a file system for connectivity (to see whether there is at least one directory entry or link for each inode or file) and discovers a file without a directory entry, fsck sends a notification to the console. The console message asks whether you want to RECONNECT. If you answer *no*, the error condition is ignored, and the file remains

inaccessible. If you answer *yes*, the orphaned file is reconnected to a file in
`./lost+found` and assigned a file name that is also its inode number.

The proper place for the `lost+found` directory is in the root directory
of each file system. For instance, if you have two mounted file systems, `/usr`
and `/own`, you should have *three* `lost+found` directories:

`/lost+found`	For the root file system. (There should always be a `lost+found` for the root file system.)
`/usr/lost+found`	For the `/usr` file system.
`/own/lost+found`	For the `/own` file system.

With this ingenious method, there is no need to lose a file even if the
rug is pulled out from under the system before it updates the disk copy of
the directory and superblock. As long as you, as system administrator, take
the time to be sure that a directory exists for `lost+found` in every file system
and that there is sufficient room in the directory to accommodate lost files,
orphaned files can be recovered. It is always a good practice to check all
`lost+found` directories for entries from time to time. This is particularly
true if you use `fsck -y` often.

What If the System Doesn't Come Up?

This section is designed to help you quickly troubleshoot your system if
you're having one of those days when *nothing* seems to work right. Sooner
or later, you will have to deal with a system that doesn't want to wake up.

Nothing on the System Works

If the console and the computer fail to communicate, examine the mechanical connections. Make sure that the cables are firmly attached to the proper
ports. Is the console cable attached to the terminal's EIA (modem) port, or
has someone made a mistake and attached the cable to its auxiliary (printer)
port? At the other end, is the cable attached to the console port, or is it
attached to just one of the *tty* ports?

The console port is the only way to get to the computer's main
processor (CPU) at the initialization stage. The console port is generally
labeled (on the back of the machine) *console*, *terminal*, *tty0*, or something
similar. Remember that when all else fails, read the manual. If everything
seems to be set up in accordance with the manual, it's time to get serious.

If you are trying to bring up a workstation or computer in which the console keyboard and display are connected directly to the machine (Personal Computer AT, PS/2, SUN, DECstation, or a similar configuration), be sure that the display is connected properly and has its power on, and that the keyboard cables are firmly in place.

If you are covered by a service contract, the safest bet is to call your supplier and have him take care of things. After all, the system is supposed to work, right? (Before you call for help, shut everything off for two full minutes, close your eyes, and try again. This has worked more times than it has failed.)

But if you are really on your own, here's what you can do. First, remove all media such as diskettes or tapes, and then turn off the power to the computer and peripherals. If your warranty is not voided by such an action, the best thing to do is a little exploratory surgery. Don't take apart anything you're not sure you can put back together. And whatever you do, don't open up any Winchester disk drives! Carefully open the computer's chassis (don't lose any of the little screws) and test each board to be sure that it is seated deeply into the (backplane) sockets. Check also that all internal cable connections are seated. Sometimes simply removing and replacing a connection or board will work. You'd be surprised to learn how many malfunctions are caused by poor cable and board connections, especially after shipment. We also advise cleaning the contacts with a recommended cleaning solution before replacing a board or connector.

The System Does Not Boot from the Boot Switch

If pressing the boot or reset switch (button) fails to bring up a boot message, the connection from the switch to the computer and power is probably not connected (or is poorly connected) to the CPU card. Test both ends of the connection and try to reboot.

Machines that use the ISA bus (Personal Computer AT and relatives) require that you install all the boards so that there are no conflicts in I/O address and interrupt numbers. Just because the hardware works as installed under MS-DOS does not guarantee that it will work under UNIX; MS-DOS does not use interrupts. A common conflict is between the video I/O address and intelligent multiport boards. To check these addresses and other boards' interrupt numbers, you will need the installation manuals for all the boards you have installed. It isn't easy to configure one of these small machines so that it has a mouse, a multiport board, a tape drive, a parallel port, and a network board. Make a list of what the settings are for all the boards, and stick it inside (taped down to the cover). This will facilitate any changes or additions. (See Chapter 15 for more information about PCs running UNIX.)

The System Boots but Does Not Execute Commands

If the system fails to execute commands, it cannot reach a very critical directory called /bin. Your shell should always know its search path. The only time that you can get a command to execute is when it is directly located in your search path, or when you have given a fully qualified path name. If the PATH variable set in your current root profile is not set to look in /bin or /etc, you will have to change the setting. Refer to Chapter 4 on configuring rc. Meanwhile, try resetting your search path with the following command if you are using the Bourne shell:

```
# PATH=/bin:/etc:$PATH ; export PATH
```

Or use this line for the C shell:

```
# setenv PATH "/bin:/etc:$PATH"
```

If this doesn't work, give full path names to your commands, such as /etc/ init, /etc/fsck, and /bin/sh.

The System Does Not Go into Multiuser Mode

If the system does not go into multiuser mode, the trick is to have the right command for the right system (see Table 2.2).

Table 2.2. Commands for invoking multiuser mode.

Systems	Command
System III and later	**init 2**
Early systems, XENIX, and SCO UNIX	Ctrl-D

If neither command in Table 2.2 works, the object is to kill the current mode. Try these keystrokes in the following order, waiting 30 seconds between them to see whether they have taken effect:

Ctrl-Z
Ctrl-C
Delete (Del)

If these don't work, try typing **exit** or **logoff**. Or perhaps your *stty* status has been garbled, so try all of these approaches again, this time followed by a linefeed (or Ctrl-J) instead of a return. Once the system enters multiuser mode, all should be well.

Handy Shell Programs

Although some of these examples seem trivial, you will find them useful. It's not a bad idea to have available in a script any system administration operations you do more than once. You will be surprised to discover how many of your problems are recurrent.

create

Often you will find it necessary to initialize one or more empty files or to truncate them to zero length. This script, `create`, does that for you by simply copying nothing into every file named on the command line:

```
for i
do
 >$i
done
```

Once you have `create`, you can put it to use in scripts like `/etc/rc` or in your everyday work, as in this example:

```
$ create /usr/adm/pacct /etc/wtmp
$ ls -l /usr/adm/pacct /etc/wtmp
-rw-r--r--   1 root      root       0 Sep 14 13:46 /usr/adm/pacct
-rw-r--r--   1 root      root       0 Sep 14 13:46 /etc/wtmp
$
```

mklost+found

`lost+found` directories must be "slotted." That is, they must have room in them for inodes to be stored while `fsck` is being run. The only way to do that is to create files and then delete them. The `mklost+found` script does that nicely, and incidentally uses `create`:

```
for i in ${*:-.}
do
   cd $i
   mkdir lost+found
   cd lost+found
   create a1 a2 a3 a4 a5 a6 a7 a8 a9 a10 a11 a12 a13 a14 a15
   create b1 b2 b3 b4 b5 b6 b7 b8 b9 b10 b11 b12 b13 b14 b15
```

```
        rm a* b*
        cd ..
    done
```

To use `mklost+found`, you can either go into the root directory of the *file system* in which you want to create the `lost+found` directory, or give as parameters as many directories as you want. The first line of the program figures out which you want:

```
# mount                    — List root directories of mounted file systems
/           on /dev/xt0a read/write on Tue Sep 24 11:30:22 1985
/usr        on /dev/xt0c read/write on Tue Sep 24 11:30:28 1985
/usr/lib    on /dev/xt0e read/write on Tue Sep 24 11:30:29 1985
/usr/spool  on /dev/xt0f read/write on Tue Sep 24 11:30:30 1985
/own        on /dev/xt1c read/write on Tue Sep 24 11:30:31 1985
# cd /usr
# mklost+found
# ls -ld lost+found
drwxrwxr-x   2 root       root 512      Sep 14 14:29 lost+found
# mklost+found /usr/spool /own
#
```

Summary

You may notice differences in booting different systems, but the main steps remain the same. The UNIX system may seem large, but it can be tamed. The basic elements of all UNIX systems are the time-sharing element (`swap` or `sched`), the file system, and the daemon for handling terminal I/O (`getty`). Terminal I/O is discussed in Chapter 10. In the next chapter, you learn how to keep the UNIX system from biting.

3

Checking
the File
System

ome computers have flat file systems: all files are in one directory or at one level. Although the files are stable and straightforward, finding a file can be a nightmare on any but the smallest system. UNIX has a hierarchical file system. It has a kind of database "manager" that you *perceive* as the file system. The entire directory structure is at your fingertips with the find command, a wonderfully convenient feature. However, if anything happens to the system before data is actually written to the disk (such as a system crash), the current, or memory, image of the directories (the true directory structure) is not saved properly on disk. Any files that are written at the time of the crash run the risk of being lost or corrupted. As a result, the directories and files are not in agreement, and the file systems need to be repaired.

The most important part of a UNIX file system is the *superblock*. It keeps track of all the free space and inodes in the file system, as well as various internal parameters such as the size of the file system. At any given time, there are at least two copies of the superblock *and* the disk buffers. One copy is in the computer's memory, and the other copy is on disk, but the copy in memory is the most accurate because it is current. Don't count on the disk copy being up-to-date! As with any other disk data, if the superblock is not updated properly, you are asking for trouble. Problems in the superblock can scramble an entire file system rather than just one or two files.

sync, *update*, and Peace of Mind

As you have seen, the superblock exists both in high-speed (core or RAM) memory and on disk. The disk version is "old" and reflects the current condition of the file system only if it has been updated in the last few seconds or if the machine is not being used. The mechanism for forcing the memory version of the superblock to be written to disk is the sync command.

sync

All data, on its way to being written to the disk, is first stored in system disk buffers in kernel data space. These buffers are areas of fast RAM or core memory set aside to hold data until enough is accumulated to write out a full disk block (or several blocks). Then the buffer is "flushed" by writing it to the disk.

If a power failure or a crash brings down the system, the disk copy probably does not accurately reflect the way the file system is *supposed* to look. The sync command forces a write of the memory version of the buffers and superblock to the disk version. Many other operating systems do not put file data to disk until the file is closed. This is an obvious invitation to disaster in the event of a power failure or a crash. UNIX avoids this potential disaster by issuing a sync call at regular intervals through either the kernel or a separate program called /etc/update. Don't feel too secure, though; even though sync may immediately return without an error, the write to disk may not be completed for several seconds.

update

On somewhat older systems is a program, /etc/update, that causes a sync to be issued every 30 seconds, so that the disks are reasonably up-to-date in the event of a crash. update is usually executed with no arguments by /etc/ rc at the time the system is brought up. However, update has an optional argument that allows an interval other than 30 seconds to be used. Theoretically, you can specify one-second intervals or even continuous syncs to make sure that the system is always up-to-date, but the system slows down to a crawl if any real work is going on.

Some systems (particularly later versions of UNIX) don't run update as a separate program, but internally run the sync system call from the kernel every 30 seconds. The sync command simply makes this system call once when it is run. Here's a short version of update for you to compile and tuck away in your bag of tricks for times when you aren't happy with the system defaults:

```
/* update.c (simple version) */
# define TRUE 1
main() {
 while (TRUE) {
 sync();
 sleep(30);
 }
}
```

A small system with only a few users can stand a 30-second (or even longer) update or sync. Larger systems, on which 30 seconds represents far more data for many more users, might stand to have a shorter interval, perhaps every 15 seconds if the disk I/O doesn't slow down processing. For fault-tolerant systems running critical tasks, you might want an interval as short as 1 second.

The *fsck* Program

The fsck command consists of several file-system reporting and repair tools. You should do any file system repairs before bringing up the system for multiuser use, because when too many directories become corrupted, a mounted disk system unravels faster than a cheap sweater. In actual practice, large, busy machines stop running more often than small machines, so file systems should be checked frequently (daily) on this category of machine. Installations that run continuously should have regularly scheduled warm starts so that file systems can be checked and repaired. (*A warm start* means bringing the system down to single-user level and bringing it back up to multiuser level without actually rebooting or powering down the system.) Many large installations do a warm start every morning precisely for this reason. You have the option of running fsck on the entire system with one command or on individual file systems. In the command line

```
# fsck /dev/dsk/hd0
```

/dev/dsk/hd0 is the name of the device holding the file system you want to check. (To see what file system device names your system is using, you execute a df.)

System crashes can radically alter a file system, but don't wait for your system to fall down before you do an fsck! Even a small power glitch can make the system a little weird. Given enough time, files that just sit and rotate on disk day after day can degrade. Cosmic radiation striking impurities in the disk substrate can change any bit's value, and if one of the important bits in the directory structure or inode gets flipped, your directory is corrupted. (No, we're not kidding; research alpha particles.) As you can see, periodically checking and repairing your file systems provide data insurance.

Most of the time, an fsck yields no errors in the file system:

```
# fsck /dev/dsk/hd0
/dev/dsk/hd0
/dev/dsk/hd0 File System: / Volume: xt1

/dev/dsk/hd0 ** Phase 1 - Check Blocks and Sizes
/dev/dsk/hd0 ** Phase 2 - Check Pathnames
/dev/dsk/hd0 ** Phase 3 - Check Connectivity
/dev/dsk/hd0 ** Phase 4 - Check Reference Counts
/dev/dsk/hd0 ** Phase 5 - Check Free List
/dev/dsk/hd0 551 files 12260 blocks 3864 free
#
```

The fsck procedure has five (or six) possible phases. In this discussion, each phase is described one at a time, along with its corresponding error messages. When something is wrong, fsck starts asking you questions that require answers. Although some of these error messages are scary, *remain calm at all times*. The worst possible error means only that you have to restore a file system from your backup tapes. If you allow panic to set in, you are setting yourself up for human error, known to have caused reformatted disks, erased backup tapes, and similar problems. Remember that if you receive a particularly frightening message from fsck, the first thing you should do is *run fsck all over again*. On many occasions, when we prepare for the worst, a rerun allows fsck to fix all the problems on its own. Newer versions of fsck have improved capability to get you out of trouble! Be sure to write down any inode or block numbers that fsck tells you about so that you can repair them later.

Phase 1: Check Blocks and Sizes

The first phase deals with the file system's inode list. Phase 1 checks inode types, examines the inode block numbers for bad or duplicate blocks, and checks the inode format. Possible Phase 1 error messages are presented here, followed immediately by explanations of the errors.

```
Unknown File Type I=1234 (CLEAR)?
```

The Unknown File Type error means what it says. An unrecognizable file type has been discovered on an inode (for example, 1234). The system can deal only with regular files, special files, and directory files. If you see this error, the only realistic option is to clear the inode and thus the file. That fills the inode with zeros, effectively wiping it out forever. Clearing the inode causes an UNALLOCATED error to show up in Phase 2 for any directory that references this file.

```
Link count table overflow (CONTINUE)?
```

fsck maintains an internal table containing a list of allocated inodes with a link count of zero (files with no directory entries). If this table overflows, it generates the Link count table overflow error. A *no* reply terminates fsck. A *yes* reply allows fsck to continue but does not allow a complete check of the system. You should rerun fsck after encountering this error.

```
Can't [stat, open, read, write, seek, create] ...
```

A message similar to any of these phrases, such as Can't read or Can't create, indicates that the disk is inaccessible in some way. You should check to make sure that the disk is physically online and not write-protected, and that you have permission to access it (to look at both the character and block device entries for this disk in the /dev directory). Are you running fsck as superuser? You should be!

```
Size check: fsize X isize Y
```

The superblock has really gotten scrambled, and the file system or inode sizes make no sense. Using great caution, you have to go into the superblock and correct these numbers (see the section "The fsdb Program" later in this chapter). If you cannot edit the superblock and correct such an error for any reason (including fear), you will probably have to reload this entire file system from your backups; take courage.

```
9999 BAD I=1234
```

If a block number doesn't make sense to fsck, it lets you know. If, for example, block number 9999 in inode 1234 is out of range, fsck tells you. (This error condition also invokes a BAD/DUP error condition in Phases 2 and 4.)

```
EXCESSIVE BAD BLOCKS I=1234 (CONTINUE)?
```

What if the BAD condition uncovers 10 blocks or more with a meaningless block number? A *no* reply to this error terminates fsck. A *yes* reply causes fsck to ignore the remaining blocks in the inode and go on to the next inode. Run a second fsck to recheck the system.

```
9999 DUP I=1234
```

This message means that inode 1234 contains a block (9999) claimed by another inode. This error also causes Phase 1B to be activated, so you get the BAD/DUP indication in Phases 2 and 4. This situation may mean that both files could be messed up. You can save one file and destroy the other. If it is text, you may be able to salvage something.

```
EXCESSIVE DUP BLOCKS I=1234 (CONTINUE)?
```

Ten or more DUP blocks are considered excessive. A *no* reply terminates fsck. A *yes* allows fsck to continue, but it is not complete. Run another fsck.

```
DUP TABLE OVERFLOW (CONTINUE)?
```

fsck's duplicate block table is full. A *no* reply terminates fsck. A *yes* causes fsck to continue. A second fsck is needed to make a complete check of the system.

```
POSSIBLE FILE SIZE ERROR I=1234
```

This message indicates a disagreement between the number of blocks used by an inode and the size of the file. The message is a warning only and is not considered a serious error. You will *always* get this error on named pipes (depending on your version of fsck); therefore, be prepared when you check the file system containing /usr/spool/lp. Still, it is nice to have an error-free run of fsck, so here is how you can clear this error for ordinary files:

1. Finish checking this file system.
2. Keep the system in single-user mode (or bring it back down to that level).
3. mount the file system on which the error occurred.
4. Find the file in question, using ncheck -i.
5. Copy the file to an unused file name temporarily.
6. sync! (You're in single-user mode, remember?)

7. Remove the original file.

8. Rename the temporary file to the original name.

9. `umount` the file system. (This automatically does a `sync`, so your work gets saved.)

An example is always more illuminating than a list of steps or rules:

```
# fsck /dev/xt0c                                    — Step 1
/dev/xt0c
/dev/xt0c File System: /usr Volume: xt0c

/dev/xt0c ** Phase 1 - Check Blocks and Sizes
 POSSIBLE FILE SIZE ERROR I=134
/dev/xt0c ** Phase 2 - Check Pathnames
/dev/xt0c ** Phase 3 - Check Connectivity
/dev/xt0c ** Phase 4 - Check Reference Counts
/dev/xt0c ** Phase 5 - Check Free List
/dev/xt0c 551 files 12260 blocks 3864 free
# mount /dev/xt0c /usr                              — Steps 2 and 3

# ncheck -i 134 /dev/xt0c                           — Step 4
/dev/xt0c:
134 /adm/pacct
# cd /usr/adm
# ls
acct cronlog.2 dtmp msgbuf sulog
aculog cronlog.3 fee pacct usracct
cronlog cronlog.4 lastlog sa
cronlog.0 cronlog.5 messages savacct
cronlog.1 cronlog.6 messages.old shutdownlog
# cp pacct temp                                     — Step 5
# sync                                              — Step 6
# rm pacct                                          — Step 7
# mv temp pacct                                     — Step 8
# cd /
# umount /dev/xt0c                                  — Step 9
# init 2
```

Why don't you simply `mv` the file to a new name? The `mv` command doesn't actually do anything more than change inode information. Because the system is "confused" as to the actual length of the file, the file must be copied to give the system another chance to get the length right.

```
DIRECTORY MISALIGNED (CLEAR)?
```

If you get this error message, you have a totally garbled directory. The algorithm testing for alignment divides the number of bytes in the directory by 16 (14 characters for the name and 2 bytes for the inode number)—in short, a mod 16. If there is a remainder, you have a problem, and clearing it is the only solution.

```
PARTLY ALLOCATED INODE I=1234 (CLEAR)?
```

A wishy-washy inode (1234) has been discovered. It is neither allocated nor unallocated. The CLEAR prompt deletes the inode if you give a *yes* reply; otherwise, the problem remains.

```
Phase 1B: Rescan for more DUPS
```

A duplicate block has been detected. The system is now rescanned to make sure that no other duplicate blocks were missed in the first pass.

Phase 2: Check Path Names

Phase 2 is designed to clean up after Phase 1. Phase 2 removes directory entries that point to files or directories modified by Phase 1. Possible Phase 2 error messages are listed here, followed immediately by explanations.

```
ROOT INODE UNALLOCATED, TERMINATING
```

Inode 2, the root inode, is out of allocation bits. This error is serious enough to cause the fsck program to quit, and you are in big trouble. You will probably have to restore the entire file system from backup media.

```
ROOT NODE NOT DIRECTORY (FIX)?
```

If the root inode is not a directory, a *no* reply terminates fsck. A *yes* forces the root inode to become a directory. Prepare for an almost infinite number of errors if you answer *yes*.

```
DUPS/BAD IN ROOT INODE (CONTINUE)?
```

Phase 1 found duplicate inodes. A *yes* reply causes the error condition to be ignored; a *no* causes fsck to terminate.

```
I OUT OF RANGE I=1234 NAME=core (REMOVE)?
```

One of the files in the directory being checked has an inode number out of range (usually caused by an inode being greater than the number of inodes allocated to the file system). A *yes* reply removes the file; a *no* ignores the condition.

```
UNALLOCATED I=1234 OWNER=root MODE=777
SIZE=64 MTIME=Fri Apr 1 00:00:00 EST 1988 NAME=tmp (REMOVE)?
```

This error message means that a directory entry has been found which has no allocate-mode bits. A *yes* reply removes the directory; a *no* ignores the condition.

```
DUP/BAD I=1234 OWNER=root MODE=777
SIZE=64 MTIME=Fri Apr 1 00:00:00 EST 1988 DIR=tmp (REMOVE)?
```

Phase 1 or 1B has uncovered duplicate or bad blocks. A *yes* reply causes the entire directory to be removed; a *no* ignores the condition.

```
DUP/BAD I=1234 OWNER=root MODE=666
SIZE=27 MTIME=Fri Apr 1 00:00:00 EST 1988 FILE=core (REMOVE)?
```

Phase 1 or 1B has uncovered duplicate or bad blocks. A *yes* reply causes the file to be removed; a *no* ignores the condition.

```
BAD BLK IN DIR OWNER=root MODE=777
SIZE=64 MTIME=Fri Apr 1 00:00:00 EST 1988
```

This message indicates that a bad block, usually caused by a file name with no zeros after it, has been found in the specified directory. You correct the error by removing the directory or bad file name.

Phase 3: Check Connectivity

Phase 3 cleans up after Phase 2. The main concern of Phase 3 is connectivity—making sure that each inode has at least one directory entry and that multiple links make sense. Phase 3 also creates error messages for unreferenced directories and lost+found directories that are full or missing. These error messages are listed here, followed by explanations.

```
UNREF DIR OWNER=root MODE=777
SIZE=64 MTIME=Fri Apr 1 00:00:00 EST 1988 (RECONNECT)?
```

The directory inode has no connection to a directory. fsck does not tolerate an unconnected full directory. A *yes* answer reconnects the inode in lost+found; a *no* allows the error to continue.

```
SORRY, NO SPACE IN lost+found DIRECTORY
or
SORRY. No lost+found DIRECTORY
```

If you forgot to run the mklost+found program presented in Chapter 2, it's too late now. The file or directory will be lost.

```
DIR I=1234 CONNECTED, PARENT WAS I=5678
```

This message shows that the inode in question (1234) has been successfully attached to the file system's lost+found directory.

Phase 4: Check Reference Counts

This phase is concerned with the link count and any alterations made in previous phases. Phase 4 lists errors resulting from unreferenced files, a missing or full lost+found directory, an incorrect link count, bad or duplicate blocks, or an incorrect sum for the free inode count. The error messages are listed here, followed by explanations.

```
UNREF FILE OWNER=root MODE=666
SIZE=27 MTIME=Fri Apr 1 00:00:00 EST 1988 (RECONNECT)?
```

A file (inode) exists without a directory entry. A *yes* reply connects the file to the lost+found directory; a *no* invokes a CLEAR error in this phase.

```
SORRY. NO lost+found DIR
```

No lost+found directory has been created. When this message appears, it's a little late to make one (for this file) but early enough to make a lost+found for next time.

```
SORRY, NO SPACE IN lost+found DIR
```

No space has been found in lost+found. Check lost+found to see whether it has any contents. It's probably full.

```
CLEAR?
```

If the file just mentioned cannot be connected to lost+found, this query appears. A *yes* reply zeros out the inode, thereby eliminating the file.

```
LINK COUNT DIR=tmp OWNER=root MODE=777
SIZE=64 MTIME=Fri Apr 1 00:00:00 EST 1988
        or
LINK COUNT FILE=core OWNER=root MODE=666
SIZE=27 MTIME=Fri Apr 1 00:00:00 EST 1988 COUNT 3 SHOULD BE 1 (ADJUST)?
```

The number of links for a file or directory is wrong. A *yes* reply corrects the link count; a *no* ignores the condition.

```
UNREF DIR=tmp OWNER=root MODE=777
SIZE=64 MTIME=Fri Apr 1 00:00:00 EST 1988 (CLEAR)?
or
UNREF FILE=core OWNER=root MODE=666
SIZE=27 MTIME=Fri Apr 1 00:00:00 EST 1988 (CLEAR)?
```

The file (inode) is not connected to a directory. A *yes* zeros out the file. A *no* ignores the condition.

```
BAD/DUP DIR=tmp OWNER=root MODE=777
SIZE=64 MTIME=Fri Apr 1 00:00:00 EST 1988 (CLEAR)?
or
BAD/DUP FILE=core OWNER=root MODE=666
SIZE=27 MTIME=Fri Apr 1 00:00:00 EST 1988 (CLEAR)?
```

Here you see the sins of Phase 1 revisited. Duplicate or bad blocks found in the first phase have yet to be dealt with. A *yes* reply clears the inode; a *no* continues the error.

```
FREE INODE COUNT IN SUPERBLK (FIX)?
```

The free inode count in the superblock does not match the free inode count found by fsck. A *yes* reply updates the count; a *no* leaves it incorrect.

Phase 5: Check Free List

UNIX is quite fastidious about maintaining a balance among the number of blocks allocated within a file system, the number in use, and the difference (known as the free block list). When fsck calculates a free block count that is not in agreement with the free block list (FREE LIST), Phase 5 reports this as an error condition. Several error messages for Phase 5 are listed here, with explanations.

```
EXCESSIVE BAD BLOCKS IN FREE LIST (CONTINUE)?
```

Too many—usually 10—"bad" blocks have been detected. A "bad" block has a block address beyond the acceptable range established by the start and finish block addresses. fsck tests about everything testable to ensure the sanity of the file system. With a *yes* reply, the rest of the free block list is ignored. A rerun of fsck is in order. A *no* reply terminates fsck.

```
EXCESSIVE DUP BLOCKS IN FREE LIST (CONTINUE)?
```

This message tells you that too many inodes have been duplicated. The proper number is 0, and 10 is considered excessive. Answering *yes* to CONTINUE makes fsck ignore the rest of the list.

`BAD FREEBLK COUNT`

This message means another accounting upset. The number of free blocks in a free list block is too low or too high (less than 0 or more than 50). This error also generates the `BAD FREE LIST` message.

`N BAD BLOCKS IN FREE LIST`

This message, which quantifies the number of bad blocks, is the final act of the `EXCESSIVE BAD BLOCKS` error message.

`N DUP BLOCKS IN FREE LIST`

This message quantifies the number of excessive duplicate blocks.

`N BLOCKS MISSING`

N unused blocks allegedly belonging to inodes were not found in the free list.

`FREE BLK COUNT WRONG IN SUPERBLK (FIX)?`

A disagreement exists between the free block count and the number in the superblock. A *yes* reply modifies the superblock into agreement; otherwise, the error remains.

`BAD FREE LIST (SALVAGE)?`

This message indicates a number of possible problems. There could be bad blocks in the free block list, duplicate blocks in the free block list, or blocks missing from the file system. In short, any of the Phase 5 errors causes this message. A *yes* reply replaces the free block list with a new one; a *no* leaves the mess as it is.

`X Files Y Blocks Z Free`

This advisory message simply reports the total number of files, blocks in use, and blocks of free space in the modified file system.

`***** FILE SYSTEM WAS MODIFIED *****`

This advisory message, which means that an error was corrected by `fsck`, appears when `fsck` is completely finished with this particular file system. (The message appears after Phase 6, if that phase is required.)

Phase 6: Salvage Free List

The last phase occurs only if something goes wrong in Phase 5 and you answer *yes* to the BAD FREE LIST (SALVAGE)? prompt. Phase 6 reconstructs the free block list.

A Special Note for Checking the Root File System

If any errors whatsoever are noted when you run fsck against the root file system, you get the following message:

```
***** BOOT UNIX (NO SYNC!) *****
```

This message means what it says. *Do NOT do a* sync *or an* /etc/shutdown. Do a cold start by pressing the reset button (or turning the key) and do it as quickly as possible before the next sync. The reason is that fsck fixes the file system by writing directly to the disk. If a sync is done, it writes the old, incorrect information from memory to disk, undoing the work of fsck and requiring a new run. Shutting down *without* a sync is necessary only when the root file system contains a problem.

Administrative Tips for *fsck*

When an error is detected by fsck, you should write down the error and note its location and address. You may decide to clear the error manually with clri. Manually fixing file system errors gives you the opportunity to check the directory entry associated with the inode. You may decide to notify the owners of the lost files. Most of these files, however, are either lost by clearing or are sent to lost+found. Because they are usually temporary files, they are normally invisible to the user who invoked the program that created them. Had the crash not happened and the process completed, they would have been automatically erased.

Generally, when you see fsck prompts that ask such questions as SALVAGE?, FIX?, CONTINUE?, RECONNECT?, or ADJUST?, it is safe to answer *yes*. Prompts that ask permission to REMOVE? or CLEAR? must be handled more carefully. Make a note of the disk ID (/dev/whatever) and the inode number so that you know where you have sustained damage. If, for example, you find that the disk in question is /dev/dd0 and it is your /tmp directory, there is little to worry about. If the damage is on a user disk, you may have a restore job ahead of you. If, for some reason, you cannot restore (from backup media) a file that fsck wants to clear, you have nothing to lose by attempting to copy the file as mentioned earlier under POSSIBLE FILE SIZE ERROR.

If you are using a CRT terminal as the system console, one day your fsck messages will scroll right off the screen before you can read them. We suggest that you ask management to buy an inexpensive, reliable printing terminal to use as the console. It will help pay for itself by logging system error messages that sometimes precede a crash.

The *fsdb* Program

If the file system or superblock is so garbled that even fsck won't touch it, you will have to go in manually and patch things up a bit. This is the computer equivalent of open-heart surgery, and your scalpel is fsdb (*file system de*bugger).

Because there are many ways in which you can get into trouble during this process, don't get too fancy using fsdb. Ninety-nine percent of the occasions when fsdb is needed, it is simply to patch one or two locations in the superblock, called fsize and isize. The isize parameter tells UNIX how many blocks were allocated for file system inodes, whereas fsize tells the total number of blocks in the file system. In a properly operating file system, these are the values reported when you run df -t:

```
# df -t /dev/dsk/hd0
 / (/dev/dsk/hd0 ): 3864 blocks 1497 i-nodes
  total: 16384 blocks 2048 i-nodes
 #
```

Here you can see that the file system has a total of 16384 blocks and 2048 inodes allocated (fsize and isize), with 3864 blocks and 1497 inodes free. When you run fsdb, this is how it looks:

```
# fsdb /dev/dsk/hd0
/dev/dsk/hd0(/): 1K byte Block File System
FSIZE = 8192, ISIZE = 2048
```

Already you're running into some sort of trouble. According to df, the file system has 16384 blocks, yet fsdb indicates that there are 8192. But wait! fsdb also said that this is a 1K file system. Could it be that df is talking about 512 bytes per block?

This system happens to use 512-byte logical blocks and 1024-byte physical blocks (the file system is earlier than SVR4), and to keep "compatibility" with even older software releases, reports things at "user level" in 512-byte blocks. (Don't be annoyed at us for not using a "normal" system. There's *no such thing* as a normal system.) Be sure to check the man page on df and du; many systems always report space in 512-byte blocks, no matter what the logical block is. As system administrator, you are supposed to remember what is really going on.

Now that you understand the block size, you can dump the superblock in decimal and take a close look at it. On most machines, block 1 is the superblock, but because this one has already proved to be a bit strange, you can start from the beginning. The idea is to know what you are looking for, so turn to the entry for filsys in Section 5 of the *UNIX Programmer's Manual*, or to the file /usr/include/sys/filsys.h (/usr/include/sys/fs/s5filsys.h if you have SVR4) on your system, and you'll see something like this:

```
/*
 * Structure of the superblock
 */
struct filsys {
unsigned short isize; /* size in blocks of i-list */
 daddr_t fsize; /* size in blocks of entire volume */
 short nfree; /* number of addresses in free */
 daddr_t free[NICFREE]; /* free block list */
 short ninode; /* number of i-nodes in inode */
 ino_t inode[NICINOD]; /* free i-node list */
 char flock; /* lock during free list manipulation */
 char ilock; /* lock during i-list manipulation */
 char fmod; /* superblock modified flag */
 char ronly; /* mounted read-only flag */
 time_t time; /* last superblock update */
 short dinfo[4]; /* device information */
 daddr_t tfree; /* total free blocks*/
 ino_t tinode; /* total free inodes */
 char fname[6]; /* file system name */
 char fpack[6]; /* file system pack name */
 long fill[15]; /* ADJUST so sizeof filsys is 512 */
 long magic; /* number to indicate new file system */
 long type; /* type of file system */
};

 #define FsMAGIC 0xfd187e20 /*if magic=this, type is valid */
```

```
/* valid values for type: */
#define Fs1b 1 /* 512 byte blocks */
#define Fs2b 2 /* 1024 byte blocks */
```

In SVR4, a number of the variable names have changed.

The general idea is simply that the first number you are looking for is isize, and the second number is fsize. Unfortunately, you cannot just look for 2048 followed by 8192. If you read a bit further in the filsys entry, you'll find that "the i-list is isize-2 blocks long." Look at the definition of isize: the size of the i-list in *blocks*. Because there are 1024 bytes per block and 64 bytes per inode, there must be 16 inodes per block. Both df and fsdb agree that there are 2048 inodes here, so there must be 2048 divided by 16, or 128 blocks' worth of inodes. Add 2 (for the "isize-2") and you get 130. Look at hexadecimal addresses 200 and 204 in the dump, and what do you see? 130 and 8192! We can't say that it's obvious, but at least it works:

```
0b.p0e                                              — Command to fsdb
0000:       8   1024    918   1858   2047   2047      3    547
0010:       3  10178     24    913     31   8356  24628    552
0020:      63    324    168    377    261   6931  24948   7049
0030:     401   5507   8621   6468   8622   6469  25028   8498
0040:     499   9465  16921   7212    560   5679   8797   6202
0050:     640   1994  25228   7793    711   8973  25308   6482
0060:     738   2293    766   1923  13059   5261  25352   4165
0070:   17194   9735    819   4345  13112   6882  25404   2182
0080:   25404   5550  25411   3945    863  10268    864   8112
0090:   25490   4938  25490   7710  25491   7846      0      0
*
0200:     130      0   8192     33      0    232      0    230
0210:       0    228      0    226      0    224      0    222
0220:       0    220      0    218      0    216      0    214
*
0370:     129    128    127    126    125    124    123    122
0380:     121    120    119    118    117    116    115    114
0390:     113     31     12    112     11      0      0   7547
03a0:   31524      5    200      0      0      0   1932   1497
03b0:   12032      0      0  29552  24946  25856      0      0
*
03f0: 0 0 0 0 -744 32288 0 2
```

In the preceding dump, the asterisks represent lines that contain either all zeros or repeated data (addresses of blocks on the free list, which are not useful to you right now). Thirty-two-bit words are used with the most significant byte zero, which is why the numbering is two by two. Counting in hex, the top line therefore represents addresses of 0, 2, 4, 6, 8, a, c, and e.

Other information can be pried from this dump. Do you see the contents of addresses 3ac and 3ae? These show the number of free blocks and inodes (tfree and tinode) reported by df previously. Again, the value 1932 found at address 3ac in the dump refers to the number of actual 1024-byte blocks free in the file system, which corresponds to 3864—the number of 512-byte blocks from df.

Now let's play with fsdb a little. In the EXAMPLES section for fsdb in the *UNIX System Administrator's Manual*, this command is listed:

```
2i.fd                                             — Command to fsdb
d0:        2   .
d1:        2   .   .
d2:        3   u   s   r
d3:        4   d   e   v
d4:      202   b   i   n
d5:      260   b   i   n   .   c   a   d   m   u   s
d6:      299   b   i   n   .   s   y   s   5
d7:      359   b   i   n   .   s   y   s   3
d8:      430   b   i   n   .   v   e   r   7
d9:      515   x   f
d10:     516   e   t   c
d11:     571   l   i   b
d12:      15   u   n   i   x
d13:     383   .   l   o   g   i   n
d14:     384   .   p   r   o   f   i   l   e
d15:     385   .   c   s   h   r   c
d16:     386   .   s   t   d   c   s   h   r   c
d17:     606   t   m   p
d18:     607   .   t   i   p   r   c
d19:       0   c   o   r   e
d20:     608   l   o   s   t   +   f   o   u   n   d
d21:     605   u   n   i   x   .   b   a   k
d22:       0   f   0
d23:     611   k
d24:     612   s   t   a   n   d   a   l   o   n   e
d25:     614   .   n   e   w   s   r   c
d26:      43   o   w   n
d27:     105   n   o   h   u   p   .   o   u   t
d28:     110   i   p   s
d29:     109   d   b
d30:       0
d31:       0
```

This listing displays the inode numbers and names of the contents of the root directory, just as the fsdb manual page says. Removed files and directories appear with the inode number set to zero (as in d19: 0 core in the preceding listing). Note calmly in passing that inode 2 points to both . and .., which is proof that this is indeed the root directory. Only the root directory can point to itself as its own parent.

Following the manual again, change to the fifth inode listed and dump the first 512 bytes in ASCII. This happens to be the directory /bin.cadmus, which contains some commands supplied by the original equipment manufacturer (OEM):

```
d5i.fc
00731c00: \? \?  .  \0 \0 \0 \0 \0 \0 \0 \0 \0 \0 \0 \0 \0
00731c10: \0 \?  .  .  \0 \0 \0 \0 \0 \0 \0 \0 \0 \0 \0 \0
00731c20: \? \?  m  a  k  e  s  t  5  2  5  \0 \0 \0 \0 \0
00731c30: \? \?  b  a  d  b  l  k  \0 \0 \0 \0 \0 \0 \0 \0
00731c40: \? \?  c  e  r  b  e  r  u  s  \0 \0 \0 \0 \0 \0
00731c50: \? \?  c  o  n  n  e  c  t  \0 \0 \0 \0 \0 \0 \0
00731c60: \? \?  d  i  s  k  f  o  r  m  a  t  \0 \0 \0 \0
00731c70: \? \?  d  l  c  o  n  f  i  g  \0 \0 \0 \0 \0 \0
00731c80: \? \?  d  l  s  u  p  p  o  r  t  \0 \0 \0 \0 \0
00731c90: \? \?  d  l  u  p  d  a  t  e  \0 \0 \0 \0 \0 \0
00731c90: \? \?  u  c  o  n  n  e  c  t  \0 \0 \0 \0 \0 \0
00731ca0: \? \?  u  m  o  n  i  t  o  r  \0 \0 \0 \0 \0 \0
00731cb0: \? \?  w  a  t  c  h  d  o  g  \0 \0 \0 \0 \0 \0
00731cc0: \? \?  u  u  h  o  s  t  s  \0 \0 \0 \0 \0 \0 \0
00731cd0: \?     u  u  q  \0 \0 \0 \0 \0 \0 \0 \0 \0 \0 \0
...
```

Now let's see how you start at a particular address, which must be typed in decimal even though it is displayed in hex, and proceed one word at a time. If you type 0+256, this gives you an offset of 256 *words* into the block, which is *byte* address hex 200. Then, by pressing Enter, you go to the next item sequentially (in this case, a word):

```
0+256
0200: 00000082 (130)
0202: 00000000 (0)
0204: 00002000 (8192)
0206: 00000021 (33)
0208: 00000000 (0)
q
#
```

In each case, the contents of the address are displayed in hex (with the decimal equivalent in parentheses). To stop displaying addresses, press Delete or Ctrl-C.

Here's what happens if you actually change one of the values and then run fsck (don't fool around with *your* root file system until you are ready to write a system administration book too!):

```
# fsck /dev/dsk/hd0
/dev/dsk/hd0
/dev/dsk/hd0 File System: / Volume: xt1a
Size check: fsize 4 isize 6313580
#
```

The fsize and isize are totally scrambled. This is the last thing you ever want to see from fsck! You will have to patch the superblock just to get fsck to run:

```
# fsdb /dev/dsk/hd0
/dev/dsk/hd0(/): 1K byte Block File System
FSIZE = 4, ISIZE = 2048
```

The first thing you notice is that fsdb isn't as upset about isize as fsck was, but fsdb agrees that fsize doesn't look healthy. Note this dump:

```
0b.p0e
0000:    8   1024    918   1858   2047   2047      3    547
0010:    3  10178     24    913     31   8356  24628    552
0020:   63    324    168    377    261   6931  24948   7049
*
0200:  130      0      4     33      0    232      0    230
0210:    0    228      0    226      0    224      0    222
0220:    0    220      0    218      0    216      0    214
```

It seems clear that fsize has been changed to 4. Because you know that it should read 8192, you must change the value. Start from hex address 200 as before:

```
0+256
0200: 00000082 (130)
0202: 00000000 (0)
0204: 00000004 (4)
```

You change the value by typing an equal sign and the value you want. Make sure that you know what you are up to, because fsdb writes *directly* to the disk and does not wait for a sync:

```
0204: 00000004 (4)
=8192
0204: 00002000 (8192)
q
#
```

When fsdb verifies the change, you type **q** to quit, and you're almost done. The safest action to take at this point is to reboot the system immediately, because you are dealing with the root file system. A reboot would not be necessary if you were patching an unmounted file system, however.

If you are confused, another, easier method is available. The other way of fixing this problem is to restore the file system from a backup. That method is covered in Chapter 8. But if your appetite is whetted for more fooling around with fsdb, think hard. Do you *really* want to fool around with your file system at that level, where one wrong key could blow the whole thing up? Having fsdb around is like having a parachute in an airplane: you may be a bit safer having it there, but using it can be pretty scary too.

Remember one more thing: the only reason that we know how to patch fsize to 8192 is that we know what it is supposed to be in the first place! Right now, go to your system, run df -t (so that you'll know how many blocks were allocated for file system inodes, and the total number of blocks in the file system), and save the output somewhere safe in case you ever run into this kind of problem.

/etc/checkall—A Handy Shell Program

If you have the dfsck program on your system, you can use it to check two file systems simultaneously. This saves time, but you must watch the console carefully. Error prompts refer to just one system at a time, but other output is interspersed and hard to read. Don't use dfsck until you are comfortable with running normal fsck, and make sure that you don't try to check two file systems on the same disk at the same time; you want to have the least number of variables for this kind of activity. The best way to do this is with a shell script like /etc/checkall:

```
fsck -D /dev/xt0a
dfsck -t /tmp/dfsck.chk $* /dev/rxt0[cef] - $* /dev/rxt1[acef]
```

/etc/checkall is generally called from /etc/bcheckrc or /etc/rc (see Chapter 4), like this:

```
# /etc/checkall -D
```

This way, any parameters passed to /etc/checkall are passed to all file systems being checked, *except root*. The root file system should *never* be checked with dfsck, and *never* using the raw device. To lose the root file system means that you lose everything.

Summary

Now that you have learned how to bring up the system, check it, and repair it, you need to know the location of all the system administration tools and files. A slightly corrupted file system can deteriorate into a disaster. If you check your file systems regularly and catch errors early, you won't ever have to do the scary stuff, such as edit the superblock.

4

Where
Everything Is
and How to
Find It

As a novice UNIX system administrator, you have a big problem: how do you find out where everything is? The UNIX file system is a relatively complex tree hierarchy, with trunks, major and minor branches, and many intertwining sticks and leaves. It takes time to get to know your way around! Eventually, you will become intimately familiar with the UNIX file system as your system administration skills mature. You will develop daily, weekly, and monthly procedures to groom, curry, and clean the entire file system. You will also learn to rely on the cron table (crontab) to do many of these weekly procedures automatically. This chapter will save you a great deal of time prowling the system so that you can do more rewarding work. Be aware that different systems may have things in different places. There are some significant differences between SVR3 and SVR4. Snoop around on your system and check out where things really are. Make a map.

Where the UNIX System Administration Files Are

You need to know the location of many files and directories in order to do your work well. The trick is to learn where to look. Files and directories in UNIX proper are grouped by type. (*UNIX proper* is the standard distribution copy of UNIX, before user-added files confuse the issue.)

System V Release 4 inherited a great deal from BSD UNIX; one important facility is the symbolic link. A *symbolic link* is a file that merely points at another file. Unlike real links, symbolic links can span across file systems. In order to maintain some compatibility with other UNIX systems, SVR4 has many symbolic links for the system administration files. For example, the scripts used for initializing the system—the rc scripts (rc0 through rc6)—can be found in the /etc subdirectory, but these are just symbolic links to the real files in /usr/sbin. However, the SVR4 model doesn't seem complete because most of the scripts invoked by the rc scripts actually reside in the /etc/rc0.d through /etc/rc6.d subdirectories. The existence of symbolic links helps bridge a limitation of the physical links but can make the graph of your file system very messy!

Table 4.1 lists some of the more important directories every UNIX system administrator eventually needs to know.

Table 4.1. The most important UNIX directories.

SVR3	SVR4	Description
/bin		Executable commands for basic UNIX operations. These commands must be available here when the /usr file system is not mounted. The noncritical utilities are usually kept in /usr/bin, though.
	/home	Personal directories for users.
/dev		Home of device files.
/dump		Home for core dumps (not standard).
/etc		System administrator's toolbox.
/etc/conf		UNIX configuration files for building new kernels and adding drivers.
/etc/default		Files that contain defaults for system programs such as mount and lp.
/etc/rc.d		Scripts for going into multiuser mode. There may be several similar subdirectories for different init levels.

SVR3	SVR4	Description
/lost+found		Where "lost" files are placed. A lost+found exists under the root of each file system.
/tmp		Repository for temporary files only.
	/var	Networking environment files.
/usr/adm	/usr/sbin	Home for some administration files.
/usr/bin		Executable commands not in /bin. These are standard UNIX utilities not critical to running in single-user/system user/system maintenance mode (init level S).
/usr/bin/X11		X Window System commands. An alternative location is /usr/X/bin.
/usr/include		Header files for C programing.
/usr/local		Commands local to your system (not standard).
/usr/local/bin		Commands local to your system (not standard, but we recommend its use).
/usr/lbin		Commands local to your system (not standard).
/usr/lib		Macros and specialized command groups.
/usr/lib/news		Commands and controls for Usenet news.
/usr/lib/uucp	/etc/uucp	Commands and controls for UUCP networking.
/usr/mail	/var/mail	Mail directory for System V.
/mnt		Mount point for temporarily mounted file systems.
/usr/src		Source code for system commands.
/usr/spool/at		Spooling directory for at command.
/usr/spool/cron		Spooling directory for cron command.
/usr/spool/lp		Printer spooler directory (System V and later).
/usr/spool/lpr		Printer spooler directory (System III and earlier).
/usr/spool/news		The top of the tree for Usenet news articles.
/usr/spool/uucp		UUCP job spooling directory.
/usr/spool/uucppublic		A publicly available directory tree for UUCP file transfers.
/usr/tmp		Another repository for temporary files.
/usr/ucb		Berkeley binaries.

The next sections describe some of these directories and show how you can use them and their contents.

The /bin Directory

In addition to keeping the system running, providing user support is part of your job. Occasionally, a user will come to you and complain that a command does not work. You must remedy the situation, but where do you start? Usually, the command won't work because, through some oversight, the directory of that command has not been placed in the user's search path.

One of the first places to look for commands is the /bin directory. As its name implies, /bin was originally intended to house *bin*ary executable files. Now it holds a few shell scripts as well. /bin holds many system administration commands and some user commands, but not all of them.

You also have to take into account the individuality of each machine when you look for commands. On most UNIX machines, there are a few commands specific to a certain OEM's machine, and these commands are usually located in a /usr/OEM/bin directory. For example, UTS is Amdahl's mainframe version of UNIX. Many virtual UTS machines can run on one actual Amdahl or IBM computer, and the command vmid identifies which virtual UTS UNIX machine you are working on. (Many virtual machines can time-share on one mainframe as if they were physically separate computer systems, and each virtual machine can support multiple users.) Obviously, the vmid command doesn't apply to UNIX on a VAX, so vmid and a few other system-specific commands are located in a special directory called /usr/amdahl/bin.

When you customize your UNIX machine, you eventually create a few commands of your own. The authors' machines have a directory called /usr/local/bin that houses customized backup routines, modem-control programs, and other specialized files.

Whether you use the name /usr/local, /usr/local/bin, /usr/lbin, or even /usr/allmine, you should use just one separate directory for locally added commands that are accessible to all users. (/usr/local/bin is the most common name for this directory.) If you keep adding programs to /bin, for instance, they could be lost in the future. System software is usually upgraded all at once from a distribution tape, and anything in /bin is in the root file system and therefore likely to be overwritten when the new distribution tape is loaded onto your system. If all of your own software is in one directory, you can always move it *en masse* to separate storage if necessary.

If you really need to find commands, you should look on your system for a command called `whereis` or `which`, which searches in known places for executable files. (Code for a similar program, `where`, is provided at the end of this chapter.) In an emergency, you can always find a file called `lostagain`, no matter where it is, with the following command:

```
# find / -name lostagain -print
```

We say "in an emergency" because the search could take a very long time on a large system; every file on the system is looked at.

The /*dev* Directory

UNIX is traditionally depicted as a series of concentric spheres with hardware at the center, users outside, and several spherical layers in between (refer again to Figure 1.1 in Chapter 1). The layer next to the hardware is usually designated as the kernel, but that layer is more accurately assigned to device drivers, which are represented by the special files in the /dev directory.

Device drivers are the software interface between UNIX and peripheral device hardware. Computers rely on devices like terminals, printers, modems, and plotters to make them complete machines. Without device drivers, computers cannot talk to these devices, and a computer without peripheral devices is about as useful as an airplane without wings. Peripherals generally store, accept, or display input/output (I/O) data, thereby allowing people to interact with computers. Because system administrators deal with drivers indirectly, this discussion first covers what device drivers are and then shows you how to work with them.

/*dev* Files Aren't What They Appear to Be

Little glory or credit has gone to the unsung heroes who write device drivers, and that is a shame. They are marvelous pieces of software. Each device driver has an upper half, written in C, that communicates with the kernel, and a corresponding lower half, written in C and assembler language, that talks directly to the hardware. The key to understanding device drivers is that the drivers are not located in /dev but are actually linked directly to the kernel. The "files" in /dev are not ordinary files at all. In fact, they are empty. Their directory and inode information is used as an index or pointer to the drivers. Obviously, the files in /dev are extremely specialized files. They are even referred to as *special files*.

People come in many different sizes, shapes, and colors, and so does I/O data. Two types of special files handle I/O data: block special files and character special files. *Block special files* handle data in blocks. In a 1K-block size machine, typical in System V, each block is one kilobyte or 1024 bytes long. This is both the buffer size and the disk-block size. All block data is buffered by the kernel. Typical block devices are disks (both hard and floppy) and tape. Block devices are used for the highest possible speeds because one operation results in the transfer of a relatively large amount of data.

Character special files handle raw data streams, one character at a time. Typical character devices are printers, terminals, and modems. The actual hardware takes care of all the details of transforming bits into characters and back, so a "character" device can be attached to either a parallel or serial port. Parallel ports send data to a device (usually a printer) using eight data wires *in parallel* to make a byte of character data. Serial ports send data over one wire, bit by bit, at a specific rate so that the receiving device can assemble the bits into a byte of character data. Serial ports are commonly used with terminals, modems, and some printers.

Now do a long listing of the /dev directory:

```
$ ls -l /dev/*
```

Character special files look like this:

```
crw-rw-rw-  1 root     1,  0 Nov 19  1989   /dev/tty
crw--w--w-  1 bruce    4,  0 Mar 28 20:23   /dev/tty0
crw-rw-rw-  1 karen    4,  1 Feb  7 19:05   /dev/tty1
crw-------  1 root     4,  2 Feb  7 19:05   /dev/tty2
crw-------  1 root     4,  3 Feb  7 19:05   /dev/tty3
crw-------  1 root     4,  4 Feb  7 19:05   /dev/tty4
crw-------  4 root     4,  5 Mar 28 20:56   /dev/tty5
c---------  1 root     4,  6 Mar 28 20:28   /dev/tty6
crw-------  1 root     4,  7 Feb  7 19:05   /dev/tty7
```

Block special files show up this way:

```
brw-r--r--  1 root     9,  0 Dec 31  1989   /dev/cd00
brw-r--r--  1 root     9,  1 Mar 23 10:03   /dev/cd01
brw-r--r--  2 root     9,  2 Dec 31  1969   /dev/cd02
brw-r--r--  1 root     9,  3 Oct 25 20:50   /dev/cd03
brw-r--r--  1 root     9,  4 Dec 13  1983   /dev/cd04
brw-r--r--  1 root     9,  5 Dec 13  1983   /dev/cd05
```

The first character in the permissions column indicates either a character (c) special file or a block (b) special file.

Examining a single, eight-column entry tells you even more:

```
crw-rw-rw-   1 karen    4,  1 Feb  7 19:05  /dev/tty1
```

The file permissions indicate that anyone on the system can write to the file. There is exactly 1 link to the file, which means that the system knows the file by only one name. The current owner is karen. The date and time of last access was Feb 7 at 19:05 (7:05 PM). The file name is tty1, the tty (terminal) located on port 1. So far, this is all pretty standard file information.

The numbers 4 and 1 located before the date are called the *major* and *minor* device numbers, respectively. Actually, these numbers are the most important information in this file entry. The major device number, 4, points to a device driver—in this case, device number 4. This lets the kernel code access the device driver program that will control the correct device. The minor number, 1, is the argument passed to that particular driver. When the device driver sees the 1, it knows to act on the port labeled 1. When asynchronous serial devices (anything that works over an RS-232 port) are involved, the minor number can be the port number.

Just to confuse you, there are also *character special drivers* for block special files:

```
$ ls -l /dev/rcd*
crw-r--r--   1 root        5,  0 Dec 31 1989  rcd00
crw-r--r--   1 root        5,  1 Dec 31 1989  rcd01
crw-r--r--   1 root        5,  2 Dec 31 1989  rcd02
crw-r--r--   1 root        5,  3 Dec 31 1989  rcd03
crw-r--r--   1 root        5,  4 Dec 13 1989  rcd04
crw-r--r--   1 root        5,  5 Dec 13 1989  rcd05
```

These are frequently called *raw devices* because you can read them "raw," or without the more sophisticated block access. Often when you are doing low-level I/O, operating on the raw device is faster. This is frequently the case when you use such commands as dd, fsck, cpio, and volcopy.

Theory aside, how are you going to deal with the files in /dev? They may be special files, but you treat them the same way you treat any other UNIX file. One of the ways a system administrator uses the files in /dev is to send a data stream to a device by way of its /dev entry. Because a tty entry in /dev acts as both a device and a file, if you type

```
# echo "hello there" >/dev/tty3
```

the message hello there appears on an operating terminal attached to port 3 on this sample system. (What would happen if a printer were on port 3 instead?) Notice that the redirection symbol > must be used instead of a pipe because the message is not sent to a process but to a file, a *special file*. You cannot direct output to `tty3` unless you are the user on `tty3` or the superuser, or unless the permissions have been left open so that anyone can write to the file.

Devices can be read also. Although there is nothing in the special file itself, reading from any device shows you the actual data coming from the device. Try reading from kernel memory space. Because this is generally binary data, it makes sense to use the `od` command so that you don't lock up your terminal by sending it the wrong combination of bits:

```
# od /dev/kmem
000 060000 001776 000000 000000 000000 002114 000000 002164
020 000000 002200 000000 002206 000000 002214 000000 002222
040 000000 002230 000000 002236 000000 002354 000000 004410
060 000000 002370 000000 002370 000000 002370 000000 002370
 . . .
```

Unless you are an expert in UNIX internals, the preceding data is close to meaningless. As superuser, you can read from the tape drive, your raw disk, the modem, or any terminal. Chapter 9 on security explains why it is important that a typical user not be able to read from all these places.

This brief examination of `/dev` gives you a glimpse of the marvelous design behind the UNIX system. `/dev` files have no contents because they are simply pointers to device driver programs. `/dev` files take or put data at one end, and send data to or from a device at the other. The actual device drivers are compiled within the kernel. However, the creators of the UNIX system cleverly designated `/dev` entries as special files so that they could be managed like other UNIX files.

Device Driver Source Code

What about the actual device drivers? When do you have to go into the kernel and modify device drivers or write new ones? Fortunately for the average UNIX system administrator, the answer is hardly ever. UNIX device drivers are extremely flexible. The drivers on an installed UNIX system, when combined with system commands and daemons, do just about anything you want them to do. (*Daemons* are programs that run continuously in the background to provide special services to other programs. Daemons are discussed in Chapter 11 on printers and probably exist right now in your system, so show some healthy respect.) There is very little that cannot be done with the existing asynchronous serial driver when it is used with `stty`.

/usr—The Mystery Directory

Do not make the mistake of approaching UNIX system administration with *too* much awe. (Convince the users that *you* deserve some awe instead.) Brilliantly conceived, sublime operating system design notwithstanding, UNIX is still in the process of being refined, and some parts of it are a bit rough around the edges. Many directories such as /usr are like closets. They contain much of what you think they should, as well as a lot of other miscellaneous stuff. /usr/spool is a collage of spooling devices, buffers, and associated commands. /usr/lib is a mixture of macros, header files, language libraries, and commands not found elsewhere. /usr directories seem to have one thing in common: they belong in /usr because they don't fit anywhere else!

/usr is actually a misleading name for this directory. Even though its name is /usr, it does not necessarily hold user files or directories. Most systems, when they are new, have some starter user directories in /usr, such as /usr/guest or /usr/demo. However, you might want to create a separate file system for your user directories; the contents of those directories change often (thanks to the users), and they are more easily backed up or moved when they are all together in one location. The common file system for the users is /home. If you have no room for new file systems, consider making another tree under /usr, such as /usr/users, /usr/home, or /home (SVR4) for your user directories.

There are some user commands in /bin, but most are found in /usr/bin. What do /usr files have in common? The answer is subtle, and it lies in the realm of UNIX internals. While UNIX is running, it is divided into two parts: kernel (or system) and user processes. Kernel activity and what is broadly classified as user activity are distinctly separated. Simply stated, the *user* classification encompasses any activity that is not kernel-resident. You might think of /usr commands as those not strictly necessary for running the system. The /bin directory, however, contains the programs necessary for running the system before anything but the default file system is mounted. You basic UNIX commands reside in the /bin directory, right under the root directory.

The /usr/bin Directory

At one time, /usr/bin was a place for putting commands that were specific (local) to one machine. Now /usr/bin has become the directory for most of the standard user programs. Don't put your locally unique programs here unless you absolutely must in order for them to work.

The */usr/local* Directory

You should put programs and support files peculiar to your UNIX installation in the /usr/local directory tree. The programs should be in /usr/local/bin. These are programs that you have written, begged, bought, or borrowed, including scripts for the system administrator, software like kermit (a file transfer system in the public domain), and various other bits and pieces of scripts and code that exist for your system alone. On some systems, the directory /usr/lbin is used instead.

The other files should go in directories such as /usr/local/lib, /usr/local/include, and so on—parallel in design to the standard UNIX files.

The */usr/lib* Directory

Most commands don't come in groups, but some do when they are related to one device or activity; examples are the UUCP programs and the printer command (lp or lpr). Such grouped commands are generally found under /usr/lib. lib means libraries, which in UNIX terminology means archives of compiled program functions. The system administrator must access them in order to deal with printers and modems attached to the computer.

There is not a great deal of consistency here. For instance, the most important uucp files and programs are found under /usr/lib/uucp, but some of the printer programs are under /usr/lib itself. Still others, such as the actual printer driver programs in System V, are found in a subdirectory of the spooler! Other items of interest in /usr/lib, aside from many function libraries, are miscellaneous help files, daemons, and reference files for Berkeley commands such as whatis, whereis, and vi. Some of the major directories under /usr/lib and their contents are described in Table 4.2.

Table 4.2. Major directories under /usr/lib.

SVR3	SVR4	Description
/usr/lib/acct		This is where you find the commands to run system accounting. The system accounting programs help you keep track of user logins, CPU use, the number of times commands have been executed, and who has been using superuser privileges.

SVR3	SVR4	Description
/lib/font /usr/lib/fontinfo	(not used)	Here are the descriptions of the different typographical modes (such as bold and italic) used by troff and its various postprocessors. There is usually a separate subdirectory under /lib/font for each output device. /usr/lib/fontinfo is used by one of the Berkeley postprocessors.
/usr/lib/macros		This directory contains the compressed and uncompressed document macro packages for use by nroff and troff.
	/usr/ucblib/doctools	This is a likely path to the documentor's tools on SVR4 systems. You may find the fonts under this path, at /usr/ucblib/doctools/font/devaps, and the macros at /usr/ucblib/doctools/tmac.
/usr/lib/news		If your system is connected to Usenet, this directory is the common path to many of the files needed to keep track of the articles flowing in and out of the system. But because Usenet is not distributed as part of UNIX, the administrator who installed the news system can put the control files anywhere.
/usr/lib/sa		Here are programs for recording the level of system activity for later analysis.
/usr/lib/spell		The programs and data files needed for the UNIX spelling checker reside here.
/usr/lib/struct	(seldom used)	This directory contains the programs used for turning f77 programs into ratfor.
/usr/lib/style		Data for the style and diction programs from Writer's Workbench is often kept here.
/usr/lib/tabs	/usr/share/lib/tabset	This directory holds ASCII files that are used to initialize tab settings on a variety of terminals and printers. Such files are generally referenced by entries in /etc/termcap. (This directory is called /usr/lib/tabset on some systems.)
/usr/lib/term	/usr/ucblib/doctoolsl/nterm	Source and binary files for nroff "terminal drivers" are found here. When properly implemented, such terminal drivers allow emulation of troff, using nroff for output on a given terminal.
/usr/lib/uucp	/etc/uucp /usr/lib/uucp	These directories have the programs and data files needed to set up and run the UUCP communications system.

/usr/lib/crontab

As administrator, you will get to know this file intimately. It enables consistent repetition of commands at any time or day you choose. Using crontab is almost like having digital timers on every appliance in your house. When the cron program starts up at system boot time, the program reads the crontab file for instructions on what commands to execute and when. Since SVR2, regular users can have their own crontab files, but they must have their names in the /usr/lib/crontab/allow file to do so.

On older systems, cron checks the crontab file every minute to see whether the file itself has been changed (presumably with new commands to execute). A different checking interval can be specified on some systems when cron is first started up. For example, running it as cron 5 forces cron to check the crontab file every five minutes.

Since System V Release 2, the crontab command must be executed to force cron to examine the appropriate file. Instead of editing the files in /usr/lib/crontab or /usr/spool/cron directly, you should create a copy of your existing cron table, using the -l option to the command:

```
crontab -l >/tmp/ctab
```

Then edit that file and resubmit the edited version with

```
crontab /tmp/ctab
```

You can remove any existing crontab entries with crontab -r.

Starting with System V Release 4, the crontab command has an option that combines this entire process: crontab -e. This option invokes the editor specified by the EDITOR environment variable. When you exit the editor, crontab submits the new table automatically.

There are six fields in every crontab entry. The entries are separated by any amount of whitespace, so you can use tabs or spaces to line things up. You can use asterisks to specify all legal values, and dashes to signify a range of values. Counting from left to right, the first field controls at what time (after the hour) the desired command should be executed. The second field specifies the hour in 24-hour time (2 or 02 means 2 AM, and 14 means 2 PM). The third field specifies a particular day of the month; this field is useful if you want to run financial accounting on the 15th or you want to back up on the 1st. The fourth field tells cron which month (1 through 12) to run the command, and the fifth field tells which day of the week you want (0 means Sunday, and 6 means Saturday). The sixth field is simply the command you want to run. Because the command is run as if it were typed into the Bourne shell, the asterisks here refer to file names as usual, and all shell constructs can be used. The following is a fairly complex crontab file taken from a working system:

```
# local stuff
00 * * * *        /bin/date
30 5 * * *        /usr/local/rmtrash
45 8 * * 6        /own/lev/gather_week
15 9 15 4 *       /bin/echo "taxes now late" > /dev/console
06 5 * * *        /bin/calendar -

# for at program and error logging
0,10,20,30,40,50 * * * * /usr/lib/atrun
5,15,25,33,45,55 * * * * /bin/dmesg - >> /usr/adm/messages
59 23 * * *              /usr/local/newcron

# for process accounting:
00 3 * * 1-6 /bin/su root -c "/usr/lib/acct/dodisk"
00 4 * * 1-6 /bin/su adm -c "/usr/lib/acct/runacct \
 2> /usr/adm/acct/nite/fd2log"
00 8 * * 1-5 /bin/su adm -c "/usr/lib/acct/prdaily ¦ lp"
03 * * * *   /bin/su adm -c "/usr/lib/acct/ckpacct 250"
15 5 1 * *   /bin/su adm -c "/usr/lib/acct/monacct"

# for uucp:
25 * * * *   /bin/su nuucp -c "nice /usr/lib/uucp/uudemon.hr"
05 23 * * 5 /bin/su nuucp -c "/usr/local/pollall"
55 23 * * 6 /bin/su nuucp -c "/usr/lib/uucp/uusub -u 168 -r -l"
56 23 * * * /bin/su nuucp -c "/usr/local/uusum ¦ mail nuucp"
57 23 * * * /bin/su nuucp -c "/usr/lib/uucp/uudemon.day"
10 05 * * 0 /bin/su nuucp -c "/usr/lib/uucp/uudemon.wk"

# for system activity statistics
3 8-17 * * 1-5 /bin/su adm -c "/usr/lib/sa/sa1 1200 3"
8 18-7 * * 1-5 /bin/su adm -c "/usr/lib/sa/sa1"
3    * * * 0,6 /bin/su adm -c "/usr/lib/sa/sa1"
11 18  * * 1-5 /bin/su adm -c "/usr/lib/sa/sa2 -s 8:00 -e
18:01\
 -i 3600 -A"

# for usenet news software
46 1 * * *        /bin/su news -c "/usr/lib/news/expire.sh"
45 2 * * *        /bin/su root -c "/usr/lib/news/trimlib"
45 3 * * *        /bin/su news -c "/usr/local/uuhosts -unbatch"
34 2,4,6 * * 1-5   find /usr/spool/news/junk -type f -print\
 ¦ xargs rm
```

```
07 1,2,4,6 * * *  /bin/su news -c "/usr/lib/news/sendbatchnews"
07 09 * * 1-5     /usr/lib/news/news.off
07 20 * * 1-5     /usr/lib/news/news.on
```

This particular file has quite a few entries. Take a look at the first entry, which is probably the easiest to understand:

```
00 * * * *         /bin/date
```

This simply says, "At 00 minutes after every hour, no matter what day it is, run the /bin/date command." How is this useful? Because a log of every command that is run is kept in the file /usr/adm/cronlog (/usr/lib/cron/log in SVR2 and /var/cron/log on SVR4), running the date command every hour serves to separate entries so that you can determine when an event took place. (On some systems, the /usr/lib/atrun program also serves this purpose if it is run exactly on the hour.) If your system isn't logging its cron entries here, make sure that the file exists and that cron is actually running.

Remember that any program run from crontab sends its output to cronlog unless otherwise specified. If you have a hard-copy console terminal and you want to keep track of the system status to the nearest hour, you can change this entry to

```
00 * * * *         /bin/date >/dev/console
```

and the date is written to the console as long as the system remains up and cron remains running. Unfortunately, there is no way to prevent output of the previous command from getting mixed with other output to the console.

On systems that allow individual user crontabs, the output is mailed to the user.

Now look at the next line:

```
30 5 * * *         /usr/local/rmtrash
```

Here cron is asked to run the /usr/local/rmtrash program every morning of every day, at 5:30. This program searches through the entire file system. If the program were run later in the day, it would slow down users' programs too much, so it is run when the system is likely to be quiet.

The next line is a little more specific:

```
45 8 * * 6         /own/lev/gather_week
```

This program gathers data from many different databases for collection and eventual transmission to another computer. The program takes almost an hour to run, so it must be run while none of the databases is active. Here cron is asked to run it every Saturday at 8:45 AM.

The next line is a silly example of how the month and day fields can be used:

```
15 9 15 4 *        /bin/echo "taxes now late" > /dev/console
```

If you are sitting at the console, you will see this message appear every April 15 at 9:15 AM. Note that the asterisk in the weekday field is still needed so that the command will be run *no matter what day of the week* April 15 falls on.

Now look at the next section of the file for these two lines:

```
0,10,20,30,40,50 * * * * /usr/lib/atrun
5,15,25,35,45,55 * * * * /bin/dmesg - >> /usr/adm/messages
```

They show how programs can be repeated at specific intervals. The first line executes the atrun program (see the manual page for at) every 10 minutes, and the second line executes dmesg also every 10 minutes. Specifying the exact times to run each program and offsetting them by 5 minutes prevent the system from being loaded unnecessarily. This might happen if both programs were run simultaneously every 10 minutes.

In fact, some administrators sort the crontab file by time (rather than by category, as in this example) so that they can easily keep track of the commands being run at a particular time. This approach prevents inadvertently scheduling two large jobs for overlapping times, or running things in the wrong order. For instance, you can't run the uusum program—which summarizes the uucp log files—after the uudemon.day program because uudemon.day effectively removes the log files! We suggest sorting by time *within* each category because that method focuses your attention on the actual programs to be run.

Note that the output from dmesg (which collects any possible system error messages) is redirected so that it is *appended* to the /usr/adm/messages log file. That way, /usr/adm/messages accumulates error messages continuously.

Finally, examine this entry:

```
00 4 * * 1-6 /bin/su adm -c "/usr/lib/acct/runacct \
2> /usr/adm/acct/nite/fd2log"
```

This entry uses the su command to execute the runacct program as if the user named adm ran it. Because cron is usually started by the system at boot time, commands executed without su are effectively run as if root typed them. This could cause a serious security breach. You shouldn't run all your normal programs as superuser; it's safer to run programs that don't need the power of root with a more restricted ownership—for example, adm. Executing runacct as adm also ensures that the accounting files and logs are actually *owned* by the adm user, so she will be able to do her job if she exists as a separate person.

73

This particular command runs system accounting at 4:00 AM every day but Sunday. The command also introduces another technique: redirecting any *error* output to a file different from /usr/adm/cronlog. In this case, any errors encountered when the runacct program is running are stored in /usr/adm/acct/nite/fd2log. If you want to save *both* normal and error output in the same file, you can create an entry like this one:

```
12 5 * * * /usr/local/program >/usr/tmp/logfile 2>&1
```

Notice that the full path name of the command to be executed should be used in crontab. You can be sure, therefore, that you are running the program you expect to, and not somebody else's program with the same name.

It is important that some files which are created by commands executed from crontab maintain that "user's" ownership. Any UUCP, news, or mail commands should be executed as a su command with corresponding name. Note this example:

```
01 05 * * * su uucp -e /usr/lib/uucp/uuclean
```

Otherwise, you find that other, interactive commands that are run with suid for that "user" will not run properly. One of the interactive commands for posting Usenet news is run as the user news, keeping the news control files protected from hacking. With 666 permissions (read and write for everyone), a script embedded in a news file could attack the control files. Those same files are manipulated by some of the news cleanup scripts. However, if these files were created or owned by root, they couldn't be manipulated by the news posting program.

You should be careful about having programs in crontab that run for a long time; cron always starts its programs at the appointed time, and it is therefore possible to have the undesirable occurrence of two copies of the same program running at the same time.

The */usr/src* Directory

UNIX source code, whether restricted by "reconfiguration rights" or full (licensed) source, is located in /usr/src. Before you run out to buy a UNIX source license, you should know that the current cost is more than $50,000! Understandably, most systems have little in /usr/src. System administrators wanting to impress their friends can create files under /usr/src—with such names as ls.c, init.c, getty.c, and so on—to appear as if they have a source license. (If you really *do* have a source license, this procedure will wipe out your source files. This is not likely to impress anyone.)

The /usr/spool Directory

One of your first major system administration problems probably will involve a spooler file that is rapidly filling right before your eyes, and you will have to figure out what to do about it. Usually, you will be made aware of this problem by an error message appearing on the system console, such as

```
Out of inodes on dev 9/4
```

followed shortly by telephone calls from users who want to know what is wrong and when it will be fixed. In this case, the notation 9/4 refers to the major device 9 and minor device 4. If you turn back to the section on the /dev directory, you'll see that this notation refers to /dev/cd04 on this system. Chapter 5, "Mounting and Unmounting File Systems," explains that cd04 refers to a specific file system.

Spoolers, and directories that act like spoolers (such as buffers), have to be emptied periodically. (Spoolers, covered in Chapter 11 on printers, enable many users to share a single device, such as a printer.) Some files are created so quietly that neither user nor system administrator is aware of the file creation. Files created this way are particularly dangerous. For example, the learn utilities provide education and practice to new UNIX users, but also leave unerased files behind that fill the /usr/lib/learn directory. Such files can keep filling the disk until the system comes down with a resounding crash, leaving you with a roomful of angry users and many broken inodes to deal with. Table 4.3 shows the locations of some of these troublesome files.

Table 4.3. Directories where troublesome files are located.

Before SVR4	SVR4	Description

/usr/spool/mail
   (Berkeley)
/usr/mail
   (System III and
   System V)
		Look (ls -lR) for mail files that are never read and emptied. You would be surprised at how many users never read their mail.

/usr/spool/adm		Accounting files and directories accumulate and must be emptied.
/usr/lib/learn		Anyone who has been in this area to use the learn facility has created files here.
/usr/lib/spell/spellhist		This is a collection of misspelled words (see "Handy Shell Programs" later in this chapter).

continued

75

Table 4.3—*Continued*

Before SVR4	SVR4	Description
/usr/spool/cons		Console notes entered by the operators and error messages end up here. Like all notes, they should be read and then thrown out with the trash. Most of the time, the system administrator ends up doing this (non-standard).
/usr/spool/news/net/junk		Here is the Usenet garbage can. If you are on Usenet, delete everything in this directory regularly without fail!
/usr/spool/rdr		This is a graveyard of files transferred by fetch commands (UTS).
/usr/spool/uucppublic		This is a gathering place for wanted and unwanted files left by uucp (Refer to Chapter 12 on modems for more information.)
/usr/spool/uucp		Here is another UUCP trash and treasure location.
/dump		This is the home for crash core dumps. It is created by mkdump and is large enough to store all of memory (nonstandard).
/tmp /usr/tmp		These are homes for temporary files. These are supposed to be erased, but you have no guarantees.
/usr/adm	/var/adm	System accounting fills up this directory.

In addition to emptying regular spooler areas, you should periodically empty some other directories, such as /tmp. This is an interesting directory because it is reserved exclusively for temporary files. An amazing number of programs create temporary files, generally with names formed by the first few letters of the command followed by the process ID:

```
$ ls -lt /tmp
total 396
-rw-rw-r--  1 dave    staff      120  May 21 01:56 ctm8017885
-rw-rw-r--  1 dave    staff     8998  May 21 01:56 ctm7017885
-rw-rw-r--  1 dave    staff      634  May 21 01:56 ctm6017885
-rw-rw-r--  1 dave    staff      634  May 21 01:56 ctm5017885
-rw-rw-r--  1 dave    staff     5426  May 21 01:56 ctm4017885
-rw-rw-r--  1 dave    staff     5426  May 21 01:56 ctm3017885
-rw-rw-r--  1 dave    staff     2762  May 21 01:56 ctm2017885
-rw-rw-r--  1 dave    staff    22347  May 21 01:56 ctm1017885
-rw-rw-r--  1 dave    staff    12425  May 21 01:56 ctm0017885
```

```
-rw-------   1 susan  staff   63488   May 21 01:52 Ex17765
-rw-------   1 susan  staff   10240   May 21 01:52 Rx17765
-rw-rw----   1 brenda staff   54184   May 19 15:45 weekly13057
```

The files beginning with ctm* are created by the C compiler; the Ex*
and Rx* files exist while a file is being edited with ex or vi, and the weekly*
file is left by a locally written program. As you can see, all system users create
temporary files at one time or another. Such files are supposed to be
removed after use by the program that created them, but "supposed to" is
a phrase familiar to system administrators. Other programs make a valiant
effort to remove unused files but are thwarted by users who kill or suspend
such programs.

Putting all temporary files in one or two directories makes it easy to
clean them all out at regular intervals. For this reason, you should encourage
users to use /tmp for all files needed for only a short while. Otherwise, their
own directories (and therefore the system's available file space) gradually
become filled. Good candidates for /tmp files include output files from
nroff and troff, redirected output from commands, and short test
programs. Educate your users to put such items in /tmp, and make sure that
all of your locally written programs use /tmp too. Depending on how your
system disks are partitioned, you may find that there is more free space in
/usr/tmp (in the /usr file system), so /usr/tmp might be more convenient
for your temporary files.

Each system also has local areas that must be emptied. For example,
some systems have the at command, which allows the user to define
processes to be run at specific times. The leftover at files and logs that show
what happened (usually found in /usr/spool/at) may need to be cleaned
out. For this task, use rmtrash (see "Handy Shell Programs" later in this
chapter).

The /etc Directory

Most user commands are in one or two directories, and most system
administration commands are in another directory, called /etc. A very
special directory, /etc is the home of the tools and files that bring up the
system. /etc programs are so specialized that they are no longer included
in the standard UNIX user documentation. Instead, they are in a manual
devoted to UNIX administration. Starting with System V, the administration
commands (labeled 1M or C) in Section 1 of the *UNIX User's Manual*, as well
as all of Sections 4 and 8, were moved to a new document: the *UNIX System
Administrator's Manual*.

77

A simple /etc listing looks something like this:

```
# ls /etc
checkall      getty    mklost+found   shutdown     ttytype
checklist     group    motd           termcap      update
cron          ident    mtab           ttys         utmp
ddate         init     passwd         ttys.2user
first.profile lpset    rc             ttys.3user
#
```

Now take a look at some of these files, starting with /etc/passwd and /etc/group, which are used to create logins and user shells. Chapter 7 covers these files in more detail, but you should learn to understand their functions as soon as possible.

/etc/passwd

In time, the /etc/passwd file becomes downright familiar to system administrators, but at first glance, it looks like Egyptian hieroglyphics:

```
# cat /etc/passwd
root:hjbHWeEt2W0RE:0:1:Super-User:/:/bin/sh
rootcsh:Dq2PskRl/PmBY:0:1:Super-User:/:/bin/csh
adm:VOID:2:1:User Administrator:/usr/adm:/bin/csh
sys:VOID:3:2:System Accounting:/usr/lib/sa:/bin/csh
bin:VOID:4:3:Owner of the System Commands:/bin:
nuucp:zL8wUerXUz/xM:5:6:UUCP Administrator:/usr/lib/uucp:/bin/csh
uucp:XLuM2jsr1tUb6:6:6:UUCP Login:/usr/spool/uucppublic:\
/usr/lib/uucp/uucico
bruce:5i4Vfgzhxs3I.:20:20:Bruce H Hunter:/us/bruce:/bin/sh
karen:MlNyd0pc7tgiE:21:20:Karen L B Hunter:/us/karen:/bin/sh
david:zCz.rpnUP1s22:23:20:David Fiedler:/us/david:/bin/csh
susan:/aik3QiekNOYU:24:20:Susan Fiedler:/us/susan:
ben:kljd8f7Njdkfjdk:24:20:Ben Smith:/usr/ben:/bin/ksh
who::50:25:The Who Command:/bin/who
```

Each line, called a *password record*, deals with one user and contains all the information necessary for the system to create a login and user shell. Each password record has seven fields. Note the fields in the following password record:

```
susan:/aik3QiekNOYU:24:20:Susan Fiedler:/us/susan:
```

The first field, susan, is the user login name. The second field, /aik3QiekNOYU, is the encrypted version of the password. The third field, 24, is the user ID, a unique integer. In UNIX terminology, it is referred to as the *uid*. It is this number, not the login name, that the system uses internally to reference the user. The fourth field, 20, is a group number or *gid*. It refers to /etc/group, the group file in which each named group has a (unique) number that associates its group name with a membership list. The fifth field, Susan Fiedler, is a comment field. It is used by programs like whois and finger to get user information, including phone numbers and office locations. The sixth field, /us/susan, is the home directory of the user.

You can use the seventh and last field to specify what program (usually a shell) is run after login. If the field is blank, as in this case, the user gets the default shell (the Bourne shell). If /bin/csh is entered for this last field, the C shell is assigned to the user. If you use the last field to specify the full path name of a program other than the shell, that will be the only program the user can use, after which she is logged off. For example, uucp logins have the executable program uucico in their last field so that they can execute the uucp protocol at login time. In the last line of the sample /etc/passwd file, this concept is illustrated with the who program.

If you encounter an /etc/passwd file in which all the passwords are either *, x, or 0, there exists an additional file for the password and other information about the user account. In that case, there will also be programs for adding and deleting users and changing their passwords. (You learn more about the password file in Chapters 7 and 9.)

/etc/group

/etc/group is the home of group information. This file is similar to /etc/passwd, but each record has fewer fields to contend with. Here is a typical /etc/group file:

```
root:VOID:1:root,rootcsh,daemon
sys:VOID:2:sys
bin:VOID:3:bin
uucp:VOID:4:uucp,nuucp
check:VOID:5:check
user:VOID:10:guest
edit:VOID:20:karen,bruce,david,susan,ben
```

Like users, groups have an internal number associated with the group name. The first field is the group name (such as check, user, or edit). The group number occupies the third field. The fourth and last field is a list of the login names of the members of the group.

What about the second field, which contains VOID in all the entries in the preceding example? This is the password field, and an encrypted password may be present for each group. Some systems have a group command to manage the group memberships (the group files and passwords), but most systems do not. You can put passwords into /etc/group (see Chapter 9), but it's not a good idea. The newgrp command lets a new user switch between groups if she knows the group password. Experience has shown, however, that while a person tends to be very protective of his own personal password, he is not as careful with his group password. Because users often allow unlimited file access to others in their working group, this practice results in poor system security! For this reason, we recommend that you put VOID, NONE, or the equivalent on every line in /etc/group. This prevents people from changing groups on their own and serves as documentation to that effect. Then the only way someone can join a group is for you, as system administrator, to enter his name on the correct line in /etc/group.

/etc/init

init is a binary executable program found in /etc. When a UNIX system is booted, /unix (the kernel) is read into memory. When the kernel executes, it brings up the swapper, known as swap, and then init. init becomes the parent of all user shells. The dozens of programs and processes that make up the UNIX kernel are all extremely important, but none has as much impact on the system as init. It is the most important process in the UNIX system because it creates the shell—the first human interface to the system.

Because there is a major difference in init between pre-System V and System V UNIX, each version of init is examined here separately.

Pre-System V and XENIX *init*

In pre-System V UNIX and XENIX, init creates itself in a single (root) user mode. It recognizes no terminals, only the *console*, which is the *tty* device the system administrator uses to bring up the system.

When you put UNIX into multiuser mode, you are actually signaling init to change its internal state (see "Going Multiuser" in Chapter 2). init performs various tasks in multiuser mode. It goes into the /etc/ttys (teletypes or terminals) file (/etc/inittab in System III) and sends login messages (by spawning gettys, or in SVR4, ttymons) to all ports specified as active in the /etc/ttys (or /etc/inittab) file.

In UNIX Version 7 and System III, init is almost invisible, although System III has a slightly more advanced init, approaching that of System V. Because init is not attached to a *tty,* init can be "seen" only by doing a ps -x or ps -e. However, init is highly visible in System V, as you shall see.

System V *init*

System V is a more mature, commercially viable operating system than earlier versions of UNIX, but it is also more complex. In early releases, UNIX (and init) ran in two modes: single-user and multiuser. Under System V, the system can run in seven levels, or modes: two single-user and five multiuser. You must choose one of them to start up the system. Most system administrators need to be concerned with only two levels, level s and level 2. (Level 3 is often used for initializing network operations.)

The s mode is single-user mode. Level 2 is a general-purpose, fits-all-does-all multiuser mode. These modes are controlled by a file called /etc/inittab. The entries in this file are a list of processes that init calls at various initiation levels. UNIX System V gets all of its process information from /etc/inittab.

Most inittab entries are a series of four fields in each record (line), separated by colons. Here is a complete /etc/inittab file for pre-SVR4:

```
is:s:initdefault:
su:s:respawn:/etc/slog </dev/console >/dev/console 2>&1
bl::bootwait:/etc/bcheckrc </dev/syscon >/dev/syscon 2>&1
bc::bootwait:/etc/brc 1>/dev/syscon 2>&1
rc::bootwait:/bin/sh /etc/rc 1>/dev/syscon 2>&1
pf::powerfail:/etc/powerfail 1>/dev/syscon 2>&1
co::respawn:getty console console
11:2:respawn:getty /dev/tty11 9600
12:2:respawn:getty -t 600 /dev/tty12 1200
13:2:respawn:getty /dev/tty13 9600
20:2:respawn:getty /dev/tty20 9600
21:2:off:getty /dev/tty21 9600
22:2:off:getty /dev/tty22 9600
23:2:respawn:getty -t 450 /dev/tty23 1200
```

Consider a single entry:

```
13:2:respawn:getty /dev/tty13 9600
```

Roughly translated into English, this entry says, "At ID 13 under init level 2, spawn a getty (create a login) on device /dev/tty13 at 9600 baud."

Now take a look at the fields, one at a time. The first field, 13, is a mnemonic or label for the process or device about to be activated. The second field, 2, is the process activation level—in this case, level 2. An s in the second field signifies single-user mode; if the field is empty, the entry is active at all levels. The third field, respawn, specifies what action to take. If the process does not exist, create it. If it already exists, go about the business of rescanning this table. The fourth and last field, getty /dev/tty13 9600, executes a getty on /dev/tty03 at 9600 baud.

The time-out -t 600 on line tty12 means that if no login is received within 600 seconds (10 minutes) after the call is connected, hang up the line. This is especially useful on modem lines, which might otherwise sit around forever if a person, instead of a modem, called by mistake.

One of the benefits of this level of system initialization is that special levels can be set up. System V's various initialization levels allow classified processing to take place with ease. On a secured system at level 1, for example, only the console and a terminal or two in the machine room are active, enabling classified information to be processed with no access to the system from the outside. At level 2, only the terminals may be set up, not modem lines or hardwired connections to other local computers. At level 3, the modem lines become active, and networking is initialized. Here is an /etc/inittab listing that shows this kind of complexity:

```
is:s:initdefault:
su:s:respawn:/etc/slog </dev/console >/dev/console 2>&1
bl::bootwait:/etc/bcheckrc </dev/syscon >/dev/syscon 2>&1
bc::bootwait:/etc/brc 1>/dev/syscon 2>&1
rc::bootwait:/bin/sh /etc/rc 1>/dev/syscon 2>&1
pf::powerfail:/etc/powerfail 1>/dev/syscon 2>&1
r0:056:wait:/etc/rc0  1>/dev/console 2>&1 </dev/console
r1:1:wait:/etc/rc1  1>/dev/console 2>&1 </dev/console
r2:2:wait:/etc/rc2  1>/dev/console 2>&1 </dev/console
r3:3:wait:/etc/rc3  1>/dev/console 2>&1 </dev/console
r3:4:wait:/etc/rc4  1>/dev/console 2>&1 </dev/console
r3:5:wait:/etc/rc5  1>/dev/console 2>&1 </dev/console
rb:6:wait:/etc/rc6 reboot 1>/dev/console 2>&1 </dev/console
co:1234:respawn:getty console 1200 la180 # hardcopy console
bi:1234:respawn:getty bip0 9600 bip # secure CRT
11:234:respawn:getty /dev/tty11 9600 tvi950 #
12:34:respawn:getty -t 600 /dev/tty12 1200 h1500 #modem
13:234:respawn:getty /dev/tty13 9600 wyse #
20:234:respawn:getty /dev/tty20 9600 wyse #
21:5:off:getty -h /dev/tty21 2400 none #printer
22:5:off:getty -h /dev/tty22 1200 none #printer
23:4:respawn:getty -t 450 /dev/tty23 1200 h1500 #modem
```

A few extra fields are shown in the preceding example. The field immediately after the baud rate (tvi950 on the tty11 line, for instance) is used to pass the TERM environment variable to the user's shell. This clears the screen on some systems so that the login message appears on the first line. As in most UNIX system files, you can place comments on a line by preceding them with a # (pound sign).

Notice that the getty has a -h flag on the two printer ports. This keeps the line from "hanging up" or reinitializing to a default baud rate, because nobody ever logs in on a printer line! Although the -h flag doesn't work on all systems, using it is good documentation and saves work if the flag becomes operational in a later software release for that system. Using a setting of off prevents a process from being started on either of these lines. Actually, a process could not start on the lines in this case unless init 5 was run.

The entries r0, r1, and r2 through r5 are pointers to the scripts that invoke the services at each of the init levels.

The rb entry causes a reboot after running the commands in rc6. You would invoke a reboot with init 6.

/etc/rc files—The SA's Custom Shop

init is a binary executable program. It cannot be altered except by recompiling it from source code, which is something most UNIX installations do not have. All by itself, init does not allow the flexibility that UNIX needs. The various rc files execute commands and scripts necessary to bring up the system in a condition suitable for a specific user community.

The init process calls the rc (for *r*un commands) files, which are executable shell scripts, as the system level moves from level to level. This structure helps customization of UNIX and adds some flexibility. Most rcs are bare-bones programs furnished by OEMs. VARs tend to add more to rcs to suit customers' applications, such as initialization and automatic recovery of special databases.

System V Release 2 and earlier distributions usually have just one rc file. Even on the more complex systems, there is an /etc/rc file for your use. rc is very much like a custom shop, and by programming rc, you are in charge of the customization of your specific UNIX machine.

When modifying rc, make sure that you do not alter any critical commands that might cause the system to hang up or loop without initializing. The safest way to add command lines to rc is to run them in the background (see the /etc/lpset line in the next code sequence); that way, if the commands fail to operate properly, the system will still come up.

rc is a system administrator's friend because it is relatively easy to use. It is written entirely in Bourne shell script and can be a straightforward series of commands to execute. Because it is not written in C, you don't have to know that language in order to program rc. rc scripts can be short, eight-line scripts, or they can run for eight pages. After initializing a few files, rc generally starts up some critical process, such as setting port characteristics and mounting disks. Here is a simple rc file taken from a Codata 3300 system running UNIX System III:

```
cp dev/null /etc/mtab
cp /dev/null /etc/utmp
/etc/update
/etc/cron
/etc/lpset &
mount /dev/cd03 /us
rm -f /usr/spool/uucp/LCK*
rm -f /usr/spool/uucp/LOGFILE
rm -f /usr/spool/uucp/SYSLOG
```

The first two lines empty a pair of files called mtab and utmp by copying literally nothing into them. Those files are used by system accounting. UNIX has a number of files that should start out empty at each system startup, including these two.

The third line, /etc/update, causes update to begin executing syncs at a specified interval. /etc/cron always runs in the background (it's a *daemon*), executing other programs at specified times from the cron tables. The next line, /etc/lpset &, executes a line-printer device initialization script in the background.

mount /dev/cd03 /us mounts logical disk 3 to the /us file tree. (On more recent systems, the mount entries are kept in the file /etc/fstab.) The next line removes all the lock files from the communication spooler:

```
rm -f /usr/spool/uucp/LCK*
```

Lock files must not exist at system startup; if they do, they prevent the desired activity from occurring.

The last two lines remove a pair of log files for the communications system:

```
rm -f /usr/spool/uucp/LOGFILE
rm -f /usr/spool/uucp/SYSLOG
```

Here is a more complex example, from a Cadmus computer running System V with about 12 users:

```
TZ=EST5EDT
export TZ

if [ ! -f /etc/mnttab ]
then
        create /etc/mnttab
        devnm / ¦ grep -v swap ¦ grep -v root ¦ setmnt
fi
        echo "Doing mounts"
        /etc/Mount

# recover vi files:
        /usr/lib/ex3.6preserve /tmp

# code for the printer ports:
        echo "Setting printers"
        nohup /usr/local/set_diablo_bd &
        nohup /usr/local/set_oki_baud &

# process accounting:
        rm -f /usr/adm/acct/nite/lock*
        /bin/su - adm -c /usr/lib/acct/startup
        echo process accounting started

# system activity:
/bin/su sys -c "/usr/lib/sa/sadc /usr/adm/sa/sa`date +%d` &"
        create /usr/adm/cronlog /usr/adm/sulog
        nice -19 cron

rm -f /usr/spool/uucp/LCK*
        rm -f /usr/spool/mail/DELIVERING
        rm -f /usr/spool/lp/SCHEDLOCK
        /usr/lib/lpsched &
exit 0
```

First, the TZ variable is set, and it takes effect here for the entire system:

```
TZ=EST5EDT
export TZ
```

The following four lines create the /etc/mnttab file if it doesn't already exist, and then initialize it with information for the root file system:

```
if [ ! -f /etc/mnttab ]
then
        create /etc/mnttab
        devnm / ¦ grep -v swap ¦ grep -v root ¦ setmnt
fi
```

The grep -v root is required on some machines in order to prevent the device on which the root file system is mounted from being included in the mount table. (Notice that the file name and technique used here are different from those in the System III example.) All user file systems are then mounted with the /etc/Mount command:

```
echo "Doing mounts"
/etc/Mount
```

These mount-related files are covered in detail in Chapter 5, "Mounting and Unmounting File Systems."

System V Release 3 and later versions use set subdirectories for the rc files: /etc/rc0.d through /etc/rc6.d. These subdirectories contain several small, single-purpose rc scripts associated with the corresponding init level. By convention, each script is named with a leading number used to determine the order in which that script is to be run along with its companions. Each subdirectory also has a corresponding master script in the /etc directory. For example, /etc/rc2 runs the scripts in rc2.d when the system is brought to init level 2.

Saving Editor Files

Assuming that the system is coming up from a crash, the command

```
# recover vi files: /usr/lib/ex3.6preserve /tmp
```

runs a special program—part of the vi package—that does the following tasks:

- Goes to the specified directory (in this case, /tmp)
- Finds all Ex* and Rx* files left there by vi or ex when the system crashed
- Reconstitutes them into editable form
- Puts them in the /usr/preserve directory
- Sends a mail message to their owner, notifying her that she can recover her files

Now take a closer look at this process, so that you can explain it to your users. Running the preserve program happens quietly enough, but the user gets a mail message like this one the next time she logs in:

```
$ mail
From root Tue Sep 24 18:53 EDT 1985
A copy of an editor buffer of your file "etc"
was saved when the system went down.
This buffer can be retrieved using the "recover" command
of the editor.
An easy way to do this is to give the command "ex -r etc".
This works for "edit" and "vi" also.
? q
$
```

The user must know what directory she was in last, unless the full path name was given on the original ex or vi command line.

The best thing to do is to proceed to that directory and carefully examine the current version of the file in question. Then determine whether that, or the recovered version, is the one you want to keep:

```
$ ls -l etc
-rw-rw----  1 susan    staff     16905 Sep 24 18:25 etc
$ ex -r etc
"etc" [Dated: Tue Sep 24 18:45:06] 704 lines, 18232 characters
:wq
"etc" 704 lines, 18232 characters
$
```

Here Susan determined that the older (and shorter) version was the one actually in her directory, and that 20 minutes' worth of work had been saved by the recover program. Writing the file out from ex gets rid of the old version. If you aren't sure which one is better, write the file out by using a different name and then use diff to see which one to keep.

Notice the special message [Dated: Tue Sep 24 18:45:06] from ex, indicating that you are working on a recovered file. Because ex, vi, and edit (as well as e and view on some systems) are all links to the same program file, using this technique works with any of them.

/etc/rc Continued

Because of an annoying bug that exists on many UNIX systems before SVR4, you cannot set a serial port to a constant baud rate unless a process (such as getty) is running on that port. Because this problem usually involves printer ports, getting around the problem is explained in Chapter 11 on printers.

The next part of the /etc/rc file deals with that problem by running special programs to fool the system. Because these programs never exit, they are run in the background with the nohup command, which keeps them going "forever":

```
# code for the printer ports:
        echo "Setting printers"
        nohup /usr/local/set_diablo_bd &
        nohup /usr/local/set_oki_baud &
```

The next set of commands removes lock files and initializes the process accounting system:

```
# process accounting:
        rm -f /usr/adm/acct/nite/lock*
        /bin/su - adm -c /usr/lib/acct/startup
        echo process accounting started
```

If the system activity programs are to be run, the next line initializes their logging file. These programs, run regularly from crontab, keep track of how heavily the system is loaded at different times of the day, and are ideal for determining when it's time to upgrade hardware:

```
# system activity:
/bin/su sys -c "/usr/lib/sa/sadc /usr/adm/sa/sa`date +%d` &"
```

Here two main log files are reinitialized, and cron is started at low priority. Then the lock files for uucp, the mail system, and the printer spooler are removed.

Finally, the printer spooler program itself is started:

```
        create /usr/adm/cronlog /usr/adm/sulog
        nice -19 cron

        rm -f /usr/spool/uucp/LCK*
        rm -f /usr/spool/mail/DELIVERING
        rm -f /usr/spool/lp/SCHEDLOCK
        /usr/lib/lpsched &
exit 0
```

If your system keeps its mail in /usr/mail instead of /usr/spool/mail, the fourth line from the bottom should read

```
        rm -f /usr/mail/*.lock
```

/etc/brc

Several additional files may be used at system startup. /etc/brc (*boot run commands*) is usually associated with checking to see whether the file system was properly synced when the system last terminated. If there is an indication that a crash occurred, brc may reset the flag after the file system has been checked (using /etc/bcheckrc).

With System V Release 4, the brc script performs administrative tasks related to file sharing on networks. The bcheckrc script should always be run before the brc script.

/etc/bcheckrc

/etc/bcheckrc is another new System V file used to handle all the file system checking before /etc/rc is called. If you have a program to set the date or time zone, it can be run from here as well. Your bcheckrc script can be fancy, with prompts requesting whether you want the file systems checked, but we prefer to do that all the time:

```
TZ=EST5EDT; export TZ
/etc/checkall -D
exit 0
```

/etc/getty and /etc/login

For systems before SVR4, getty (which is called by init) is the process that sets the baud rate, asks for a login name, and executes the actual login program (generally located in /etc/login but sometimes found in /bin/login or /usr/bin/login). login then comes back and asks for a password, turns off echo while getting the password, encrypts it, validates it (retrying if necessary), and finally gets around to giving the user a login. The arguments passed to getty in normal usage are the *tty* number, the baud rate (transmission speed), and the time getty should allow for an entry to shut down or time out.

getty must deal with /etc/gettydefs. Without getting into agonizing detail yet, you should know that gettydefs provides a series of stty and ioctl settings to getty. (These settings are explained in Chapter 10 on terminals.) One of getty's many purposes is to retry serial asynchronous lines (ttys) for different baud rates until it can successfully get login data. After control is passed to the login program, login must do other tasks, such as change the ownership of the tty to root, and then, when the login is successful, change the ownership to that of the user.

Service Access Controller

System V Release 4 (SVR4) does not use `getty` and `/etc/gettydefs`. Instead, it includes a port administration subsystem, the Service Access Controller (SAC). The purpose of SAC is to manage all *tty* (serial ports) and psuedo-*tty* (network and window system access). SAC is started from the appropriate `rc` script when the system goes multiuser. Most of the control files reside in `/etc/sac` and `/etc/saf` subdirectories.

As with most modern additions to UNIX, SAC is a complex, multilayered, configurable mishmash of administrative commands and daemons. The top of SAC is handled by `sacadm`, the *service access control adm*inistration program (you guessed it?). The underlying daemons are *port monitors*, but there is a middle manager, `pmadm`.

The SAC programmers must have studied with the `lpadmin` programmers because the style is so similar; `sacadm` and `pmadm` are members of the do-all-program design club. The `sacadm` program does the following tasks:

- Adds and removes port monitors

- Starts and stops port monitors

- Enables and disables port monitors

- Prints port monitor information

- Installs and replaces SAC configuration scripts

    The `pmadm` program performs these tasks:

- Adds and removes services

- Enables and disables services

- Prints services reports

- Installs and replaces service configuration scripts

The most common port-monitoring daemons in SVR4 are `ttymon` (the serial/terminal port and pseudo-*tty* services daemon—the SVR4 replacement for `getty` and `uugetty`) and `inetd` (the IP services daemon). The SVR4 replacement for `/etc/gettydefs` is `/etc/ttydefs`.

A third administrative utility is `ttyadm`, which is used to administer the `tty` and `ptty` ports. Usually, all the utilities have a front end that uses system administration menus and forms.

Handy Shell Programs

Like the files and directories you have examined so far in this chapter, the mix of shell programs presented here is somewhat eclectic. All the programs are easy to adapt to your own needs.

morning

Here is a program you should run when you first log on in the morning, either as a matter of habit or through your `.profile` or `.login` file. Customize `morning` to your liking; the commands provided are only a starting point:

```
( who ; df -t; tail -24 /usr/adm/messages ) ¦ ${PAGER:-more}
```

ftype

You won't appreciate `ftype` until you use it a few times, but it's perfect for prowling around places like `/usr/lib`. To use `ftype`, you have to be familiar with the shell construct `` `program` ``. (Notice that grave accents are used; see Chapter 13 on networking for more details.) This shell construct lets you run an arbitrary program and send the output to the shell command line. The effect is like a sideways pipe. Here is an easy example:

```
$ cat chapter
All
bin
dev
etc
shellprogs
summary
usr
where
$ ls -l `cat chapter`
total 90
-rw-rw----  1 dave     staff       142 Sep 15 01:02 All
-rw-rw----  1 dave     staff      2968 Sep 15 00:59 bin
-rw-rw----  1 dave     staff      9896 Sep 17 00:06 dev
-rw-rw----  1 dave     staff     16371 Sep 15 01:22 etc
```

```
-rw-rw----  1 dave      staff         180 Sep 17 01:30 shellprogs
-rw-rw----  1 dave      staff         977 Sep 15 01:01 summary
-rw-rw----  1 dave      staff       11548 Sep 17 01:08 usr
-rw-rw----  1 dave      staff        2123 Sep 15 00:59 where
```

Notice that the ls program found the names of the files to display by running cat chapter. In this way, the output of one command can be used as the arguments to another command. This is the ftype program:

```
file * ¦ grep $1 ¦ sed 's/:.*$//'
```

Here's how you use it. Go into /usr/lib and try to look at the contents of every file with cat, more, or even head. What you will get is a headache, as the screen fills with binary garbage. You want to look at only ASCII text files, to see what's inside. The file command tells you what kind of file you are looking at:

```
$ file /usr/lib/*
/usr/lib/accept:      shareable executable with symboltable
/usr/lib/acct:        directory
/usr/lib/acctcon:     shareable executable with symboltable
/usr/lib/atrun:       shareable executable with symboltable
/usr/lib/crontab:     ascii text
/usr/lib/ctextlib.a:    archive
/usr/lib/deroff:      shareable executable
/usr/lib/dict.d:      commands text
/usr/lib/dprog:       shareable executable
/usr/lib/edwhatis:    ascii text
/usr/lib/eign:        ascii text
  ...
/usr/lib/whatis:      roff, nroff, or eqn input text
/usr/lib/whereis.dirs:   English text
/usr/lib/winlib.a:    archive
```

Because you want to see only text files, notice that such files always have the word text in their description (from running file). This is how ftype determines what to do. You can see the result in this example:

```
$ cd /usr/lib
$ ftype text
crontab
dict.d
edwhatis
eign
  ...
```

```
whatis
whereis.dirs
$ head -3 `ftype text`
==> crontab <==
# this crontab file assumes that the system runs day and night
# the # is a comment character
# min hour day-of-mos(1-31) mos(1-12), day(0-6, 0=sun)

==> dict.d <==
ing behavior
 ability to
 a great deal of
==> edwhatis <==
g/\\-/s//-/
g/\\\*-/s//-/
g/ VAX-11/s///

==> eign <==
the
a
and
 ...

==> whatis <==
A.OUT 5      a.out \- assembler and link editor output
A68 1        a68 \- MIT assembler
ABORT 3C     abort \- generate an IOT fault

==> whereis.dirs <==
WHEREIS LOOKS INTO THESE DIRECTORIES
 This file is read out line by line.
 1. Commentary, Format: free
```

Besides using ftype for exploring, you can use it for system administration tasks. For example, removing symbol tables from programs can save
a surprising amount of space. strip won't disturb files that aren't in the
correct a.out format, so the lazy way is to do something like this (do not
strip files that may produce core dumps if you want to analyze the dumps):

```
# strip /usr/bin/*
strip: /usr/bin/append not in a.out format
strip: /usr/bin/basic already stripped
strip: /usr/bin/checknews already stripped
strip: /usr/bin/hdial already stripped
```

```
strip: /usr/bin/help not in a.out format
strip: /usr/bin/indent already stripped
strip: /usr/bin/inews already stripped
strip: /usr/bin/initmodem not in a.out format
strip: /usr/bin/pick already stripped
strip: /usr/bin/postnews already stripped
strip: /usr/bin/readnews already stripped
strip: /usr/bin/rmtrash not in a.out format
strip: /usr/bin/rnews already stripped
strip: /usr/bin/scomp not in a.out format
strip: /usr/bin/spell not in a.out format
strip: /usr/bin/today already stripped
```

See all the error messages? The right thing to do is to strip only the files that have unwanted symbol tables:

```
# cd /usr/bin
# strip `ftype symboltable`
#
```

This avoids error messages and also assumes that strip never acts on the wrong file by mistake.

On some systems, the message from the file program may say executable not stripped instead of executable with symboltable, so you could run the following instead:

```
# cd /usr/bin
# strip `ftype stripped`
#
```

findbig

Large directories are inefficient, and you should keep track of very large files. The findbig program mails you the details about each one:

```
find / -type d -size +5 -print ¦ xargs ls -ld ¦ mail root
find / -type f -size +$1 -print ¦ xargs ls -l ¦ mail root
```

Although directories greater than 10 blocks long are the problem, reporting them when they reach 5 blocks alerts you to directories that are growing. findbig should be executed from crontab once a week with an argument to specify the minimum size of the ordinary files to report. Remember that the default operation of find uses the number of blocks, not bytes:

```
07 03 * * 0 /usr/local/findbig 500
```

This reports all files larger than 256000 bytes (for 512-byte block systems) or 512000 bytes (for 1024-byte block systems).

rmtrash

Not only do certain directories fill up, but files with certain names keep popping up all over the system, no matter how useless they are. The rmtrash program, which can serve as a model for your own version, should be run every night in the wee hours to clean things up:

```
find / \( -name core -o -name dead.letter \) -mtime +1 -print \
    ¦ xargs -t /bin/rm
find /tmp /usr/tmp /usr/preserve -type f -mtime +1 -print\
    ¦ xargs -t /bin/rm
find /usr/spool/uucp /usr/adm/acct -type f -mtime +3 -print\
    ¦ xargs -t /bin/rm
```

The first line shows you how to find and remove several different file names in a single pass through the file system. The line removes all dead.letter and core files more than one day old. (You don't want to remove someone's core file while he is running adb or sdb on it!) The syntax is tortuous but effective. (See Chapter 13 on networking for more details on find.) Notice that this example, as well as the preceding one, uses the xargs program available on most systems. xargs collects the output from find with the -print option and executes its command argument just *once* on each file named by find. This avoids the alternative

```
find /tmp -type f -mtime +1 -print -exec /bin/rm {} \;
```

which executes /bin/rm whenever a file is to be removed, slowing the system down unnecessarily. (Our thanks to Fred Yankowski of AT&T Bell Laboratories for pointing this out.) The -t flag for xargs prints the file names as they are removed; they will be left in /usr/adm/cronlog as an audit trail.

spellcount and dospell

spellcount is a handy one-liner that shows you the words misspelled most often by your system's users of the spell program. The command is

```
sort /usr/lib/spell/spellhist ¦ uniq -c ¦ sort -nr
```

(On SVR4, the list resides in /var/adm/spellhist.) Because the output of spellcount shows the most frequently found words first, these words are probably correctly spelled words that do not appear in the dictionary. After running spellcount, you can create a file containing the correct words and add them to the dictionary by whatever process works on your system. Would we leave you without a program to do that? Call it dospell, and here it is:

```
cd /usr/lib/spell
cp hlista hlista.old
sort -u $1 ¦ hashmake > newhash
hashcheck < hlista > oldhash
sort -u newhash oldhash > sorthash
n=`wc -l sorthash ¦ sed "s/^ *//" ¦ sed "s/ .*//"`
spellin $n < sorthash > hlista
rm newhash oldhash sorthash
```

Of course, you run dospell by typing

```
$ dospell new_words
```

new_words is the name of the file you created after running spellcount.

newcron

Once you start using cron seriously, the /usr/adm/cronlog file (/var/cron/log on SVR4) rapidly fills up. You could clean it out regularly, but reviewing the entries for a particular day is often useful. The newcron program helps you manage cronlog by splitting it into smaller daily files. You can extend this idea as far as you like if you prefer to keep logs even longer than a week. The newcron program is simple but still useful:

```
cd /usr/adm
mv cronlog cronlog.last
touch cronlog
uniq cronlog.last cronlog.`date +%a`
rm cronlog.last
chmod o-r cronlog cronlog.???
```

The construct `date +%a` tacks on a file suffix (such as .Sun or .Mon) that indicates which day of the week the log covers. This works with only the date program versions that allow date's output to be formatted. And make sure to run newcron every night at 23:59!

where

This highly useful C program is one you will use often. where looks in your PATH for executable files with the same names as the arguments on the command line and shows you their full path names if found:

```
$ where spellcount vi where
/usr/local/spellcount
/bin/vi
/usr/ucb/vi
/usr/local/where
$ where foobar
No foobar in :/bin:/usr/bin:/bin.cadmus:/bin.ver7:/bin.sys3:
/bin.sys5:/usr/ucb:/usr/games:/etc:/usr/local:/own/lev:
/usr/lib/news:/usr/lib/uucp:/usr/lib/acct:/usr/lib/sa:
/own/stat/bin:/usr/lib:/usr/lib/spell:.:
$
```

Although where does not look for commands in obscure places the way the Berkeley whereis program does, where is much faster than its almost-equivalent which. Even if you have whereis or which, you will like where more:

```
/*
 * where.c
 *
 * by Larry Barello, Teltone, Bellevue, WA
 * ..!uw-beaver!{tikal,teltone}!larry
 *
 */

#include <stdio.h>
char *getenv();
char *index(); /* use strchr() on System III and later */

main(ac,av)
char **av;
{
 char *origpath, *path, *cp;
 char buf[200];
 char patbuf[512];
 int quit, found;
```

```
        if (ac < 2) {
        fprintf(stderr, "Usage: %s cmd [cmd, ..]\n", *av);
        exit(1);
        }
        if ((origpath = getenv("PATH")) == 0)
        origpath = ".";
      av[ac] = 0;
        for(av++ ; *av; av++) {
        strcpy(patbuf, origpath);
        cp = path = patbuf;
        quit = found = 0;

      while(!quit) {
        cp = index(path, ':');
        if (cp == NULL)
        quit++;
        else *cp = '\0';

      sprintf(buf, "%s/%s", (*path ? path:"."), *av);
        path = ++cp;
        if (access(buf, 1) == 0) {
        printf("%s\n", buf);
        found++;
        }
        }
        if (!found)
        printf("No %s in %s\n", *av, origpath);
        }
        exit(0);}
```

Here is a simpler version of where (from Bruce Dawson) for the
Bourne and Korn shells:

```
        path=`echo $PATH | sed -e 's/:/w/q'`
        for i in $path
        do
            if [-f $1/$1 ]
            then echo $i/$1
            fi
        done
```

Summary

In the past, most operating systems had flat file systems. Modern multiuser operating systems use a hierarchical file system, which has a significant advantage: it enables the system's users to deal with a large file system in an organized way. But there is a price. The file system hierarchy must be maintained. In the next chapter, you learn how to mount and unmount these file systems.

5

Mounting and

Unmounting

File Systems

UNIX is not a homogeneous entity—it is divided into several working parts. The smallest UNIX system deals with a minimum of two separate file systems. One file system is the standard UNIX distribution (/unix: the kernel, /dev, /etc, and /bin and the user files), and the other file system is for the swapper (for swapping executable binaries in and out of memory as needed). Usually, the user files reside in their own file system. Each of these file systems is stored on its own separate section of the disk, a section called a *disk partition*. The swap area is not mounted and is actually not a file system.

Larger UNIX systems have huge disk capacities and thus many more mounted file systems. In fact, on very large UNIX systems, there are many separate user file systems, and even UNIX proper may be divided into smaller partitions on the hard disk. A UNIX system can be partitioned a number of ways, depending on the size of the system and the implementor's fancy.

When you come up in single-user mode (init s in System V), you are working with disk partitions—UNIX proper and the swap disk. These are already created when you receive your UNIX system. However, when you go into multiuser mode (init 2 – 5 in System V), init calls rc, and rc mounts any other file systems it has been told to mount. Here is where you, the system administrator, enter the picture. In order to get `rc` to mount a file system, first you need to create a disk partition for it on one of your disks. Then you create the file system (with `mkfs`) and `mount` it. Finally, you edit the appropriate file in `/etc` to add the `mount` command so that the system will be mounted automatically as it comes up in multiuser mode.

UNIX System V Release 4 supports many different kinds of file systems, including Berkeley, Sun NFS, and XENIX, besides the standard System V file system. Right now, you don't need to be concerned with these other flavors, just aware that they exist.

This chapter shows you how to do all these tasks, explores some UNIX file theory in the process, and explains how to unmount a file system. But before getting in any deeper, you need to examine some essential concepts.

What Is a Mounted File System?

First of all, what is the difference between mounted and unmounted file systems? Each mounted UNIX file system is a user file tree that has its own root—not to be confused with *the* root (UNIX proper). The file system is attached to the UNIX file tree and, consequently, is accessible for the usual UNIX operations—reading files, writing files, and so on. An unmounted file system is *not* attached to the UNIX file tree. Unmounted, a file system can be created and formatted by the system administrator, but it is noninteractive and essentially useless for system use. Once mounted, the file system officially becomes part of the working UNIX system.

A Little UNIX File System Theory

Although the actual process of mounting and unmounting file systems is straightforward enough, the theory behind it is not. You are far more effective as a UNIX system administrator if you know not only what to do but also why you do it.

UNIX is a multiuser system, capable of being quite large indeed. Mainframe UNIX implementations deal with billions of bytes of data and hundreds of users. Regardless of the actual number of users, an operating system must maintain data integrity, which is no easy task on multiuser systems. Hence, file systems are kept not only separate but also inviolate. UNIX is extremely particular about crossing the boundaries of mounted file systems. Each file system has its own separate disk partition, and communication between file systems is rigidly controlled by UNIX proper. If you try to use the ln (link) command from one file system to another, you quickly find that the system refuses to allow links across disk boundaries (although you can create *symbolic links*). By selectively isolating data in this manner, data corruption is prevented, and data security is facilitated.

In order to adapt to the demands of a busy multiuser system, you are more effective, as a system administrator, if you have the freedom to mount and unmount file systems to suit specific needs. UNIX gives you this freedom. On small UNIX systems, although system administrators seldom need to create more than a few mounted file systems, having the ability to do so makes even the smallest UNIX system more versatile and expandable. For example, if you run out of room on your hard disk, you can get the additional space you need for more user file trees by simply purchasing another disk drive and mounting it as a separate file system.

In addition, as you learned in earlier chapters, the reason for doing most system administration tasks in single-user mode is that user file systems are unmounted at that time. Occasionally, even the system administrator of a small system may find it necessary to unmount a user file system manually to prevent inadvertent data damage during crucial system administration operations. UNIX fortunately makes unmounting file systems an easy task.

Naturally, the larger the UNIX system, the more variables are involved in system administration, and the greater the potential for creativity. File systems can be mounted to UNIX proper one at a time, or they can be stacked one on top of another. (/usr/spool, /usr/src, and /usr/man are typical stacked file systems. On very large machines, /usr is mounted as one file system to which /man, /src, and /spool are attached as separate file systems.) On the largest systems, the system administrator may create duplicate file trees as an alternative backup strategy for critical areas. On systems heavily loaded with users, the system administrator often has to create custom-sized file trees to manage existing disk space. Your system supplier usually provides a layout of the disk partitions available on your system. An example is shown in Figure 5.1.

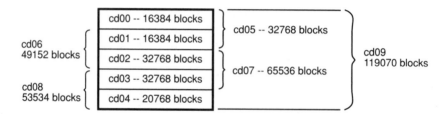

Figure 5.1. Disk devices can incorporate other disk devices, the partitions.

These partitions are simply entry points in the device driver code that tell the driver where each partition begins and ends on the disk. By using partitions cd02 and cd03 separately, you get two reasonably sized file systems of 32768 blocks each. But by addressing the partitions jointly as cd07, you have one large 65536-block file system if you need one. Similarly, you can use the *entire disk* as a giant 119070-block file system by simply calling it cd09.

Now that you know a little of the theory behind mounting user file systems, you learn how to mount them in the next section.

File System Creation and Implementation

Before you can create a file system, you have to set aside a special area for it on the hard disk. As noted earlier, this area is called a disk partition (or predefined disk subsystem). The birth of every file system starts with two possibilities: using an existing disk partition or making your own from scratch. New owners of UNIX systems need to keep in mind that most OEMs partition and format the disk and make (mkfs) a file system to start you off. Finding it may take a little detective work, however.

Because UNIX proper and the swapper are already installed and mounted, your first problem as system administrator is to find out whether the rest of the hard disk has been predefined with disk partitions. By doing a df -t, you can see how much total disk space (in blocks) is available to the system. If the total is substantially less than the potential size of the disk, either you have a predefined disk system, or a large block of disk is unused:

```
$ df -t
/usr    (/dev/cd01 ):     32266 blocks     4059 inodes
                total:    32768 blocks     4096 inodes
/       (/dev/cd00 ):      3888 blocks     1489 inodes
                total:    16384 blocks     2048 inodes
```

Note that the information is given separately for each file system. In this case, the /usr file system is clearly underused. Only 502 blocks are in use out of a possible 32768.

Now the detective work begins. If you are in pre-SVR2 UNIX, go into the /dev directory (or a subdirectory below there, such as /dev/dsk) and look for a set of block special files with approximately the same file name but increasing numbers (for example, cd00 through cd37). These are your hard disk partitions:

```
brw-r--r-- 1 root 0, 0   Dec 31   1989    cd00
brw-r--r-- 1 root 0, 1   Jun  9 20:31    cd01
brw-r--r-- 1 root 0, 2   Dec 31   1989    cd02
brw-r--r-- 1 root 0, 3   Oct 25   1990    cd03
brw-r--r-- 1 root 0, 4   Dec 13   1990    cd04
brw-r--r-- 1 root 0, 5   Dec 13   1990    cd05
```

Now find a corresponding set of character special files (these might be in /dev/rdsk) with a similar name and the same set of numbers. These are "raw" disks (rcd00 through rcd37). They are there to handle tasks requiring character I/O, such as formatting:

```
crw-r--r-- 1 root 5, 0   Dec 31 1989    rcd00
crw-r--r-- 1 root 5, 1   Dec 31 1989    rcd01
crw-r--r-- 1 root 5, 2   Dec 31 1989    rcd02
crw-r--r-- 1 root 5, 3   Dec 31 1989    rcd03
crw-r--r-- 1 root 5, 4   Dec 13 1990    rcd04
crw-r--r-- 1 root 5, 5   Dec 13 1990    rcd05
```

Now go to / (root) and nose around for a directory that looks like a match:

```
# ls -l /
total 359
drwxr-xr-x 2 root      3040   Oct 14   1984    bin
-rw-rw-rw- 1 root     14336   Jun  1 12:29    core
drwxr-xr-x 2 root      1856   Feb 24 11:59    dev
drwxr-xr-x 2 root       480   Feb 11 14:46    etc
-rwx------ 1 root        49   Nov 19   1989    fdload
drwxr-xr-x 2 root       496   Jan  1   1990    lib
drwxr-xr-x 2 root      4608   May 22 20:31    lost+found
drwxrwxrwx 2 root        32   Dec 31   1989    mnt03
drwxrwxrwx 2 root       208   Jun 11 21:08    tmp
-rwxr--r-- 2 root     77656   Aug 13   1989    unix
-rwxr--r-- 2 root     77656   Aug 13   1989    unix.cd.dm.i
drwxr-xr-x16 root       336   Feb 17 18:44    usr
```

Can you find the directory in question? It's `mnt03`, an OEM-created directory. It is empty and located in the root directory—a natural place to mount a new file system. Note that any directory with a displayed size of 32 bytes is empty. You need 16 bytes per file name (14 for the name and 2 for the inodes), and a directory always has a minimum of 2 entries—1 pointing to itself (.) and 1 pointing to its parent (. .). If the disk partition is made into a file system, it shows its size when the `df` command is used. When you mount `/dev/cd03` to `mnt03`, you have the beginning of a file system:

```
# mkfs /dev/cd03 16384
# mount /dev/cd03 /mnt03
#
```

(On System V Release 2, the disks have their own directory in `/dev`, called `/dev/dsk`.) If you want to change the name of the file system to something more readable—say, from `/mnt03` to `/us`—use the `mv` command to do that, and then you can mount `/dev/cd03` on `/us`:

```
# mv mnt03 us
# mount /dev/cd03 /us
#
```

Creating a Disk Partition

If no predefined partition or subdisk is available, you have to make one. At this point, anyone not trained in operating system theory may be surprised to find that UNIX usually does not do this task. Disk partitions must be created with special partitioning and formatting utilities. Creating partitions varies from machine to machine.

UNIX relies on a host operating system to bring it up. The host operating system may be something as sophisticated as VM/SP (Amdahl and IBM), or as primitive as a simple PROM-based monitor with no purpose other than providing minimal facilities to support UNIX. With few exceptions, the host system provides the means of partitioning and formatting disk subsystems for UNIX. Some hardware support systems, like AT&T's 3B2 firmware, are quite sophisticated. Very large systems, such as UTS UNIX under VM/SP, even allow partitioning "minidisks," or partial disks, by absolute addressing. Check your manual to see what needs to be done on your machine. (Sometimes all of these functions can be performed directly from within UNIX, such as on SCO and Interactive Systems UNIX, where you have the partition utility `fdisk`.)

Formatting is also done from the host system. Small 68000-based machines format from the boot PROM system. Exceptions include UTS UNIX, which formats from UTS itself. There is no standard method; each system is different. You must exercise great care when either formatting or making a file system (mkfs) because both actions are highly destructive of any data already existing within that area. As one manual puts it, "data will be mercilessly destroyed."

format is not a standard UNIX command for hard disks but is commonly used for diskettes (floppies). When found on UNIX systems, format is supplied by the OEM as an extension of UNIX proper. format allows hard disks to be formatted from UNIX rather than by the boot operating system. This approach is much easier for the system administrator because she is working with UNIX more often than not.

Formatting prepares the disk for a file system, zeroing out old data and creating a disk format compatible with the host UNIX system. Don't confuse this process with mkfs, which creates the inode and file structure necessary for a UNIX file system. And don't forget that *either* process wipes out all data on the section of disk you are dealing with!

Creating a File System with *mkfs*

Before the actual mounting process takes place, you need two necessary ingredients: a file tree or system ready to mount, and a directory to mount it on. You make a file system with the mkfs command, and you make a directory with the mkdir command.

mkfs creates a UNIX file system. UNIX demands that a file system have its superblock and inode information initialized before putting a file or directory on disk. UNIX goes to a default formula unless you, the system administrator, specify otherwise, but you must specify the size of the file system. With UNIX System V, you have the additional option of being able to specify the number of inodes you want as well as the most efficient disk block spacing.

Being able to control file system size is handy if disk space is at a premium. File systems vary in flavor and texture, depending on their purpose. If you have lots of small files, such as data files for an accounting system billing operation that are seldom more than a few hundred characters each, the number of inodes should be close to the number of blocks. If, however, you are dealing with massive text files such as book chapters or reports, the number of inodes should be substantially less than the number of blocks. Remember that at least one inode is needed for each file, no matter how small, but large files may contain many blocks. Even inodes take up disk space.

If the number of inodes is unspecified when you run mkfs, the number defaults to the number of physical blocks in the file system divided by four. Experience has proved that this is more than sufficient in most cases. Because of the many small files, the file system used to hold Usenet news-posting files (generally /usr/spool) should have twice this many inodes, however. Actual use and continual checking (df) will show you the best ratios.

Don't continually reformat or re-mkfs your disks. One day you will forget to back up something, and you'll wipe out several months' work. Unless the data is quite unusual—from Usenet on one extreme to large graphics bitmap files on the other—stick with the default formula.

You create a file system with the mkfs command:

```
# mkfs /dev/cd03 1000
```

/dev/cd03 is the block special file, and 1000 is the number of blocks in the new file system.

In System V Release 2 (and later), the command line looks like this:

```
# mkfs /dev/dsk/cd03 1000:500
```

500 is the number of inodes you want.

More Than You Ever Wanted to Know about Disk Drives

In the manual page for mkfs, two other parameters are listed: *gap* and *blocks*. (There is also a procedure mentioned for automatically creating an entire file system, including a boot program, from a specification file; but this is so tricky, we don't advise using it.) These parameters refer to the actual physical disk you are using, and they are really quite simple.

All data on a disk is written and read in blocks of 512, 1024, 4096, or some other multiple of bytes at once for efficiency. The disk is constantly spinning, and the read/write head moves backward and forward to go from track to track.

If the head stays in one place for a while, all the data on a track will eventually pass underneath the head to be read. As the data you want (perhaps block 5 of track 0) passes under the head, it is read and transferred to a buffer area in the disk controller. This takes a short but significant amount of time, during which several other blocks of data pass under the head. If the blocks are numbered sequentially on the disk and you want block 6, the disk has to spin an entire turn before block 6 comes up again.

So system designers measure the time needed to transfer data, and they calculate the number of blocks skipped when reading or writing. Then, by starting at block 0 and skipping two blocks before assigning block 1, the head is ready to read data immediately. This block numbering is shown in Figure 5.2.

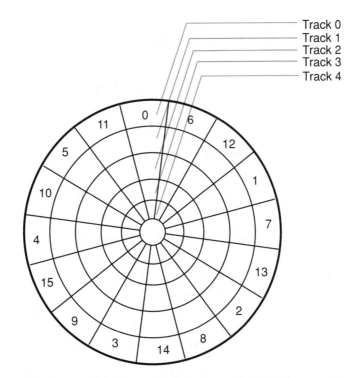

Figure 5.2. *Sector skewing or interleaving. This disk has an interleave factor of 2.*

The trick of skipping sectors is known as *sector skewing* or *interleaving*, and the *gap* is simply the number of blocks skipped—in this figure, two. Disk operations are speeded up considerably with interleaving.

Here the term *blocks* refers to the number of blocks per cylinder. A *cylinder* is an imaginary vertical slice of disk comprising all tracks of the same number on each usable disk surface. Cylinder 1 contains all track *1*s on all disk surfaces, cylinder 2 contains all track *2*s on all disk surfaces, and so on.

For example, if a disk has 6 "platters" of which only 4 are usable (on both sides), there are 8 usable disk surfaces. If each track has 20 blocks, there are 20 * 8 or 160 blocks per cylinder.

The figures for both gap and blocks should be specified to you by the system supplier, or mkfs should have been modified by the supplier so that it automatically supplies the correct values. By now, you should have enough information to figure out the values yourself, if necessary, from the disk drive specification sheet.

Once the formatted subdisk is prepared and you make the file system with mkfs, the groundwork is completed. Now a subdisk exists that is defined and formatted and has all the file and inode structures needed to make a system run once it is mounted.

Mounting a File System

You attach a file system or a tree to another file system by mounting it. The command to mount a file tree is mount:

```
# mount /dev/xt0f /usr/spool
```

Any data on the special file /dev/xt0f is now part of the file system /usr/spool. Be careful when using mount because when one file system is mounted on top of another, any files already there seem to disappear! For example, if the text file /usr/spool/README exists before the /usr/spool file system is attached, /usr/spool/README seems to vanish until /usr/spool is unmounted. However, the file is still there and using space (see Figures 5.3 and 5.4).

A df shows whether the system is mounted:

```
$ df /dev/xt0f
(/dev/xt0f ): 21554 blocks 7801 inodes
```

The df command displays free disk space, showing that the /usr/spool system is not only mounted, but also has 10+ megabytes free (21554 blocks of 512 bytes divided by 2).

The mount command without arguments also shows all mounted systems:

```
# mount
/          on /dev/xt0a read/write on Tue Sep 10 17:19:03 1985
/usr       on /dev/xt0c read/write on Tue Sep 10 17:19:07 1985
/usr/lib   on /dev/xt0e read/write on Tue Sep 10 17:19:08 1985
/usr/spool on /dev/xt0f read/write on Tue Sep 10 17:19:09 1985
/tmp       on /dev/xt1b read/write on Tue Sep 10 17:19:23 1985
```

```
/own        on /dev/xt1c read/write on Tue Sep 10 17:19:10 1985
/ips        on /dev/xt1e read/write on Tue Sep 10 17:19:11 1985
/db         on /dev/xt1f read/write on Tue Sep 10 17:19:12 1985
```

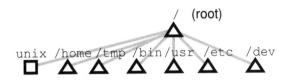

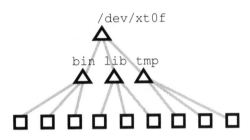

Figure 5.3. The /dev/xt0f *file before mounting.*

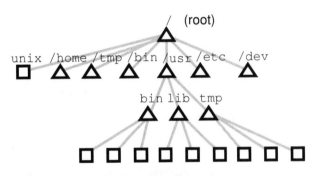

Figure 5.4. The /dev/xt0f *file after mounting.*

Mounting a file system under System 5.2 is a little more complex, but not much. Each file system created by mkfs can be further partitioned. A file system starting point, usually 0, must be specified in the mount command. Here is a typical System 5.2 mount command with arguments:

 # mount /dev/dsk/330s0 /usr/man

The s0 offset on the /dev entry shows that you are dealing with the *zero*th partition of /dsk330. You can also mount a file system as read-only, so that it cannot be written on. Generally, you do this when mounting a

111

backup disk, to prevent wiping it out by mistake. (Of course, people who wipe out file systems by mistake also usually forget to mount a file system as read-only in the first place.) The way to do it is simply to add the read-only flag at the end of the `mount` command:

```
# mount /dev/cd03 /us -r
```

Unmounting a File System

File systems must be unmounted from time to time. Whenever you do a disk frontal lobotomy (a `format` or `mkfs`), you have to unmount the system. `fsck` is best done on a quiescent system, and an unmounted system is even safer. Fortunately, the `umount` syntax is simple. It takes only one argument—the name of the special file (device) to be unmounted:

```
# umount /dev/cd03
```

Whatever `/dev/cd03` was attached to is now a free directory, and `/dev/cd03` is unreachable by the users. You will not be able to `umount` a file system if any of the following conditions are true:

- You don't have write permission on the device on which the system is mounted. You must have superuser privileges to unmount a file system in almost all cases.

- Anyone is using it. This includes you! Generally, you must be in the root file system to `umount` other file systems.

- *Anyone* is using it. This means that if any user has a file open on the file system in question, even the superuser will not be able to unmount it.

- *Anyone is using it*. This means that if the *system* has a file open on that file system, you will also be blocked from unmounting it.

How can the system have a file open? Suppose that someone is editing a file with `vi`, and you are trying to unmount the `/usr` file system. Because `vi` is located in the `/usr/ucb` directory (on most systems), as long as `vi` is being executed, the system has the binary file `/usr/ucb/vi` open! The user must get out of `vi` for you to be able to unmount `/usr`. Or, for an even trickier example, you won't be able to unmount `/usr/lib` until you kill the printer daemon (`lpdaemon` or `lpsched`) because the daemon's home directory is `/usr/lib`. There is no easy way to determine whether someone is using a file system. It is best to get everyone off the system if you are going to `umount` a file system.

/etc/mnttab

In the /etc/mnttab file, the system keeps a binary record of what file systems are mounted and when they were mounted. As you have seen, executing the mount command with no arguments prints this information in readable form. When the system is brought up after a crash, /etc/mnttab still exists, and if the mount table is not reinitialized, the data is there several times over. You get the following sort of nonsense:

```
$ mount
/         on /dev/xt0a read/write on Mon Oct  1 14:02:38 1984
/usr      on /dev/xt0c read/write on Mon Oct  1 14:02:43 1984
/usr/lib on /dev/xt0e read/write on Mon Oct  1 14:02:43 1984
/xf       on /dev/xt0f read/write on Mon Oct  1 14:02:44 1984
/usr      on /dev/xt0c read/write on Thu Jan 31 17:35:31 1985
/usr/lib on /dev/xt0e read/write on Thu Jan 31 17:35:32 1985
/xf       on /dev/xt0f read/write on Thu Jan 31 17:35:32 1985
/usr      on /dev/xt0c read/write on Thu Jan 31 22:39:50 1985
/usr/lib on /dev/xt0e read/write on Thu Jan 31 22:39:50 1985
/xf       on /dev/xt0f read/write on Thu Jan 31 22:39:51 1985
```

If this is the case on your system, make sure that /etc/mnttab is being properly erased on each reboot. The simplest way to do that is to put the following lines in your /etc/rc file:

```
> /etc/mnttab
devnm / ¦ setmnt
```

Handy Shell Programs

As system administrator, you will do many processes again and again. The shell programs presented here will help you with tasks involved in mounting and unmounting file systems.

/etc/Mount

The ideas behind /etc/Mount and /etc/Unmount are similar. Try to isolate the details of your normally mounted file systems in a pair of command files. Then, when you are in single-user mode and you want to test a program, you can mount all file systems by simply typing

```
# Mount
```

113

This command eliminates the common error of forgetting to mount a file system, which is especially important in this case because two file systems are mounted *on top of* /usr, and order is therefore important. You can also use the Mount program in /etc/rc when mounting all file systems. Naturally, you must substitute the commands to mount *your* file systems properly on *your* devices. The Mount script is simply a list of the mount commands you execute when you bring up your system to the multiuser run level. *Don't copy ours*, which looks like this:

```
mount /dev/xt0c /usr
mount /dev/xt0e /usr/lib
mount /dev/xt0f /usr/spool
mount /dev/xt1b /tmp
mount /dev/xt1c /own
mount /dev/xt1e /ips
mount /dev/xt1f /db
```

/etc/Umount

This is the same program in reverse, of course. You wouldn't get far if you tried umount /dev/xt0c before /dev/xt0f, so now you won't do that by accident. The following script represents our file systems (yours should reflect your file systems in the same way that Mount does):

```
umount /dev/xt1f
umount /dev/xt1e
umount /dev/xt1c
umount /dev/xt1b
umount /dev/xt0f
umount /dev/xt0e
umount /dev/xt0c
```

free

The df command lets you know how many free blocks you have on each file system. Some systems—such as XENIX, UTS 2.x, and 4.2 BSD—tell you what *percentage* of free space you have left. Knowing the percentage can be more useful; having 4000 blocks free may be either good or an imminent disaster, depending on how big your system is. The following little program, called free (a combination of awk and shell), tells you the number of free kilobytes, the number of free blocks, and the percentage of free space on any or all file systems:

```
while true
do
  echo ${1:-Total}"\t\c"
  df -t ${1:-} ¦ awk '{
    if (( NR % 2 ) == 1)
    bl += $4
    else total += $2
    }
  END { kb = bl / 2 ; avg = 100 * (bl/total) ;
  printf "%d KB (%d blocks) free or %d%% of usable space\n"\
,kb,bl,avg}'

 if test $# -gt 1
 then shift
 else exit 0
 fi
done
```

If no parameters are given, free automatically totals the information for all file systems (otherwise, free works for the file systems named on the command line):

```
$ free
Total 28341 KB (56682 blocks) free or 28% of usable space
$ free / /usr /tmp
/     1910 KB (3820 blocks) free or 23% of usable space
/usr 1239 KB (2478 blocks) free or 7% of usable space
/tmp 7349 KB (14698 blocks) free or 89% of usable space
```

Note that this program was written for older (pre-System V) systems, where 512-byte blocks were used, so some arithmetic is done to figure out the number of free kilobytes. If you use 1K blocks, you can change the line beginning with END to

```
END { kb = bl ; avg = 100 * (bl/total) ;
```

If you use 4096-byte blocks, you can change that line to

```
END { kb = bl * 4 ; avg = 100 * (bl/total) ;
```

The system on which this program was written returns df output like this:

```
/ (/dev/xt0a ): 3822 blocks 1491 i-nodes
```

If your `df` output has no whitespace between the name of the device and the closing parentheses, change the line

```
bl += $4
```

to

```
bl += $3
```

You may also need to tweak this command script a little to reflect the peculiar output format of your `df` utility.

Summary

Although there are usually automatic scripts and control files for mounting and unmounting all the file systems normally used on most systems, you may need to do these tasks manually when you are doing file system maintenance. There are also special cases for mounting and unmounting remote file systems on your local system file tree. Remote file systems are discussed in Chapter 13 on networks. In the next chapter, you look at one of the most vital system administration tasks—how to shut down the system gracefully (and carefully).

6

Hangup, Crash, and Shutdown

Life as a system administrator has some special challenges. Processes can get hung or turn into zombies. Devices can get in an irreparable state of confusion. The whole system can even come crashing down. Before you study how these disasters might occur and how you can recover, you need to consider what constitutes a normal system shutdown.

How to Be Nice to Your System

Stopping the system "cold" by simply cutting power not only is an invitation to disaster but also almost guarantees damage to the UNIX file system. Bringing down the system nicely is an absolute necessity. Because the file system's directory and inode information exist in RAM as well as on disk, the disk version must match the one stored in RAM when the system comes down. You must also have provisions to prevent additional users from logging onto the system after the shutdown warnings have gone out. You should consider many factors, but first take a look at the basics of a voluntary system shutdown.

Shutdown Fundamentals

In the simplest terms, you shut down a UNIX system by updating each disk's file system information with a `sync` command and doing a soft kill on `init`. (A *soft kill* is an interrupt number 15 or a SIGTERM, generally done by a command such as `kill -15 1`.) Most systems, though, have a shutdown script created by the computer supplier. The script is usually in /etc/ shutdown (/sbin/shutdown on SVR4) and must be performed from the root login and on the system console. This procedure is best done after all users have logged off and all background processes have been stopped.

UNIX System V Release 3 and later versions have an underlying script that is part of the init structure. If this script is part of your system, the shutdown script should use init 0 instead of killing the init process (1) directly. The default shutdown script takes care of warning users. The rc0 and associated scripts under /etc/rc0.d (/sbin/rc0.d on SVR4) take care of shutting down the system in an orderly manner, including shutting down servers and preventing new logins. The final lines of rc0 invoke *seppuku*, ritual suicide.

The system administrator should develop procedures for bringing down the system in an orderly way with as little discomfort to the users as possible. If the system is brought down nightly, it should remain up during normal working hours and be brought down at a reasonably consistent time every night. If the system is usually up around the clock, it should be brought down from time to time for maintenance. These shutdowns should be scheduled, and the users given ample warning. As a general rule, never go more than a week without throwing out excess baggage, testing the file system for consistency, and making general repairs.

Because shutdown starts out as a canned shell script, you should gradually develop your own shutdown script. This is not as hard as it sounds. Use the original script as a pattern and add to it as you develop scripts for your particular installation. Be sure that your version does at least what the original canned version does. For example, you will be adding mounted file systems as your system expands. You are going to want to unmount them before shutting down the system (killing init), and what better place than in shutdown? To make things easier, use as a guide the /etc/Unmount script from the last chapter.

Don't be afraid to customize your own system. UNIX is uniquely plastic. It was created to be readily programmable, so no two UNIX systems need to be exactly alike. In fact, a good UNIX system administrator molds her machine to fit the needs of her particular installation.

Warn Your Users Ahead of Time

Unless all of your users are within shouting distance, you should place a message in /etc/motd (the *message-of-the-d*ay file that users normally see when they log in) to warn users of the scheduled shutdown. In addition, wall (*w*rite all) the users at reasonable time intervals before the shutdown, and once more immediately before initiating the shutdown procedure. Give at least a five-minute "grace" period before shutdown begins. System administrators usually put all this in /etc/shutdown. In its simplest form, it looks something like this:

```
echo starting shutdown
/etc/wall<<XX
Please log off. System coming down in 5 minutes.
XX
sleep 300
/etc/wall<<XX
System coming down now!!
XX
sleep 15
cd /
/etc/Unmount
sync; sleep 1
sync
sleep 5
sync
sleep 5
kill -15 1
```

Remember that once the shutdown procedure has started, make sure that you have made provisions to exclude users from logging on. Some systems have a file called /etc/nologins or /etc/maxusers, which prevents new logins simply by being on the computer (this file is usually created by /etc/shutdown). On other systems, you physically turn off all incoming modems. If someone logs on while the system is coming down, they get logged off immediately.

Scheduled shutdowns are the most desirable, but panic shutdowns are inevitable, particularly on large systems. Hanging logins, unsuccessful mount requests, and runaway processes can confuse the system so much that your only hope is to bring it down and restart it again. When you do this, give as much notice as possible, even if it's only a few seconds. The fewer people left stuck in editors, the less work you have when the system comes back up. Generally, when things start acting funny, type sync from the nearest terminal. (Any user can sync the system; you don't have to be root.) Let the users close their files and log off if possible.

Recovering from System Catastrophes

The system administrator must jump into the heat of battle when system catastrophes occur. They can range from minor problems such as hung terminals or processes, to major disasters such as a head crash. You must keep your head while the world around you comes unraveled.

Your first step is to ascertain exactly what happened. The next step is to formulate a recovery plan. If you make too hasty a move, you may find yourself picking up the shattered remains of your system.

About Processes

Each program that runs on your system, no matter how small, is run as a *process*—a separate program with its own input, output, and "parent" program that can control it. The user who starts a process is the *owner* of that process and all subsequent children. The owner of a process can terminate (kill) it at any time. Root has the power to kill any and all system processes.

To get information about the processes on the system, you use the ps (process status) command. ps takes a "snapshot" of the system's process table at the instant it is executed. When ps is run without arguments, it shows you information about all your own processes:

```
$ ps
  PID   TTY   TIME   CMD
 25371  12    0:14   -csh
 26023  12    0:14   vi shutdown
 26054   ?           <defunct>
 26055  12    0:00   sh -c ps
 26056  12    0:02   ps
$
```

The leftmost column, labeled PID, displays the individual *process identification* numbers, which are the unique numbers that UNIX assigns while processes exist in the system. The count starts over again after 32767. The TTY column tells you which *tty* (or terminal line) the process was initiated from—in this case, /dev/tty12. TIME is simply the total amount of system CPU time that has been used by each process.

In the CMD column, ps attempts to print the command line used to start the process. At this point, you are logged in under csh, editing a file with vi, and running the ps command under the Bourne shell. This last Bourne shell is actually a subshell created expressly to run the ps command while in vi, which is why the process shows up as a separate sh -c ps. <defunct> marks a process that ended its existence just before ps could determine any information about it aside from its pid.

Now look at a more complex report. ps -elf (or ps -ax on Berkeley UNIX) shows a great deal of information about all processes running in the system, not just your own. This is what you will usually run as system administrator:

```
$ ps -elf
S UID    PID  PPID PRI NICE  SZ  WCHAN  TTY   TIME  CMD
S   0     0    0    1   20    0  12b094    ? 129:38  swapper
S   0     1    0   39   20   40  200000    ?   3:05  /etc/init
S   0 21224    1   28   20   36  128a22   co   0:02  getty console console
S   0 20781    1   28   20   36  128a74   11   0:02  getty /dev/tty11 9600
S   0 19024    1   39   39   24  200000   12   2:02  cron
S  12 25371    1   39   20  124  200000   12   0:14  -csh
S   0 20783    1   28   20   36  128b18   13   0:02  getty /dev/tty13 9600
S   0 22697    1   28   20   36  128b6a   20   0:02  getty /dev/tty20 9600
S  12 26023 25371  26   20  260  1119d2   12   0:39  vi shutdown
S   0    63    1   26   20   56  111502    ?   0:07  /usr/lib/lpsched
R  12 26047 26040  65   20   88           12   1:15  uucico -r1 -swhuxcc
S  12 26037    1    0   20   44  115bd8   12   0:01  poll whuxcc
S  12 26040 26037  30   20   44  115c40   12   0:00  poll whuxcc
Z  12 26101 26023  20   20    0   10000    ?         <defunct>
S   0 22927    1   28   20   36  128f42   bi   0:01  getty bip0 bip bip
S  12 26102 26023  30   20   44  115f7c   12   0:00  sh -c ps -eLf
R  12 26103 26102  70   20   28           12   0:04  ps -eLf
```

(In the preceding sequence, some columns have been excised because of width restrictions.) Looks marvelous, doesn't it? All the gory details for every column are written up in the manual, so they won't be repeated here. The important columns for you to examine are S, UID, PID, PPID, NICE, SZ, and WCHAN.

The S column shows what process is running at the exact moment of executing ps; this column always shows ps and perhaps something else as well. (Only one process actually runs at a time, but even ps isn't perfect.) The S column is useful for spotting problems. In this case, the process that was noted before as being <defunct> has the flag Z, known colloquially as a *zombie* because it has been killed but refuses to die. When this happens to a process, you should become superuser and attempt to kill it. If you can't kill the process as superuser, it is destined to haunt your system until the next reboot, which may be sooner than you think if the process is large and growing. Sometimes zombies die when a device they are waiting for changes state, such as a tape drive or printer. Other letters that are likely to appear here, as detailed in the manual, include R (for a running process), S (for a sleeping process, which will run either when its turn comes or when it stops sleeping), and T (for a process that has been stopped, usually by someone using the C shell).

The UID column shows who owns the process (by user ID number or user name). You know what PID means now, and PPID is the *previous* process ID, or the "parent" of the process. If the parent process is killed, all child processes started by the parent should also die. Note that in this longer listing, you can trace the evolution of the various processes started from the original csh with PID 25371.

All processes waiting in line for the CPU don't have the same priority. A lower priority number means that the process can cut in line. The NICE column shows the "niceness" of a process (default is 20). The NICE number is related to the priority number; when a program is run with nice, its priority number goes higher. If you know you will be running a large or long program, you run it with a higher NICE in order to be "nice" to other users. As superuser, you can also start processes off at negative niceness to get them done as quickly as possible:

```
# nice − 30 nroff important.file
```

If you have the Berkeley program renice, you can change the priority of a program after it has already started (as superuser only):

```
# renice 26023 10
```

This raises the niceness of the vi process to 10, making response time faster for editing.

The SZ, or size column, shows how much actual memory each process takes up. If you add up all the process sizes, you can get a good idea of how much memory is being used. If the total is more memory than you actually have available, your system will slow down because the swapper has to move processes in and out of memory in order to run them. If you are lucky enough to have a virtual memory system, only *page*-sized chunks (usually 4 KB) of program get moved out, greatly speeding system operations.

On some systems, programs have *shared text*. In other words, if the same program is being run more than once (even by different users), its "text," or program area, is shared by all processes running it. Note the following illustration:

Process = text (shared) + data area + context
+ stacks (user and kernel) + user structure

So even though several processes are listed as running `getty`, each taking up 36 KB, the *actual* amount of memory in use from all of these processes is still only 36 KB, plus a bit extra for nonshared space specific to each process. To check this, you can run the `file` program on system programs:

```
$ file /bin/*
/bin/adb:       shareable executable
/bin/as:        commands text
/bin/awk:       shareable executable
/bin/calendar:      c program text
/bin/cat:       shareable executable
/bin/cc:        shareable executable
Interrupt
$
```

Because the binary executable files are marked shareable, you have the shared text feature. On other systems, `file` may return a string saying "pure text" or another phrase that means the same thing.

The total memory usage, as reported by the previous `ps`, is 744 KB. If you find that your processes often add up to more memory than you have available (as reported by the kernel at boot time), you may want to buy more memory for maximum speed.

The last column to examine is `WCHAN`. It tells what device, or "channel," each process is waiting for. On most systems, what appears in the `ps` listing is a number that is the kernel address of the device driver in question. To use the information in `WCHAN`, you need an address map of your kernel. Some enlightened suppliers have added a routine to the `ps`, such as `/dev/lp`, which prints the name of the device being waited for.

Hung Processes

A hung process usually manifests itself in a terminal echoing whatever you type, does nothing useful whatsoever, and cannot be killed or stopped. Like a mad dog, a user's process that becomes hung must be destroyed. The proper method is to kill the user's process. It takes three steps.

The first step is to run the `who` command to get the *tty* number of the process. The second step is to find the process ID number by executing the process status command `ps -e` (`ps -ax` on Berkeley systems). Look for all processes attached to the *tty* onto which the user is logged. The last step is to kill the hung process. It may also be necessary to kill other processes— owned by the same user—that might be affected. In fact, when you want to be absolutely sure that the hung process is destroyed, you kill all of the user's processes, including his login shell, and then let him log back on again. If the user is hung in `kermit` (a communications program), the only way to kill the process and free the user is to kill the user's shell. (This is true of some implementations of `cu` as well.)

Imagine that one of your users, Chad, comes to you with his editor hung. No amount of coaxing to `vi` will get the editor to do anything, so you must play Grand Exalted Process Executioner. First, figure out where Chad is logged in:

```
$ who
karen      console  Mar 18 19:08
bruce      tty0     Mar 18 18:54
chad       tty1     Mar 18 18:56
```

Next, do a `ps -a` to find Chad's process numbers:

```
$ ps -t tty1

PID TTY TIME CMD
250 1   0:07 -sh
298 1   0:19 vi mor.let
```

If you know Chad's login name, a shortcut is to use the `-u` option of the `ps` command:

```
$ ps -u chad

PID TTY TIME CMD
250 1   0:07 -sh
298 1   0:19 vi mor.let
```

Finally, issue a *sure kill* to all of Chad's processes. You do this by becoming superuser and issuing the `kill -9` (terminate with extreme prejudice) command followed by the process numbers:

```
$ su
Password:
# kill -9 298 250
```

Chad's CRT should complain righteously with a "killed" message followed by a polite new login.

Here is the quick and dirty method to accomplish the same thing on some terminals: simply turn off the terminal and then turn it back on. This method logs him off and kills all of his processes in most cases. Never do this on IBM and IBM-type (Lee Data) synchronous terminal equipment, however. It upsets the hardware controllers.

Hung Devices

Computers and their peripheral equipment are a long way from being perfect. The combination of imperfection talking to imperfection often results in a peripheral getting hung. Hung terminals go deaf and dumb, neither taking nor displaying data. Modems get hung sending data to themselves or sitting off hook without doing anything to recover. Printers go crazy typing unintelligible graphics. All of these devices have the same problem: they can no longer communicate intelligently with the computer.

Usually, two steps are required to bring your peripherals back to sanity. The first step is a hardware reset. You reset most devices by shutting them off for about 15 seconds and then turning them back on. Some, such as IBM 3270 terminals, have a reset key. If resetting the device fails to return it to its senses, kill the process associated with the device. If you have the `fuser` command, it comes in handy here:

```
# fuser -k -d /dev/tty3
```

You must have the process running under the superuser ID. (The `-d` option is not supported on all systems.) This command line does an automatic "seek and destroy" on all processes, using `/dev/tty3`.

Killing a process related to a device is not without its repercussions. A killed printer process, for instance, can leave a lock file that prevents further printer activity until that file is removed (see Chapter 11 on printers for more details). A terminal that is reset may have the opposite problem— no activity can occur until the process using the terminal has been killed, which then allows a new login message to be displayed.

Paradoxically, modems are hung when they refuse to hang up! Here a little skill goes a long way. Talk to the port that the modem is on by accessing it with the `cu` command. Send the modem its hangup sequence. In the case of a Hayes or compatible modem, try the following sequence:

```
$ su
Password:
# cu -l /dev/modem
Connected
ATH
OK
~. [ronin]
#
```

Or try the direct approach:

```
# echo "ATH" > /dev/modem
```

Either sequence attempts to send the letters *ATH* to the modem, which should cause it to hang up the phone. If neither sequence works, turn off the modem and then turn it back on (a surefire method). As with the printer, lock files may still have to be removed (see Chapter 12 on modems).

System Crashes

Small UNIX systems seldom crash. They core dump at the drop of a hat, but they don't crash. The tri-nightly crashing of microcomputers went away with MMUs. (*M*emory *M*anagement *U*nits prevent wild address pointers from bringing the system crashing down like a falling redwood tree. The problem was caused by programs with bugs that used impossible or improbable memory addresses. They wouldn't just die; they would crash the entire system.) Large systems are more sophisticated, so they seldom core dump, but they do crash with painful regularity. Getting a million dollars worth of silicon, copper, gold, aluminum, and steel to play the same song is not possible at all times and under all circumstances. When a large system gets confused, it has only one action left to defend itself—it crashes. Elegant systems do a great deal of precrash juggling, such as closing files and writing open editor files out to error files to be recovered later. Such systems then attempt to log the cause of the crisis.

But even the most sophisticated systems seldom do that final sync. The last sync puts a good copy of the directory and inode information on disk. Because many crashes occur so quickly, nothing gets updated, no files get closed, and the total result is a disaster. Consequently, the file system becomes the major victim of the crash. Broken inodes lay scattered around the system, and the system administrator is left with the cleanup job.

A crash is *imminent* when the system begins slowing down precipitously, when people start getting logged off mysteriously, when almost every command yields a core dump, or when garbage starts appearing on people's terminals. At this point, get as many people as possible logged off and head for the console. If you have a chance, type **sync** a few times for luck. If time is really tight, remember that sync works from any terminal—you don't have to be superuser to run sync.

A crash is *complete* when everything stops. Sometimes your terminal echoes characters, but nothing runs. Sometimes the disk makes a repetitive sound of seeking but doesn't find anything. At this point, you are safer rebooting than letting strange broken programs run. They might erase your disk! Note to advanced administrators: if the system hangs, you may want to force a dump as the final act of the crash so that you can analyze it with the crash command later.

To recover from a system crash, your first step is to bring the system back up into single-user mode and leave it there while doing an fsck (or equivalent). Do *not* get in the habit of relying on the -y option. As broken inodes appear, make note of the disk partition and location of the node that has to be cleared, if possible. Expect to see many temporary files irrevocably lost. These files are usually invisible to the user, and their loss will not be mourned.

The two areas most subject to damage are the root and spooler areas. If damage is severe, you will have to reboot UNIX, perhaps a number of times, while doing an fsck. Some lost files are saved in lost+found directories. Files that are lost "forever" have to be restored from the previous evening's backup tape (or disk). System crashes are the best argument for regular system backups.

Summary

You have seen how to bring up and shut down a UNIX system. Chapter 5 took the mystery out of mounting and unmounting file systems. Now you should be familiar with processes. Besides warning the users, shutdown involves little more than killing processes and unmounting file systems. With these basics behind you, you are ready for a longer view of the day-to-day running of a UNIX system.

7

Adding and
Removing Users
from the System

A user has his mark all over the UNIX system. He has an entry in the password file (/etc/passwd); another entry in the group file (/etc/group); a mail box in /usr/spool/mail (pre-System V), /usr/mail, or /var/mail (SVR4); and a home directory where he lives, containing at the very least a profile (.profile for Bourne shell or .login for C shell) that instructs UNIX about his environment.

Adding New Users

To officially add a new user to the system, the system administrator must create all of these entries and files. How do they fit together when a user logs in? The login program goes to the /etc/passwd file to get information about the user. /etc/passwd gives login the user's home directory and tells login which shell to execute—Bourne shell, C shell, or restricted shell. Armed with this information, login moves to the user's home directory and starts up his shell, which then executes his .profile (or .login). The profile executes a series of commands initializing the user's environment, usually his prompt, the type of terminal he is using, the settings for his editor, and his search path. As you can see, information critical to a user's environment is also critical in creating the files needed for the login process.

Although UNIX system administration tasks vary a little from machine to machine and from installation to installation, such tasks as adding (and removing) user logins are common to every UNIX machine.

Keep It Simple, SA

Imagine that it is 3:30 on Friday afternoon. You are an average user, busily completing an intensive programming project. Putting the final touches on your intricate program, you relish the thought of getting it all done today so that you can enjoy the first peaceful weekend in months without the project on your mind. Suddenly, you notice that the response time on your terminal slows to a snail's pace. Although you try to go on with the project, the response time becomes intolerably slow, and your blood pressure starts to rise. Impatiently, you do a succession of

```
$ ps -e
```

commands to see what is slowing down the system, revealing what you suspected all along: one user is hogging the system with a CPU- and disk-intensive task (usually nroff or one of the language compilers). Time drags on as you wait for the user to finish, but he continues to hog the system, oblivious to the needs of other users. If you don't find out who the user is, you can throw your plans for a peaceful weekend out the window. By doing a who command, you have access to the current users (by login name), terminals, and login times:

```
$ who
susan      tty10      Sep  2 14:15
david      bip0       Sep  2 12:39
pecos      tty14      Sep  2 15:27
```

If the login names are clearly descriptive, such as last names or identifiable first names, you can easily locate the user in the company's phone directory and yell at the person for hogging too much CPU and disk space. The user should then yield his piggy process so that you can finish your project on time, and this little story will have a happy ending. But what if that user's login name is "wizard" or "mouse"? Finding the user is going to waste not only much of your time but the system administrator's time as well. Your project won't be completed on time, and the story will have an unhappy ending.

The moral of this story is to keep user login names simple and straightforward. It's better for you and for your users. If the most efficient system administration possible is your prime directive, even pedestrian tasks like adding users to the UNIX system require some forethought. Reliable and clearly descriptive login names make life easier for everyone, especially in large systems with hundreds of users. Most /etc/passwd file formats include a "comment" field; use it for the full name of the login account owner. Enough said.

Some UNIX systems provide a self-explanatory, menu-driven, screen-mapped utility for doing *sys* administration tasks—in particular, adding users to the system. On more recent System V releases, the program is called sysadm or sysadmsh. (System V Release 4 has a menu-driven program to customize your own system administration menus.) Many other systems have a special script (frequently called adduser) to add users to the system. This script is found in /etc. On other UNIX systems, you must do the job manually with root privilege. In this chapter, you first examine the slow, manual way to enter users, and then take a look at an adduser program you can type and use.

Entering a New User to the */etc/passwd* File

First things first. The manual entry of a new user starts at the password file, requiring superuser privilege. You start by opening /etc/passwd with an editor. (Do not hold /etc/passwd open for very long; it can be fatal to your system.) Before you enter any data to passwd, be sure to do a search on the new user's last name to make sure that she won't get mixed up with someone else. grep or a simple search within the editor does this nicely. (Sophisticated adduser utilities do this for you automatically.) Even more important is to make certain that the new user ID number does not match one currently on the system. If two users have the same user ID number, only the first one (as you read the /etc/passwd file) is the official owner of any files created by either user.

Once you have established the uniqueness of the new user's proposed login name and user ID number, you are ready to enter data. /etc/passwd entries have the following fields:

- Login name

- Encrypted password

- User ID number

- Group ID number

- Home directory

- Login shell

Fields are separated by colons (:). A typical /etc/passwd entry, when completed, looks something like this:

```
khunter:bm%q4Bc03A?:12:14:Karen Hunter:/home/khunter:/bin/csh
```

Now look at each field, one at a time. khunter is the name under which Karen Hunter will log in as user. It is good practice not only to use a straightforward login name (such as the user's first initial and last name), but also to be consistent with your other login names. Inconsistencies are easier to pinpoint that way.

The second field, bm%q4Bc03A?, is the password field, unintelligible because it is stored in encrypted form. If your password entries are all stars (*) or xs, see the next section, "Systems with More Security." There are several ways to install user passwords. One method is to leave the password field empty, letting the user add his own password voluntarily. To do this, you type every field but the password field, like this:

```
khunter::12:24:Karen Hunter:/home/khunter:/bin/csh
```

The empty password field is a "null password." Now the user can enter her password into the system with the passwd command. Of course, you have to be prepared to go back and check the password file to verify that a password was added. The user may try to duck out of entering a password so that she can log on quickly! On pre-System III UNIX, you can stop a user from doing this by adding anything to the password field to prevent her from logging on. The word *VOID* does very nicely and is also clearly visible:

```
khunter:VOID:12: ...
```

Karen Hunter will not be able to log on until she sees you. Then you can make sure that she enters a password.

System III and later UNIX versions let you handle the user password installation another way: by providing you with an elaborate series of password-aging commands. To make sure that the user enters her password, you can add a comma and two periods to the password field when you make a new user entry in /etc/passwd:

```
khunter:,..:12: ...
```

This makes the null password obsolete immediately by telling the login program that the password is aged. A new password will be requested from the new user the moment she logs on.

System V Release 3 put all of this information in the /etc/shadow file. The details are described in Chapter 9 on security.

Yet another way to enter a password is to use the passwd command as superuser. When you run the passwd command as an ordinary user, UNIX responds by asking you for your old password in order to be sure that you are who UNIX thinks you should be. UNIX then asks you for the new password twice. When the superuser uses the passwd command, it takes on a different flavor. Although the superuser cannot read another user's password, he can change any password on the system by using the passwd command with the name of the user as an argument:

```
# passwd jsmith
New password:tribble        —Password is not actually displayed
Retype new password:tribble —Password is not actually displayed
#
```

The superuser will not be asked the old password name. He just needs to enter the new password name twice. If a password is entered that the system feels is too short, it asks repeatedly for a new one that is long enough. Many systems insist on a six- to eight-character alphanumeric mix.

The third field, 12, is the user ID field. It must be an integer less than 65535, and it is usually the next available sequential user number. This *uid* number is used internally by the system to designate all file and directory ownerships. If you are entering users manually, sometimes the addition of a new user ID number requires visually scanning the list and taking the next available number. On larger machines, employee numbers might be your best bet. (These are especially handy if you ever need to merge machines.) Each *uid* must be unique, or two login names will refer to the same files. The user's employee or badge number is a good candidate for a unique *uid* number.

The fourth field, 14, is the group ID number, taken from the /etc/group file. Use the number of the specific group required. (For example, if the system has an editing group designated as group number 12, each member of the editing group has 12 as the group number in that member's /etc/passwd entry.) Even if you don't need groups right away, it is a good idea to indicate an other category for this field, using an arbitrary integer such as 100. That way, searching and replacing a specific number is easier later on. Of course, you have the option of leaving this field blank.

The fifth field, Karen Hunter, is a comment field. Usually, the user's full name is inserted here to positively identify the user with her login name. Other data, such as department name and phone extension, is also helpful.

The sixth field, /home/khunter, is the user's base or home directory. When the user logs on, she is automatically placed in this directory. It is also the directory defined as HOME in the user's .profile file.

The last field, /bin/csh, is the shell assigned to the user when logging in. It is usually /bin/sh for the Bourne shell, /bin/csh for the C shell, or /bin/ksh for the Korn shell. If the shell field is left blank, most systems default to the Bourne shell.

There are two places in which you can specify that a certain shell be used at login time: in the last field in the /etc/passwd file and in .profile. The /etc/passwd file is a much better place to do the job. When /bin/csh is found by login in the /etc/passwd file, the C shell becomes the user's shell immediately. Then all it needs to do is search for .cshrc and .login in the user's HOME directory. However, if /bin/csh is executed from .profile, an extra process is spawned needlessly, which makes the login process slower. (Unless login is told otherwise, the user's shell automatically becomes the Bourne shell. If the C shell is specified when .profile is executed, you must create another process to accommodate the change to the C shell before it goes to the user's HOME directory to look for .login and .cshrc.) Therefore, specifying shells in /etc/passwd entries is more efficient.

Any executable program can be used as a shell. If you have a user who wants to work with just the wondercalc program, simply use the path name /usr/local/bin/wondercalc instead of /bin/sh. But if a shell is execed from .profile (or in any other way), the .profile is not reread. Only the login shell (specified in passwd) executes the .profile.

Here are some typical /etc/passwd entries with various shells in the last field:

```
bruce:jlc4EEKiPwiRw:20:20:Bruce H Hunter:/home/bruce:
karen:MlNyd0pc7tgiE:21:20:Karen L B Hunter:/home/karen:/bin/sh
david:zCz.rpnUP1s22:23:22:David Fiedler:/home/david:/bin/csh
susan:/aik3QiekNOYU:24:22:Susan Fiedler:/home/susan:
chad:Vzqv.YMBLNDe2:27:30:my kid:/home/chad:/bin/rsh
```

If you are going to designate the Bourne shell, you might as well leave this field blank, because login gives you the Bourne shell first.

Note a final warning: don't keep the password file open any longer than necessary. If /bin/passwd or any other program that writes to /etc/passwd is called, the system will get confused. One day on a UTS machine, an expensive UNIX consultant we brought in left the passwd file open for over an hour. The system got terribly confused, losing track of root's *uid*. Finally, the system crashed (a major disaster on a mainframe), putting two hundred users (and the consultant) out of business on the spot. We had to rebuild the entire machine from the bits and pieces that were left.

Systems with More Security

In the late 1980s, it became popular to beef up the security of UNIX systems. System V Release 3.2 no longer kept the encrypted password in /etc/passwd because that file has global read permission. Instead, the encrypted password was moved to the more secure /etc/shadow file. The features of this enhancement to UNIX security include password-aging information, discussed in Chapter 9 on security. Similar in design to the /etc/passwd file, the /etc/shadow file has the following fields:

- The user login ID

- The encrypted password for the user

- The number of days between 1/1/70 and the last day the password was changed

- The minimum number of days allowed before the user can change her password again

- The maximum number of days before the password must be changed

- The number of days before a warning is sent to the user that the password is getting old

- The number of days of inactivity allowed for the account before it should be removed

- An absolute date on which the password will expire

- A flag, the use of which is not yet defined

Instead of editing this file directly, you should modify it indirectly with useradd, usermod, userdel, and passwd. In this type of security system, the passwd command is also used to read the aging information.

SCO UNIX and some other systems have an entire directory of information about users' access history and passwords.

Adding the New User to the */etc/group* File

Once the user has been entered to the /etc/passwd file, you need to add her to /etc/group. The /etc/group entry is similar to the /etc/passwd entry. They both use the colon as a field separator. Each group entry has the following form:

group_name:*encrypted_password*:*group_id_no*:*user1*,*user2*,*user3*

As superuser, you enter the data with an editor. A typical entry looks like this:

edit:VOID:12:hogan,singer,weaver

When a new member needs to be added to the group, you simply add the name to the end of the /etc/group entry.

Notice that the *encrypted_password* field is VOID. Group memberships are usually determined by the system administrator. This prevents people from crossing groups, because no password will work. (See Chapters 4 and 9 for more information.) When a group has an encrypted password field and directories restricted to that group, the group's files and directories cannot be entered by nonmembers.

Creating a Directory for the New User

Now you need to create the home directory for the user. To create Karen Hunter's home directory and give her ownership of it, go to the directory above the intended home directory and follow this command sequence:

```
# cd /user
# mkdir khunter
# chown khunter khunter
# chgrp edit khunter
# cd khunter
# cp /usr/local/stdprofile .profile
# chown khunter .profile
```

The mkdir command is used to create the directory, and the ownership of the directory is given to Karen Hunter by the chown (*change own*er) command. A .profile is created using the cp command to copy /usr/local/stdprofile, already created earlier by the system administrator as a standard profile for new users. (Your system may already have standard .profile in /etc/stdprofile.) A typical stdprofile might look like this:

```
PATH=:/bin:/usr/bin:/usr/ucb:/usr/games:/usr/local:.:
EXINIT='set shell=/bin/sh noai redraw bf opt wm=12 scroll=22'
PAGER=more -c
EDITOR=/bin/vi
MAIL=/home/${LOGNAME:?}
export PATH EXINIT PAGER EDITOR MAIL
```

Ownership of the file is given to the user by the command line chown khunter .profile. The user is now free to modify her .profile further to suit her personal needs.

Creating a Mail File for the New User

Now go to /usr/mail (/usr/spool/mail in pre-System V) and create a mail file for the new user. To give a mail file to Karen Hunter, do the following:

```
# cd /usr/mail
# create khunter
# chown khunter khunter
# chgrp mail khunter
# chmod 660 khunter
```

Once this new user has an empty file in /usr/mail, she can receive mail. Changing the file mode to 660 prevents anyone else from reading her mail. (See the section on permissions in Chapter 9.) The line chown khunter khunter gives her the ownership of that file.

The End Result

All these operations result in a complete computer work environment for the new user. She has a password file entry in /etc/passwd that locates her home directory and assigns her a shell. She has a HOME directory, a profile, a group file entry, and a mailbox. Karen Hunter is ready to start work on the UNIX system. If she chooses, she is free to add to or modify this computer work environment to suit her needs.

Removing Users from the System

Removing users from the system is also a day-to-day administration task involving two essential steps: saving all the user's files on offline backup media and removing the user from the system. Sophisticated UNIX systems have utilities (usually called rmuser, deluser, or userdel) to remove the user's file tree, password entry, group entry, and mailbox. If these utilities are absent from the system, you need to do the job "from scratch."

Back Up Data Before You Remove It

Before removing anything, copy the user's entire tree to tape or diskette. A user's contribution to a company represents a significant company investment. Perhaps a new user will come in expecting to start where the former user left off. An efficient backup system allows you to present new users with all the information they need in order to breathe new life into old projects. Backing up data before you destroy it is always a good idea. You might need it again! For this special case, the fastest way to back up is to use find with the -cpio option:

```
# find /home/khunter /usr/mail/khunter \
  -user khunter -cpio /dev/tape
```

137

If the new user is starting work right away, simply change the old user's login name and home directory in /etc/passwd, and change the password. Then you're done. No chown commands have to be issued because the actual user ID number is the same (unless employee numbers are used).

Look Before You Leap

After copying the user's file tree, you need to go just above the user's home directory. Because you are doing a mass deletion, be sure that you remove only what is necessary. Always use the ls command before removing any files so that you know exactly what you are removing.

To remove Karen Hunter from the system, do the following:

```
# cd /home
# ls -al khunter
total 125
drwxr-x---  12 khunter       576 Sep  8 05:13 .
drwxr-xr-x  27 bruce         512 Jun 28 05:13 ..
-rw-rw-rw-   1 khunter       455 Aug 28 03:16 .cshrc
-rw-rw-rw-   1 khunter        76 Jun 20 00:41 .login
-rw-rw-rw-   1 khunter         8 May  6 20:50 .logout
-rw-r--r--   1 khunter         0 Feb  6  1984 .news_time
-rw-rw-r--   1 khunter       899 Sep 10 17:07 .newsrc
-rwxr-xr-x   1 khunter       326 Feb 27  1985 .profile
drwxrwxrwx   2 khunter       176 Oct 18 20:42 C
drwxrwxrwx   2 khunter        32 Oct 10 16:19 Doc
drwxrwxrwx   2 khunter       160 Oct 15 19:52 HCR
drwxrwxrwx   2 khunter       224 Oct 18 19:23 Letter
drwxrwxrwx   2 khunter        80 Oct 17 21:45 Sysad
drwxrwxrwx   2 khunter        64 Oct 15 18:36 bin
-rw-r--r--   1 khunter     18737 Oct 17 10:03 chron
-rw-r--r--   1 khunter     18666 Oct 14 13:50 chron.bak
-rwxr-xr-x   1 khunter        37 Oct 15 19:28 dsp
```

You can easily see and inspect all 16 khunter-owned files and directories.

Search and Destroy

Now you can use the rm command to quickly remove all khunter-owned files and directories in this area—that is, in this subdirectory and all those below it:

```
# cd /home
# rm -rf khunter
```

Using rm instead of rm -r or rm -rf adds an extra cushion of safety because rm forces you to go into each subdirectory, one at a time, to remove the contents, until you finally end up at the base directory. Remember that the rm command with the -rf option does a no-questions-asked recursive removal of all files and directories, so you have to be extra careful when using this command—*particularly when you are superuser!*

After you have removed the directories and files from /home/khunter, go to /etc/group in an editor and do a global removal of the user's login name:

```
# ed /etc/group
247
1,$s/[\,,:]khunter//g
w
231
q
#
```

In the preceding command line, you are substituting the null string (or nothing) for the string khunter. Now go to /usr/spool/mail and remove the khunter mailbox from the system:

```
# cd /usr/spool/mail
# rm khunter
```

Finally, when you remove the user's entry from /etc/passwd, she is gone from the system. Should you fail to complete each one of these steps, you will leave bits and pieces of trash all around the system to clutter and confuse you later. To make sure that no extra files are lying around, check with the find command:

```
# find / -user 12 -print
```

Any file that is still owned by user ID 12 (khunter's old *uid*) will be reported. It is especially important to remove *all* the files owned by an earlier user ID 12 before recycling that number to a new user.

Changing Passwords

Passwords have a limited life span. Naturally, some users get careless after a while. It is not uncommon to type a password instead of a name in response to the `login` prompt. Then anyone who happens to be standing near the terminal can see what the password is! You also have to be on the alert for the usual system mischief by system abusers. Your users may fall victim to the old Trojan horse technique—a shell script written by a curious system abuser that sneakily emulates the login and password sequence for the purpose of capturing user log names and passwords. Determined system abusers often pick up passwords by glancing over the shoulder of a user entering his password. Changing passwords fairly often is therefore good insurance. You learn more about that in Chapter 9 on security.

Handy Shell Programs

Most modern UNIX systems come with tools, programs, or menu-driven systems for managing the users on the system. If you have to manage more than a few accounts, you will probably need even more aids. Here are some shell scripts you can add to your collection.

fickle_finger

Although not as fancy as Berkeley `finger` or UTS `whois`, the `fickle_finger` program makes it a bit easier to find information about a user from the password file. Naturally, the more information stored with each entry, the better. Here is `fickle_finger`:

```
grep $1 /etc/passwd ¦ cut -d: -f5
```

Why not call it `finger` (or `whois`) if you don't have a program by that name already?

sortpw

If you keep adding users manually, your password file will eventually start looking confusing, even if it really isn't. Although the `sortpw` program won't do anything for the system, it will make your job easier. `sortpw` sorts the password file by user ID, leaving a backup copy in /tmp just in case. Because `sortpw` modifies the password file, the program should be run only when you are the sole user on the system:

```
cp /etc/passwd /tmp
sort -nt: +2 /tmp/passwd > /etc/passwd
```

adduser

Here's a simple little adduser program. It doesn't even look in the password file to find the next user ID, instead letting the administrator make that determination. But adduser gives you an easy-to-understand starting point for your own modifications:

```
MAILDIR=/usr/mail
USERBASE=/home # where all your user directories will go
if [ $# -lt 1 ]
then
 echo "Login Name: \c"
 read NAME
else NAME=$1
fi
echo "Userid Number: \c"
read UID
echo "Group number: \c"
read GRP
echo "Extended Finger Information: \c"
read FINGER
echo "Login shell (enter /bin/sh (default) or /bin/csh): \c"
read SHELL
echo "Updating /etc/passwd..."
if mkdir /etc/ptmp # fails if passwd command running
then
 cp /etc/passwd /etc/pw$$
 echo "$NAME::$UID:$GRP:$FINGER:$USERBASE/$NAME:$SHELL" \
 >> /etc/pw$$
 ln /etc/passwd /etc/opasswd
 ln /etc/pw$$ /etc/passwd
 rmdir /etc/ptmp
else
 echo "/etc/passwd file in use, try again later"
 exit 1
fi
echo "Now set initial password..."
passwd $NAME
echo "Initializing Home Directory"
mkdir $USERBASE/$NAME
chmod 775 $USERBASE/$NAME
echo "Initializing mail directory"
```

```
cp /dev/null $MAILDIR/$NAME
chmod 660 $MAILDIR/$NAME
echo "Initializing default .profile"
cat >>$USERBASE/$NAME/.profile <<!
HOME=$USERBASE/$NAME
TERM=
MAIL=$MAILDIR/$NAME
export TERM MAIL HOME
!
echo "Initializing .cshrc"
cat >>$USERBASE/$NAME/.cshrc <<!
source /.stdcshrc
setenv HOME $USERBASE/$NAME
setenv MAIL $MAILDIR/$NAME
!
echo "Changing ownership..."
chown $NAME $USERBASE/$NAME
chgrp $GRP $USERBASE/$NAME
chown $NAME $MAILDIR/$NAME
chgrp mail $MAILDIR/$NAME
chown $NAME $USERBASE/$NAME/.profile $USERBASE/$NAME/.cshrc
chgrp $GRP $USERBASE/$NAME/.profile $USERBASE/$NAME/.cshrc
```

Summary

If your system has only a few experienced users, you probably will be able to manage just by setting up the accounts and then forgetting them. But if you are the system administrator of a department or company-wide UNIX system, managing user accounts takes a great deal of time and skill. Be sure that you have everything set up in your defaults to make the job easier, and don't forget security (covered in Chapter 9).

With new users comfortably on the system, you need to consider how best to preserve the data they use. In the next chapter, you learn how to back up the system.

8

Backups and

Archives

Computers exist to create, store, and disseminate data—the heart of a business. Backups preserve that precious data and keep you in business. There are many ways to back up data in UNIX, but whatever the method, you back up a system so that you can put it all back together should the system come crashing down or should data be lost or corrupted. All files, directories, and file systems can be restored fully *if* your system is properly backed up. Backing up is more useful and inexpensive than a complete DP center insurance policy.

Backup Philosophy

Data loss is far more common than you might think. Often it occurs because of accidents and just plain carelessness by users, but data loss is not confined to users alone. When those with superuser power lose data, they generally do it in a big way, such as losing an entire file system! Data loss occurs also when the system crashes. Small single-user systems seldom crash, but large ones do with frightening regularity. The more users you have, the more potential you have for crashes. UNIX system administrators on large machines need to be prepared to restore the system, piece by piece, at the drop of a hat.

Fortunately, UNIX is a versatile operating system, so there are many backup and archive commands that allow you to back up all of the system or just part of it, from one file to an entire file tree. Some of these commands are `cpio`, `dd`, `dump`, `find`, `tar`, and `volcopy`.

Although you can use these commands directly on a command line, you probably will choose the commands you want for your system, and incorporate them into your own customized backup shell scripts. This approach keeps backups consistent—an important point when you want to restore data.

Determining the best backup technique for your system depends on many factors. The time you decide to spend on backups must be balanced by the time required to do a restore. In other words, a quick, easy backup scheme will backfire on you when you end up spending hours restoring the system. Small UNIX systems can get by with a nightly, cyclic backup approach, but larger UNIX systems require a more sophisticated set of overlapping backup programs to protect data adequately in the event of a hardware crash. Two hundred users working on 4 completely different projects require a backup technique different from that used by 20 users working on 1 project. Data processing installations are data-intensive and require specific backup approaches that are not necessary on program development installations.

Database applications have very dynamic files that require special care in backup and restoration. Never back up a database system while transactions are being processed. If backup utilities are part of the database system, use those utilities instead of the standard UNIX backup utilities when you back up the data. The data needs to be written to separate media (tapes).

As you can see, in order to devise the best backup strategy, a system administrator needs to be armed with more than just a list of UNIX backup commands. She needs to be able to make intelligent choices. So before you look at the backup commands, consider some behind-the-scenes backup strategies.

A Little or a Lot?

Two basic backup options are available to you: backing up all of the system or just part of it. A *full* (unqualified) system backup backs up everything on the system, including UNIX itself. A *partial* system backup backs up anything less than a full system backup. There are three kinds of partial backups:

- A *qualified backup* backs up all file systems other than root, along with some UNIX files and directories that are subject to frequent modification, such as /etc/passwd, /etc/group, and /etc/inittab.

- An *incremental backup* is a specialized form of partial backup, copying files based on the last time each file was modified, written, or read.

- A *walking backup* copies different parts of the file systems on different nights.

Because of the flexibility of UNIX, you can perform each backup method in a variety of ways. Consider the full backup. If you do a `tar` dump from the root file system, you can do a full backup of the entire system, but you will probably run out of tape first! (Many implementations of `tar` do not support multiple tapes or diskettes.) However, full backups can also be made up of a series of partial backups. On mainframes and superminis, the magnetic medium is reel-to-reel tape. Full backups could never fit on one tape, so they are done in sections, each one sized to fit comfortably on a single tape. Now take a look at these approaches in more detail.

Full Backups

Full backups are *unqualified*. This means that they copy everything, including UNIX proper and all user areas—something like eating a watermelon whole (rind, seeds, and all). Full backups are often done to checkpoint and document the system status at particular times. On the average, full backups can be done every month for systems with over 36 simultaneous users, and every 3 to 6 months for smaller systems. Some SAs choose to do one full backup a day. It's up to you and the management to decide what is best for your site. (If all else fails, don't forget that you can restore UNIX proper from the original distribution tape or diskettes, instead of from a full backup. The distribution tape is neither tired nor degraded from constant use.)

Of the two major backup approaches, a partial backup is more practical for most types of everyday work. It gives an up-to-date copy of the rest of the system, including parts of UNIX that are modified frequently, such as `/etc/passwd`. One thing that even a full backup won't do is to copy the system so that it can be reloaded if your disk is completely erased. A *system* restore from the distribution tape is necessary to get UNIX running again so that a *file system* restore can be done.

Partial Backups

Partial backups are the most versatile backup method open to system administrators. They are one of the many ways that SAs begin customizing and optimizing their system operations.

What if you have a system with two user areas, each one about half the size of a backup tape? Should you try to cram them both on one tape with a "best fit" algorithm, or should you use two tapes, one for each file system?

It is always best if partial backups are separated along mounted system divisions. Best-fit algorithms that cram as much data on tape as possible have their uses, but not in this case. Should the system go down, restoring it is much faster and easier when each file system is on its own clearly labeled tape. Otherwise, you waste a great deal of time sifting through directories and then cutting and pasting your file systems back together. Tapes are cheap compared to the time that you and other users waste while the computer is down.

Incremental backups are selective partial backups. The modification date of a file is the date the file was made or modified (touched), and this date is the one on which incremental backups are based. A Tuesday evening backup covers all files touched on Tuesday. An incremental backup on Monday evening should cover three calendar days (Saturday, Sunday, and Monday) to take care of the work performed by weekend workers. Be sure to run backups that cover holiday periods too.

Incremental backups save tape and time, and at first they seem to be a tremendously appealing backup method. You copy only what has been touched or modified, thereby preserving a constant file update. Why not rely on nightly incremental backups supplemented with monthly permanent backups? Although this practice is common, you must be aware of potential hidden pitfalls.

Picture a user coming to you with a tale of woe about a lost directory. You look for it on yesterday's incremental backup, and it is nowhere to be found. Interrogation of the user reveals that he doesn't remember when he last accessed the directory, but it was a long time ago. Now you have a big problem. How many permanent monthly tapes are you going to have to go through before you find the darned thing?

This story is far from unusual. The larger the system, the greater the incidence of user carelessness, such as forgotten passwords and misplaced directories. Qualified backups take longer, but they work better. If your system falls down, restoring it is faster and easier with qualified backups. In the event of a head crash, which is the worst disaster of all, a qualified backup, along with the UNIX distribution tape, will have you back in business as soon as a replacement disk can be found. If your system has enough hardware redundancy (a spare disk on hand), you can be back in business in a few hours, even on the largest systems.

Backup Schedules

In an ideal world, with an unlimited supply of free tapes and an infinite storage area, backups would be no problem whatsoever. Unqualified backups of the entire system would be done every night and stored permanently! In the real world, backup media cost money, and you quickly run out of storage space. So you fudge a little.

An overlapping backup strategy is always the safest way to go, even on small systems with only one to eight users. Combine two or three backup techniques, and you increase your chances of being able to rebuild your system. Most backup schemes combine regularly scheduled qualified backups with one or two supplemental partial backups. In addition, one current set of full-backup tapes should *always* be stored off premises in case of a fire or major disaster. (In this context, the word *tape* refers to removable backup media, including tapes and floppies.)

Now take a look at two hypothetical backup schedules in detail, one for a small UNIX system and one for an extremely large one.

Backing Up a Small UNIX System

Small UNIX systems have about 80 megabytes of disk space with about 4 megabytes of memory. Systems of this size generally have 1 to 5 active users. A safe, minimum backup schedule involves 4 backup steps:

Nightly:	Partial backups done nightly and reused week to week
Weekly:	Incremental backups covering the preceding week and stored off premises until the end of the month, when they may be reused
Monthly:	Incremental backups done monthly and stored off premises until the next full backup
Quarterly:	Full backups stored off premises

A nightly backup is done each day of the week to ensure that all new files are captured. At the beginning of a new week, you write over your old tapes. (On Monday you write over the preceding Monday's backup, on Tuesday you write over the preceding Tuesday's backup, and so on.) To reinforce the weekly backups, you have another set of permanent backups, done monthly, and stored off premises for an indefinite period. The weekly tapes allow you to recycle the daily tapes without worry.

As long as your UNIX system is stored on removable media away from the physical system, you are safe from disaster. You can reuse monthly tapes after 3 to 6 months or so, depending on the value of the media and your site's needs. Naturally, you should do a full backup at that time. Assuming that you do the full backups after 3 months, you will need 12 tapes altogether: 5 for the dailies, 4 for the weeklies, 3 for the monthlies, plus however many tapes (usually 2 or 3) are required to make the full backup *times 2*. If, for example, a full backup takes 3 tapes, you will need at least $12 + (3 \times 2) = 18$ tapes for 3 months' worth of backups. Why? What happens if your system crashes while making the full backup (it has happened to us)? So you make the *new* full backup on the extra tapes, after which you can recycle the monthlies and the old full-backup tapes. Buy 20 tapes when you get your system, and you will not only get a quantity discount but also have enough for emergencies. Remember *not* to reuse your *old* full-backup tapes until you have verified that the new ones are readable.

You can replace your hardware with a check from the insurance company, but once your data files are lost, they are lost forever! Incidentally, it takes all day to do a full floppy backup of a small system, but it takes less than an hour on one extended-length cartridge tape.

Backing Up a Large UNIX System

Large UNIX systems are another animal altogether. Mainframe UNIX systems with more than one bank of disk drives are not uncommon. Administrators on large UNIX installations must stay alert to keep data safe. A minimum backup schedule for one mainframe UTS UNIX system with about 200 users runs something like this:

Nightly:	Partial backups done nightly and reused week to week
Weekly:	Partial backups stored until the next month and then recirculated
Monthly:	Full backups stored permanently off premises

All of these backups are *supplemented* with some kind of specialized backups of the user file systems, such as incremental backups.

On systems with overlaid operating systems like V-VM (UTS/VM), a byte-for-byte copy technique is often used in addition to a standard UNIX copy technique. The VM DDR copy command copies a disk pack verbatim.

Because the boot track on these systems is not in UNIX format, that track has to be DDRed so that it can be copied. Doing a partial backup of a mainframe UTS UNIX system takes about 12 tapes and a little longer than 1 hour, including mounting and unmounting tapes.

Backup Media

The size of your computer system generally determines the backup medium the manufacturer provides. Small systems typically come with a floppy drive or a cartridge tape drive. If you have the option (and the money), we recommend 8mm cartridge tapes for any computer system serving over 16 simultaneous users. Available backup media include the following:

- One-half-inch, reel-to-reel tapes
- Floppy diskettes
- Removable disk packs
- Removable cartridge disks
- Cartridge tapes, including 8-mm tape and DAT

Now consider the pros and cons of the types of backup media.

Reel-to-Reel Tapes

There are two types of reel-to-reel tape: conventional (start-stop) and streamer. The two types operate differently. A start-stop tape writes a buffer's worth of data at a time, leaving gaps between the blocks of data. A streamer sends data in a constant stream to the tape. The "best" UNIX backup medium is conventional (start-stop) 9-track, 1/2-inch, reel-to-reel tape at 1600 bpi. 1600 bpi is the only tape density guaranteed to be universally readable from one system to another. Streamers might be better for your application because they are faster and can store more data per tape, but *only* if they can also function in conventional mode for portability.

Tapes run quickly and quietly in the background with no attention required from the system administrator or system operators except for mounting and unmounting. Tapes are very fast. IBM and Amdahl mainframes read in tape at 200 feet per second. Tape-to-tape copies can be made in 5 minutes. Tape is the cheapest magnetic medium available—at $23.00 a tape (2,400 feet long), a dollar's worth of tape can store over 7 megabytes! (That equates to $0.14 per megabyte.) Unfortunately, the hardware for these tapes is quite expensive, with a decent unit costing at least $10,000. For this reason, reel-to-reel tapes are used only with larger computers.

Floppy Diskettes

The slowest, most inconvenient backup method is the use of floppy diskettes. Floppies cost about $2.00 each, so the cost is about $2.00 per megabyte. They are much more expensive than any other backup medium. They require constant attention, and several *cartons* of floppies and hours of time are required to do an unqualified backup of even a small UNIX system. Their only saving grace is that floppy disk drives are the cheapest backup hardware available at a few hundred dollars. Therefore, floppies are commonly used on small systems.

Removable Disk Packs

Disk packs are the *de facto* standard type of storage on most large minicomputers. Although more expensive than Winchester drives, disk packs compensate by their extremely high speed and the fact that the entire disk medium may be removed from a drive in seconds. Full disk-to-disk copies are done in a few minutes, greatly simplifying backups.

Disk packs are also rather heavy and easy to damage, not an inconsequential problem when you consider the $1,000 price tag per pack. Disk packs look like 6 or 8 LP records stacked on top of each other, and the drives themselves closely resemble top-loading washing machines.

The term /usr comes from the days when UNIX was run on systems with such removable disk packs. Most of UNIX proper (kernel, /bin, /etc...) was kept on a fixed disk. The /usr file system contained all user files on disk packs. Even though the system didn't have enough storage for all the user files, you could change disk packs. One set was for accounting, another was for engineering, and so on.

Cartridge Disks

Cartridge disks are a cross between Winchester (sealed) disks and (open) disk packs. Cartridge disks consist of several disk platters encased in plastic (the whole assembly resembles a pizza in a traveling case), and they can be removed and changed in a minute or so. Cartridge disks were popular on minicomputers several years ago but are almost obsolete now because of the low cost of Winchesters. One particular cartridge disk (called the Bernoulli Box) is popular as mass storage and fast backup on IBM PCs.

Cartridge Tapes

Cartridge tapes are a good compromise between reel-to-reel tapes and floppy diskettes. Each cartridge slips easily into the drive slot like a video cassette. They are reasonably fast, and a standard-sized tape holds anything from 60 to 250 megabytes. You can back up a standard distribution system on one cartridge tape. Each 60 MB cartridge is $20.00, so the cost is about $0.33 per MB. The drives cost about $3,000 each and are available in streamer and start-stop models. Because virtually all cartridge drives at this writing have their own format, try to get the fastest kind available if you have a choice.

There are now two new forms of cartridge tape that are far more convenient than any other medium: DAT (*d*igital-*a*udio *t*echnology) tape and 8-mm tape. The DAT tape system is less expensive than the 8-mm system, but the reliability of the DAT system has not yet been proved as of this writing. The tiny 8-mm tape system is a pricey unit, but you will quickly appreciate its convenience: a single 8-mm cartridge holds more than 2 gigabytes of data! That is 2000 megabytes. One tape is capable of backing up an entire network of workstations.

Write Protection

There are various methods of physically write-protecting magnetic media to prevent accidental erasure of information. Physical write protection differs slightly from protecting the data through software under UNIX (using permission bits or mounting a file system as read-only). Physical write protection prevents writing unless actual damage is done to the unit, whereas software protection is not as secure.

You should note that although these methods prevent you from writing over data by using the computer hardware, you can erase any magnetic medium at any time by using a permanent magnet or strong magnetic field (such as those found near motors, terminals, and fluorescent light ballasts).

Reel-to-reel tapes cannot be written on unless the soft plastic "write ring" is present on the back of the reel hub. These rings are generally a bright color, such as red or yellow, and are used by system operators on the night shift for impromptu games of ring toss during backups.

You write-protect floppy diskettes (the 5 1/4-inch square variety) by putting a sticker on the write-protect notch cut on the side. You write-protect smaller floppies (the 3 1/2-inch size in a rigid plastic case) by sliding a plastic tab off a small window.

A cartridge tape has a little slot on top at the left that can be turned, using a screwdriver or your finger, toward the word *SAFE*; turning the slot prevents the drive from writing on the tape. Disk packs have a write-protect switch on the drive itself. If you get a write error when trying to make a backup, always make sure that the write-protect mechanism has not been activated.

Archive Programs versus Copy Programs

Technically, there's a small but important difference between an *archive* program and a *copy* program. Copy programs, such as dd, copy data, plain and simple. Archive programs store all critical data for reference, and the information is filed so that the archive can re-create the entire data structure. Both tar and cpio are excellent archivers, and they are excellent for backups as well.

To be safe, you should incorporate a dual copy-and-archive scheme on your system. If you do, you will have a 100-percent-reliable method of restoring lost files. A copy program stores the data, but archivers keep track of it. Archives are necessary when users are moved (known as a "rollover") to another system or a file system. Archives are necessary also to do a file system compression: you gain back disk space by taking data off the system and putting it back on by recursive copy. (*Recursion,* in programming, is a process calling itself. In a recursive copy, as each directory is copied, all the files within it are copied. Each subdirectory in that directory is copied, all the files within the subdirectory are copied, and so on.)

Restoring Data—A Reminder

Shortly, you will be examining a few UNIX backup and archive commands in detail. First, remember that backup and archive commands are used for two purposes: to read data out onto magnetic media (back it up) and to read data from the magnetic media back into the system (restore it). Whenever anyone loses or corrupts a file, directory, or tree, you will have to find it on the backup tape and read it back into the system. The trick is to read in only what you want so that you don't overwrite good data.

Imagine that a careless user, Mr. A, loses a two-block file, his third one this month. He is reluctant to reveal that he lost another file, because he will get yelled at by the system administrator. However, Mr. A convinces his friend, an operator on the system, to find the file for him. The operator, Mr. B, is new at his job, but he is a loyal friend, so he mounts yesterday's `tar` backup tape on the system and does an unqualified extract:

```
tar x
```

This reads the entire contents of the tape back into the system, overwriting all the file systems. As a result, all the work for the last 24 hours is wiped out! Mr. A and Mr. B have to hide behind the tape drives to escape the wrath of the system administrator and 200 angry users!

If you back up and restore your data in a thoughtful, methodical way, you should have few problems.

Wear a Belt and Suspenders Too

Although keeping duplicate copies of your backup tapes is probably not necessary, it never hurts to have a healthy suspicion of all your backup media. When you use media that must be formatted (that is, all floppy diskettes and many cartridge tapes), it pays to verify that you'll be able to read your precious backups at a later date. The safest way to do this is to read the entire blank tape or disk after it has been formatted. This shows that the formatting was done correctly.

As an example, the Cadmus 9790 uses a Cipher ST525 streaming cartridge tape drive for backup. This particular drive (also used on the AT&T 3B2 series) actually emulates a floppy disk interface, so it must be formatted before use. To read the entire tape for checking purposes, note the following sample command line:

```
# dd if=/dev/rst525 of=/dev/null bs=17k count=1470
1470+0
1470+0
#
```

The output from the `dd` command shows that the full 1470 blocks (corresponding to the 25589760-byte capacity of the tape) were read from this tape. A defective tape would have had an I/O error indication and an incorrect block count.

You can use the same method for any medium if you know the exact capacity. Use a block size (`bs=17k` in this example) that matches the hardware buffer size of the device for best efficiency. If you really want to be careful, do the same check again after you have made the backup onto the tape. That way, you can be sure that the data itself is readable. If you have ever been unable to read a backup when you needed it, you will be completely paranoid, so check the logical data as well to be on the safe side. This is demonstrated separately for each command covered in the next section and is a recommended procedure for all weekly, monthly, and full backups.

UNIX Archive and Backup Commands

The standard programs for archiving and backing up your file systems are tar, dd, cpio, and volcopy. There used to be a standard all-purpose backup utility called dump, but it is no longer part of the UNIX distributions. In fact, a new dump command that has nothing to do with backups is now available; you use it for inspecting the output of compilers, which are machine-language object files.

tar—The Tape Archiver

tar copies just about anything you want to copy to tape, floppy diskette, or hard disk. tar once was the number one UNIX tape archiver but is currently being phased out in favor of cpio, which was introduced with System III. Pre-System V systems are set up so that tar defaults to the largest removable storage device. If the system has 1/2-inch, reel-to-reel tape, tar defaults to /dev/rmt0 (rmt stands for raw magnetic tape). If the only medium available is floppy diskette, that is the default medium. (On many systems, the default drive is defined in the file /etc/default/tar.)

Some *tar* Flags

The following command line copies all of UNIX, tape quantities permitting:

```
# tar c /
```

The c flag means to start the copy from the beginning of the tape. Other flags, such as r, copy to the end of the tape, but you may run out of tape if you are not careful. For this reason, the c flag is safest for backups. For archives of a large file tree, you should rewind the tape and start the copy from the beginning.

Often you will want to watch the progress of the copy operation. tar's v flag is the *verbose* option, which writes everything to the standard output as it is copied. The following command line copies the entire /home file tree, starting at the beginning of the tape, and sends the path name of each /home file to the terminal:

```
# tar cv /home
```

tar's syntax is simple enough, but *where* you start your tar copy is critical. If you start from root, the file paths on the archive start at root also. Thus, the file names will be fully qualified, as in

```
/usr/system/hunter/monitor/monitor.dat
```

If you start at the base of the file structure, /usr/system/hunter/ monitor, the archive starts there also, and the file is stored as ./monitor.dat. When reshuffling data (moving data from system to system or tree to tree), you definitely want the shortest path. This allows you to move the data without having to create extra directories.

tar is fully recursive. It climbs its way down each file tree, from the base directory given as an argument, and copies everything all the way to the bottom. Because tar is an archiver, it insists on putting each file back where it came from, even if it has to make up directories as it goes along to do so. Don't be surprised when you occasionally find a set of directories you never (deliberately) created.

For example, if you want to use tar to archive a file tree such as /5650/ accounting/jones so that you can transfer it as /home/jones to another system, doing a tar copy from root or /5650 will be a disaster. On the target system, the command sequence

```
# cd /
# tar x /5650/accounting/jones/*
```

forces tar to make the directory

```
/home/jones/5650/accounting/jones
```

or die trying. The trick is to cd to the base of Jones' home directory (/home/ jones) on the old system, and start the copy from there. There will be no qualified path name to deal with, and the transfer will go smoothly. The command sequence on the source system should be

```
# cd /5650
# tar cv ./accounting
```

and on the destination system

```
# cd /home/jones
# tar xv ./accounting
```

A Bourne Shell Script That Uses *tar*

Here is a Bourne shell script that backs up all user files plus critical UNIX system files that are subject to frequent change:

```
# backup script
cd /etc
tar cvf /dev/rmt0 /home /usr/local passwd rc ttytype ttys group
exit
```

Notice the three flags:

```
tar cvf /dev/rmt0 ...
```

The c and v flags have been covered, but the f flag is new. It means that the argument following is the file or device where the archive is being written—in this case, /dev/rmt0, the raw magnetic tape. The last arguments are the names of the trees and files to be copied.

Notice that by keeping your users' files away from /usr or any other file systems in the standard distribution, you can copy pertinent system files more easily. If you have /usr/tom, /usr/dick, and /usr/harry, the only way to get a copy of each to tape or diskette without copying everything else in /usr is to specify each directory individually. This is not convenient, so it invites data loss by oversight. If all users are in a separate directory (tree) just below root level—like /home/tom, /home/dick, and /home/harry—you need to specify only /home to copy all of them, and no users will be left out by mistake.

On systems that require more than one tape to do a backup and on systems with floppy diskettes (using tar), a separate copy script is necessary for each tape or floppy:

```
tar cf /dev/floppy /usr
echo change floppy, press return when ready
read $ready
tar cf /dev/floppy /own
```

Restoring Data with *tar*

Restoring a file from a tar archive or backup tape is perhaps the easiest of all restoration methods. The syntax is

```
tar x file.name
```

Imagine that a novice user (Jones) comes up to you with a sad tale. He was in his home directory thinking he was in $HOME/junk, did a rm -r *, and lost everything. Now you have to restore him. Mount last night's tar backup tape (or diskette) and read back his lost file tree with

    tar xv /home/Jones

x is for extract, removing data from the tape. In this example, you will also see all the files that are being restored, because of the v flag.

tar's t flag is used to get names of the files on tape and then put them out to the standard output. The following command line verifies that all the files you wanted are on tape, and puts them out to the printer as well:

    # tar t ¦ lp

The absence of an argument means everything and is better than the equivalent of

    # tar t * .* */* .*/* .*/.* */*/* ...

Adding the v flag enables you to check all logical data in the tape and to get even more information than you could get with just the t flag:

    # tar tv ¦ lp

Many different implementations of tar exist. The newer ones support a variety of ways for archiving on a series of diskettes or tapes (a necessity on small systems that use diskettes for backups). When backing up to a series of diskettes or tapes, be sure to label each with its position in the series—for example, disk 1 of 5, disk 2 of 5, ..., disk 5 of 5. If you don't specify the e flag when doing multivolume backups, files may be split across two volumes. Even though this makes the maximum use of your media, it is risky. We recommend using the e flag to prevent breaking a file across volumes.

Another feature of newer versions of tar is a configurable table of devices and their block sizes for an abbreviated command. For example, remembering (and entering)

    # tar cv2 ./*

is much easier than using

    # tar cvfb /dev/fd096ds15 20 ./*

These device descriptions are found in the file /etc/default/tar.

Table 8.1 lists the tar options you may find on your system. The *archive* is the data structure tape, a diskette, or even a file on the disk. Not all options are available on all implementations of tar.

Table 8.1. Tar options.

Option	Action
r	Replace (write to end of the archive)
x	Extract (read) from the archive
t	Table (list the contents of the archive)
u	Update (add the files if they are not already part of the archive)
c	Create a new archive

Modifier	Description
0,..,999	Drive number (as defined in /etc/default/tar)
v	Verbose mode (report on activity as it is done)
w	Wait for confirmation before doing each activity
f	Next argument is the device to use
b	Blocking factor (default is 1, maximum 20)
l	Complain if a link cannot be resolved
F	Take the arguments from the file indicated in the next argument
m	When restoring from the archive, do *not* use the file modification time that is stored with the archived file
k	Maximum size for each volume in a multivolume archive (not applicable to tapes; intended for diskettes)
e	Prevent files from being split across volumes
o	Take on the user identifier and group identifier of the user running the extraction
L	Follow symbolic links
n	Archive is not a tape (speeds up diskette read access)
p	Extract files *with* their original permissions
A	Convert all absolute path names to become relative from the current director

You can use tar for more than just putting files on tape or diskette. You can combine many files into a single file by specifying a dash (for standard output) as the device and then redirecting the output to a file or even another process. Note this example:

```
$ tar cvf - oldtree > oldstuff.tar
```

Here a single file, oldstuff.tar, will be created from all the files in the directory subtree oldtree. This technique is often combined with a compression program to produce files for distribution on the public Usenet network and archive sites that are around the world. To complete this process, the line

```
$ compress oldstuff.tar
```

produces the file oldstuff.tar.Z, which may be even less than half the size of the original oldstuff.tar file.

The reverse process is

```
$ uncompress oldstuff.tar.Z
$ tar xvf - < oldstuff.tar
```

which re-creates the original file subtree oldtree. Once you have checked that every file came through the transition without error, you may want to save space by deleting the *.tar file. You don't need to have two copies around.

The *dd* Command

As all-purpose data copy programs go, dd is one of the most useful. With dd, you can copy data, convert it from ASCII to EBCDIC (used on IBM mainframes) and back, convert uppercase to lowercase, skip a given number of records, and even read blocked records from other operating systems.

For backup purposes, however, dd's uses are limited to making exact (byte for byte) copies of tapes, floppies, disks, or even disk partitions. With a little imagination, dd can still be an extremely handy program to have around.

Suppose, for example, that you have a precious boot floppy you would like a backup of, but you have only one floppy drive, so there's no way of copying the disk. Just use dd to read the *entire* floppy into a temporary file, and then write the data back out to a backup floppy. The format of the floppy data doesn't matter as long as your equipment can physically read and write it:

```
# dd if=/dev/fdsk of=/tmp/floppy.image
dd read error: I/O error
1900+0 records in
1900+0 records out
# ls -l /tmp/floppy.image
-rw-rw---- 1 root  staff  972800 Nov 4 19:16 /tmp/floppy.image
#
```

The I/O error shouldn't startle you. Because we didn't specify to dd how many blocks it should read, it simply read until it reached the end of the floppy. Reading past the end of most block devices causes a harmless I/O error because you are asking the hardware to do something it can't. Now you have the information necessary to make the backup. Simply put a clean, formatted floppy in your drive and type

```
# dd if=/tmp/floppy.image of=/dev/fdsk count=1900
1900+0 records in
1900+0 records out
#
```

You can speed up the transfer if you know the number of sectors per track on your floppy. If you have 12 sectors per track and 1024 bytes per sector, a 12 KB buffer allows an entire track to be transferred at once. You could use this command line instead:

```
# dd if=/dev/rfdsk of=/tmp/floppy.image bs=12k count=80
80+0 records in
80+0 records out
#
```

How did we know to use a count of 80? Partly by dividing—972800, the file size, divided by (12 times 1024) equals 79.166, so we have to round up—and partly by the fact that there are 80 tracks on a double-sided, 5 1/4-inch diskette. If you miscalculate, do it again.

Notice that we had to use the *raw* floppy device (/dev/rfdsk). Disk drives are accessed by a driver that uses blocking. Blocking groups output into blocks of data, each data block consisting of a certain number of bytes. The block size depends on the system. Old UNIX systems (Version 7) use 512-byte blocks. System V uses 1024-byte blocks. UTS UNIX systems use 4096-byte blocks. However, all block devices also have a raw or character interface that allows a system administrator to perform little magic tricks like this.

Because we're specifying to dd exactly how much to read at a time, we can't let the block device feed us data at one rate and try to read at another. Actually, we can, but it would take a lot longer. In a practical test, it took about 75 seconds to read a floppy using the raw disk and 12 KB blocks, almost 2 minutes using the default (512-byte blocks and the block device), and 6 1/2 minutes using 512-byte blocks and the raw device. This shows that you shouldn't bother fooling with the raw device unless you know how to use it!

In a similar way, you can back up an entire disk with dd. You usually do this with disk packs or cartridges, which can be removed and stored safely. Here is how you might do such a backup on a DEC RK07 cartridge drive:

```
# dd if=/dev/rhk07 of=/dev/rhk17 bs=22x512 count=2575
```

The block size, 22x512, corresponds to a full track of data (22 blocks of 512 bytes each), and the count corresponds to the number of total blocks on the disk (53636) divided by the number of tracks. This kind of information is available for most drives on the appropriate manual page in Section 4 (HW) of the *UNIX Programmer's Manual*. For example, we found the information for the RK07 on the page called hk(4), because the device is known as hk on the system. (The section numbering and naming scheme varies among systems.)

A disk partition can also be backed up with dd to another disk or tape. Using RK07 again as an example, you can copy the first partition of the disk to the corresponding part of another cartridge with

```
# dd if=/dev/rhk00 of=/dev/rhk10 bs=22x512 count=438
438+0 records in
438+0 records out
#
```

or to a tape with

```
# dd if=/dev/rhk00 of=/dev/rmt0 bs=22x512 count=438
438+0 records in
438+0 records out
#
```

Again, the information regarding the size, partitions, and number of the disks is taken directly from the manual. Notice that different device numbers refer to different partitions: when you copied the entire disk, the use of rhk07 signified disk 0, partition 7 (meaning the entire disk); and now the use of rhk00 means disk 0, partition 0 (just the root file system).

cpio

cpio made its appearance on System III and is also present in XENIX. Its name stands for "*copy i*nput to *o*utput," and it does just that while archiving everything passing through. cpio ingeniously makes the most of the attributes of UNIX by using the standard input as its source of file names and the standard output as the archive output. The list of file names to be copied comes from stdin.

Watch how cleverly cpio takes advantage of the existing attributes of UNIX. With either ls or the find command to get a list of file names, you can use a pipe to direct the results to cpio. Use the command line

```
# ls ¦ cpio -o > /dev/floppy
```

or

```
# find . -depth -print ¦ cpio -o > /dev/rmt0
```

Several options are available, and the first two are used for archiving purposes:

-o   For copy out

-i   For copy in

-p   For "pass" mode (in and out in one operation).
        The -p option is versatile, but it's not an archive
        command.

Using find as a source of the file list gives more control than ls because find can be selective, qualifying by size, date, and so on. In this case, you are working from the current directory (.). Using find with the -depth flag causes a descent of the directory hierarchy to be done so that all entries are acted on before the directory itself. This approach gets around the problem of copying directories without write permission and is handy when you're in a hurry. Redirection and pipes are used both to get the list of files into cpio and to send the archived output to a device.

Backups and Recovery with *cpio*

Here's an example of how to use cpio for selective backups. The following backup script is used on one of the authors' systems for nightly, weekly, and monthly incremental backups. It finds and archives all files that have been modified in the number of days specified on the command line, with one day as the default:

```
# backup
# incremental backup script for infopro machine
days=$1
echo "backing up last ${days:=1} day(s) -- kill if wrong"
```

```
sleep 10
cd /
find . -type f -mtime -$days -print | cpio -ov > /dev/tape
```

On some systems, the find command itself has a -cpio option, so that the last line of the backup script could be written as

find . -type f -mtime -$days -print -cpio /dev/tape

With this syntax, the program is more efficient, saving memory and an extra process while doing the same thing. We consistently use the -type f flag; otherwise, cpio will back up FIFOs (named pipes) and device special files. This is just a waste of good backup media, and there's no reason to risk clobbering one of your device files during a restore.

The backup script can be used in any of the following ways:

```
# backup
./usr/lib/crontab
./usr/lib/news/sys
./usr/lib/news/active
./usr/lib/news/history
./usr/lib/news/seq
./usr/lib/news/log
./usr/lib/news/ohistory.Z
./usr/lib/news/moderators
./usr/lib/news/backbone
./usr/lib/news/mapsh
  ...
#
```

Or you can specify the number of days to back up:

```
# backup 7 >/dev/null
#
```

Here the list of file names is thrown away (>/dev/null), so they are not displayed on the terminal. When you are running monthly backups, it's a good idea to save the names of all files being backed up. The easiest way is just to pipe the output of backup to the printer spooler:

```
# backup 31 | lp
#
```

Anyone interested in saving paper can do this instead:

```
# backup 31 | pr -3 -w132 | lp
#
```

To verify that you have all logical data on a cpio tape, you simply read it back in with the correct flags. Here's what we do when running important (monthly or full) backups with cpio:

```
# backup 31 >/tmp/tape.out
# cpio -itv </dev/tape >/tmp/tape.in
# tail /tmp/tape.out
./ips/book/ch13/All
./ips/book/ch13/ideas
./ips/book/ch13/create
./ips/book/ch13/extra
./ips/book/ch13/misc
./ips/book/ch13/philos
./ips/book/ch13/storage
./lpinterface/diablo
./lpinterface/oki
././.stdlogin
# tail /tmp/tape.in
100660 dave      46 Oct 25 18:59:01 1985 ips/book/ch13/ideas
100666 dave    6295 Oct 25 18:59:01 1985 ips/book/ch13/create
100666 dave    3031 Oct 25 18:59:01 1985 ips/book/ch13/extra
100666 dave    5466 Oct 25 18:59:01 1985 ips/book/ch13/misc
100666 dave    9163 Oct 25 18:59:01 1985 ips/book/ch13/philos
100666 dave    9757 Oct 25 18:59:01 1985 ips/book/ch13/storage
106751 root     463 Oct  6 15:42:34 1985 lpinterface/diablo
106755 root     859 Oct  6 15:42:34 1985 lpinterface/oki
100644 dave      28 Oct  3 10:20:57 1985 .stdlogin
48072 blocks
# pr /tmp/tape.in ¦ lp
#
```

Running the tail program on the log files shows that what was read in from the tape matches what was put on the tape in the first place. Then printing the tape.in file gives us a hard-copy record of not only the file names but also their sizes and times of modification. The extra time spent is worth it.

Those log files come in handy when you need to recover a file. All you have to do is determine the file name or names you want, and use our handy recover script:

```
# recover
# selective file recovery script
# for use with backup program above
```

```
# D. Fiedler
cd /
cpio -ivdmu $* < /dev/tape
```

Use the script like this, leaving off the initial slash (/) of each path name:

```
#  recover  etc/passwd  'etc/*rc'  usr/lib/crontab
etc/passwd
etc/bcheckrc
etc/brc
etc/rc
usr/lib/crontab
48072 blocks
#
```

Notice that file name substitution (a la the shell) can be used to match names of files. And that brings us to the one major problem with cpio for a backup method: if the file to be recovered is not named, it won't be pulled off the tape. So if you lose an entire directory (or even a file system), you will have to know the name of every file to be recovered, use file name substitution (very carefully), or recover the entire system (by specifying no argument at all). For this reason, you should regularly supplement incremental cpio backups with qualified backups of each file system. These qualified backups can be done with cpio, tar, or volcopy. Here's a quick example of how to do a qualified backup of the /usr file system with cpio:

```
# cd /usr
# find . -type f -print ¦ cpio -o > /dev/tape
```

Notice that we always cd to a directory before running the backup. Keeping all path names relative is useful if you ever have to move an entire file tree unexpectedly, or even restore to a different disk.

tar versus *cpio*

Each UNIX command has its unique advantages and disadvantages, which you will discover with use. The simplicity of tar's syntax is hard to beat. Although cpio's syntax is a little clumsy, it is far more versatile, however.

To make a long list of files to be copied with tar, you go to the directory in question and make a file of the file names. In the following command line, all file names in /usr/doc are appended to file.list:

```
$ ls /usr/doc >> file.list
```

165

Chapter 8: Backups and Archives

When the file list is complete, you go into it with an editor and remove any unwanted files before you copy. To copy all of those files with `tar`, use

```
# tar cv `cat file.list`
```

The argument `` `cat file.list` `` supplies each file name to `tar` as if it were a list of names entered on the command line (whitespace included). If the list is too long for `tar`, it fails with the complaint "list too long." The list will be too long if the number of files causes the name buffer to fill.

`cpio` does the same thing, but better. In the following example, a file list is read into `cpio` by a pipe. The file list can be any length (you won't get a "list too long" error):

```
# cat file.list ¦ cpio > /dev/rmt0
```

There is no default other than standard input for a file list or standard output to archive. Therefore, you have to specify the tape as a device (as in `/dev/rmt0` earlier). Another advantage of `cpio` is that it will often retry automatically if a tape error is encountered during an attempt to recover files.

volcopy

`volcopy` copies an entire file system (or `volume`) to tape or to another disk (generally a disk pack). This program is very fast because it uses a large internal data buffer and deals with raw devices. Another advantage of `volcopy` is that it can check machine-readable labels of the tape or disk, preventing an error during backing up or restoring.

The main disadvantage of `volcopy` is that you must use a separate tape to back up each file system. If you have partitioned your disk into many small file systems, using `volcopy` will be expensive in terms of media; even if you could fit all your data on one tape, you will still have to use one tape for each file system. Another problem can occur if `volcopy` fails while restoring data from tape: you could end up with a scrambled file system and be in even worse trouble. Finally, single files or groups of files cannot be recovered with `volcopy`; it's the whole file system or nothing. One way of getting around this problem is to restore the file system onto a spare section of your disk, and then just copy the files you want.

Running `volcopy` without a script can be frustrating because the manual is not completely clear about what arguments are expected where. Here's a handy guide to `volcopy` arguments:

```
volcopy filesystem raw-device-from vol-from raw-device-to vol-to
```

filesystem is the file system you want to copy, such as /usr, /usr/ spool, or the root file system (/). The volcopy command can be confusing because you are *not* expected to enter the exact name (such as /usr). Instead, you are supposed to make up your *own* name of less than six characters for the file system; you must do this *beforehand*, entering the name with the labelit command (don't worry, we'll show you how).

raw-device-from is the raw device (generally a disk partition if you are making a backup) that you want to copy *from*.

vol-from should uniquely identify the particular volume involved, especially if the medium is removable. On fixed disks, use the device name of the partition. For disk packs or tapes, use the last few digits of the serial number (if there is one) or number each one uniquely with permanent markers. On daily backup tapes or packs, use the day as the volume name so that the wrong backup isn't used by mistake.

raw-device-to is the raw device you want to copy *to*—usually a tape drive.

Finally, *vol-to* is your own unique name for the volume being copied to. For a tape, use the serial number or some other identifier.

Here is a simple example that shows how all this works:

```
# volcopy root /dev/rxt0a xt0a /dev/rxt1a xt1a
```

The first partition (a) of disk 0, containing the root file system, is being copied to the corresponding partition of disk 1. Because this example deals with fixed (Winchester) disks, each volume is the name of the corresponding partition.

Now take a look at something a bit more complex but realistic: a complete backup of the root file system onto tape. The first part of the process checks the machine-readable labels on the disk and tape to make sure that they correspond, using labelit. (Note that labelit is not on all systems.)

```
# labelit /dev/rxt0a
Current fsname: root, Current volname: xt0a,
Blocks: 16384, Inodes: 2048
FS Units: 1Kb, Date last mounted: Wed Oct 2 20:08:31 1985
```

Well, that looks reasonable. How about the tape?

```
# labelit /dev/rst525
Current fsname: 626Qmo, Current volname: d.rec.,
Blocks: 1949199727, Inodes: 29464
FS Units: 512b, Date last mounted: Thu Sep 24 12:08:05 1998
```

A few strange pieces of information, eh? It turns out that the last time this tape was used, it was for a cpio backup, so a new tape label is needed:

```
# labelit /dev/rst525 root tape01 -n
Skipping label check!
NEW fsname = root, NEW volname = tape01 -- DEL if wrong!!
#
```

Giving the new file system name and volume name on the labelit command line, followed by the -n flag, forces a new tape label to be written (that's what the message Skipping label check! means). labelit echoes what it thinks you are trying to do, and delays 10 seconds to allow you to kill the command if anything seems incorrect. Nothing is, so you can let labelit run to completion. Now the new tape label is checked:

```
# labelit /dev/rst525
Volcopy tape volume: tape01, reel 0 of 0 reels
Written: Wed Nov 6 02:21:42 1985
Current fsname: root, Current volname: tape01,
Blocks: 0, Inodes: -16
FS Units: 512b, Date last mounted: Wed Nov 6 02:21:42 1985
#
```

The negative inode count Inodes: -16 might seem alarming, but inodes mean nothing on tapes because they are not mounted file systems. Now it's time to run volcopy:

```
# volcopy root /dev/rxt0a xt0a /dev/rst525 tape01
You will need 1 reels.
(The same size and density is expected for all reels)
From: /dev/rxt0a, to: /dev/rst525? (DEL if wrong)
#
```

Again, volcopy gives you a chance to stop before it starts writing all over your output device. This feature is handy if you suddenly discover that you've switched input and output by accident!

By prompting, volcopy will also lead you through if anything important doesn't match. Thus, you will be able to override almost any incorrect combination of labels or file systems. This gives you the option of continuing if something was typed badly, but also allows you to make serious mistakes. We recommend starting over with the correct information because overriding changes the labeling on the output device, possibly causing more and bigger errors.

To restore a volcopy backup from tape, simply use the tape as the input (*vol-from*) device, and the appropriate disk partition as the output (*vol-to*) device. Now is the time when you will appreciate volcopy's insistence on the correct label. If you have heeded our warnings about how to choose your volume names, you won't make a mistake and restore onto the wrong disk.

Backup Shell Scripts

This section shows you some backup scripts for an Amdahl mainframe (IBM 370 architecture) running UTS UNIX. A few nonstandard UNIX commands are used in the scripts. Using these commands is unavoidable when you are dealing with a bay of tape drives. But essential UNIX commands are the same.

Backing Up a Mainframe in Three Easy Steps

You can back up a UNIX mainframe system with three quick scripts: tape_mount, tape_copy, and tape_print. The first script, tape_mount, causes a tape request to go to the system's main console. (Note that the script uses tape, a nonstandard UNIX command.) tape_mount also sets the parameters for having the tape mounted with a write ring and run at maximum density:

```
# tape_mount
# tape mounting command
tape -w -d 6250 -b tape.utsa
exit
```

You must use tape because the drives must be mounted from VM, not UTS. The tape command line says, "Mount a tape called tape.utsa as writable (-w) at 6250-bpi density (-d 6250) and bypass label processing (-b)." The reason for making a script out of a one-line command invocation is to guarantee that the mount request is done properly. Then the operator needs to type only the name of the command:

tape_mount

The next script, tape_copy, causes the actual copy to occur:

```
# tape_copy
# copy user file trees to
# UTSystem administrator nightly backup tape
tar c tape.utsa /ddf /491 /idf /pas /rdf /system /etc/passwd
exit
```

There it is in its beautiful `tar` simplicity. The system creates a file known as `/dev/tape/tape.utsa` and writes to it all the specified file trees (`/ddf` through `/system`) as well as the password file. When the `tape_copy` script is completed, the tape is not rewound.

The last script, `tape_print`, rewinds the tape, extracts every file name from it, and sends the names out to the system printer:

```
# tape_print
# make a listing of the files on the backup tape created by
# mount and copy
tm tape.utsa rew
tar t tape.utsa ¦ pr -3 -w132 ¦ lp
tape -u tape.utsa
exit
```

`tm`, the tape manipulator, is instructed to rewind (`rew`) the tape so that it can be reread. `tar` uses the `t` option to get the file names from the tape. This option is used instead of the `v` option to verify that the files have indeed been copied. The `-u` option with `tape` is used to logically dismount the tape.

These three scripts guarantee that a good set of backups are done consistently. The listing is usually made on wide green-bar paper in three columns for a total width of 132 characters. It is left on the system administrator's desk at night, and in the morning he has visual proof that the file systems are backed up. The listing is also available for users. They can look for files to verify that their work is on last night's tape. These listings are usually kept for no less than seven days.

tapefit

Any storage medium is finite. Imagine spending 30 minutes writing to a tape on a slow system and then finding out that because you have so much data, you have run off the end of the tape. This is a common backup problem. Yesterday's data distribution may not work today, especially after someone has just imported a few megabytes of text in mm format, processed it, and left the formatted output in a file! So what do you do?

Most of your shell scripts will be pedestrian and straightforward, but occasionally you will come up with something stunningly elegant. The following `tapefit` shell script was written by Brett Robblee to predetermine the number of tapes required and file distribution for backups. The script takes advantage of the `df` (disk free) command with the `-t` option to display both the number of blocks used and the total blocks available. This program is worth its weight in core memory when it comes to tape fitting:

```
# NAME
#       tapefit - report file system block usage
# SYNOPSIS
#       tapefit [ file-system ... ]
# DESCRIPTION
#       tapefit reports the number of blocks used for all
#       or selected mountable file systems. also displays
#       the device name, file-system name, and what
#       percentage of a tape(s) the file-system will use up.
# FILES
#       tapefit uses "pipelining" throughout. No intermediate
#       files are created.
# SEE ALSO your UNIX manuals on the following:
#       ascii(1), awk(1), df(1m), echo(1), printf(3s), sed(1),
#       sh(1), sort(1).
# NOTES
#       tapefit doesn't know if arguments passed to it are
#       valid file systems. It blithely passes all arguments
#       to "df" which, in turn, handles all error reporting.
# VERSION
#       bpr 6/29/85 version 1.0
echo "Report Number of 512-byte Disk Blocks Used"
echo "Version 1.0 6/29/85 bpr"
echo
echo "blocks used     device name     file system     tapes needed"
echo

df -t ${*:-} ¦ grep -v vio0 ¦ grep -v src ¦ \
 awk 'BEGIN { TAPEBLOCKS = 60000 }
     { if ((NR % 2) == 1)
       { tree[NR] = $1
       special[NR] = $2
       used[NR] = $3
       }
     else
       {   sum[NR-1] = $2
           {
           printf "%6d\t\t%17s\t%-12s\t%4.3f\n", \
             ((sum[NR-1]-used[NR-1]) * 8), special[NR-1], \
             tree[NR-1],  (((sum[NR-1]-used[NR-1]) * 8) \
             / TAPEBLOCKS )
           }
       }

     }' ¦ sort +0nr -1 exit 0
```

tapefit takes shell programming to an advanced state, cleverly using awk's capability to create arrays. The name of each file tree, its special file name (in /dev), the number of blocks used, and the total number of blocks for each file system are stored in single-element arrays called *vectors*. The modulus operator (%) is used to test each line in the df output to see whether it is even or odd. The even-numbered lines contain totals and require a different assignment than that of odd-numbered lines. A constant, TAPEBLOCKS, is defined to store the number of 512-byte blocks on the tape. Here the program is set up to deal with 2400-foot tape running 6250-bpi density. There are 8 "UNIX blocks" (of 512 bytes) per system hardware block (4096 bytes). *These numbers have to be changed to meet your system's parameters.* Remember that System V uses 1024-byte blocks, Version 7 uses 512, and UTS UNIX for mainframes uses 4096. On most systems, because the blocks are the same size, no multiplier is needed. Look at BSIZE in /usr /include/sys/param.h to find the value for your system.

Note that two file systems have been deliberately filtered out: /src, which is illegal to copy; and /dev/vio0, a memory device used by /tmp. The final output is sorted in the first field so that the output is from the largest file system to the smallest.

Typical tapefit output looks like this:

Report Number of 512-byte Disk Blocks Used
Version 1.0   6/29/85 bpr

blocks used	device name	file system	tapes needed
109416	(/dev/dsk/318s0):	/d5	1.824
40448	(/dev/dsk/560s0):	/5460	0.674
36584	(/dev/dsk/520s0):	/5520	0.610
28640	(/dev/dsk/220s0):	/	0.477
26784	(/dev/dsk/802s0):	/5802	0.446
18496	(/dev/dsk/540s0):	/sysgrp	0.308
13464	(/dev/dsk/544s0):	/system	0.224
4256	(/dev/dsk/5a0s0):	/sys	0.071
3504	(/dev/dsk/530s0):	/5530	0.058
2896	(/dev/dsk/599s0):	/ds	0.048
2032	(/dev/dsk/542s0):	/pass	0.034
1856	(/dev/dsk/502s0):	/project	0.031
152	(/dev/dsk/300s0):	/5300	0.003
144	(/dev/dsk/740s0):	/5740	0.002
136	(/dev/dsk/502s0):	/pdl	0.002
128	(/dev/dsk/512s0):	/ids	0.002
128	(/dev/dsk/dd0s0):	/dump	0.002

As you work with your system, you gain insights about the needs of the system and the needs of your users. Gradually, you will develop backup and archiving routines of your own. The scripts to run them don't need to be fancy, only effective.

Summary

As you learned in this chapter, there are many ways to back up your system. Besides selecting from a wide spectrum of media, you can use different formats for writing the data. You can create your own schedule, but you need to back up regularly. If you forget to back up just *once*, you will be in a world of trouble! Remember, you've been warned.

Now that you have seen how to preserve and back up the system's data, you need to learn how to protect the data on the system from mischief, espionage, and theft.

9

Security

An important but often overlooked feature of running a computer system is the maintenance of its security from outside intrusion, internal sabotage (known as "mischief" outside the commercial environment), and just plain user stupidity. This chapter covers the basic information you need for understanding and making use of UNIX security features.

The Running System

Multiuser systems need security features. Because a system is potentially open to anyone who walks by a terminal or has a terminal and modem, the system must be protected from intrusion by unauthorized individuals. To be universally useful, system security features must be flexible. Otherwise, they are so specialized that nobody can use them. UNIX security features accomplish this without too much difficulty.

Although some of the techniques in this chapter may seem overly paranoid at first reading, all of them have been used to break into UNIX systems at one time or another. Underestimating the cleverness of a "bad guy" is a poor mistake, and so is assuming that he won't decide to wipe out your system once he becomes root. Because few systems can be totally secure, your best chance is to know exactly what the problems are and to know your users.

Be as careful about security as you want, but if you have an incoming modem, you should also have a full, current set of backups. The minute you run an outside line into the system, the potential for mischief increases dramatically.

Security Basics

The ability to access files or go through file systems is called *privilege*. The permissions of a specific file show not only who has the privilege of accessing that file but also the degree of access. Permissions also indicate whether a file can be executed or a directory traversed. Three types of privilege are usable in three different areas:

r   Only *r*ead a file

w   *W*rite (create and modify) a file

x   E*x*ecute (run a program)

These privileges can be applied to three areas, or different types of users:

u   A file's owner, called *u*ser

g   Members of a *g*roup who share privilege for this and other files

o   All *o*thers (any current and potential system user)

The preceding two categories are combined to form the various privilege designations you see whenever a long listing is performed:

```
$ ls -l /bin/ls
-rwxr-xr-x 3 bin adm 21108 Jan 23 16:22 /bin/ls
```

This is a long listing of the ls command as it resides in /bin. The string -rwxr-xr-x, which shows the settings of the *protection bits*, is broken down into three segments of three letters each. (The leftmost character does not relate to security and is set to - for ordinary files, d for directories, c for character special files, b for block special files, or p for FIFOs.) Here are the three segments:

User	Group	Other
rwx	r-x	r-x

These settings mean that the owner, bin, has *read*, *write*, and *execute* privileges, while members of the adm group and all others on the system have *read* and *execute* privileges only. A hyphen signifies that a privilege is denied (in this case, *write* privilege).

Changing Ownership of Files and Directories

If a person has neither group nor ownership rights to a file, the system will not allow him access. This is as it should be, but when you, as administrator, create files and directories, how are you going to assign ownership to the intended user? The command to change ownership is chown, and its syntax is

```
# chown logname filename
```

chown is used like this:

```
# chown david bruce.file
```

You have now changed bruce.file's owner to david. In another case, suppose that you copy a .profile to a new user's home after creating the home directory while acting as superuser. Both the home directory and the profile now have root as the owner. The user can neither execute the profile nor change it. chown rectifies the problem in seconds:

```
# chown singer .profile /us/singer
```

On some systems, the use of the chown command is restricted to root to avoid the sushi security hole described later in this chapter. On other systems, chown has been fixed to prevent this problem. On most systems, you are left wide open.

Changing Group Ownership

Analogous to the chown command is chgrp. It allows you to change group ownership of files, directories, or devices. Usually, the group ownership of files created by a given user is that of his group as assigned in /etc/passwd (or his effective group if running under the newgrp command):

```
$ whoami
david
$ grep david /etc/passwd
david:TDDc8H8ZFlA9I:12:7:David Fiedler:/own/dave:/bin/csh
$ grep david /etc/group
staff:VOID:7:susan,brenda,debbie,unique,root,david,chris
$ cp /etc/passwd /tmp
$ ls -lg /etc/passwd /tmp/passwd
-rw-r--r-- 1 root      root      3673  Dec  7 17:33 /etc/passwd
-rw-r--r-- 1 david     staff     3673  Dec  7 21:47 /tmp/passwd
```

```
$ chgrp other /tmp/passwd
$ chgrp other /etc/passwd
/etc/passwd: Not owner
$ ls -lg /etc/passwd /tmp/passwd
-rw-r--r-- 1 root     root     3673  Dec  7 17:33 /etc/passwd
-rw-r--r-- 1 david    other    3673  Dec  7 21:47 /tmp/passwd
$
```

Protection Bits

The chmod command uses file protection bits to establish protection levels. The levels are expressed in octal (base 8). Each octal number has its own individual meaning, and the sum of the bits incorporates all the meanings associated with each octal number.

Read	4	4	4			
Write	2	2		2	2	
Execute	1	1	1		1	
Sum	7	6	5	4	3	1

Octal 4 (r--) means *read*, octal 2 (-w-) means *write*, and octal 1 (--x) means *execute*. Thus, octal 7, when applied to permissions, means that the file can be read, written to, and executed. You generally use three octal digits when changing the permission bits with chmod—one digit each for user, group, and others. This set of bits is called the *mode*. With the bit system, you can quickly set permissions with the chmod command, using the syntax

```
chmod octal-bits file-name
```

Thus

```
$ chmod 751 my.file
```

gives read, write, and execute privileges to the owner; read and execute privileges to the group members; and just execute privilege to all others. Root can use chmod to modify privilege on any files, but a regular user may modify the protection on her own files only. The result from the preceding command might look like this:

```
-rwxr-x--x 1 penny 128 Apr 18 my.file
```

Most people do not like to fool with octal bits. On most systems, you can also use *symbolic modes* with the chmod command. Symbolic modes let you add or remove permissions by using letters—such as u for user; g for group; o for other; a for all (user, group, and other); and of course r, w, and x. Using symbolic modes is simply a matter of specifying first *who* should get their permissions changed (the default is the a flag), then a plus or minus sign (for giving or taking away permission), and finally the specific permission you are referencing. As usual, showing is easier than telling:

```
$ chmod o+r my.file          — Add read permission for others
$ ls -l my.file
-rwxr-xr-x 1 penny           128 Apr 18 my.file
$ chmod g-x my.file          —Take away group execute permission
$ ls -l my.file
-rwxr--r-x 1 penny           128 Apr 18 my.file
$ chmod a+w my.file          — Give everyone write permission
$ ls -l
-rwxrw-rwx 1 penny           128 Apr 18 my.file
$
```

Symbolic modes are useful for turning a specific permission on or off without having to calculate octal numbers, but as an administrator, you will gradually learn to use octal.

Permission bits work a little differently for directories because a directory is actually just a file with special data in it about other files:

- *Read* permission for a directory means that you can look at the file names in the directory, even if you can't actually cd to it.

- *Write* permission for a directory means that you can alter the contents of the directory. With write permission, you can add files to a directory, but you can also wipe out files in the directory, even if you have no write permission for those files!

- *Execute* permission for a directory means that you can cd to the directory or use it as part of a path name. You *cannot* access files that don't have execute permissions on all the directories in the path.

As you can see, directory permissions can permit security breaches if they are not understood. If a directory is set with

```
drwxr-x--x    root    bin 56 May 27 05:30 /usr/lib/src
```

even a lowly user can type something like

```
$ cat /usr/lib/src/secret.c
```

and look at any file within that has read permission for other, as long as he knows its name. If you do not want others in a directory, set the mode accordingly:

```
# chmod o-wx /usr/lib/src
# ls -ld /usr/lib/src
drwxr-x---     root      bin 56 May 27 05:30 /usr/lib/src
#
```

umask

Most people do not like running chmod every time they create a file, so it's nice to be able to set default permissions. You do this with the umask command. umask is sometimes difficult to understand because it implies a *logical inverse*. The easiest way to calculate the umask is to think of it as *taking away* permission. Suppose that you want your files set to mode 660, and your directories to the equivalent 770. Think of "taking away" as subtraction, so 777 minus 770 equals 007. Figuring this out relative to *directory* permissions allows both files and directories to be created with appropriate modes.

The command that gives full permission to just owner and group is chmod 770, and its equivalent is umask 007. (You must explicitly give execute permissions to files unless they are generated by a program designed for generating executables—for example, a compiler.) Note the following example:

```
$ umask 007
$ > zero
$ mkdir nothing
$ ls -l zero nothing
-rw-rw----  1 david      staff     0 Nov 23 15:07 zero
-rwxrwx---  2 david      staff    32 Nov 23 15:07 nothing
```

Because read and execute permissions to other are established by chmod 775, the equivalent is umask 002, as shown in the following code:

```
$ umask 002
$ > one
$ mkdir another
$ ls -l one another
-rw-rw-r--  1 david      staff     0 Nov 23 15:08 one
-rwxrwxr-x  2 david      staff    32 Nov 23 15:08 another
```

Full permissions are generated with umask 000:

```
$ umask 000
$ > two
$ mkdir pair
```

```
$ ls -l two pair
-rw-rw-rw- 1 david      staff      0 Nov 23 15:09 two
-rwxrwxrwx 2 david      staff     32 Nov 23 15:09 pair
$
```

The best place to set umask is in your .profile or .cshrc file so that umask is always in effect. The most common settings are shown in Table 9.1.

Table 9.1. Common umask settings.

umask	Yields	Purpose
077	-rw------- -rwx------	Most restrictive and private (directory and executable)
007	-rw-rw---- -rwxrwx---	Working with groups in sensitive environment (directory and executable)
002	-rw-rw-r-- -rwxrwxr-x	Working with groups in academic environment (directory and executable)
022	-rw-r--r-- -rwxr-xr-x	A reasonable default (directory and executable)
000	-rw-rw-rw- -rwxrwxrwx	For people who trust everyone (directory and executable)
277	-r-------- -r-x------	For people who don't trust themselves (directory and executable)

To set the default umask for everyone on the system, put the setting you want into /etc/profile and /etc/default/cshrc. Anyone who cares can change his .profile himself.

Some Very Special Modes

Besides read, write, and execute bits, there are three remaining permission bits:

- Set-user-ID (setuid or SUID)

- Set-group-ID (setgid or SGID)

- The "sticky" bit

The first two bits solve an otherwise unsurmountable problem, and the last bit can speed up system response time.

The Set-User-ID Bit

How does the system deal with a command like passwd? passwd allows a user to change her password. It lets her write a new encrypted password to the file /etc/passwd. Yet /etc/passwd cannot be modified (written to) except by root. The trick is that when the passwd command is executed, the user is given the same privilege as the owner of the passwd command, root. When a user uses /bin/passwd, the system acts as if /etc/passwd is being modified by root. This trick is accomplished with the set-user-ID bit. Look at the permissions of the program file itself:

```
$ ls -l /bin/passwd
-rwsr-xr-x 1 root          17136 Nov 19 1982 /bin/passwd
```

The listing looks normal except for the strange s in the x field of the owner's permissions. The s shows that the set-user-ID bit is active. You set it with chmod in this way:

```
# chmod 4755 /bin/passwd
```

The 4000 bit sets the user ID to the same *effective* user ID as the owner (root) of the program file, *but only while the program is being run*. In other words, while the program is running, it acts as though its owner (root) was running it, rather than an ordinary user. This wondrous bit of magic (pun intended) is the brainchild of Dennis Ritchie and is actually patented (U.S. Patent #4,135,240). The chmod program is written so that only root or the owner of a program can make it SUID. Thus, any user can create an SUID program.

What is most dangerous, of course, is a program that is SUID and owned by root, especially if that program is general-purpose, rather than specific in nature. For instance, passwd operates only on the /etc/passwd file, but an editor that is SUID and owned by root lets anyone edit /etc/passwd or any other file.

A Bit of Sushi

The first thing any bad guy will do if he gains access to the root login, even if only for a minute, is to execute these commands:

```
# cp /bin/sh /own/badguy/sushi
# chmod 4755 /own/badguy/sushi
```

Now he logs off from being root and goes back to his original identity. The copy of the shell he just created is SUID and owned by root, so merely executing it gives him untraceable root privileges. Whenever he wants, he can become root:

```
$ pwd
/own/badguy
$ sushi
#
```

sushi (*su*peruser *sh*ell, *i*nteractive) illustrates how careful you must be with SUID programs, as well as with the root password. Here are some rules that protect you from dangerous sushi (if you get caught, you will join the ranks of *fugu—f*ooled *U*NIX gurus *u*nited):

1. Never let anyone else use your root password or login. Even close supervision is not good enough.

2. No program that is SUID root should be writable by anyone but root. If you fail to guard against this, someone will copy the shell onto that program quicker than you can say "Chopsticks, please."

3. Don't use any SUID shell programs. Some versions of UNIX allow even shell programs to be SUID, and for various technical reasons, these can be compromised no matter how the permission bits are set. They cannot be traced with the accounting either, making them hard to monitor!

4. Don't expect to protect yourself by looking for programs named sushi! When testing the security of various systems, one of the authors would move the stolen shell to a file called .profile or junk. Even if the administrator found this file, he would tend to ignore it because of the name. The only safe method is to run a program similar to checksecure (provided at the end of this chapter) regularly.

5. The only programs that should be SUID root are those that are delivered this way with the system and are documented as needing SUID root privilege. When a user comes to you with a program that he says must be SUID root, assume that he has hidden a security hole inside unless he can prove otherwise by going over it, line by line, with the best system programmer you know (and trust).

6. Only single-purpose programs (like passwd) should be SUID root. Anything with a shell escape—especially any interactive program— will give you a problem.

7. To ensure that only the owner of an SUID file has write permission on it, always use the command chmod 4755 instead of the symbolic equivalent chmod +s when creating it.

8. If the chown commands are accessible to normal users on your system, test them to make sure that the old security holes have been fixed. After setting a test program to mode 4755, chown it to root (while a normal user). The mode should be reset automatically to 755 to prevent unexpected raw fish dinners.

Watch Your *crontab*

The /usr/spool/cron/crontabs/* files (and earlier versions /usr/lib/cron/crontabs/* and /usr/lib/crontab) are quite useful, but you must use them wisely. A dedicated bad guy can find many holes by studying them. First of all, if anyone besides root can read the system administration crons, you are running the risk that a bad guy may write a program to look at the modes of every program executed through cron, and copy his own code on top of any of these programs that are writable. Most crons execute their commands as root (even System V Release 2 has a cron file for root) and as such are extremely dangerous.

An even bigger problem relates to the at program found on many systems. This facility allows the average user to schedule execution of programs at a later time. To accomplish this, a daemon called /usr/lib/atrun is started by cron every 10 minutes or so. When the user runs at, a file is created in the /usr/spool/at directory containing the commands to be executed. Because the daemon has to be able to execute any program, it is SUID root. The bad guy has several options:

- Run the commands to create the sushi program, using at.

- Run a harmless program with at but edit the spool file (the one at puts in the /usr/spool/at directory) to add the sushi code.

- Make a copy of the spool file, add the sushi code to this copy, and give the copy a name that tricks atrun into executing it at a particular time.

The approach he picks depends on what holes have been left open. Sometimes changing the ownership of the spool file to root is enough to fool at. To guard against an at attack, make sure that the /usr/spool/at directory is owned by root with mode 755. Now log in as a normal user and try all of the preceding methods. If any of them works, the only solution is to disable the atrun daemon or to remove its SUID status. Naturally, a complaint to your system supplier is also in order.

The Set-Group-ID Bit

Just as the set-user-ID bit allows a user to have the same power as the owner of a file, the set-group-ID (SGID) bit allows a user to have the same power as any member of the group to which the file belongs. An example of the use of the SGID bit is the creation of a special program to allow an otherwise restricted user to access certain files in a predetermined way.

For instance, a system operator might be given an SGID program that would allow him to copy all of a particular group's files to tape for backup, and nothing more. If written correctly, the program would not permit him to print or even examine the files. Here the SGID feature allows greater access (to all files belonging to the group) without greater risk. The alternative would probably be to give the operator root privilege through an SUID program, so SGID limits the potential for danger in case there *is* an undiscovered security hole in the program.

The Sticky Bit

The third special type of permission bit is the sticky bit, or the "save text image after execution" bit. To understand the sticky bit, you have to remember that UNIX loads the program files into system memory by reading them from the file system. To do this, UNIX must find every block of the file (which may be randomly scattered all over the disk), load all the blocks into memory, and then begin executing the file. (On some systems with virtual memory, execution can begin before the entire file has finished loading.) This could take a noticeable amount of time, especially for large files. When not enough memory is on the system to hold all active processes simultaneously, UNIX "swaps out" a process "text" (program) area by writing it *sequentially* to a special area on the system disk.

The sticky bit is used only on large executable programs that are called constantly, like screen editors, the C compiler, and the shells. It tells the system to leave the program's text on the swap area permanently (or until the system is rebooted). The next time someone tries to execute the program, the system will load it from the swap area much faster than the program could be loaded from the file system. Furthermore, the system will swap the text out only once—after that, the system knows that the copy is out there and doesn't have to be copied out again. Having the sticky bit doesn't make a program run any faster; it just means that the program will start (load) faster after the first time.

To make a file sticky, you should use the symbolic mode +t of the chmod command to avoid changing any other permission bits:

```
# ls -l /usr/ucb/vi
-rwxr-xr-x 3 bin    sys   131078 Sep 28 13:26 /usr/ucb/vi
# chmod +t /usr/ucb/vi
# ls -l /usr/ucb/vi
-rwxr-xr-t 3 bin    sys   131078 Sep 28 13:26 /usr/ucb/vi
#
```

Now, on a quiet system, type vi and time how long it takes before your screen is set up; then exit vi and time it again. The program should load noticeably faster. If it does not, you might as well remove the sticky bit.

When using the sticky bit, be sure to avoid getting carried away and making too many programs sticky. If that happens, you could run out of swap space, which would crash your system. As a general rule, the total size of your sticky programs should not exceed 25 percent of your available swap space.

Sticky Memory

Because of the decrease in the size and price of RAM chips, many UNIX systems, especially small ones, have more RAM available than disk swap space. To take advantage of this, VenturCom, the supplier of the VENIX (real-time) operating system, developed the concept of *sticky memory*.

A program that has its sticky memory bit set (denoted by an m instead of a t in column 10 of an ls -l listing) will be kept in RAM as long as there is sufficient room for it. This allows virtually instantaneous reloading of the program and enables a VENIX system to have all the advantages of the RAM-disk concept (used on personal computers) without having to set aside a fixed amount of memory for the RAM disk.

Passwords

Security is impossible without passwords. In UNIX, a password is the key to otherwise locked doors. The first password a user sees is his own login password. When a user attempts to log on the system, he must enter his login name and then his password. The password is encrypted and is compared to the encrypted version stored in /etc/passwd; if they match, the user is allowed to log in. Because only the encrypted version is stored in /etc/passwd, it's safe to allow all users to read it.

The biggest problem with passwords is human frailty. Given a choice, the average user selects a password that is easy to remember and type. Such a password is also easy for an intruder to guess. Studies have found that, on almost every system tested, *someone* uses his first or last name, his friend's or pet's name, or another easy-to-guess password.

A person who uses his own name for a password is called a *joe*. Running under your usual login, test other people's passwords regularly to see if they qualify. The authors have a program called `joetest` that automatically checks all logins for this and similar problems (such as using last name, department name, and so on), but `joetest` is too easily abused to publish. Commercial versions of this same concept are available.

The `passwd` program tries to encourage people to use passwords longer than just a few letters. Remember, though, that only the first eight characters of a password are actually used by the `passwd` program. You should go further and encourage people to use more complex passwords, yet still easy to remember. Some good methods are these:

- Use two short words with a space or underscore between them, such as `kiss me` or `darn_it`.

- Replace letters by mnemonic digits. For example, if your name is David, use `dav1d`, or `r00t` instead of root.

- Throw in extra punctuation, such as `whosez?` or `egg;roll`.

- Capitalize letters within the words—for instance, `hIlda` or `gArbAge`.

- Use several methods at once, such as `y0u T00!`

Newer UNIX systems have a rule base for making passwords. For example, SCO UNIX (which incorporates many other security measures), has a password rules-checking program, `goodpw`. The rules and messages are contained in files and subdirectories below `/usr/lib/goodpw`. General rules for acceptable and forbidden passwords are described in the files `/usr/lib/goodpw/match` and `/usr/lib/goodpw/reject`, using regular expressions. Further definition files exist in the subdirectory `usr/lib/goodpw/checks`.

Aging

Some systems allow *password aging*, so that a password expires after a certain number of weeks. This is not a bad idea in theory because eventually even the best password may be guessed or otherwise compromised. Unfortunately, older UNIX password-aging implementation requires the administrator to edit the password field manually for each user. Errors are almost inevitable because of the complex series of obscure codes used by aging.

Another problem is that aging forces you to select your new password at login time (once the old password has expired, of course). Most people are in a big hurry to log in, so they tend to select an "easy" password at this point, negating all your careful planning. Or they select two passwords and switch back and forth between them at expiration time. This common practice is called *password toggling*.

We suggest using a regular program of gentle reminders to users instead of forced aging. Use the `mall` program (provided at the end of this chapter) or `/etc/motd` to alert people to change their passwords. Do this with `crontab`, and you won't even have to think about it again.

Newer systems have password-aging information in the `/etc/shadow` file (along with the encrypted password) or in another separate database. In these cases, the `passwd` command is what you use, as system administrator, to manage password aging. For example, with UNIX V.4 and SCO UNIX, you set the maximum number of days that a password is valid by using the following syntax:

passwd -x *n* *name*

n is the number of days between changes that a password will be valid, and *name* is the user ID of the account you are setting. Also built into the newer password-management utilities is the capability to warn users when their passwords are about to expire (the gentle reminder). This helps avoid last-minute password creation.

The `passwd` options for System V.4 are shown in Table 9.2.

Table 9.2. `passwd` options for System V.4.

Option	Description
-l	Lock password entry
-d	Delete password
-n *days*	Set the minimum number of days before the pass word can be changed
-x *days*	Set the maximum number of days the password can be used before it must be changed
-w *days*	Set the number of days (before the expiration date) that warnings will be given to the user
-a	Report on all `passwd` entries (use with -s)
-s	Show password attributes
-f	Force the user to change the password at his next login

Of course, to speed things up, you will want to use a script or menu interface to do your password management.

Group Privileges

The concept of groups extends the usability and versatility of UNIX. With properly set group privileges, members of a group may share files with some people while excluding all others from them. A group called edit can set up privileges in this way:

```
-rw-rw-r-- 1 susan     edit 9870 Apr 18 20:56 chapter9
```

The owner, susan, and any member of the group edit can read and write to the chapter9 file. Anyone else can only read it. Group privilege is meaningful only when the group file, /etc/group, is carefully edited to be sure that only the members of the intended group are attached to the group and that the group entry is protected.

Note some typical group entries:

```
edit:876cAt07dbeh:20:bruce,karen,david,susan
people:3hqE02n1Md33:30:bruce,karen
dragons:4hQ83zO3Fm9A:40:david,susan
```

Here 20 is the unique number assigned to the group edit. The edit group privilege becomes valid for a user only when her login name is entered into this file. Only when a person (susan) is part of an active group (edit), or uses newgrp (with the correct password) to join the group temporarily, do the group permissions for the members' files (such as chapter9) become functional.

The group number assigned to a user in her /etc/passwd file entry is the default group for that user. If she is listed as a member of several groups in /etc/group, she may switch between those groups at will by simply executing the newgrp command with the name of the group she wants. If she is *not* listed as a group member—for example, for group people—she may newgrp to people only if she knows the group password associated with people:

```
$ whoami
susan
$ create test
$ ls -l test
-rw-rw-r-- 1 susan     edit        0 Apr 18 20:56 test
$ newgrp dragons
$ whoami
```

```
susan
$ create another
$ ls -l another
-rw-rw-r-- 1 susan     dragons     0 Apr 18 20:57 another
$ newgrp people
Password:
$ whoami
susan
$ create yetanother
$ ls -l yetanother
-rw-rw-r-- 1 susan     people      0 Apr 18 20:59 yetanother
$
```

A Note on Group Passwords

There is still no consistent way to apply group passwords. Older UNIX systems had no provision whatsoever for group passwords. Some later UNIX systems have group commands that encrypt the group password in /etc/group just as passwd encrypts the login password. Other systems simply allow an unencrypted password to be placed in the password field in the /etc/group file, but in such cases care must be taken to prevent anyone other than root from reading the group file. If an encrypted password is needed in /etc/group and no command supports it, here is how to add one:

1. Make a dummy entry in /etc/passwd:

```
# ed /etc/passwd
751
$
a*
dummy::999:999::::
.
w
770
q
#
```

2. As root, create an encrypted password for dummy:

```
# passwd dummy
# New password:

#
```

3. Look at the new dummy entry in /etc/passwd and carefully copy the encrypted password on a piece of paper:

```
# tail -1 /etc/passwd
dummy:2ux8ha#4%bc:999:999::::
#
```

4. Edit the /etc/group file and enter the encrypted password there:

```
# ed /etc/group
S8
/edit/
edit::20:bruce,karen,david,susan
s/::/:2ux8ha#4%bc:/p
edit:2ux8ha#4%bc:20:bruce,karen,david,susan
w
74
q
#
```

5. Delete the dummy entry from /etc/passwd:

```
# ed /etc/passwd
770
$
d
w
751
q
#
```

For best security, you should disable the group passwords completely. As noted earlier, people do not protect group passwords as vigorously as their own personal accounts. If group passwords are disabled, only root can assign people to groups. This means more work for you, but also a much more secure system. On most systems, simply having *no* password for a group in the /etc/group file disables passwords and prevents people from switching groups with newgrp. But we recommend, if only for the sake of reminding yourself, that you put the word VOID or something similar in the password field of the group file.

rsh—The Restricted Shell

Although most users believe that they are heavily restricted by security administration (compared to root), the average user has enough privilege to get into plenty of trouble. The ideally secured system has no lines outside the console and no users other than the administrator. However, such a system is incapable of producing much work. To tighten up a system's security and prevent damage either from those who lack expertise in UNIX or from those who have too much, a restricted shell is available.

Another command named rsh (remote *sh*ell) is on some systems, particularly Berkeley systems. This command is used for executing commands on remote (across the LAN) systems. Don't confuse the Berkeley rsh with the restricted shell. If your system has no rsh file, make a link from /bin/sh to /bin/rsh and execute rsh to see whether it works as described.

The restricted shell acts very much like the standard Bourne shell, with several exceptions. The person confined to an rsh cannot do the following tasks:

- Change the directory

- Reset his search path variable PATH or his SHELL environment variable (this depends on the version)

- Use the / character in a path name, thus effectively eliminating trips outside the home directory

- Redirect output because the > and >> forms of redirection are unavailable

- exec a program (again, this depends on the version)

On some systems, a companion editor red is provided to give similarly restricted use in editing.

The administrator can further restrict an rsh user by making a special restricted directory, /usr/rbin, linking in only those programs needed by the restricted user and setting the PATH for that user to /usr/rbin.

Does this sound like a lot of trouble? As time goes on, a restricted user will probably ask for more commands than you have given him. At this point, you have the following options:

- *Refuse*. This option is safe but might get you in trouble with management.

- *Give in*. Put the desired commands in /usr/rbin. Each new command is a potential security hole. Do you have time to check them all?

- *Give up*. Giving the restricted shell user a normal shell might open a can of worms but is likely to force the issue. If the user is a bad guy, you will probably find out fast.

Unfortunately, the security goals of the system administrator are not always in line with the goals of management. In fact, running a tight system may put you at odds with both the user community and management. Taking any privilege away, once granted, makes you a bad guy with management. Compromising security to avoid run-ins with management is tempting, but such compromises leave the system open to all sorts of potential security breaches.

One method of providing restricted access to a single program is to use that program as a user's shell, as in this passwd entry:

```
joe:hsdfkyeiuky:59:100:Joe Editor:/own/joe:/usr/ucb/vi
```

Joe can now use only vi. Or can he? By typing :sh from within vi, Joe gets a regular shell and can then do whatever a normal user can do. A better way is to execute vi from a restricted rsh:

```
# grep joe /etc/passwd
joe::hsdfkyeiuky:59:100:Joe Editor:/own/joe:/bin/rsh
# cd /own/joe
# ls -la
total 3
drwxr-xr-x  2 root     bin       64 Mar 9 1984 .
drwxr-xr-x 27 root     bin      512 Nov 22 19:18 ..
-r-x--x--x  1 joe      bin      223 Mar 7 1984 .profile
# cat .profile
PATH=/usr/rbin
SHELL=/bin/rsh
export PATH SHELL
/usr/ucb/vi
exit
#
```

Now even if Joe figures out how to escape to the shell, all he will get is rsh. Notice that Joe can execute his own .profile, but he can't change or erase it.

One thing you should know is that the restricted shell available on your system may not be truly restricted. New holes are found periodically, and new versions of the restricted shell are written to deal with them. Because there is no guarantee that even the newest rsh doesn't have a way out, it should never be used to contain a potentially hostile user.

Data Encryption

Another way to prevent data from being read is to make the data unreadable to anyone accessing it. You do this by coding or encrypting it. The `crypt` command is a software version of the old German Enigma code machine used in World War II. (`crypt` may not be available on all sites because the exporting of `crypt` from the United States is restricted. The design actually originated in Europe, so there are publicly available versions on European and Asian UNIX archive sites.) `crypt` uses a single rotor with 256 elements. Although it is not impossible to break a coded file made with `crypt`, it is difficult enough to keep all but the most serious intruder at bay. `crypt` is a filter that encodes or decodes as it takes in data. It relies on the use of a key, as in this example:

```
$ cat no_code ¦ crypt passw1 > coded
```

Here the file `no_code` is passed to `crypt` with the key `passw1` and encoded. The output is then redirected to the file `coded`.

To decrypt the file, you reverse the process:

```
$ cat coded ¦ crypt passwd > no_code
```

There are several problems with this, however. The first is that both the encrypted text (the file called `coded`) and the clear text (the file `no_code`) are left on the system. Thus, it's much easier for a potential spy to decrypt any future messages, because almost everyone who uses `crypt` tends to use the same key over and over again.

The solution is never to keep the clear text on the system. You do this by using the editor (`ed` or `vi`) with the `-x` encryption option, so that the file is always stored encrypted and can be decrypted whenever it is again edited or examined:

```
$ ed -x coded
Key:
a
Hello there everybody.
.
w
23
q
$ cat coded
bcx5@fuoiwe47h139po9803
$ cat coded ¦ crypt bigjohn
Hello there everybody.
$
```

Another problem with this way of using `crypt` is that the key is given on the command line. Any good spy can simply run `ps -af` and see your key. To prevent this, force `crypt` to prompt you for your key:

```
$ cat coded ¦ crypt
Key:
Hello there everybody.
$
```

Encryption seems to be a nearly perfect solution to the security problem. The superuser can access any file and directory in the system, but even she cannot ordinarily read the contents of an encrypted file. A problem arises if a user's files are encrypted and he leaves the company or forgets the key. His files are inaccessible! For this reason, the `crypt` command is restricted on some systems.

Another security flaw of `crypt` is that a dishonest superuser could compromise it by modifying it so that it secretly writes the user's name and key to a hidden file. This can even be done without the source code, although we won't mention how. Because it is hard for the average user to determine whether this has been done, truly top-secret material should not be entrusted to a multiuser system.

The last problem of `crypt` stems from U.S. government restrictions on its distribution. If you try to send `crypt`ed files out of or into the United States, you may find that the versions of `crypt` are different. Be sure that you have the same program as well as the same key word at both ends of the communications link.

High Security

The protection offered by `crypt` will generally prove sufficient for end-user populations. If you have C programmers (especially systems programmers) on your system or you have sensitive material, you cannot afford to be complacent.

Each of the techniques presented in this section has been used successfully to break into a UNIX system. Although some of them require great technical skill, others do not. By presenting the details, we intend to shock you into action rather than make it easier for the bad guys. Most of these methods are well known already, though we know a few more that aren't (unfortunately, they are beyond the scope of this book).

Exploring the Limits

A bad guy has all the time he wants to crack your security at leisure. Some bad guys try to find system limitations in order to exploit them. For example, in UNIX Version 6, a bad guy could open so many files that the system's file table had room for only one more to be opened. Opening the final file made him root automatically. In another case, the su program was written so that entering an extremely long password (even though incorrect) would write over an internal buffer, forcing the long password to "match."

Although both of these system bugs have been fixed, you can never be certain that a new one has not been introduced or that an old one hasn't been found yet. Method of protection: none!

Device and Conquer

The /dev directory is a potential gold mine for bad guys with enough knowledge. All devices should be as fully read- and write-protected as possible. Consider a simple example. Suppose that you have carefully protected your source code directory (as you should, because you might be held liable if someone stole the code). You examine the permissions and the disk partitions involved:

```
$ mount
/ on /dev/xt0a    read/write on Sat Dec  7 20:34:09 1985
/usr on /dev/xt0c read/write on Sat Dec  7 20:34:13 1985
/src on /dev/xt1b read/write on Sat Dec  7 20:34:15 1985
$ ls -ld /src
drwx------15 bin       sys           1104 Nov 22 02:04 /src
$ ls -l /dev/*xt1b
crw-r--r-- 1 root      bin        84, 17 Dec  4 1984  /dev/rxt1b
brw-r--r-- 1 root      bin        73, 17 Nov  8 20:33 /dev/xt1b
$
```

Although the ownership and permissions of the /src directory have been carefully set, the device that this file system is mounted on is readable by anyone. Therefore, *anyone* can write a program to read the device, extract the inode information, and read any file he wants! If the disk device is writable by anyone, then *anyone* can do what he wants to the entire file system. This can range from wiping it out to changing permissions and SUID bits on any file. Method of protection: all entries in /dev pertaining to disks should be mode 600 and owned by root.

Overly Intelligent Terminals

Modern CRT terminals are able to do much work on their own. A short sequence of control characters can be sent to a terminal to make it delete or insert a line, position the cursor, and so on (see Chapter 10 on terminals). Thus, writing screen-oriented text editors and other programs is relatively easy.

Unfortunately, many such terminals also make it easy for bad guys. For example, the following command line forces a Wyse 50 terminal to transmit the command `rm -r *` to the computer:

```
echo "\0338rm -r *\0339\033s"
```

If this command is typed by a bad guy and *redirected to your terminal*, the computer will think that *you* typed the `rm` command and will merrily begin removing all your files. The bad guy can even send the "lock keyboard" command to your terminal, preventing you from halting the runaway command. Instead of removing your files, he can send a series of commands that give him a `sushi` program owned by you.

Naturally, if you are root when this trick is sprung on you, the results will be even worse. Method of protection: if you use a terminal that can be forced to transmit information to the host computer by a code sequence (most can), the only defense is to disable other users and processes from writing to your *tty* line. The simplest way to do this is to execute the command

```
mesg n
```

when you log in (from your `.profile` or `.cshrc` file). This has the unfortunate side effect of preventing interterminal communications through the `write` command.

Handy Shell Programs

These scripts do not guarantee security but are offered as a starting point from which you can expand. If you have such scripts, periodic checks of your system will not be as much of a chore as hand checking. You might consider using `crontab` to keep your security checking regular.

checksecure

This program should be run by cron as root, as often as you think necessary for your installation. checksecure will send you information by mail on setuid programs owned by root and on programs in root's execution path that may be written by others:

```
find / -user root -perm -4000 -exec ls -l {} \;                    \
      ¦ mail root # setuid
find `echo $PATH ¦ tr ":" " "` -perm -0002 -exec ls -l {} \; \
      ¦ mail root # writable
```

Here is the sample output:

```
From root bin 14488 Oct 13 1983 /usr/lib/lpd
-rwsrwsr-x 1 root  bin    15490 Mar 15 1984      /usr/lib/atrun
-rwsr-x--- 1 root  news    9012 Sep 14 00:57     /usr/lib/news/mapsh
---s--s--x 1 root  uucp   28012 Mar  8 1984      /usr/lib/uucp/xqt
-rwsrwxr-x 1 root  bin    16838 Dec 16 1983      /usr/lib/jobdaemon
-rwsrwsr-x 1 root  bin    38234 Jul 23 1984      /usr/lib/lpadmin
-rwsrwsr-x 1 root  bin    13020 Jul 23 1984      /usr/lib/lpshut
-rwsrwsr-x 1 root  bin    29790 Nov 28 1984      /usr/lib/lpsched
-rwsr-xr-x 1 root  bin    23928 Jun 28 1984      /usr/lib/ex3.6recover
-rwsr-xr-x 1 root  bin    17468 Jun 28 1984      /usr/lib/ex3.6preserve
---s--x--x 1 root  bin    14804 Mar  7 1984      /usr/bin/uulog
-rwsr-xr-x 1 root  bin    22512 Mar 10 1984      /usr/bin/mail
-rwsr-xr-x 1 root  bin    19082 Dec  3 1984      /bin/login
-rwsr-xr-x 1 root  bin     5768 Dec  3 1984      /bin/mkdir
-rwsr-xr-x 1 root  bin    12078 Dec  3 1984      /bin/passwd
-rwsrwxr-x 1 root  bin     6170 Dec  3 1984      /bin/rmdir
-rwsr-xr-x 1 root  bin    15588 Dec  3 1984      /bin/su
-rwsr-sr-x 3 root  uucp   29974 Dec  4 1984      /bin/mail
-rwsrwsr-x 2 root  sys    22176 Dec  4 1984      /bin/lp
```

The output can be saved in a hidden file owned by root with mode 600, and run through diff with each new invocation of checksecure to look for changes, which will probably be real threats.

sticky

Similar to checksecure, sticky finds all files on the system with the sticky bit set:

```
find / -perm -1000 -exec ls -l {} \;    \
      ¦ mail root # sticky bit
```

```
From root Tue Sep 24 23:06 EDT 1985
-rwxr-xr-t 3 bin     sys     131078 Feb 15  1985 ex
-rwxr-xr-t 3 bin     sys     131078 Feb 15  1985 vi
-rwxr-xr-t 3 bin     sys     131078 Feb 15  1985 view
-rwsr-sr-t 2 news    news     63558 Dec 22  1984 inews
-rwsr-sr-t 2 news    news     63558 Dec 22  1984 rnews
```

Note that only two programs were actually found because each link
shows up separately. (ex, vi, and view are actually the same program, as are
inews and rnews.)

mall

This is a cute one-liner. Just as wall writes a message to everyone on the
system, mall mails a message to everyone on the system:

```
mail `cut -f1 -d: /etc/passwd`
```

Unfortunately, this has the side effect of generating mail for every
separate login entry, including uucp logins and administrative logins that
are generally forwarded to root.

syssnoop

syssnoop monitors user activity. It executes once a week, getting the
system's (System III's) user accounting and disk usage data:

```
#                       syssnoop
# a program for weekly system usage statistical gathering
#                   bh hunter 12:12:83
#
> /tmp/tmp.$$
df >> /tmp/tmp.$$
echo >> /tmp/tmp.$$
disku -ams ¦ sort -rn >> /tmp/tmp.$$
echo "                    BLOCKS / USER" >> /tmp/tmp.$$
disku -adtsm >> /tmp/tmp.$$
echo >> /tmp/tmp.$$
disku -ams ¦  awk '{sum = sum + $1}
END {print "total system file blocks ", sum}' >> /tmp/tmp.$$
echo >> /tmp/tmp.$$
echo "                    USER ACCOUNTING" >> /tmp/tmp.$$
echo "user   dept   connect   #commands   cpu   records" \
 >> /tmp/tmp.$$
```

```
echo "id     no      time         issued        time   r or w'tn" \
 >> /tmp/tmp.$$
au ¦ sort -nr +5 -6 >> /tmp/tmp.$$
echo >> /tmp/tmp.$$
ac >> /tmp/tmp$$
lpr /tmp/tmp.$$
rm /tmp/tmp.$$
exit
```

The disku, au, and ac commands might not be available on many systems. You may need to delete them from your version of the security checking script.

The data output provides the system administrator with valuable disk usage and user information needed to plan his system administration activity for the following week.

By the way, a seasoned system administrator can also catch system abusers by reading the output of this script. Normal activity shows a balance of CPU time and disk I/O. If you find a correlation between high CPU time and high file activity, you probably have a busy user. If there is a disparity, the user may be making unauthorized or time-wasting use of the system. (Activity such as calculating *pi* to 10 places does not involve disk writes. Therefore, this activity shows as high CPU tasks with no disk I/O.) He merits watching.

Summary

Despite the many security features on UNIX, some of which are quite elaborate, you have seen that there are ways around most of them. Because UNIX was originally designed to help programmers share work together, you should not be too surprised.

When all is said and done, UNIX probably isn't any more insecure than other multiuser operating systems. In fact, many systems since the late 1980s are designed with very high levels of security. But no system is totally secure; it just has holes that haven't been found yet. Knowing the security problems of UNIX gives you a head start on the bad guys. It is up to you—with the understanding and cooperation of your users—to keep your system safe.

10

Terminals

erminals, the source of nearly all original data, are the windows to the system from the outside world. But quiet, polite CRT terminals were unknown to the original UNIX. It had a teletype instead. This slow, indestructible, oil-dripping, noisily clanking escapee from the Smithsonian was the only terminal available for most early computers, including the little PDP-7 that Ken Thompson used to give birth to his MULTICS variant, UNIX. In those days, programmers had to live with any terminal device that could be scrounged, begged, or borrowed. As a result, UNIX has a versatile terminal interface second to none, with provisions for all sorts of tty (*teletype*) oddities such as delays for formfeeds, tabs, carriage returns, and linefeeds.

This UNIX past affects us today. Imagine that you bought a terminal to attach to your UNIX system that emulates a VT100. All you have to do is attach the terminal by cable and "make it run." On most operating systems, this can be a trauma. Sometimes it involves writing an addition to the computer's Input/Output system in assembly language and recompiling the entire thing. Making a terminal talk to UNIX is nowhere near that difficult.

Few operating systems have as much versatility as UNIX in dealing with asynchronous serial devices (ports). For everyday devices such as terminals, teletypes, printers, and modems, UNIX provides device drivers which are so versatile that it is seldom necessary to write special drivers. In addition, UNIX provides a way to reset a device's characteristics dynamically. You can change characteristics "on the fly" if you have to.

UNIX System V Release 4 (SVR4) has changed the port management from previous releases. The behavior appears the same for the user, but the daemons and configuration structures are significantly different.

Screen Control

UNIX loves dumb terminals. The primary editor, ed, does not care what your terminal looks like; nor does vi's parent editor, ex. People, however, are not as fond of dumb terminals. People like Teletype 5420s, DEC VT102s, TeleVideo 950s, Wyse 60s, and just about everything else that costs more than $200 a tube. (Installing the *really* expensive tubes, X terminals, is discussed in Chapter 15.) Most people also prefer visual editors like vi, and software that requires character-mapped screens. All of this requires that the user's environment understand exactly what kind of terminal is being used or emulated. termcap is one special type of software that allows this information to be passed into the user environment.

termcap

termcap is one of Berkeley's finest contributions to UNIX. It enables programs that require screen control to have the information necessary to put the characters where you want to see them. To help a new user set up her initial environment, you may need to put a statement in her .profile or .login script, telling the shell what the terminal is. (Some systems have an /etc/ttytype file or can define the terminal type in /etc/inittab. In these cases, the default terminal is defined for each port.) First, you need to find out the termcap name for the terminal. Because you can spend all afternoon wading through the voluminous /etc/termcap file, put UNIX to work and have grep filter out the information for you:

```
$ grep vt100 /etc/termcap
d0¦vt100¦vt100-am¦vt100¦dec vt100:\
 :rf=/usr/lib/tabset/vt100:ku=\EOA:kd=\EOB:kr=\EOC:
d1¦vt100¦vt100-nam¦vt100 w/no am:\
 :am@:xn@:tc=vt100-am:
 :al=99\E[L:dl=99\E[M:ip=7:dc=7\E[P:ei=\E[4l:
di¦vt100-23¦vt100 for use with vt100sys:\
 :li#23:is=\E[1;23r\E[23;1H:tc=vt100-am:
dt¦vt100-w¦dec vt100 132 cols (w/advanced video):\
 :co#132:li#24:rs=\E>\E[?3h\E[?4l\E[?5l\E[?8h:tc=vt100-am:
dt¦vt100-w-nam¦dec vt100 132 cols (w/advanced video):\
 :co#132:li#24:rs=\E>\E[?3h\E[?4l\E[?5l\E[?8h:vt@:
vt100am:tc=vt100-am:
vt100nam:tc=vt100-nam:
vt100s:tc=vt100-s:
vt100w:tc=vt100-w:
```

You see? There is more than one way to skin a DEC.

Needless to say, `termcap` makes even the `/etc/passwd` file look simple. Essentially, `termcap` entries consist of coded actions or descriptions, followed by sequences of ASCII characters necessary to get the terminal to perform those actions. For example, here is a complete entry for a Cadmus graphics tube emulating a "normal" 24x80 terminal:

```
bi¦bip¦pcs bitmap:\
    :li#24:co#80:cl=\f:ho=\EH:sf=\ES:sr=\Es:\
    :sg#0:ug#0:pt:cm=\EM%r%+ %+ :\
    :so=\ER:se=\Er:us=\EU:ue=\Eu:cd=\EJ:ce=\EK:\
    :nd=\EC:do=\EB:up=\EA:bs:am:al=\EO:dl=\EX:
```

The first two items show the number of lines and columns, respectively (24 by 80, remember?). The next item (`cl`, for clear screen) tells a program that sending a formfeed character (Ctrl-L, often written as `\f`) will clear the screen. Following this is `ho` (home cursor or move it to the top left position), which can be performed by sending *escape* code (notated as `\E`) followed by H. Need we interpret the entire entry?

At least one entire book has been written about creating and maintaining `termcap` entries (see the Bibliography in this book), so we can just begin to give you a flavor of what is involved.

If all this looks too complex, get a programmer to do any necessary `termcap` maintenance for you. Try to avoid extra work whenever possible. If a new terminal appears on your system, look through the `termcap` file for others of the same brand. Often a company will use the same control sequences from model to model. Failing that, see whether the terminal will emulate an already existing `termcap` entry. At worst, you will have to read the `termcap` documentation in Section 5 (F) of the manuals if you want to craft your own `termcap` entry.

Now you can put this information to use by setting up a `.profile` that allows for three different kinds of terminals on the system. The ports are fixed (the terminals will not move from port to port). By knowing which port the user is on, the system will know what kind of terminal the user has, as you can see from the following profile:

```
TTY=`tty`
if [ "$TTY" = /dev/tty0 ]
then
        TERM=vt100
elif [ "$TTY" = /dev/tty1 ]
        TERM=tv910
*else
        TERM=viewpoint
```

```
fi
PATH=:/bin:/usr/bin:/usr/local:.
HOME=/home/joanna
EXINIT="set wrapmargin=10 autoindent"
export TERM HOME EXINIT PATH
```

If the user is on port 0, she is on a DEC VT100. On port 1, she is on a TeleVideo 910. At any other port, including the console, she is on an Adds Viewpoint terminal. This type of program is especially handy for dial-up lines, when you work from home on a terminal unlike the one in your office.

Notice that a set of commands is passed into the environment to set up the visual editor, vi. This particular EXINIT environment variable tells vi (and ex) to set wraparound at 10 characters from the left of the screen limit and keep the auto indent feature on. But most important is the TERM variable. If it is not exported into the environment, it will not take effect, and programs will not know what to do. On some systems, you may also have to export the location of the termcap file:

```
TERMCAP=/etc/termcap
export TERMCAP
```

On some systems, you won't have to go to these extremes to specify which type of terminal is attached to which port. For example, on SCO UNIX systems, the file /etc/ttytype defines the terminal.

terminfo

termcap seemed irreplaceable until AT&T introduced terminfo in System V Release 2. terminfo is a termcap work-alike, but it is much larger and better organized in many ways. It is located in /usr/lib/terminfo. There is a directory for each letter of the alphabet, and for each number 1 through 9. The quick way to find a terminal is to go to the directory that starts with the number or letter corresponding to your terminal. Use the model name, not the name of the manufacturer. Suppose that you are looking for an Adds Viewpoint:

```
$ ls /usr/lib/terminfo/v ¦ grep view
viewpoint
$
```

terminfo works with the curses(3x) library. You can create your own entries and modify existing ones, but the actual files are not text files that you can edit like termcap. For speed in loading, terminfo files are compiled down to a binary data file. The command for compiling terminfo source files into the binaries is tic.

Hardware Installation—
From Theory to Reality

There are two sides to installing computer hardware: the hardware side (making cables and setting switches) and the software side (entering data on /etc/ttys or inittab and setting other characteristics with stty). Large computer installations usually have many hardware engineers, so the system administrator handles only the software portion of installing hardware. However, if you are on a smaller UNIX installation or if you have your own UNIX machine at home, eventually you are going to have to come to grips with the hardware. Besides, at smaller computer sites, you may be expected to do some hardware installation on the machine, as well as perform your system administration tasks.

This section applies some of what is covered in this chapter and in Appendix B, "The RS-232 Blues," to a real-life situation. Talking in general terms about /etc/ttys, inittab, and stty is one thing, but actually installing a terminal is quite another story. Here you are going to "install" a terminal on a UNIX system, with ample discussion provided along the way.

Before starting, you should remember three informal hardware installation rules:

1. Most terminals are default-set at 9600 baud. If, however, your system is heavily loaded, keep the console at 9600 baud and slow the other terminals down to 4800 or less so that the system "appears" more responsive.

2. Some devices, such as modems, set themselves. A 300-baud modem is 300 baud, but a 300/1200/2400/9600-baud incoming modem may operate at any one of those speeds. This is a job for gettydefs or for the modem's setup registers. SVR4 uses /etc/ttydefs instead of gettydefs. This system administration file is more easily accessed through the sysadm menus and input screens than through direct editing.

3. Printer baud rates depend on the speed a printer is able to receive. You usually set it a little faster than the printer can receive *unless* you don't have hardware handshaking, in which case you set it a little slower.

Imagine that you just picked up a Liberty 50 terminal for $150 at a computer flea market. As you take it out of your car and bring it into the house, the sweet success of getting a bargain begins to turn into concern. How much work is required to interface this terminal to your UNIX system?

Before you look in the hardware manual, don't forget to look at the back of the terminal, because only on rare occasions are the switch settings explained in detail on the back. Fortunately, the Liberty 50 is one of those few terminals that has labels for the dip switches. The switch settings that change line speed, and hardware and software handshaking are among the things listed there.

Generally, terminals are default-set at 9600 baud. Most UNIX systems are default-set at 9600 when they come out of the box. UNIX is a full duplex ASCII system that uses newlines without returns (no carriage return/linefeed pairs). You are safe to assume that the switch settings you want are full duplex with auto linefeed off. (Refer to your hardware manual.) stty does not default to xon-xoff protocol for nonlogin ports, nor is it very fussy about parity. So set parity off. You have a choice of either 8 data bits transmission with 1 stop bit, or 7 with 2. It's a coin toss. Using 7 guarantees that the characters received and sent are in the ASCII set.

Now review the plan:

- Baud rate 9600

- Parity off

- Duplex full

- Auto lf off

- Data bits 7

- Stop bits 2

This is all the information you need in order to initialize the port and set characteristics.

With confidence high, you expect to have the terminal installed shortly. Unfortunately, your confidence dwindles when you try to find a Liberty 50 in termcap or terminfo. It isn't there. Fortunately, the good point about inexpensive terminals is that they are almost always emulators. The manual for the Liberty terminal shows that it emulates a number of common terminals recognized by termcap. One of the emulation modes in termcap is TeleVideo 910. If you have terminfo instead of termcap, you may not even find the TeleVideo 910, but the Liberty emulates the Hazeltine 1420 also, so look for that in terminfo. Put the TERM information in the .profile of the users using that port, or modify the /etc/inittab or /etc/ttytype file.

The next logical step is to "sex" the terminal. Common sense tells you that a terminal should be a DTE (Data Terminal Equipment), but you can't always rely on the common sense of hardware manufacturers. For example, DEC uses male connectors on the back of its VT series instead of the standard female connectors. Now you need a spirit of adventure, a lot of patience, and a breakout box. Use Hunter's $1.98 pin tester if you have nothing else (see Appendix B). To sex the terminal, test pins 2 and 3 against pin 7. A DTE has pin 2 asserted low— otherwise, pin 3 will be low (making it a DCE instead). Test the computer the same way. Chances are that it will be a DCE with pin 3 low, but you never know unless you have tested it before.

If you have a conventional marriage (DTE on one and DCE on the other), you may be able to use a straight ribbon cable, 25 wires, all pins in. If this is the case, consider yourself lucky. Unfortunately, cabling is hardly ever this easy. The more sophisticated the terminal and the fussier the computer, the longer cabling is going to take. Attach 25-wire ribbon cables to both the computer and the terminal with a breakout box in the middle. Suppose that the Liberty shows pin 2 low (DTE), and pins 4 (ready to send) and 20 (data terminal ready) high. It is telling you that it's a male (DTE) and ready to go. DTR and RTS set high provides a good source of positive voltage if the computer needs a signal source. The smaller AT&T 3B computers need pins 5 and 6 pulled up, so pin 4 on the Liberty is a good source. A machine set up for easy cabling, such as the Codata 3300, is no problem—a 3-wire (2 to 2, 3 to 3, 7 to 7) cable does just fine.

Once you have your cable made, you need to get the computer ready to talk to the terminal. This is part of the software end of hardware installation. Go into /etc and set up the /etc/ttys file (old UNIX and XENIX) or /etc/inittab for the new terminal. The baud rate is 9600, and you want to spawn a getty (ttymon if you have SVR4). Pick an unused port by number. If the computer is a Codata running System III and port 4 is open, the /etc/ttys entry is

    1dtty4

If the computer is a 3B2/300 and port 4 is open on board 1, the entry in inittab is

    14:2:respawn:/etc/getty tty14 9600

To get the system to recognize the new port setting, type **init q** in System V. If you have an SCO UNIX or a XENIX system, you must execute

    # **enable tty4a**

or an equivalent for the appropriate port.

Back to the hardware end. You still have a little more testing to do before you can complete your cable. The easiest way is to borrow a functioning cable from another terminal port, but assume (for this example) that this is your first. With a getty waiting patiently for a terminal to talk to, start jumpering the breakout box. With both pieces of equipment being sexed opposite (DCE to DTE), pins 2 and 3 are straight across. The ground pins, 1 (if used) and 7, are straight across as well. If both pieces of equipment are of the same sex, a null modem (pins 3 to 2, 2 to 3) is necessary. If these 3-wire connections are sufficient (as they are 90 percent of the time), the `login:` message appears on the terminal. If no login message appears, it's "dart board and common sense" time. Pin 4 (RTS) on the Liberty is ready to do assertion for the asking. Jumper it on the breakout box to pins 5 and/or 6 on the computer. This should get the desired results and bring on the login message. Should this fail, continue bringing up signal pins (4, 8, and 20) until data flows. Once you get your login, put your cable together, and you are in business.

Back to the software part of hardware installation. Now you need to make an entry in the user's `.profile` or `.login` file for the terminal type so that `vi` can work. If you have `termcap`, ask it what it thinks about 910s:

```
$ grep 910 /etc/termcap
v0|tvi910|910|televideo910:\
$
```

It will tell you that `termcap` calls your new terminal a `v0`.

Try the same trick on System V.2+ by asking `terminfo` to talk about the Hazeltine 1420:

```
$ ls /usr/lib/terminfo/h | grep 1420
h1420
```

The Hazeltine emulation is OK, so set the emulation switches for the 1420 and go for it.

Summary

The UNIX system has enough versatility with `ttys` or `inittab`, with `stty`, and with `termcap` or `terminfo` to handle just about anything in the way of terminals or other asynchronous serial devices. The complexity lies in the property descriptions of the hundreds of different terminals and display devices, but a little familiarity with these files and commands goes a long way toward interfacing with the world.

11

Printers

Once your system is running smoothly and your users start working, someone will want to print a file. If your system is like most other systems, each user doesn't have the luxury of a CRT terminal with a printer attached. You probably have just one or two printers for all your users. As administrator, you have an immediate problem: how do you hook up a printer so that it can be used? You will quickly discover that your next problem is how to prevent two people from using one printer at the same time. Before you handle these problems, though, you must get your printers running.

Getting Your Printers Running

The user and the system administrator deal with the printer from different perspectives. To the user, invoking the printer seems simple, whether with Version 7 and BSD's lpr command, or with System V's lp command. In either case, the nomenclature (lp and lpr) refers to a *line printer*, which can range from an inexpensive dot-matrix printer that prints one character at a time to a very large, expensive laser printer that prints an entire page at a time. A user sends a file to the printer with one of two possible commands:

```
$ lpr filename                          — Version 7, BSD
$ lp filename                           — System V and later
```

Although these two commands accomplish the same results, the internals of lp and lpr are quite different.

As a UNIX system administrator, you get to see the hidden complexities involved when dealing with the printer. Although pre-System V UNIX versions handle only a single printer per system, System V can run several different printers, even different printer types, on the same computer. Yet in neither case does the file go directly to the printer. Instead, the file is intercepted and managed by a software mechanism known as a spooler. (SPOOL is an acronym for *S*imultaneous *P*eripheral *O*perations *O*n-*L*ine.) This chapter presents an overview of the spooler for Version 7/BSD and then for System V.

What Is a Spooler?

Daisywheel printers and many dot-matrix printers have an effective character transmission rate of 120 characters per second (CPS) or less. In order for you to use the printer, you must have direct access to that printer for as long as it takes to print your file. In other words, the printer port has to belong to you as owner of the process, or you must have write permission for it. Whenever you have to get character transmission out to a relatively slow device such as a printer, you must wait for the transmission to complete before your terminal is free for other tasks. What you want to be able to do is free up your terminal so that you don't have to get old waiting for the printer to finish printing your file! Of course, on UNIX you can simply put the process in the background. But suppose that your system has one printer and four users, all of whom start writing to the printer at once. You guessed it—everybody's output appears jumbled together on the same sheet of paper.

Here's where the spooler comes in. A *spooler* is a mechanism for buffering or storing data on its way to a specific destination. The purpose of a printer spooler is to hold files to be printed until the line printer is ready to receive and process those files. When the printer command (lpr or lp) is used, each file to be printed is transmitted to the printer spool buffer. The file is held there until the spooler program senses that the printer is free; at that time, the spooler program sends the file, one character at a time, to the printer. The end result of all this is that the spooler does all the printing and device management, which leaves you free to do something else. On UNIX, spooling is done by copying the data to be printed into a spool area on the disk (/usr/spool/lp) and then using a daemon to print the spooled data.

What Is a Daemon?

Daemon is the fanciful name given to a program that emerges to do your bidding when it's needed, and then disappears, as if by magic. In the case of the printer spooler (pre-System V), lpr sends its input to the /usr/spool/lpd directory, which then causes /usr/lib/lpd (sometimes found as /etc/lpd instead) to be activated. /usr/lib/lpd is the *line printer daemon* that does nothing except go to its assigned directory (/usr/spool/lpd) and send every file it finds there to the file (or device) called /dev/lp, and then the daemon disappears.

On System V and later versions, the daemon is lpsched, which runs continuously in the background, waiting for files to be fed to it by lp so that it can schedule and pass them on to another program, one at a time. The various spooler control and filter files reside in the directory tree starting at /usr/spool/lp.

Attaching a Serial Printer to the System

Before you look at some of the specifics of UNIX printer internals, you should know how to hook up a printer, tell the system that the printer is there, and test the printer.

The first thing you do when putting a printer on the system is to find an open port for the device. Older systems use serial interfaces for printers, in which case it's generally best to put the printer on the last port of the I/O card, where it has the lowest priority on the computer's interrupt structures. The reason is that the printer will probably be the slowest peripheral on your system, and you want it to use as little of the system resources as possible. If the I/O card has 8 ports, the printer port is 07, since numbering typically starts from 00. In a perfect world, the physical connection is an easy attachment of ribbon cable with male DB-25 connectors between the computer and the printer, and with the printer baud rate set to something reasonable for both the printer and the computer. If the printer runs at 200 characters per second (CPS), a baud rate of 1200—about 120 CPS—does not use the printer's full speed. Baud rates *over* 2400 make the computer wait for the printer most of the time. 2400 is the only *reasonable* baud rate in this situation. The rule of thumb is this: CPS = baud rate divided by 10.

Unfortunately, connecting a serial printer is not usually that easy, although in theory all that is needed to make a printer print is one wire from pin 2 (data send) of the computer hooked to pin 3 (data receive) of the printer, and a logic ground on pin 7; problems arise when the computer considers itself Data Terminal Equipment (DTE) and/or the printer considers itself Data Communications Equipment (DCE). Other problems occur when devices that need special pins (like clear-to-send) are enabled. These problems are beyond the scope of this chapter, so see Appendix B, "The RS-232 Blues."

Once you have selected a printer port, you need to get the system to recognize that port as a printer port when the system comes up. If the port is marked port 07 on the back of the computer, it is probably known as /dev/tty7, /dev/serial07, or something along that line—UNIX systems generally treat any serial device attached to the I/O card as a tty device. Go to your /dev directory and see whether you already have a printer device defined as a serial port. If you do, and you take a look at a long listing of /dev/lp and the /dev/tty files, you may notice that both /dev/tty7 and /dev/lp have the same major and minor device numbers—for example, 4 and 7:

```
$ ls -l /dev/lp /dev/tty*

crw-------  2   daemon    4,  7 Dec 2 10:24   /dev/lp
crw-rw-rw-  1   root      1,  0 Nov 19 1982   /dev/tty
crw-------  1   root      4,  0 Dec 2 08:49   /dev/tty0
crw--w--w-  1   bruce     4,  1 Dec 2 12:33   /dev/tty1
crw-------  1   root      4,  2 Dec 2 08:49   /dev/tty2
crw-------  1   root      4,  3 Dec 2 08:49   /dev/tty3
crw-------  1   root      4,  4 Dec 2 08:49   /dev/tty4
crw-------  1   root      4,  5 Dec 2 08:49   /dev/tty5
crw-------  1   root      4,  6 Dec 2 08:49   /dev/tty6
crw-------  2   daemon    4,  7 Dec 2 10:24   /dev/tty7
```

This means that both device names have the same driver and port. In fact, they are simply different names for the same device. Notice also the ownership of these files. /dev/lp belongs to the printer daemon. Because the daemon owns and runs the printer, this is a sure indication that the system is ready to deal with lpr, lpd, and /dev/lp as a continuous series of "devices" that takes a file from the print command lpr to the physical printer. (As a general rule, if you have a /dev/lp entry defined as a device, with major and minor nodes, and its nodes do *not* match those of any tty devices on your system, it's probably a Centronics printer device. If you are using a serial printer, rename /dev/lp to /dev/Centronics to save it for future use.)

Creating two different names for the same device is a useful system administration technique. You use this technique for two reasons: fooling the system software and making life easier for yourself. Suppose that someone sells you an old Version 7 system with poor documentation, and there's no /dev/lp device on it. You attempt to use the spooler, having plugged a serial printer into /dev/tty7 as suggested:

```
$ lpr /etc/group
/etc/lpd: cannot open /dev/lp
```

Now what? You don't even *have* a /dev/lp. (If you had run this as the superuser, you would have created a *file* called /dev/lp, which would have silently collected all the output destined for the printer until the disk filled and your system crashed!) Well, because *your* printer is on **tty7**, all you do is this:

```
# ln /dev/tty7 /dev/lp
# ls -l /dev/tty7 /dev/lp
crw-rw-rw- 2    daemon    bin 13, 7 Nov 15 21:12  /dev/tty7
crw-rw-rw- 2    daemon    bin 13, 7 Nov 15 21:12  /dev/lp
#
```

Making the link (ln) between tty7 and lp means that they are exactly the same file (in this case, device). Now when you write to /dev/lp, you also write to /dev/tty7, and the output goes to your printer with no one the wiser. "No one" in this case includes your spooler program, which has no other way of knowing how to reach the real printer.

Is this the "right" way to do things? You bet it is! What would happen if you had the full source code to UNIX? You would proudly go to the directory with the source code for the spooler program, find the line that said /dev/lp, change it to /dev/tty7, recompile the program, and install the new version. Apart from the fact that this would take you at least 25 times longer than just making the link, it doesn't help you when you have to change ports for some reason or install a new word processing program that wants to write to /dev/lp. By standardizing /dev/lp as the name for the system default printer, you can always make sure that /dev/lp addresses the real working printer on your system by linking it to the correct serial port.

You should use this same technique for each individual printer you have. (But first be sure that these device names don't already exist!) You can easily forget which of your printers is actually /dev/lp if you have three of them, but not if you make links for each printer name:

```
crw-rw-r-- 4    lp    bin    13,  5 Nov 15 21:12  /dev/lp
crw-rw-r-- 4    lp    bin    13,  5 Nov 15 21:12  /dev/lp0
crw-rw-r-- 4    lp    bin    13,  5 Nov 15 21:12  /dev/oki
crw-rw-r-- 4    lp    bin    13,  5 Nov 15 21:12  /dev/tty21
crw-rw-r-- 3    lp    other  13,  6 Nov 15 21:17  /dev/diablo
crw-rw-r-- 3    lp    other  13,  6 Nov 15 21:17  /dev/il
crw-rw-r-- 3    lp    other  13,  6 Nov 15 21:17  /dev/tty22
crw-rw-r-- 2    lp    other  13,  7 Nov 15 21:17  /dev/epson
crw-rw-r-- 2    lp    other  13,  7 Nov 15 21:17  /dev/tty23
```

You should also do this for your other devices. Add a `/dev/modem` link to your outgoing modem line, and add `/dev/tape` and `/dev/floppy` to those strange devices called `/dev/mt0` and `/dev/fdsk0`.

To make a `tty` port safe for printers, you first make sure that logins (actually, `gettys`) to all the printer ports have been disabled, as explained in Chapter 10 on terminals. The kernel's character device switch accesses a device driver that is usually intended for a terminal, but as mentioned earlier, the UNIX kernel is written so that `tty`-related commands can also work with printers.

Next, you make sure that each printer port has the correct characteristics, such as baud rate and tab expansion. If these are not provided for in your UNIX distribution, you must do the job yourself. It should be done at system startup from either `/etc/rc` or from another program called by `/etc/rc`, such as `lpset`. The `lpset` file usually contains a delay statement (such as `sleep 5`), which is used to give the system time to act on commands remaining in the background from `init` and `rc`, and an `stty` command. `stty` is used here to set up the characteristics for the printer port on the computer. Note a sample `/etc/lpset` file:

```
sleep 5
stty 300 -raw -echo -nl tabs ixon ixany nl0 cr0 < /dev/lp
stty 1200 -raw -echo -nl tabs ixon ixany nl0 cr0 < /dev/tty6
```

The redirection (`<`) may seem backward, but `stty` affects only the `stdin` of devices.

Each `/dev` entry that supports a printer on a `tty` port must have an `stty` command, as illustrated here. Although it may seem more efficient to do the initialization from `/etc/rc`, it is better to do it from a separate file, like `lpset`, in order to keep the internal details isolated.

Attaching a Parallel Printer to the System

Centronics parallel printer ports are found on most modern systems. In many ways, a Centronics parallel port is less difficult to work with than a serial port because all the protocols and pins are predefined. The port name for the parallel port in `/dev` is generally self-descriptive (as in `/dev/lp`, `/dev/centronics`, or `/dev/parallel`). Cabling is a matter of buying a Centronics parallel cable with the necessary combination of male and female fittings (these usually cannot be longer than 50 feet). Of course, you must hook the cable up to a printer (or plotter) with a Centronics parallel interface. No baud rates have to be set; just plug it in and go.

Printer Troubleshooting

Testing a newly installed printer can be a suspenseful experience. Make it easy on yourself by simplifying the process at first. You can test that you have the correct port by redirecting the output of some command to the port to which you think you are connected. Note the following example:

```
# ls /etc > /dev/lp
```

Don't concern yourself with what the output looks like, just that you get output. Print spooler programs will include operations to ensure that the proper sequence of CRs (carriage returns) and NLs (newlines) are sent to the printer. This is a test that you have the correct port and that the cable and printer are properly connected. By sending the output directly to the port, you bypass the lp (or lpr) command. If the output on the printer doesn't match what you get on your screen when you do an

```
# ls /etc
```

several things may have happened and should be corrected either by reconfiguring your printer or the port, or by modifying the printer device script for that printer. (These scripts are discussed in "Writing Printer Interface Programs" later in this chapter.) Here are some possible problems:

- Double-spaced output

  UNIX separates each line of text with a newline character—an ASCII linefeed (LF), hex code 0a. Some operating systems use a pair of characters—a carriage return (ASCII CR, hex code 0d) followed by a linefeed—and the printer may have been set accordingly. Your printer will almost surely have a switch, usually labeled Auto LF or CR/LF, to take care of this condition. Check the manual for your printer; sometimes the switch is internal or on a separate serial interface card. If you cannot find such a switch, you can fix the problem with software. Try different stty settings, using flags such as onlcr or nl (and their negations -onlcr and -nl) in combination, if necessary, until the output is correct. Then incorporate the final settings in your printer interface script or lpset file.

- Output all on one line

  This problem is simply the opposite of the preceding one: the printer refuses to recognize an LF code unless it is preceded by a CR. Just find the switch and flip it the other way.

- Garbage output

  If sending a text file to the printer produces strange graphics or
  alien names or causes the paper to feed without printing, and you
  have a serial printer connection, the baud rate of the printer does
  not match the serial port. Check the settings, recycle power to the
  printer if you have changed any settings, and try again. If you still
  get garbage, go to the next section, "Real Devices and Fooling
  `stty`." If you get garbage on a parallel connection, your printer is
  not configured for the ASCII character set.

- Missing output

  Suppose that you test the printer by sending it a short file, but later
  you find that longer printouts have some missing or garbled text.
  Most likely, the computer is sending data to the printer too fast. Go
  to the section "Handshaking" later in this chapter.

- No output

  You may have sent the output to the wrong port, but check the
  following:

Printer switch settings	Printer turned on and plugged in? Paper in printer properly? If serial connection: Baud rate OK? Parity off? Seven data bits, not eight?
Computer settings	Does daemon (or `lp` for System V) have write permission for `/dev/lp`? If serial connection: Baud rate OK? Parity off? Seven data bits, not eight? Is `/dev/lp` linked to the port into which the printer is plugged? Try substituting a working terminal for the printer (set the terminal baud rate to match). Has the `getty` been disabled on the printer port?
Cable	Is the cable (or cable adapter) right for the printer? Did you try a terminal cable? Does the printer need extra pins hooked up?

Real Devices and Fooling *stty*

Generally, everything goes as advertised. The printers and terminals are plugged in, the baud rates are set, and everyone can start working. But sometimes peculiarities about certain computers, devices, cables, serial ports, or even software releases cause headaches for the new or unwary administrator.

One example may be found on some computers running early versions of System V. Suppose that you have a printer plugged into port tty23, and it's set to 1200 baud. You carefully make sure that its inittab entry is also set to 1200 baud and doesn't force a login on that line. Now you bring the system up. You send a file to the printer and get a long stream of garbage. After checking the baud rate on the printer itself, you attempt to verify that the port is indeed set to 1200 baud:

```
# stty < /dev/tty23
speed 9600 baud; -parity
brkint -inpck icrnl -ixany ixoff onlcr tab3
echo echoe echok
#
```

What's wrong? It turns out that when System V doesn't have a tty open, it attempts to reset that tty line to some default setting. So you have to fool stty by holding the line open while the system comes up. The following shell script has worked when other simpler ones have failed. It may look like magic, but if this is your problem, give it a try:

```
while true
do
 (sleep 60 >/dev/tty23;\
 stty clocal -echo 1200 -parity ixon -ixany tab3 opost \
 < /dev/tty23; \
 chmod 666 /dev/tty23) &
 sleep 10 >/dev/tty23
 stty clocal -echo 1200 -parity ixon -ixany tab3 opost \
 </dev/tty23
 sleep 32767 >/dev/tty23
done
```

We call our version `set_baud` and run it from `/etc/rc` with a line like this:

```
nohup set_baud &
```

Naturally, make sure to substitute the name of *your* port for `/dev/tty23`.

Handshaking

If you hook a printer rated at an honest 120 CPS to a 1200-baud line, you should be able to send data to it all day without dropping a letter. But suppose that you buy a fancy new line printer that goes 800 CPS. Plug it into a 9600-baud serial port, and 960 characters per second will pour out of that port. Even if your printer has a 4 KB buffer, disaster will strike in less than 30 seconds as all of the extra characters leak out of the cable onto the floor.

The way to prevent this problem is to have the printer tell the computer, "Slow down, please, I'm getting rather full." The technical term for this is *handshaking*, because both the computer and the printer must agree on how to accomplish it. Two methods are possible on UNIX, one based on hardware and the other on software.

Hardware handshaking is the best way to prevent printer overflow. (In parallel communications, handshaking is built-in.) The computer may not respond fast enough to software handshaking when heavily loaded, but hardware can physically force it to stop sending characters. With serial ports, the usual way to do this is with the RTS (pin 4) and CTS (pin 5) lines (see Appendix B). You will have to check the manual for your printer and also verify that your computer supports these handshaking lines. Many computers do *not* support any RS-232 lines other than the few basic ones necessary to transmit data. Other computers have full RS-232 support on just one or two ports, usually reserved for modems. If that is your case, you are probably better off using software handshaking, because the modems need full control more than the printers do.

Software handshaking on UNIX is simple, at least in theory, because every `tty` line is set up to recognize the ubiquitous XON/XOFF protocol. (A note for trivia buffs: XON/XOFF stands for external device *on/off* and was used on teletype machines to start and stop the paper tape reader.) XON/XOFF, sometimes called flow control, is what you are using when you press Ctrl-S (really the ASCII XOFF or DC3 code) at your terminal to temporarily halt data from coming to your screen. Pressing Ctrl-Q (ASCII XON or DC1) resumes the flow of data.

In a similar way, most serial printers automatically (or at the flip of the appropriate switch) send XOFF to the computer when their input buffers are getting full, and send XON when the buffers are almost empty and sending data is again safe. The trick is to get UNIX to honor the protocol. You can do that in the file where you initialize your printers by adding the modes -ixon, -ixoff, and -ixany to your stty line.

Don't try to enable *both* hardware and software handshaking at the same time. Some device is liable to get confused. If you have a UNIX Version 7 system, you will almost always *have* to use the hardware handshaking or lower your baud rate; XON/XOFF was not part of stty back then. The exceptions are systems on which the tandem mode was added to stty; this specifically enables XON/XOFF.

Testing the Spooler

If the printer was functional when you sent the data directly to it, but the command line

```
# lc /etc ¦ lp
```

doesn't work, look in /usr/spool/lp for the answer. (Pipe to lpr for spoolers on BSD and before System V.) Data and lock files should exist and be readable by daemon. If the printer installation is new, your cup of problems runneth over. Before you enter the software maze of print spoolers, check all your hardware settings and port settings once again; be sure that the connection works *without* the spooler.

Version 7 and Early BSD *lpr* Spooler Internals

The spool directory in which Version 7 and System III print-output files are stored is called /usr/spool/lpd. (Although the print spooler of modern BSD systems is also called lpr, it is considerably different from these early versions. The modern BSD spooler is not covered here because the focus of this book is UNIX V Release 4.) This is an ordinary directory, and when no user printer requests are present, it is quite empty. When a printer request is made, such as

```
# cat /etc/rc ¦ lpr
#
```

the output created by the list command is sent to a file in the /usr/spool/lpd directory and stored with a unique alphanumeric combination *file* name like cf00084. Another file is created as well; it is a lock file and has no permissions. The purpose of the lock file is to retain the exclusive use of a device (in this case, a printer) for one user (in this case, the printer daemon). Using a lock file prevents such conflicts as your code listing becoming intertwined with someone else's strudel recipe. A directory listing of /usr/spool/lpd looks like this while the print job is running:

```
$ ls -l /usr/spool/lpd
total 26
-rw-r--r-- 1  bruce          13080  Dec 2 10:24  cf00084
-rw-r--r-- 1  bruce             50  Dec 2 10:24  df00084
---------- 1  daemon             0  Dec 2 10:24  lock
$
```

The df00084 file is a "data file" that tells the spooler the name of the user who requested the printout and what file to print. The daemon owns the lock file because it actually does the printing.

When the file to be printed is finally sent to the printer, the print file, data file, and lock file are removed from /usr/spool/lpd, and the printer is free to print something else. Usually, all goes well with this arrangement, and there is nothing for the system administrator to do but enjoy a well-thought-out system. Occasionally, something does go wrong, and you have to open the hood on the spooler, look inside, and fix it.

Imagine a scenario in which a user sends a file to the printer and suddenly realizes that the file is not the one he wanted to send. It is 60 pages long, so it could tie up the system's only printer for a long time. When a process is in deep trouble, the first thing you usually do is type ps (process status command) to get the process identification number. Then you issue a kill on the process. In this scenario, however, a kill stops the printer, but the problem is far from being solved. In fact, *you are in worse trouble than ever*, because the next request to the printer spooler fails to produce the expected results—namely, a printout. What happened, and what is the cure?

A lock file is present when a file is being sent to the physical printer. The lock file's purpose is to prevent two or more files from trying to go to the printer simultaneously. When anything interrupts the process, such as a soft kill or system crash, the lock file is left in the spool directory, and that's why the printer won't print. On pre-System V UNIX, there is no way to cancel a print request; as long as the lock file is there, nothing can be sent to the printer. As a result, printer files accumulate in the spool directory.

The cure is easy enough when you understand the workings of the spooler. You simply remove the lock file. A typical repair session looks like this:

```
$ su
Password:
# ps -ax
```

```
PID TTY TIME CMD
0 ? 139:50 swapper
1 ? 3:16 /etc/init
27547 ? 0:00 getty -t 600 /dev/tty12 1200 h1500
24937 co 0:10 -csh
42 co 0:01 sh /usr/local/set_oki_baud
24718 11 0:11 -csh
24925 20 0:13 -csh
24930 bi 0:15 -csh
24717 13 0:11 -csh
70 co 0:00 sleep 65535
27729 ? 0:03 /usr/lib/lpd cf0084
27774 bi 0:03 ps -ax
3156 bi 5:09 cron
# kill 27729
# cd /usr/spool/lpd
# ls
cf0084 df0084 lock
# rm -f lock cf0084 df0084
#
```

Getting no output through the spooler is another possible problem, even though the printer works when redirecting to it. The first thing to check is that the data and lock files are being created; if they aren't, the spool directory doesn't exist or its permission bits prevent the daemon from writing into it. The /usr/spool/lpd directory should be owned by daemon, and the actual spooler daemon program (/usr/lib/lpd or /usr/lib/lpdaemon, or sometimes the program is under /etc rather than /usr/lib) should be SUID and owned by the daemon:

```
# chown daemon /usr/lib/lpd /usr/spool/lpd
# chmod 775 /usr/spool/lpd
# chmod 4755 /usr/lib/lpd
#
```

Another possibility is that the spooler itself (/bin/lpr) is not executable by the average user (it should be mode 755). Of course, the daemon should be running! Do a **ps -ax** and check for lpd. If you're still not getting printouts after checking all this, make sure that the daemon has permission to write to the printer device. The safest way is to give ownership of the printer to the daemon:

```
# chown daemon /dev/lp
#
```

Naturally, in order for you to give ownership to the daemon login, it must first exist. Take a tip from System V and create the login daemon, with a password of VOID, and a home directory of /usr/spool/lpd.

Because UNIX Version 7 has no accept/reject command pair to stop spooler input, it is possible to queue up so much output that the spool directory overflows. You will notice this when console messages saying "no space left on device" appear, especially when you check and find that the device in question is where the spool directory is, and then you go in there and see dozens of big files. There might be one user who is merrily trying to print every file on the entire system (his login name will be apparent by the ownership of the spool files). If so, you should deal with him appropriately, considering both your company's regulations and the laws against homicide.

If the spool files being printed are indeed useless, you can simply remove them, and all will be well. However, if legitimate requests have simply gotten ahead of the printer, the best thing to do is to prevent further spooling for a while. You can do this informally (using the wall program or the telephone, asking everyone politely to stop spooling temporarily) or with brute force (making /bin/lpr, the printer spooler, nonexecutable until the printer catches up).

UNIX System V *lp* Printer Internals

lpr, the Version 7 and early BSD printer spooler command, was quite simple. It accommodated only one printer, one printer spooler, and one printer port. Thus, UNIX systems running those versions of UNIX were unable to spool to more than one printer. You could always get around this by plugging a printer into one of the remaining output ports and then reach it with any file transfer command, but that is file transfer, not spooling. UNIX System V's lp spooler, however, is happy to deal with more printers than you can possibly afford. It's part of AT&T's answer to the complaint that "UNIX just isn't a commercial system."

Nowadays, a typical commercial computer environment, even a relatively small one, has more than one printer. A laser printer is often found at modern installations. Another printer is usually reserved for handling multipart forms. In small installations, an inexpensive, relatively fast dot-matrix printer is often used. Another printer (such as a daisywheel, inkjet, or laser printer) is then reserved for handling high-quality printing tasks. Additional printers may be added for various reasons. One large mainframe or supermini may service users in several buildings, so printers need to be added in each building. Because most computer environments now have more than one printer, a special printer system is needed that is capable of dealing with a variety of printer types and printer ports.

Printers versus Devices

In System V, AT&T makes a syntactic distinction between a printer and a device; the distinction can be confusing unless you get the terms straight. A *device* is the mechanical device that does the actual printing, such as a Hewlett-Packard LaserJet III. A *printer* is a connection to the mechanical device—specifically, the port or interface program to which the file is sent on its way to the LaserJet. It might be considered a "virtual" printer.

Another term to understand is *class*. A class is a group of similar *printers* that are known by one name. For example, if your system has three identical Epson MX100s (a popular dot-matrix printer), they can be grouped into one `class` called `matrix`, and printing requests sent to `matrix` might reach any of the three Epsons, depending on which was busy at a given moment.

The names of files to be printed are stored in `/usr/spool/lp/requests` and are eventually sent to either a printer or a class. (The actual files are copied if the user uses the copy option, `lp -c`.) Those files sent to a printer (port) continue on to a device (like the LaserJet) where the actual printing process takes place. Those files sent to a specific class then go on to any one of several printers, and then to the actual physical device (like one of the three Epsons) where the printing process takes place. All devices in a class must be similar. On the mainframe, there is further confusion because of classes for paper types that are run from separate spool areas at specified times of the day.

To the user, `lp` appears to work almost the same as `lpr`, but he can now specify a particular printer for output. If a printer is named `laser`, for instance, the user can send a file to it with the command line

```
$ lp -dlaser filename
request-id is laser-4856 (1 file)
$
```

where `-d` is the option signifying destination. If a printer (such as an Epson) has been declared as the default printer, invoking the default printer is even simpler:

```
$ lp filename
request-id is epson-4857 (1 file)
$
```

223

When a file is sent to the spooler, the lp system sends an ID number back to the user's terminal, as shown. (If you find this annoying, use the -s flag to lp to suppress the messages.) Suppose that in this case the number is epson-4857. This ID number identifies the print "job" and is necessary in case you decide that you don't want to print that file after all. As long as you know the ID number, the cancel command stops the file from reaching the printer. The syntax is

```
cancel id_number
```

and it is used in this way:

```
$ cancel epson-4857
request "epson-4857" cancelled
$
```

To understand fully the usefulness of the cancel command, assume that you accidentally sent an executable binary file to the printer, rather than its documentation. If you don't cancel the request, the printer has a dilemma and prints a paper box full of blanks, odd characters, and graphics! cancel arms the average user with the necessary tool to stop any unwanted printing process. The system administrator needs more sophisticated tools, so now take a look inside the lp system.

How the *lp* Printer Spooler Works

The System V lp spooler system is relatively complex, and to understand it, you need a helpful analogy. UNIX has often been compared to a set of plumbing devices, and it's an apt comparison, particularly because you are dealing with a character stream that flows throughout the entire system (see Figure 11.1).

Requests to send a file to a printer are processed with the lp command. lp is represented by the hopper or funnel at the top of the spooler tank. Notice that the cancel command is pictured as a small, valved drain pipe that, when turned on, drains the printer request right out of the lp funnel. The spooler buffer, /usr/spool/lp, is represented by the tank. Files stored in /usr/spool/lp have their destinations as part of their file names. These files are queued in the spooler, waiting for an opportunity to reach the printer. If the printer is available, the file is sent immediately. Now take a look at the valve located between the spooler tank and the lp funnel, the position of the accept/reject command pair. accept allows a specific printer or class to accept files from the lp command. The off position of accept is reject. These two commands either allow or prevent the spooler from accepting any more files.

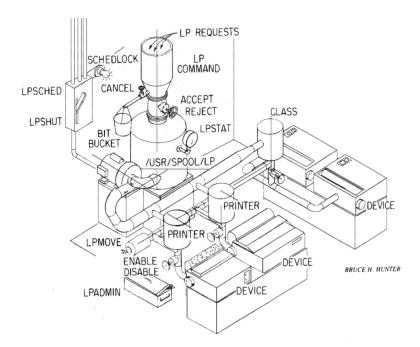

Figure 11.1. *The System V* lp *spooler system.*

Plumbing systems have a number of pumps and valves. The main pump in the lp system is lpsched. It enables the entire process, just like turning on the power to the main pump at an industrial installation. The off position of lpsched is lpshut, which shuts off the entire system. The activation of lpsched is usually written into rc, the program called by init when the system is brought up. Notice the SCHEDLOCK flag positioned on the lpsched/lpshut pump. In reality, SCHEDLOCK is a lock file, and its presence indicates that the spooler daemon is (or should be) running. SCHEDLOCK prevents more than one lpsched from running at a time.

Controlling the character flow at the end of the lp system is also important. A paper jam or an out-of-paper condition necessitates shutting down the device but not at the cost of rejecting files to the spooler. Under normal circumstances, the spooler should be capable of accepting any files, and the brief amount of time required to service a specific printer should not cause the spooler to fill. To keep this from happening, you need a set of commands at the printer end of the lp system to control the flow of files. This command pair is enable and disable.

A couple of lp commands vital to the system administrator are lpadmin and lpstat. lpadmin is the system administrator's printer tool box, and it is used to configure the entire lp system. Although lpstat is pictured as a gauge located on the spooler tank, it actually gives you the status of the entire lp system. Imagine that you are just coming into work, and five users greet you with the information that the printers aren't working. No matter what the assumed cause, the first thing you do is an lpstat -t. It not only tells you of the printers' activity but also lets you know how long the devices have been active. Perhaps its most useful purpose is to tell you what is and is not enabled:

```
# lpstat -t
scheduler is running
system default destination: oki
members of class okidata:
 oki
 oki_lq
device for oki: /dev/oki
device for diablo: /dev/diablo
device for oki_lq: /dev/oki
oki accepting requests since Jun 13 15:56
okidata accepting requests since Nov 27 17:09
oki_lq accepting requests since Jun 13 15:56
diablo accepting requests since Jul 5 14:24
printer oki is idle. enabled since Dec 25 19:59
printer oki_lq is disabled since Jun 12 18:23 -
 reason unknown
printer diablo is idle. enabled since Jul 16 11:14
```

Notice that two "virtual printers" share the same physical device (/dev/oki). This technique is useful when different paper stocks (such as invoices and labels) are to be used with interface programs that can take advantage of them, or when you want both draft and letter-quality output from the same printer (as in this case). If you set up two spoolers for the same printer, it's important to remember that these are all different printers to the spooler system. Unfortunately, the system doesn't check that they all go to the same device and will happily mix your printouts together. So you should disable the printers not being used.

Now that you have some idea of the general structure of the lp system, you can put the theory into practice by considering what you'll actually have to go through to set up lp on your system.

Setting Up *lp* on a New System

Creating a functional lp system on a System V machine is a bit more work than enabling lpr on Version 7, System III, and early BSD systems. This is the price of having multiple printer capabilities, yet being able to create your own special printer drivers makes the effort worthwhile.

First of all, in order to do system administration work on the lp system, you must log on as lp (line printer administrator), not root, so there must be a separate lp login. If your system was not distributed with a login for lp (along with root, bin, uucp, and so on), you have to create one. Don't forget that lp needs a home directory (which should be /usr/spool/lp) and a password as well. For reasons that will become apparent, the default execution path for lp should include /usr/lib, where many printer commands reside.

On systems with virtual terminals (such as UTS with Session), the lp login should be up whenever the system is up. As a matter of fact, if you have a spare terminal, you may want to use it to maintain an additional active lp login, because when errors are encountered in the operation of the printer system, the error messages are sent to lp's terminal, making any necessary troubleshooting easier for you. Most installations do not have the luxury of an exclusive lp terminal, so when problems are encountered with the printers, you either log off and log on as lp, or you do a substitute user ID (su) to lp to allow the error messages to be displayed. All subsequent commands in this chapter that use the lp: prompt are assumed to be issued from the lp login.

Attaching Printers to the System

You have to make the UNIX system aware of each printer physically attached to the system. In the following example, a printer is being added to a typical microcomputer system. The printer is attached to a serial port at /dev/tty22. The command to attach the printer as a logical device to the system is lpadmin and is executed as

```
lp: lpadmin -poki -v/dev/tty22 -mdumb
```

In this example, the printer is an Okidata 84. The argument -mdumb is used to let the lp system know that it's using the standard ("dumb," no special features) printer interface program. When the -m (for model) flag is used, lpadmin knows to look for a file by that name in the /usr/spool/lp/model directory. If you have a program in a different place, you can use the -i (for interface) flag and specify the full path name of the program you want to use:

```
lp: lpadmin -poki -v/dev/tty22 -i/own/dave/testprog
```

In either case, the program is copied into the directory named /usr/spool/lp/interface.

The -p flag names the printer oki, so subsequent lp commands should appear as

```
$ lp -doki file1 file2
request-id is oki-4385 (2 files)
$
```

if the commands are meant to print on this particular printer.

You won't be able to issue many lpadmin commands while the daemon (lpsched) is active, so you will have to run lpshut first. lpadmin will notify you of this if you forget. However, it *won't* tell you that after you have attached the printer, you still cannot use it until you run accept and enable and restart the daemon:

```
lp: lpadmin -poki -v/dev/tty22 -i/own/dave/testprog
lp: accept oki
destination "oki" now accepting requests
lp: enable oki
printer "oki" now enabled
lp: lpsched
lp:
```

All the lp administration commands for SVR3 and later reside in /usr/lib. If this is not in the PATH for the spooler administrator, the full path must be included in each command, as in /usr/lib/lpsched and /usr/lib/lpadmin.

Making One Printer the Default Printer

If a default printer is not specified, each invocation of the lp command requires that the printer be specified with the -d flag, as mentioned earlier. This quickly becomes tiresome, so the most frequently used printer should be designated as the default printer. The command to create a default printer is also lpadmin:

```
lp: lpadmin -doki
```

The printer called oki has been set as the default printer by use of the -d flag of lpadmin.

A Closer Look at */usr/spool/lp*

The directory /usr/spool/lp is the heart of the lp printer spooling system. This directory is a mix of the commands and directories that make it possible to spool multiple files to multiple printers. The locations and directory names may vary from one OEM's system to another, but the purpose of these files and directories is the same on all UNIX systems. Table 11.1 provides thumbnail sketches of files and directories located in usr/spool/lp.

Table 11.1. Files and directories used by lp.

File	Description
/usr/spool/lpSCHEDLOCK	This is the lock file. If it is present when the lpsched command is issued, lpsched aborts. SCHEDLOCK prevents damage to a running lp system by reinitializing it.
fifos/FIFO	This is a named pipe used by the lp commands to communicate with lpsched.
default	/usr/spool/default holds the name of the default printer.
/var/lp/logs or /usr/spool/lp/logs	This directory holds the logs of lp system administration and all requests.
outputq or /etc/lp/printers or /usr/spool/lp/requests	This directory (or file) holds the queue (list) for all printers and classes of printers.
qstatus (Older systems only)	This data file looks very much like outputq and holds the current status of the printers and printer classes.
seqfile (Older systems only)	This file has a single entry: the next printer request number.

continued

Table 11.1—*Continued*

Subdirectory	Description
`requests`	`/usr/spool/lp/request` has a subdirectory for each printer and printer class. On the way to the printers, the output files for each printer are spooled to that printer's subdirectory.
`/etc/classes` or `/usr/spool/lp/class`	This directory holds information pertinent to the printer classes.
`/etc/lp/interfaces` or `/usr/spool/interface`	This directory is the home of the executable interface programs for each printer or printer class.
`member`	`member` contains a file for each printer or class. Each file contains the name and path of the character special device file (in `/dev`)—for example, `/dev/printer00e`.
`/usr/spool/model` or `/usr/lib/lp/model`	This is where the sample interface programs are kept.

Troubleshooting the *lp* Spooler System

Imagine that your printer spooler is rapidly running out of space. Picture yourself logging on as `lp` (the printer administrator), checking the spooler, and finding out to your horror that a couple of users are printing private copies of the system manuals, while at the same time two bureaucrats-at-heart are making multiple copies of a mountain of internally generated specifications. On medium to large UNIX systems, `/usr/spool` is a separately mounted file system, and a `df` clearly shows that the remaining space is nearly exhausted. However, with this much printer activity, you don't need the sophistication of UNIX on a mainframe to tell you what is happening: the spooler has nearly filled all the remaining allocated disk space.

To add to the suspense, imagine that your other users are sending files to a printer faster than the printer can put them on green-bar paper. The spooler has to be stopped from taking any more printer requests, at least for a while. The trick is to shut off the 1p command. The cancel command won't do the job. You don't want to shut off the entire 1p system because you still want to keep other printers running. What you want to do is stop any new requests from coming into the spooler so that it has a chance to send its remaining output to the printer.

reject and *accept*

The command you want is reject, and here's how you use it:

```
lp: reject -r"spooler full" system matrix letter
destination "system" is no longer accepting requests
destination "matrix" is no longer accepting requests
destination "letter" is no longer accepting requests
lp:
```

This command prevents any further printer requests to the printers (or classes) named system, matrix, and letter. Like all printer commands, and most UNIX commands in general, reject has a number of flags and options. In this example, the -r option sends a message to the users' terminals when they attempt to use any of these printers, telling the users that the spooler is full.

To reactivate that portion of the system and allow more printer requests to enter the spooler, you use the accept command:

```
lp: accept system matrix letter
destination "system" now accepting requests
destination "matrix" now accepting requests
destination "letter" now accepting requests
lp:
```

Although it's not obvious, and perhaps it goes against common sense, running reject for an entire class of printers does *not* stop people from sending output to any printer in that class! For instance, if matrix (in the preceding example) were a class of printers including okidata, epson, and tally, only general requests such as

```
$ lp -dmatrix filename
```

would be rejected, although people could still successfully execute

```
$ lp -depson filename
```

disable and *enable*

accept and reject halt input *to* the spooler temporarily, but what if a printer jams or needs a paper change? Then you have to halt output *from* the spooler to the printer. For this task, you should use the disable command, which is similar in syntax to reject:

```
lp: disable -r"paper jammed" okidata
printer "okidata" now disabled
lp:
```

Because disable is used to deal with a specific printer (device), you must use the printer name, not an entire class, as an argument. When a printer is disabled, any file that is running on that printer will be rerun when it is enabled. disable also has an optional -c flag that cancels any print jobs running on the named printer(s). enable, the opposite command, starts the printer going again:

```
lp: enable okidata
printer "okidata" now enabled
lp:
```

Other Problems

Suppose that you can't get anything to spool or print. Here are a few things to look for:

outputq	This file must exist in the /usr/spool/lp directory.
permissions	Everything at the level of /usr/spool/lp and below should be owned by lp.
SUID	All lp programs should have the set-user-ID permission (mode 4755) on to enable them to work properly. In addition, the lpsched and lpadmin programs should be owned by root.
lpsched	This daemon *is* running, right?

In cases in which file protection is especially tight, such as a file with mode 600 in a directory with mode 700, you will *not* be able to print files with the command

```
$ lp filename
```

The result in such a case will probably be a printout with an error message like `no permission`. To circumvent this, simply use input redirection with `lp`:

```
$ lp < filename
```

Writing Printer Interface Programs

One of the best features of `lp` is that you can modify the interface programs to create your own custom "printer drivers." No C programming experience is needed because shell programs work fine. In fact, the system is generally delivered with shell interface programs. But if you plan to write your own, you need to understand some of the undocumented features.

Basic Interface Internals

When a print job is spooled, a single line of ASCII data is passed to the printer interface program, consisting of a minimum of seven fields. Some of these fields may be blank (the so-called "null string"), so you should *not* use the shell $* construct to examine the line, but instead get the data by position ($1, $2, and so on). Here's a guide to what you will find for this sample command line:

```
$ lp -depson -n2 -o12 -tTitle programs
```

The data line passed to the interface program contains

```
interface/epson epson-3126 david Title 2 12 /ch11/programs
```

When broken down, the data line looks like this:

Field 0	This is the subdirectory (in `/usr/spool/lp`) and name of the actual interface program to which the data is being passed. If the printer name is `epson`, field 0 contains the string `interface/epson`.
Field 1	This is the request-ID or print "job number." It might say something like `epson-3126`.
Field 2	This is the login name of the person who made the `lp` request.
Field 3	If a title for the listing was requested (through the `-t` option to `lp`), this field contains the title. Otherwise, it is empty.

233

Field 4	This is the number of printout copies requested, which defaults to 1.
Field 5	If any special options were requested (through the -o flag), *all* of them will appear in this field, separated by spaces.
Field 6	This is the *full* path name of the file or files to be printed. If the original command line looked like lp *filename*, this will be the path to *filename*. If the command line was lp -c *filename* or cat *filename* ¦ lp, a copy was made in the spooling directory, and this field now looks like

```
/usr/spool/lp/request/epson/d0-3126
```

If more than one file was requested, the other file names will follow, separated by a single space.

Three Interface Programs

With all that in mind, now look at a simple interface program:

```
shift; shift; shift; shift; shift # get file names
                                  # to beginning of line
pr $*
exit 0
```

We *did* say simple! Are you surprised? The spooler system is set up so that when you attach a logical printer to a device by using lpadmin, standard output from the interface program goes right to the device you want.

Here's a slightly more complex example, using more of the supplied parameters. This version prints out a header page and processes the number of copies wanted and any title that was requested on the lp command line:

```
echo ; echo ; echo
banner $2
echo ; echo ; echo
echo lp request is: $1
echo ; echo ; echo
title=$3
number=$4
```

```
shift; shift; shift; shift; shift # get file names
                                  # to beginning of line
echo $*
echo "\014\c" # formfeed to eject header page
j=1
while [ $j -le $number ]
do
 if [ -n "$title" ]
 then pr -h "$title" $*
 else pr $*
 fi
 j=`expr $j + 1`
done
exit 0
```

The third program doesn't print headers (which are useful mostly at large installations with many people). It's meant to *follow* an invocation of the pr program (as in pr *file1 file2* ¦ lp). What's so special about this program, then? It illustrates how to adapt your program for the features of a specific printer, such as pitch control. It also shows you how to print nroff output by using the termcap database (of all things)! This program is written for the Okidata 84, but the technique involved works on any printer:

```
pitch=10
number=$4
for p in $5
do
 case "$p" in
 -12 ¦ 12 ) pitch=12;;
 -15 ¦ 15 ) pitch=15;;
 esac
done

case "$pitch" in
 10) echo "\036\c" ;;
 12) echo "\035\c" ;;
 15) echo "\034\c" ;;
esac

shift; shift; shift; shift; shift
files="$*"
j=1
while [ $j -le $number ]
```

```
do
 for file in $files
 do
 ul -Toki84 "$file" 2>&1
 echo "\014\c"
 done
 j=`expr $j + 1`
done
echo "\036\033\060\c" # reset to normal
exit 0
```

The echo commands send the octal control sequences to the printer, enabling it to change to 10, 12, or 15 pitch based on the value of the -o flag to the lp command. (On some systems, you will need to use /bin/echo.) For instance, the following command prints a file in 12 pitch:

$ **pr file ¦ lp -o12**

And the next command is perfect for getting tiny nroff output:

$ **nroff letter.file ¦ lp -o15**

Notice that the printer was reset to a known default value at the end of the file. Although the pitch changes are pretty clear, how does this program allow the printing of nroff?

The secret is in the use of the ul program. (With luck, you have ul on your system. ul actually isn't all that common.) Developed at Berkeley, ul was meant to interface with termcap so that files with bold or underscore sequences could be viewed on CRT terminals that support those features. If you make up a termcap entry for your printer, entering the control sequences that force the printer to perform bold and underscoring and then feeding a file through ul automatically generates the proper control codes at the proper times. Here's the complete termcap entry for the Okidata:

```
ok¦oki84¦okidata microline 84 printer:\
 :co#136:li#66:hc:ul:so=\EH:se=\EI:us=\EC:ue=\ED:
```

If your system doesn't have ul, you have several alternatives. One is to ask your system supplier for either ul or an equivalent, such as ncrt. Another is to write your own, but that could take quite a long time.

uroff—Underline Filter for Printers

Here's a nice C program from Usenet that allows most printers to underline (the program won't work with CRTs). With a little work, you might be able to get the program to do bold also:

```
/* uroff - produce nroff underlining for not-so-smart printers */
/* introduction */
/* uroff -------------------------------------------------- **
**
** uroff - produce underlining for nroff documents for printers that
** do not do backspacing.
**
** This program works with any printer that can handle text
** followed by carriage return followed by some spaces and underscores.
**
** This program is simple-minded, but quick. It uses buffered I/O and
** classes characters into very simple categories.
**
** usage: uroff [ file... ]
**
** If no file names are specified, it will filter standard input.
** If a file name is dash (-), standard input will be read at that
** point.
**
** Permission is granted for use and distribution, as long as you
** include the following notice:
**
** (c) 1985 Steven M. List
** Benetics Corporation, Mt. View, CA
** {cdp,greipa,idi,oliveb,sun,tolerant}!bene!luke!itkin
**
** -------------------------------------------------- */
#include <stdio.h>

char *pgm;
```

```
#ifdef BSD
#define strrchr rindex
#endif
extern char *strrchr ();

/* main - control loop */
main (ac, av)
int ac;
char **av;
{
 register FILE *in; /* input stream */

 /* ------------------------------------------------------------- */
 /* set the basename of the program name for logging */
 /* ------------------------------------------------------------- */

if (pgm = strrchr (av[0], '/')) pgm++;
 else pgm = av[0];

ac--; av++;

/* ------------------------------------------------------------- */
/* arguments are file names - if none, use standard input */
/* ------------------------------------------------------------- */

if (ac == 0)
 {
 dofile (stdin);
 }
else while (ac--)
 {
 if (!strcmp (*av, "-"))
  {
  in = stdin;
  }
 else if (!(in = fopen (*av, "r")))
  {
  fprintf (stderr,
  "%s: cannot open %s for read\n", pgm, *(av-1));
  }

 av++;
```

```
 if (in)
  {
  dofile (in);
  if (in != stdin) fclose (in);
  }
 }

exit (0);
}

/* dofile - process an input file */
/*
 * dofile
 *
 * Read each character from the input file. Put it into the buffer
 * appropriate for the type. Flush the buffers on newline or eof.
 *
 *****************************************************************/
dofile (stream)
register FILE *stream;
{
 /* ------------------------------------------------------------- */
 /* some convenient defines */
 /* ------------------------------------------------------------- */

# define BUFSIZE 256
# define BACKSPACE '\b'
# define NEWLINE '\n'
# define FORMFEED '\f'
# define RETURN '\r'
# define UNDERSCORE '_'
# define TAB '\t'
# define SPACE ' '
# define NUL '\0'
 register unsigned char anyund = 0;
 register unsigned char backup = 0;
 register char c;
 register int i;
 register char *tp;
 register char *up;
```

```
char tbuf[BUFSIZE];
char ubuf[BUFSIZE];

/* ------------------------------------------------------------ */
/* initialize BOTH buffers to all spaces */
/* ------------------------------------------------------------ */

for (i = 0, tp = tbuf, up = ubuf; i < BUFSIZE; i++)
 *(tp++) = *(up++) = SPACE;
 tp = tbuf; up = ubuf;

/* ------------------------------------------------------------ */
/* process each character in the input file */
/* ------------------------------------------------------------ */

while ((c = getc (stream)) != EOF)
 {
 switch
  {
  case BACKSPACE:
   backup = 1;
   break;
  case UNDERSCORE:
   if (backup) *(up-1) = c;
   else
    {
    *up = c;
    up++; tp++;
    }
   anyund = 1;
   backup = 0;
   break;
  case NEWLINE:
   *tp = *up = NUL;
   fputs (tbuf, stdout);
   if (anyund)
    {
    putchar (RETURN);
```

```
    fputs (ubuf, stdout);
    }
  putchar (NEWLINE);
  anyund = 0;
  for (i = 0, tp = tbuf, up = ubuf; i < BUFSIZE; i++)
   *(tp++) = *(up++) = SPACE;
  tp = tbuf; up = ubuf;
  break;
 case SPACE:
 case TAB:
 case FORMFEED:
  *(up++) = *(tp++) = c;
  break;
 default:
  if (backup) *(tp-1) = c;
  else
   {
   *tp = c;
   up++; tp++;
   }
  backup = 0;
  break;
 }
 }

if (tp != tbuf)
 {
 *tp = *up = NUL;
 fputs (tbuf, stdout);
 if (anyund)
  {
  putchar (RETURN);
  fputs (ubuf, stdout);
  }
 putchar (NEWLINE);
 }

return;
}
```

One Last Thing

If you have gotten this far, you deserve a bonus. Although it's called the lp spooler system, nowhere are you forced to use this wonderful invention just for printers. With a little imagination and some good interface programs, you can use the lp system to queue output to plotters, graphics output devices, voice synthesizers, or even your own fleet of robots!

In fact, you are not even limited to hardware. If people are overusing CPU-hogging programs such as troff, you could hide the actual binary file and then set up a shell interface program that would feed input to the binary, while letting the user specify an output file. After you set up a "printer" called troff, only one person at a time is able to run troff. Be sure that troff is owned by lp and set to mode 500. Give it a try.

lpstart—A Handy Shell Program

Although the textbook way to initialize the System V lp spooler is just to run lpsched, this may be an oversimplification. We have found that lpsched doesn't always start running right away, especially when the system is heavily loaded. What is worse is that lpsched can fail to initialize properly.

The lpstart script is designed to start up the spooler in a positive manner. The script first attempts to shut down any current spooler daemons, and loops until it does. The script then forcibly removes any lock files, runs a single instance of lpsched, and checks to see whether it initialized properly. If the scheduler is running properly, the script exits; otherwise, it kills the daemon and starts again. The best time to run lpstart is while you are logged in as lp. To start the spooler up at boot time, add this line to your /etc/rc file:

```
/bin/su lp -c "/usr/local/lpstart" &
```

The script is so complex because of a defect in the lpshut program. lpshut does not actually look in the process table to ensure that all lpsched daemons are dead (there *can* be more than one running, despite what the manual says). The SCHEDLOCK file contains the process number of the daemon that created it; this daemon is the only one that lpshut eventually kills. Because there is room for just one SCHEDLOCK file, other daemons might well exist. Checking the output of ps to find whether any daemons are actually running is the only way to be sure.

Similarly, lpstat -r doesn't really tell whether the scheduler is running, but only whether the files in /usr/spool/lp seem to have been set up correctly. So both ps and lpstat are used to verify that the scheduler is up:

```
# lpstart
# by D. Fiedler
# the opposite of lpshut; gets the lp spooler started
# replace ps -ax by ps -e on System V

until test "$status" = "scheduler is running"
do
  /usr/lib/lpshut >/dev/null 2>&1
  while true
  do
    line=`ps -ax ¦ grep lpsched ¦ grep -v grep ¦ head-1`
    if test "$line"
      then kill -9 `echo $line ¦ cut -c1-6`
      else break
    fi
  done
  rm /usr/spool/lp/SCHEDLOCK >/dev/null 2>&1
  /usr/lib/lpsched
  line=`ps -ax ¦ grep lpsched ¦ grep -v grep`
  if test "$line"
    then status=`lpstat -r`
  fi
done
echo $status
```

Summary

Unquestionably, print spooler systems have become more complex over the years. If you take into consideration the schedulers and the sophisticated printers with multiple printing methods (such as standard print control characters and PostScript), as well as the different text filters, formats, and device control programs, printer administration can appear to be the most complex UNIX subsystem. But once the printer spooler is active and bug-free, its maintenance is quite simple. Unlike other spooling systems (such as E-mail), the printer spooler is self-cleaning. After a file has been printed, it is removed! There are no crontab entries to create, and you don't need to do a periodic check of the spooler. The only time the system needs attention is when it fails to produce a printout or when you are adding new devices.

12

Modems

NIX is a communicating operating system. It is capable of extending far beyond the immediate surroundings of the basic CPU box and local terminals by reaching out to remote terminals and systems. It can extend itself through local (real-time) and long-distance networks (both real-time and batch). AT&T has a package called the Basic Networking Utilities. This product is commonly known as HoneyDanBer UUCP and is the standard UUCP of System V Release 3 and later. UUCP is a suite of programs responsible for what we call "batch" networking: systems establish links only when required. Its basic communications programs, cu and uucp, come with any implementation worthy of calling itself UNIX. LANs (real-time networks) are covered in Chapter 13.

How to Talk to the World

If you set up cu and uucp on your system, you have already laid the groundwork for your ability to talk to almost any other computer with communications capability.

cu is a basic communications program that lets you dial into another system as a remote terminal on that system. When you log on to the other system, you are as much a part of it as any other logged-in user. To accomplish this, you use the facilities of your own computer. cu not only allows the local terminal to be remote but also enables text file transfers in both directions. If the computer you are calling is another UNIX system, certain protocols are followed to provide the best results with little or no work on your part.

Have you ever needed help with your system? Whether you are a novice or guru, software support is a necessity. You pay for it when you buy your system, and you should expect it. With a UNIX system, you can get a technician to look at your system by having him call in through cu or by your attaching him through ct. The technician can work on your system as if he were sitting at the terminal next to you. Although cu does have capabilities for file transfer (put and take), that facility falls more into the realm of uucp.

ct is somewhat the opposite of cu. Instead of letting *you* call out to another computer, ct calls a remote terminal and sends a login message to it. This approach can ensure security, because your system is not open to just anyone to attempt a login but instead calls a known telephone number of a (presumably) trustworthy person.

uucp is nothing like cu. Whereas cu is a real-time communications package, uucp is the basis of a store-and-forward service, network protocol, and a few other things. Although uucp is technically one command that copies files from one UNIX system to another, most people use the name UUCP when they mean the whole range of facilities that a UUCP link provides. uucp sends jobs to be executed on remote systems (uux), sends and receives remote mail (rmail), and transfers files in either direction. And uucp can execute these activities on a time schedule, thus allowing complete control over your phone costs.

uucp is similar to most store-and-forward services, such as CompuServe and BIX, but stores the data in your own system, your friend's system, and other system nodes along the way. The cost is lower than commercial store-and-forward services—your only cost is the phone bill.

uux allows you to run commands on remote systems. It is most often used as part of the operations for forwarding mail or feeding the Usenet news files, but uux can be useful for remote administrative work as well.

The UNIX mail command is a quick and convenient way to send messages and files from one terminal to another, but what if you want to send mail to someone 2,000 miles away? Remote electronic mail is almost as easy to send as local electronic mail, and that capability is included once you are set up for UUCP. UUCP is the connection method that makes remote mail possible. As you will see, simply typing the name or path to a remote system activates the UUCP spooling process, which transmits the mail to the other system for you.

cu and UUCP are interrelated in some ways, however. In order to debug your modem port, you need cu running reliably. Otherwise, you don't stand much chance of getting UUCP going. The first thing you want to do as system administrator, then, is to set up cu.

Getting from Here to There

You need to consider three different physical methods of connecting systems when you are dealing with UNIX networking capabilities: direct serial; LAN (*Local Area Network*); and DDD (*Direct Distance Dialing*), also known as the phone system. In addition, there are multiplexers (MUXes), RJE, X.25, and many other networking protocols that are fascinating but beyond the scope of this book. This chapter covers only two methods: direct lines and DDD lines. LANs are discussed in Chapter 13.

Direct Lines

Direct lines are hardwired lines used for relatively short distances (50 feet or less on an RS-232 cable). If you have two or more computers in the same room, the same building, or even the same block, the computers can be cabled together with direct lines.

Setting up a hardwire serial port is one-tenth the work of setting up a modem port. A simple but effective method of tying together two systems in close proximity is a *null modem hardwire connection*: a wire (cable) connection from one system to another. You need to be aware of the limits in distance and speed. The maximum transmission speed is determined by the serial board's UARTs and the length of the wire. The RS-232 specification "allows" transmission for only 50 feet, but greater distances (up to 500 feet at 9600 baud) can often be obtained by using shielded low-capacitance cables. For even greater speed and longer distances, more costly and sophisticated methods are required, such as installing *repeaters* or *short haul modems* in the data line, which boost the signal back to standard levels.

ACU Lines

In UNIX documentation, there are often references to devices called ACUs (*Automatic Calling Units*). Such devices go back to the days when modems were expensive to build, and if you wanted automatic dialing, it was left to a separate ACU device on another port. Some large minicomputers and mainframes still use ACUs with rack-mountable modems, but virtually all modems today have internal dialers. Part of the trick in setting up UUCP is to get UNIX to understand that the modem and the ACU (dialer) are the same device.

The Problem of Transmitting Data

Telephone lines are seldom perfect. Everybody is familiar with irritating background noise and echoes in voice transmissions, otherwise known as "spurious signals" that cause "dirty lines." The amount of "dirt" is usually in direct proportion to the distance traveled and the number of switching stations along the way. Satellites are also notorious for echoes, which are an absolute disaster for data transmission. If you use cu to transmit data over a long distance and you see curly braces mixed in with the text, the line is probably too noisy to transmit reliably. (The left curly brace, {, corresponds to a typical noise burst on most 1200-baud modem designs.)

In our experience, we've found that AT&T has the best lines for long-distance data transmission. Premium discount services are better than most, but as of this writing, they are still not 100-percent reliable. The rule of thumb is this: the cheaper the service, the worse the transmission; the shorter the distance, the cleaner the line.

Data can be transmitted in several ways, but packet transmission has a built-in safety check. Packet transmission breaks up the data stream into packages called packets. Each packet contains a *checksum*, a number derived from an algorithm that adds the bit patterns of the characters going out. The receiving system runs the same algorithm. If the checksums don't agree, the receiving system has the sending system resend the packet. Packet transmission is the closest thing to 100-percent-guaranteed data transfer.

Making the Initial Connections

Even professional hardware engineers who do nothing all day but grapple with networks and peripheral connections have occasional problems in wiring together two devices. The procedure is easy only if you have a no-problem cable connection, such as an AT&T modem, cable, and computer—all matched with the proper AT&T RS-232 cable adapter. But you probably have a mix-and-match connection, such as a Prometheus modem installed to an AT&T 3B2/300. Mix-and-match connections are crapshoots. Expect them to take a little more time.

Setting Hardware Switches

Before you can run cu (or UUCP for that matter), you have to set a few hardware switches. No data is going anywhere until the ports allow transmission. Modems have many switches that must be set correctly so that cu and UUCP work properly. (Older modems have actual switches located behind the front panel, on the bottom, or on the back. Modern modems require you to set the switches by using a terminal or communications program from a computer.) The modem must be set to autoanswer if it is to receive incoming calls. The computer and UUCP have to know whether the modem is ready—in other words, the modem must send back result codes to the computer. For example, UUCP expects a Hayes protocol modem to send back OK after it has sent the modem an AT to see whether it is active. Additional switches must be set to cause this to happen. Other switches that might be set are the number of rings (to hear before answering) and redialing if the line is busy (a nice idea for personal computers but almost useless to UUCP).

Here is how one of the authors had to set up the switches on a Hayes modem. (Setting up Telebit modems is discussed in the section "Telebit Modems" later in this chapter.) The switch settings are explained so that you can make the necessary adjustments if you have another type of modem. Note carefully the settings with asterisks; they might have to be set differently for your system.

For *outgoing* modems (dialing out with cu or UUCP), use these settings:

Switch 1 — UP*	Forces the modem to hang up the phone line when the DTR (*D*ata *T*erminal *R*eady) line (pin 20) is asserted low.
Switch 2 — UP	Forces the modem to send result codes to the computer as strings. If the switch is down, only digits are sent (easy to miss when parsing).
Switch 3 — DOWN	Enables the result codes to be returned to the computer. If this switch is up, you will get no result codes, overriding any setting of switch 2.
Switch 4 — UP	Allows commands to be echoed as they are entered. If the switch is down, you can see what you are doing.
Switch 5 — DOWN	Prevents the modem from answering calls (unnecessary on an outgoing-only modem).

Switch 6 — DOWN*	Forces CD (*Carrier Detect*—pin 8) high (to fool the computer) so that commands can be sent *to the modem*, even before the connection is made to a distant modem.
Switch 7 — UP	Setting needed for normal installation to a single-user phone jack.
Switch 8 — DOWN	Allows the modem to recognize and execute commands.

For *incoming* modems (allowing logins), use these settings:

Switch 1 — DOWN*	Forces DTR high so that the modem is fooled into answering the phone, because this computer drops DTR momentarily when the modem picks up the line, which would otherwise disconnect the call.
Switch 2 — N/A	
Switch 3 — UP	Prevents result codes from going to the computer, because no commands are anticipated.
Switch 4 — DOWN	Prevents commands from being echoed.
Switch 5 — UP	Forces the modem to answer calls.
Switch 6 — UP*	Allows state of CD (*Carrier Detect*—pin 8) line to be passed to the computer so that the getty program will know when a call has been received.
Switch 7 — UP	Same as for outgoing modem.
Switch 8 — UP	Prevents the modem from executing commands.

Sometimes the most important switches to set are those that "lie" to the modem. These are the ones marked with asterisks in the preceding list. RS-232 signal pins like CD and DTR allow the computer and the modem to send signals to one other to see whether they are alive and whether a carrier (modem on the other end) has been detected. (You may want to refer to Appendix B, "The RS-232 Blues," while reading this section.) You need to make sure that each device "thinks" that the other device is ready, and that's where the lie comes in. Simple connections do not use these signals, but if you want to take advantage of full modem-control capabilities, you have to deal with these pins.

Modem Control

What is modem control, and why is it so important? As you have seen with terminals, generally only three lines (data in, data out, and ground) are necessary to send data back and forth. Modems, which operate at random intervals over phone lines, are a little more complex.

Consider a few potential problems. First, someone logs in and works for a while, and then hangs up without logging off. In such a case, you would want him automatically logged off because he broke the connection, so that the next person to log in does not get the first person's shell and privileges.

Second, your computer places an outgoing call in the middle of the night, and the answering modem picks up the phone, yet the computer on the other end is down. You would want the phone line to be hung up after a while, to avoid a nine-hour phone charge to the other side of the country, wouldn't you?

Finally, another computer calls your system but never gets to log in because of noise on the line. If your computer does not sense this condition, your incoming line will be tied up until someone on either end notices.

All of these annoying problems can be avoided by the proper use of *modem control*, which simply refers to the few extra status lines that allow sensing of various phone line conditions and subsequent control of the modem by the computer. One runaway phone call can easily cost more than a modem, so pay attention!

The two main modem-control lines are DTR (pin 20) and CD (pin 8). The function of DTR is to signal the modem that the computer attached to it is ready for data. If DTR is low, the modem will either hang up (if a call is already in progress), or refuse to answer or initiate a call. DTR is normally low if the computer is down or turned off. DTR is low also (or will go low momentarily, which is just as bad) if the computer doesn't properly support modem control.

In such a case, DTR must be held high for the modem to operate at all; you do this by flipping an internal switch or by wiring the cable so that DTR is asserted high. Afterward, it will be *impossible* for the computer to hang up the line by software, so jumpering DTR high is *unacceptable* for unattended outgoing use.

The CD line from the modem indicates whether the remote modem has connected. CD is used on incoming lines to signal to getty that a login message should be sent. The problem arises on outgoing lines. Because there is no remote hookup before the call takes place, CD will be low, and the driver may refuse to open the line. Unless the device driver has been written to ignore the CD signal when you attempt to open the port for output, you have to fool the modem by wiring CD high or by flipping a switch. This in turn prevents the same modem from being used for incoming calls. In order to get away with fewer than two modems on your system (one permanently incoming and one permanently outgoing), you must therefore have one of the following:

- A correctly designed computer and operating system

- A system with the uugetty program or an equivalent

- A modem that ignores CD when necessary

Setting the Computer

You usually do not have to set any hardware switches at the computer end, but the I/O board may have to be "jumpered," particularly if you find that you need more modem control. For example, pin 5, Clear To Send (CTS), allows data transmission only if it is high (or true). When pin 5 goes high, it causes pin 20 (DTR) to go high as well, thus allowing another signal to work the modem. If pin 5 (CTS) is internally true (that is, if your computer sends data with or without an external CTS high), you have to extract the board from your computer and jumper CTS to accept an external signal and act on it (see Figure 12.1).

Clear To Send (CTS)
Jumpered External

Clear To Send (CTS)
Jumpered Internal

Figure 12.1. *CTS jumper on I/O board.*

If you move the shorting device or jumper from INT to EXT, the internal true signal is defeated, and the computer responds to an external signal. Now when no signal is present, no data flows. When the CTS pin goes high (true), data bits are able to flow from the computer end *if* the modem end is also ready. If DTR goes high, it allows further control as you get more sophisticated.

As you can see, even the initial stages of connecting modems can be a difficult affair. If you are a novice and are having too many problems getting started, try setting all the signal pins high (set switches 1 and 6 down for the Hayes). This will probably get you going. You may have to switch the modem off manually or software-switch it to hang up, but at least you will be transmitting data.

Once all the necessary hardware switches have been switched and jumpers have been jumped, you are ready to go to the software stage, setting ports in /etc/ttys or inittab. When you have set up the ports, you can start trying the connections for the first time. Modems are particularly tricky because you have more pins to deal with. The next discussion shows you what's involved when you are trying out your first shaky modem connections.

Trying an Outgoing Modem for the First Time

With breakout box in place, queue some data on the computer port. There are different protocols for different modems. If the device is a Hayes-compatible modem, type

```
$ cat </dev/modem &      —You need to see the modem's prompt
$ echo "AT" >/dev/modem
```

When you press Enter, the prompt may fail to come back because the connection hasn't been made. Jumper the breakout box until data flows. (Don't forget to kill the background cat program.)

If the computer is a DCE, you have a crossed connection, and pin 2 must be connected to pin 3 on the opposite side. Pin 7 on the computer *always* goes to pin 7 on the modem.

The rest varies from system to system and modem to modem, but a good example is pin 8 (CD) of the modem side of the connection, going to pin 5 on the computer side to bring up Clear To Send (CTS) and activate the computer into sending. A straight-through connection (pin 2 to pin 2, pin 3 to pin 3, pin 7 to pin 7, and so on) should always be tried first. When the computer has sent the message to the modem, the prompt comes back on the terminal.

Now try talking to the modem with cu. If all goes well, you might as well make a semipermanent cable, but don't put on hoods or strain reliefs. You are probably not through yet. A few more factors need to be considered. Although cu is undemanding and simple to deal with, UUCP is fussy and requires more handshaking. Plan on making some subtle changes in the cable connections before you finish the job.

Testing *cu*

Depending on your particular implementation, one of the following command lines should cause some action (dialing, the return of result codes, or at least lights blinking) on your modem:

```
$ cu
$ cu -t
$ cu -l
$ cu -l /dev/modem
$ cu -l /dev/modem -s 1200
$ cu 9991212          — Use a known good modem phone number
```

If the last variation worked, and you dialed a functioning modem line, a login message from the other computer should appear on your screen. Otherwise, you merely made a connection to your own modem, and now you have to send your modem the command sequence to get it to dial out. In the case of the Hayes, that might look like the following:

```
$ cu -l
Connected            — cu has connected to the modem
AT                   — Wake up the Hayes
OK                   — Return code from Hayes
ATD5551212           — Hayes dialing sequence
CONNECT              — The Hayes has reached the remote modem
login:               — Message from remote computer
```

At this point, you are hooked to the remote system and should log in.

The first thing you should know about cu is how to disconnect. All cu commands start on a new line with the tilde (~), and the disconnect sequence looks like this:

```
~.
Disconnected
$
```

The $ prompt is from your own system because you've just exited the cu command. If your modem control is working, the phone line will also disconnect when you exit cu. (Check the modem lights.) Otherwise, you will have to physically turn off the modem to ensure that the connection has been broken. If you log off the other system, and simply logging off drops the line, then the other system has its modem control working properly.

Using *cu*

Although the actual use of cu is covered pretty well in the manual page, the tricky part is to keep track of the context—whether you are talking, at any given moment, to your local system or to the remote. Once in cu, you are generally talking to the remote. Typing a command line that begins with the characters ~! runs that command on your local system, with the output going to your terminal only (the remote system doesn't know that the output was typed). Typing a command line that begins with the characters ~$ runs that command on your local system but sends the output of the command to the remote system, as if you were typing the output. So if you are logged on to a non-UNIX system and you want to send it a file, put the other system in a mode in which it is ready to receive, and then type

```
~$cat myfile
```

Your local system will send myfile—not to your terminal as usual, but to the other system. When cat is finished, you are talking to the other system again, automatically.

One trick that is not obvious relates to keeping a log of your remote session. Although personal computer owners have to deal with such things as "capture buffers," all you need on UNIX is the right command—in this case, tee:

```
$ cu 5551212 ¦ tee save.file
Connected

Faraway login:
~.
Disconnected
$ cat save.file

Faraway login:
$
```

Direct (Computer to Computer) Connection

Hooking two computers back-to-back can allow data transfer up to 38400 baud (and higher on some systems). Instead of a modem, we use a null modem. A *null modem connection* is similar to a standard modem connection, only much simpler. It's nothing more than a cleverly wired cable. As a bare minimum, two wires are required to carry data (one in each direction, connecting pins 2 and 3), and one more wire is used for signal ground (connecting both pin 7s). This connection is illustrated in Figure 12.2.

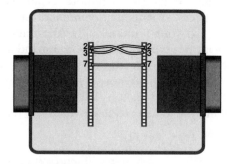

Figure 12.2. *A minimal modem connection.*

If your equipment is matched, only stock cables are required, but mix-and-match equipment is not as easy. If both systems are identical, the connections are at least symmetrical. Start with a 25-pin ribbon connector attached to the sending port of one system, and another similar cable attached to the receiving port of the other system. As explained in Appendix B, place a breakout box in the center so that the connection is now port to cable to breakout box to cable to port. Then check the use of pins 2 and 3 on both ends. The pin asserted on the port tells the story. If pin 2 is asserted low, the port is a DTE (a terminal type). If pin 3 is asserted low, the port is a DCE (communications type). If both pin 3s are low, they are both DCEs, and pin 2 must be crossed to pin 3 at the other system—a null modem connection. If the ports are opposite types, DCE to DTE, a straight connection fills the bill.

The plan is to get the sending system to retrieve a login from the receiving system. After ensuring that a getty process is running on the port of the receiving system, type

```
# cu -l /dev/modem
```

at the terminal of the sending system.

If cu returns immediately, you have opened a port that requires modem control. The prompt will not return to this terminal until the connection has been successfully made. With pins 2, 3, and 7 jumpered, the trick is to see which signal pins have to be pulled up at either end to make the connection complete. Find one of pins 4, 5, 6, 8, or 20 asserted high at either end or both ends. Use it initially to pull up one or more of the unasserted signal pins until data flows. Pin 5 or pin 6 (or both) usually has to be asserted high in order to get things going. Pin 4 (RTS) and pin 20 (DTR) are generally high and make a good source for a signal. Once data flows, the prompt comes back on the sending system and a login request follows, unless you have failed to set the receiving port for a getty. Write down the jumper connections on a worksheet. Log in on the remote system and then drop the connection with a

```
~.
Disconnected
$
```

Now reconnect by typing your cu command again. If your login is still active on the remote system, you will want to redo the cables for modem control so that an interruption of signal generates a hangup (SIGHUP) on the remote system. As usual, the safest way is to connect all wires straight through (except for possibly having to cross pins 2 and 3) and then try the connection. If this doesn't work, a typical bit of hardware engineer's magic is to take an active (asserted) pin 4 (RTS) on one system and jumper it to an unasserted pin 5 (CTS) on the other. Similarly, you can wire pin 20 (DTR) across to the other system's pin 8 (CD). Now when you software-disconnect, one signal pin going off or low drops the whole connection and kills the login. Figure 12.3 shows a complete null modem wiring.

This may sound like a lot of work, but it is worth it. Since the beginning of time (1970) in UNIX, there has always been a problem concerning the login remaining in an active state long after a remote terminal has hung up. This "unshakable login" is not unique to UNIX but exists on many LANs as well. The trick is to make sure that the receiving system (the one with the getty) can sense and act on a hardware hangup. Otherwise, even a sure kill (kill -9 process ID number) to the stuck login cannot kill it. Only a reboot of the system clears up this problem.

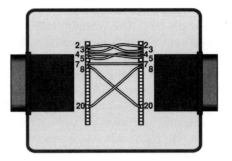

Figure 12.3. Null modem cable with modem control.

The Easy Route

If you are new at cabling, you may want to take the easy route by jumpering either the cable or the I/O board so that pins like CTS and DSR are always high or true (see Figure 12.4). Then a three-wire connection makes the unit work. You will not have full control, however. You may suffer with unshakable logins when using direct hardwire connections. In other words, you won't be taking advantage of the full handshaking capabilities available to you. An imperfect connection that works is better then a shaky one that doesn't, so go with whatever works for now and refine your methods as you become more experienced. If the cable configuration works, make your cable without strain reliefs and hoods. Just let the pins hang out and connect the cable.

The Software Side

Bidirectional logins are possible over a single port only in HDB UUCP, using a special program called uugetty at both ends. If uugetty is available at only one end, it cannot be used. For all versions of UUCP before HDB, two ports are required. An "in" port must have a getty, and an "out" port cannot have one. This is true for modem connections as well as null modems. (Later you learn how to turn a `getty` on and off if you can afford only one modem or port.) Even so, with two systems connected locally, you can have one system call the other at 15-minute intervals all day, so it hardly matters.

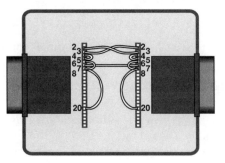

Figure 12.4. *Guaranteed null modem.*

A typical line speed for a hardwire connection is 9600 baud. Some systems can't handle 9600 baud reliably; if this is true of your system, try 4800. In fact, UUCP internal overhead often limits actual transfer rates to about 750 characters per second, no matter how high the baud rate is. We recommend that you set up hardwire connections at 1200 baud initially and then turn up the speed later.

The *incoming* port setup in /etc/ttys looks like this in Version 7 and earlier UNIX versions:

```
19tty6
```

/etc/inittab looks like this in System III:

```
2:6:c:/etc/getty tty6 3 60
```

It looks like this in System V:

```
6:2:respawn:/etc/getty -t 60 tty6 1200
```

For bidirectional ports, the line in /etc/inittab is

```
6:2:respawn:/usr/lib/uucp/uugetty -r -t 60 tty6 1200
```

For *outgoing* lines, you must turn off the `getty` in Version 7 by using

```
09tty5
```

In System III, use

```
2:6:k:/etc/getty tty6 3 60
```

In System V, use

```
5:2:off:/etc/getty tty5 1200
```

See Chapter 10 on terminals for more information about `getty`.

Letting UNIX Know about Your Connections

UNIX Version 7 is simple and forgiving. To add an outgoing modem, just modify `/etc/ttys` to disable the login on that port (this trivial task is covered in Chapter 10). If there is something at the other end of the port to talk to, `cu` puts you in business.

UNIX System III and Version 7 were ill-equipped to deal with modems. If you didn't have a DEC modem, you had to rewrite `uucico`. Early Unisoft ports were so poor at handling UUCP that you couldn't use them to call out, and calling in was spotty at best. HDB UUCP, available on recent releases of System V, is very tolerant, recognizing Hayes, Micom, Telebit, Rixon, and Vadic modems (among others), as well as LANs. Later you learn a trick to get your modem to dial out automatically even if it's not supported.

HDB UUCP is far more stable, much more commercially oriented, but not nearly as forgiving. Before you can use `cu`, HDB wants the `/usr/lib/uucp` files to know about the port. The `Devices` file has to have an entry for each port or modem that `cu` and UUCP use. A typical `Devices` file might look like this:

```
ACU tty11 - 1200 Hayes
ACU tty11 - 300 Hayes
hunter tty12 - 9600 direct
ACU tty13 - 1200 Hayes
ACU tty13 - 300 Hayes
```

Modem lines begin with `ACU` or another `Devices` name; different port types usually have different `Devices` names. Direct lines begin with the node name. The port name is next. It should be the name of a device in `/dev`. Typically, you should use `tty11` if you mean `/dev/tty11`. The next field for normal connections is a `-`. The fourth field is the baud rate. The last field is the name of the device. `tty11` and `tty13` have only one modem each. By putting a single modem in `Devices` at different baud rates, you can use the modem at any of those rates.

Check the file `/usr/lib/uucp/Dialers` to be sure that there is an entry for your modem. If you bought a Snark XVII and it doesn't emulate a brand that UUCP knows about, you will have to enter its *expect* sequence here (be patient; the method is explained shortly).

Believe it or not, that's about all there is to cu and anything short of UUCP. For UUCP, you have completed most of the work as well. Congratulations!

Setting Up *cu* under HDB

On older UNIX versions (System III and earlier), cu had some remarkable features that were easily taken for granted before HDB UUCP came along. For example, cu could be used to address a port. By typing

```
cu -l /dev/modem
```

you talk directly to the modem port. Send the port the modem dialing sequence, and if all goes well, you are in the communications business. A user or an administrator can use cu to talk to a printer, a tty, or any device attached to a port. This flexibility is highly advantageous because it allows you to easily test devices attached to ports, thus making system administration easier.

If you have a modem on a port, it is customary to use cu to "direct dial," as in

```
cu -l /dev/tty14 12015551234
```

or

```
cu system
```

The -l option specifies the *line* (port) on which UNIX dials the named system for you. With only an ACU-style entry for the port in /usr/lib/uucp/Devices, you can't talk directly to the modem port. An attempt to reach the port, such as

```
cu -l /dev/tty14
```

will be met with the error message

```
DEVICE NOT AVAILABLE
```

and an understandable amount of frustration. You need to make an entry for the modem port as a direct device as well as an ACU. In the following example from /usr/lib/uucp/Devices, port 13 is set up as a conventional UUCP port for an ACU, port 12 is a hardwire port, and port 14 is set up for a direct connection to the modem:

```
ACU     tty14 - 1200 Hayes
Direct  tty14 - 1200 direct \D
Direct  tty12 - 9600 direct \D
hunter  tty12 - 9600 direct
ACU     tty13 - 1200 Hayes
```

Note the two entries for tty14, one Direct and the other ACU. By adding this extra Direct entry, a user or an administrator can cu directly to the port and thus to the modem, manipulate the device on the port before dialing, and then process as if it were a modem connection in the mode of Version 7.

So that you can understand the syntax of the Dialers file, look at the entry for Hayes that is referenced in the preceding Devices file:

```
Hayes     =,-,  "" \M\dAT\r\c OK\r \EATDT\T\r\c\m CONNECT
```

Like the other tables used by UUCP, the Dialers table entry starts with an entry name—in this case, Hayes. (You can also have a special Dialers entry name that begins with the ampersand, &, for resetting the modem *after* the connection is complete. For example, the reset table for Hayes would be named &Hayes, but you had better test this before relying on it—not all implementations of the dialer know to look for a reset script.) Each entry is composed of three parts: the entry name (this one is easy), a phone-number command translation (in this example, the little string =, - ,), and a "chat" script between the dialing program and the modem (here everything between "" and the CONNECT).

The phone-number command translation string consists of character pairs: the first element of the pair is what is expected in the phone number in the cu command or Systems entry; the second element is what the modem expects for the equivalent action. In this example, the string =, - , consists of two pairs, =, and - ,. In other words, if a phone-number string is received that is 9=1-212-555-1212, the dialer program will send the modem the dialing string 9,1,212,555,1212. In the general parlance of phone numbers, the equal sign (=) means to wait for a dial tone, and the dash (-) means to pause. Well, this Hayes doesn't have a single-character, wait-for-dial-tone command (many modems do), so the "pause" command (,) is sent for both situations.

Now look at the chat script:

```
"" \M\dAT\r\c OK\r \EATDT\T\r\c\m CONNECT
```

There are plenty of backslashes in the chat script. Table 12.1 describes them so that you can better understand (and write) dialers.

Table 12.1. Dialer escape characters.

Characters	Description
" "	Empty string (nothing)
\p	Pause 1/4 to 1/2 second
\d	Delay 1 to 2 seconds
\D	Send phone number *without* translation from dialcodes
\T	Send phone number *with* translation from dialcodes
\K	Send BREAK
\E	*Enable* echo checking
\e	*Disable* echo checking
\M	Turn *off* modem control interpretation of hardware lines
\m	Turn *on* modem control interpretation of hardware lines
\c	Prevent carriage return or linefeed
\r	Send carriage return
\b	Send a backspace character (BREAK on BSD systems)
\s	Send a space character
\t	Send a tab character
\n	Send a linefeed character
\nnn	Send character represented by octal *nnn*

The chat script is made up of expected messages from the modem and the responses to send to it. This script always starts with a message expected from the modem. In this example, the Hayes entry starts with any empty string (represented by " "). In other words, don't expect anything from the modem; just proceed to the first string to send: \M\dAT\r\c. This string starts with the command to turn off modem control (\M) and the two-second delay (\d). After the delay, the dialer will send the characters AT to the modem, followed by a carriage return without a linefeed (\r\c—unless specified, all strings sent end with a linefeed).

The dialer then waits until it receives the expected OK message from the modem followed by a carriage return.

To continue, the dialer needs to send the dial command string and the phone number. These are specified by the string \EATDT\T\r\c\m. The string breaks down this way: enable echo checking (\E); send the characters ATDT, followed by the phone number *with* translation (\T) and a carriage return without linefeed (\r\c); and end by turning modem control back on (\m).

The CONNECT message from the modem tells the dialer that it is done.

You can add some additional abbreviations of your own, using the Dialcodes file. If you deal with dialer scripts one byte at a time, the scripts make sense.

L-devices

The corresponding file to Devices in the old UUCP is called L-devices. It is similar to the HDB Devices files and looks like this:

```
DIR tty5 0 1200
DIR tty5 0 9600
ACU cul0 cua0 1200
```

The two entries for tty5 allow you to run the modem at either speed. The entries cul0 (that's *ell zero*, not *one zero*) and cua0 are a Version 7 anachronism. As mentioned earlier, dialers used to be known as ACUs and were separate physical devices from modems. If your modem dials out in response to commands, you have to fool the system into recognizing the old names as being the same as your modem device. To do this, you simply make links in your /dev directory, like this:

```
# cd /dev
# ln tty5 modem
# ln tty5 cua0
# ln tty5 cul0
# ls -l tty5 modem cu?0
crw-rw-rw- 4 nuucp staff 13, 5 Nov 23 12:30 cua0
crw-rw-rw- 4 nuucp staff 13, 5 Nov 23 12:30 cul0
crw-rw-rw- 4 nuucp staff 13, 5 Nov 23 12:30 modem
crw-rw-rw- 4 nuucp staff 13, 5 Nov 23 12:30 tty5
#
```

Now any program that tries to access any of these old names will simply talk to your real modem on /dev/tty5.

Setting Up UUCP

UUCP is a magnificent tool for both networking and communications. Until recently, however, its splendor was unavailable to most UNIX system owners simply because installing UUCP was difficult. It is said that installing UUCP takes a day and a half the first time, and 15 minutes each time thereafter. That is pretty close to the truth. Systems with menu-driven administration, like AT&T's "simple administration" and SCO's sysadmsh, make installing UUCP nearly painless. In fact, on AT&T's UNIX PC, you don't even realize that you are setting it up. This discussion focuses on bringing up UUCP the long way.

Definitions

All UNIX systems have a node name. In this context, the word *node* means a link in the communications network; it's simply the name by which your computer will be known to others. On many UNIX System III and earlier systems, the node name of the system is entered in `/usr/lib/uucp/SYSTEMNAME` or `/etc/systemid`, where the name may be easily changed. You may be unlucky, and it has been compiled right into the kernel! If that's the case, look in a file like `/usr/sys/name.c` or `/usr/include/whoami.h` for an entry that corresponds to `sysname` or `nodename`, and edit accordingly. Then you have to relink the kernel—a procedure that is different for every system.

In case you are wondering, you don't need a source license to relink the kernel. Suppliers that allow you to relink the kernel have made it possible for you not only to change the node name but also to add or take away drivers and otherwise reconfigure your system. Such people are good to deal with. However, if you can't reconfigure the kernel, you will have to manually patch a copy of the `/unix` file. Because this is something of a trick, a `sysname` program is included at the end of this chapter that does all the hard work for you.

On System V, the node name can be displayed with the `uname` command:

```
$ uname -n                          — The n stands for node
infopro
$
```

And on an AT&T 3B2, the node name can be changed as easily as this:

```
# uname -n
netsuke
# uname -S hunter
# uname -n
hunter
#
```

On some systems, the equivalent is provided by the command setuname -n *nodename*. Other computers have the uuname command rather than uname. uuname -l displays the node name of your system, whereas typing just uuname reveals the names of all other computers your system can call.

Initiating a data call to another system is known as *polling* the other system. With no modification of how the UUCP utilities are set up, use of any of the UUCP commands or remote mail forces immediate polling of the other system. Later you will learn a way to stop that from happening, which you will surely appreciate when your phone bill arrives.

The way UUCP works is fascinating; some highlights are touched on here. The uucico (*UNIX-to-UNIX copy-in-copy-out*) program is the one that actually performs polling. When the remote system picks up the phone, your system takes any strings the remote system puts out. The remote system is expecting a login message. When it gets a substring that is acceptable to the *expect-send* sequence in its Systems file, it sends the *send* message, which is the login name on your system.

Pause here and remember that the data coming and going between any two systems, the modems, all that phone equipment, the satellites, and the switching gear is very "noisy," and stray characters will probably be interjected. This is an important consideration when you expect to transfer files on a nonpacketizing system like cu.

Once a log name is sent and acknowledged, uucico sends the password. If the login is accepted, the real fun begins. The link has been set up, and both systems can communicate. Unless told otherwise, the sending system completes any queued-up business first. The operation then shifts to the work directory, /usr/spool/uucp. (In pre-HDB UUCP, files have the name of the remote system embedded in the file name, such as D.roninB1234. In HDB UUCP, each node has its own directory.) Now all files to be transferred, all remote mail to be sent, and all remote commands to be executed go out. Next, the process reverses, and the called system does the same—sending files, mail, and commands for remote execution. When all work is complete, uucico hangs up the phone, writes to the log file, and goes away.

The *Systems* File

If you have followed all the steps explained in the preceding sections, you are close to getting UUCP working. Now you need to create your UUCP systems file. This file tells UUCP what systems it can call and how to call them. On HDB UUCP, it is `/usr/lib/uucp/Systems` and looks like this:

```
dragon Any hunter 9600 - in:--in: bruce word: reptile
infopro Any ACU 1200 12015551234 in:--in: Uhunter word: UVideo
ronin Any PEP 9600 16035550000 in:--in: Uhunter word: UUpasswd
```

In older UNIX versions, the corresponding file is `/usr/lib/uucp/L.sys`, and here's how it looks:

```
dragon Any tty12 9600 - in:--in: bruce word: reptile
infopro Any tty11 1200 tty11 12015551234 ogin:-EOT-ogin: Uhunter \
 ?sword: UVideo
ronin Any tty13 9600 tty13 16035550000 ogin:-EOT-ogin: Uhunter \
 ?sword: UUpasswd
```

Here the node names are `dragon`, `infopro`, and `ronin`. The second field in the `Systems` file is the time of day when calls are allowed to that system. For cost and security reasons, you may want to limit call time, and this is the field in which to do it. An entry of `Never` or `None` prevents all calls to that system, so *they* have to poll *you*. Any allows calls at any time. Days are entered as one or more of

```
Su Mo Tu We Th Fr Sa Wk
```

where `Wk` stands for every day, Monday through Friday. You can enter time as a range, further modifying which days to call. The classic 9-to-5 is entered on a 24-hour clock basis so that 0900-1700 is the equivalent of 9:00 AM to 5:00 PM. Thus, the entry

```
SaSu0615-1800
```

means Saturday/Sunday dialouts only from 6:15 AM to 6:00 PM. The most inexpensive time to call is late evening to early morning, which can be entered as

```
Any2301-0759
```

Note that no spaces are allowed in this field.

The third field in the HDB Systems file is the type of device that UUCP must deal with. If the device is a modem, it is usually called ACU. (Notice that the Devices name for ronin is PEP. It could be anything as long as you have defined it in the Devices file. In this case, the Devices entry forces Telebit's high-speed PEP protocol.) If the Devices entry is a network, use a name, like micom or devcon, that is recognized by the Devices file. If the connection is direct, use the system node name (a link to dragon has dragon in this field). The word Direct is not applicable in this field because even a direct line has to be to a system with a node name.

On older systems that use an L.sys file instead of a Systems file, you may need to enter the tty line like this:

```
dragon Any tty12 9600 - in:--in: bruce word: reptile
```

The fourth field is class or speed. It normally has the baud rate or (line) speed of the ACU or line. This field may have a letter as well, such as D1200 or C1200. The letter is a reference to the Devices file and stands for a type of PBX such as *D*imension or *C*entrex.

The fifth field is the phone number. It can be straightforward, such as

```
12135559876
```

which translates to

```
1 (213) 555-9876
```

Or this field may use substitute strings from another file, /usr/lib/uucp/Dialcodes. An example is

```
LA5559876
```

where LA was defined in Dialcodes as

```
1 213
```

L.sys files have an extra field before the phone number, where you should again put the tty line.

The rest of the Systems line is a bit tricky. It consists of a sequence of entries that are subfields and have the format

expect send

An expect-send sequence looks like this:

```
ogin: uucp
```

The *expect* is a substring. Thus, Login: or login: satisfies the substring ogin:. Once the expected string is received, uucico sends the log name uucp.

All this is fine in theory, but in practice a single expect-send won't work. The reason is that systems send a lot of garbage when a login starts, such as

```
Welcome to Mos Eisley 5 with Unisys 3.1
```

so a series of repetitive expect-sends must go out. This is especially true if more than one baud rate may be used on the system being called. A pair of hyphens (--) causes the expect-send to repeat, so

```
ogin:--ogin:
```

repeats the expect sequence after about 30 seconds if it isn't received properly the first time. The *send* is the full log name expected by the getty at the other end. You need to enter the password sequence, if any, with an expect-send as well. Note an example:

```
ogin:--ogin: bond sword: jb007
```

As for dialer scripts, you can use a number of convenient escape characters and strings with special meanings. These are listed in Table 12.2.

Table 12.2. Escape characters and strings for the Systems file.

Characters/String	Description
" "	Empty string (nothing)
\N	Null
\b	Backspace (BREAK on BSD systems)
\c	Suppress newline (like echo)
\d	A two-second delay
\p	Pause (about 1/4 to 1/2 second)
\n	Newline
\r	Carriage return
\s	A space or 020 hex
\t	Tab
\\	An escaped \
EOT	ASCII EOT (end of transmission or Ctrl-D)
\ddd	A sequence of octal digits like \006 for ACK
BREAK	A break

Not all the escapes work on all systems, but give them a try. A handy string is BREAK or BREAK1. It sends out the *break* character, useful for switching baud rates on systems that use more than one connection baud rate. If the first expect-send pair is not satisfied, you might be at the wrong baud rate. The following line can start the sequence of baud rates over again:

```
gold Any tty2 1200 5551212 ?login:-BREAK1--?login: uucp
```

Fooling *uucico*

If your modem isn't directly supported and your system uses L.sys instead of Systems, uucico won't know how to send out the proper dialing sequences. But because the L.sys file sends out arbitrary strings on the basis of other received strings, you can put the dialing sequence right in the L.sys file. Here's how a typical entry looks when used with a Hayes modem:

```
hunter Any tty2 1200 tty2 ATDT5551234 ?login:--?login: uucp
```

Very simply, uucico sends out the Hayes ATDT dialing sequence once the line to the modem is opened. This technique has proved successful on many systems with different modem brands.

UUCP Logins

The password file /etc/passwd has to be modified. It requires an entry for UUCP and traditionally for nuucp, as well as for any users that are allowed to dial in through cu. Here you see some entries from a passwd file:

```
uucp:4gq5h:5:4:UUCP:/usr/spool/uucppublic:/usr/lib/uucp/uucico
Uinfopro:yS75hb:5:4::/usr/spool/uucppublic:/usr/lib/uucp/uucico
Uintel:f13d8h:5:4::/usr/spool/uucppublic:/usr/lib/uucp/uucico
nuucp:iZ3W4Nf(CWhaIeg:4:4:uucp Administrator:/usr/lib/uucp:
david:zCQrpnUP1s22:23:22:David Fiedler:/us/david:/bin/csh
```

Notice that the nuucp entry has no conventional shell but instead uses /usr/lib/uucp/uucico as a shell. *This is imperative.* uucico is the workhorse program of UUCP and must be brought up when UUCP logs in. UUCP's home directory (top line, sixth field) should be /usr/spool/uucppublic on most systems because that's the default place to put files received by UUCP.

For security reasons, you should give every computer that calls you its own UUCP login. If everybody uses the login name uucp, it's hard to track specific system logins. Don't even try to make the uucp login name the same as the system node name; terrible things will happen. Use a leading U or u as we've done. Notice that all UUCP login entries can share the same uid and gid numbers. Many systems are set up so that nuucp is the UUCP login name, and uucp is the administrative login. Either way will work; we advise that you set up your system the way the supplier intended.

Saving Big Bucks

As delivered, the uux and UUCP programs usually activate uucico immediately, which means that your system will attempt to dial out whenever mail or a file is sent. You can alter this method of operation with a -r flag option to these programs (undocumented on most systems), which stops uucico from being automatically executed. In this way, you can run uucico from the cron at regular intervals so that all mail queued within that interval goes out at once. If you don't have the source code for UUCP, the only way to change the operation of uux is to create a "phony" uux that calls the real one with the flags you want:

```
# ls -l /bin/uux
-rwsr-xr-x 1 nuucp sys 28130 Dec 4 1984 /bin/uux
# cat > /usr/local/uux
exec /bin/UUX -r $*
^D
# chmod +x /usr/local/uux
# ls -l /usr/local/uux
-rwxr-xr-x 1 root bin 20 Dec 11 15:36 /usr/local/uux
# mv /bin/uux /bin/UUX
# cp /usr/local/uux /bin/uux
#
```

Now the "real" executable uux program is safely stored as /bin/UUX, and your shell version passes to it any flags it was called with, *plus* the -r flag you want. Now you must make sure that uucico is executed every hour or so in a manner that causes it to dial out only to systems with work pending. For this, we recommend using the following lines (or their equivalent) in a file called /usr/lib/uucp/uudemon.hr, to be run every hour from cron:

```
cd /usr/lib/uucp
/usr/bin/uulog
exec uucico -r1
```

The uulog command consolidates any pending log information, and executing uucico with the -r1 flag performs the necessary phone calls. (This is provided as part of HDB UUCP.)

Telebit Modems

Currently, the most popular modems for UNIX systems are Telebit modems and modems that support V.32/V.42 error correction. Telebit modems have built-in data transfer methods that make high-speed transfers possible on voice-grade phone lines. In addition, Telebit modems have built-in protocols for error checking, including the UUCP, kermit, and xmodem protocols. But even the simplest Telebit modem is *very* sophisticated.

As with all modems that use "soft switches," Telebits use internal *registers* (memory) to hold the configuration information. The Telebit T2500 has more than a hundred registers. Some register settings are simply ON(1)/OFF(0), but most settings hold values from 0 to 255. Each register holds a separate configuration parameter—for example, the number of rings before answering an incoming call (register 1). In addition, there are some Hayes modem type settings, such as Quiet Enable (register Q). You can save two different configurations in nonvolatile memory; saving does not overwrite the factory default read-only memory (ROM), which you can always reload as the current configuration.

Because a Telebit modem can operate in many different modes, it is valuable to have different dialer/device scripts for each mode, or at least a sophisticated, single program to handle all the possibilities. SCO provides a compiled C program (and source code) for a Telebit dialer. But you may need to install a Telebit on some systems for which there are no ready-made programs.

Telebit modems have a default connection to the local computer (DTE) of 9600 baud. For you to set the registers in a Telebit, you must establish a 9600-baud direct connect entry in your /usr/lib/uucp/ Devices file. While you are at it, make an entry for using the dialer/UUCP connection. Note the following example:

```
Direct tty1A - 9600 direct
ACU tty1A - 9600 dialTBIT \T
```

For safety's sake, before using this direct line to the modem (in this example, on /dev/tty1A), be sure that a getty isn't running on that port. The /etc/inittab entry should look something like this:

```
t1Aa:23:off:/etc/getty tty1A m
```

(You can be sure that this entry is being used by issuing an init q.)

Now, to begin setting the registers in the Telebit, use the cu program to talk directly to the modem:

```
cu -1tty1A -s9600 dir                              — Don't include the dir on HDB

Connected
at                                        — Confirm that the modem sees us
OK                               — The modem's response to all valid commands
atn?                                    — Let's look at all the registers

E1 F1 M1 Q0 P V1 W0 X1 Y0 &P0 &T4      Version GF7.00-T2500SA
S00=001 S01=000 S02=043 S03=013 S04=010 S05=008 S06=002 S07=040 S08=002 S09=006
S10=007 S11=070 S12=050 S18=000 S25=005 S26=000 S38=000
S41=000 S45=000 S47=004 S48=000 S49=000
S50=000 S51=255 S52=000 S54=000 S55=000 S56=017 S57=019 S58:002 S59=000
S61=150 S62=003 S63=001 S64=000 S65=000 S66=000 S67=000 S68=255 S69=000
S90=000 S91=000 S92=000 S93=008 S94=001 S95=000 S96=001 S97=000 S98=003
S100=000 S101=000 S102=000 S104=000 S105=001 S106=000 S107=020
S110=255 S111=255 S112=001
S121=000 S130=002 S131=002
S150=000 S151=004 S152=001 S153=001 S154=000 S155=000 S157=000 S158=000
S160=010 S161=020 S162=002 S163=003 S164=007 S169=000 S255=000
OK
```

Next examine the registers listed in Table 12.3.

Table 12.3. Important S (switch) registers in Telebit modems.

Use	Register
Eight-bit comparison for local DTE	S48
Local interface speed	S51
DTR interpretation	S52
Break signal interpretation	S54
Flow control used by DTE	S58
Lock interface speed	S66
Flow control used by DCE	S68
Guard tone selection	S92
Data-carrier detected interpretation	S131

To continue this session with the Telebit legion of registers, set the S (switch) registers with the syntax s*n*=*N*, where *n* is the switch register number and *N* is the value you set to. All commands start with the attention string AT:

```
ats48=1                                     — All 8 bits are used for checking
OK
ats51=255                                   — Automatic speed select, 9600 default
OK
ats52=2                                     — Modem bangs up, resets, and will not
OK                                              answer if DTR is switched off
ats58=2                                     — Use hardware (RTS/CTS) flow control
OK
ats66=1                                     — Lock interface speed and use flow
OK                                              control
ats68=255                                   — Flow control for PEP, mode same as
OK                                              specified in S58
atn?                                        — See what we have done
E0 F1 M0 Q4 P V1 W0 X3 Y0 &P0 &T4     Version GF7.00-T2500SA
S00=001 S01=000 S02=043 S03=013 S04=010 S05=008 S06=002 S07=040 S08=002 S09=006
S10=007 S11=070 S12=050 S18=000 S25=005 S26=000 S38=000
S41=000 S45=000 S47=004 S48:001 S49=000
S50=000 S51:254 S52:002 S54=003 S55=000 S56=017 S57=019 S58:002 S59=000
S61=150 S62=003 S63=001 S64=000 S65=000 S66=000 S67=000 S68=255 S69=000
S90=000 S91=000 S92:001 S93=008 S94=001 S95=000 S96=001 S97=000 S98=003
S100=000 S101=000 S102=000 S104=000 S105=001 S106=000 S107=020
S110=255 S111=255 S112=001
S121=000 S130=002 S131:001
S150=000 S151=004 S152=001 S153=001 S154=000 S155=000 S157=000 S158=000
S160=010 S161=020 S162=002 S163=003 S164=007 S169=000 S255=000
at&w                                        — Save registers in nonvolatile memory
OK
~.                                          — Exit cu connection
```

The commands for setting the registers can actually be strung together in a single AT command:

ats48=1s51=255s52=2s58=2s66=1s68=255&w

This syntax can be used in chat scripts and set/reset strings, but if you are carrying on an interactive session with the modem, you should send a single command at a time. In this way, you can see which (if any) commands produce errors or problems. For example, if you don't have a proper cable for hardware handshaking between the computer and the modem, the command s58=2 will produce an unfortunate situation: *you will no longer be able to communicate with the modem!* Be sure to locate the power switch on your modem, and don't forget that the ~. is used to exit cu, even in this situation.

All of this may seem esoteric, but you will realize the value of these settings as you work with these high-performance (and highly configurable) modems.

HDB Dialers for Telebits

Telebits become very flexible if you take advantage of the Dialers file. A simple Telebit dialer entry might be

```
telebit =W-, "" ATs50=0 OK ATDT\T CONNECT
```

which says, "Map the wait-for-dial-tone (=) to the W command, and map the pause to the comma (,). Without receiving anything from the modem, send the string ATs50=0 for automatic speed determination between the local and remote system. When the Telebit responds with an OK, send the dial sequence ATDT\T and wait for the CONNECT."

This chat script has one problem: the modem has no way of determining what communications are to be used between itself and the local computer. Ah-ha! This can be taken care of easily (after all, this is a SMART modem). Just send a few As to the modem with some pauses. The modem can figure out at what speed it is connected to the computer from the characters you send. Here's a better chat script:

```
telebit =W-, "" A\pA\pA\pATs50=0 OK ATDT\T CONNECT
```

So far, the local Telebit and the remote modem (not necessarily a Telebit) have determined at what speed (and protocol) the two of them are going to communicate. Actually, with this chat script, the remote modem picks the communication parameters, and your local Telebit automatically follows suit. But what if you know that the remote modem is capable of using Telebit's PEP high-speed communications protocol? You want to force the local modem so that it will acknowledge only PEP, and the remote modem will follow the local Telebit. Don't delete your telebit entry in Dialers, but instead add the new entry

```
tbpep =W-, "" A\pA\pA\pATs50=255 OK ATDT\T CONNECT
```

where the name (tbpep or anything else) is different, and the s50 register is set to 255 instead of zero. You will want to have a new entry in your Devices file that references this Dialers entry. Call it something other than ACU, such as

```
PEP tty1A - 9600 tbpep \T
```

275

and you can use this device in your `Systems` file for any systems with Telebit modems in order to ensure that you get the maximum data-transfer rates possible (for file transfers). A typical use of PEP in a `Systems` entry might look like this:

```
ronin Any PEP 9600 16035550000 in:--in: Uhunter word: UUCPpasswd
```

One problem remains. When you have completed the PEP connection, the local modem is still set to accept only PEP connections (s50=255); it has not been reset to automatic speed determination (s50=0). If s52=2 and DTR drop, the modem resets by itself. Now you can understand the use for a `Dialers` hangup script, one that starts with an ampersand (&). For example, the hangup script for the `tbpep` dialer might be

```
&tbpep =W-, "" +++A\pA\pA\pATHS50=0 OK
```

V.32 Communications

PEP mode may be excellent for file transfers, but it is not very good at online communications in which the data moves back and forth, one character at a time. The reason is that PEP is optimized for large blocks of data (packets); the overhead of PEP slows down single-character blocks. For high-speed, single-character communications, you probably want V.32 protocol. There are many modem manufacturers that make models which support V.32. The Telebit T2500 is one such modem. (It does it all—standard communications, PEP, and V.32.)

Here is an example of a Telebit V.32 `Dialers` script:

```
tbv32 =W-, "" A\pA\pA\pATs50=6 OK ATDT\T CONNECT
```

Here is a `Devices` script:

```
V32 tty1A - 9600 tbv32 \T
```

And here is a `Systems` script:

```
ronin Any V32 9600 16035550000 in:--in: Uhunter word: UUCPpasswd
```

Finishing Up the Telebit Installation

Without starting up a `getty` or `uugetty`, try connecting out to another system. Try connecting with both `cu` and `uucico`. When you are sure that things are working, go ahead and change your `/etc/inittab` entry to something like this:

```
t1A:2:respawn:/usr/lib/uucp/uugetty -r -t 60 tty1A 9600
```

Pay attention to the 9600-baud reference to your /etc/gettydefs; be sure that one is defined. You may want to make some changes to it—for example, watch for IGNPAR or PARENB. As a side note, Telebits can communicate with the local computer at 19200 baud, but many computer serial ports are not reliable at this speed. If you have serial ports that can handle 19200 (with hardware handshaking), take full advantage of the Telebit by setting its local communications rate with register S51=254 and an equivalent inittab entry.

Using *uucp*

You use the uucp program for copying files to and from other systems. It is limited to working only with systems that connect directly to the local system, not for transferring files to systems that are several "hops" away. (The mail system and Usenet are capable of doing this.)

Copying Files to Another System

The simplest use of the uucp command is to transfer a file from your system to a remote system. Once you have established a reliable connection with another system, you should try to transfer a file:

```
$ uucp /etc/group remote!/usr/spool/uucppublic
```

Running this uucp command does not actually transfer the file directly. It creates a "workfile" in the same spooling directory used by uux. When a uucp command is issued, it executes uucico to perform the actual phone call. If your system returns a prompt, as indicated here, your /etc/group file has been queued for copying to the remote system. This illustrates one of the problems of the UUCP facility: unless you take certain steps, the security of your system can be compromised. Meanwhile, if an error message occurs, do this instead:

```
$ cp /etc/group /usr/spool/uucppublic
$ cd /usr/spool/uucppublic
$ chmod o+r group
$ uucp group remote!/usr/spool/uucppublic
```

Now go into the proper spooling directory for the system called remote (/usr/spool/uucp/remote for HDB versions or /usr/spool/ uucp for all others). You will see the workfile there, with a C prefix:

```
$ cd /usr/spool/uucp
```

```
$ ls -lt
total 169
-rw-r--r-- 1 nuucp uucp 72 Dec 11 15:48 C.remoten4KAd
---------- 1 nuucp uucp 0 Dec 11 15:48 dummy
-rw-rw-rw- 1 nuucp uucp 8013 Dec 11 15:48 LOGFILE
-rw-r--r-- 1 nuucp mail 56 Dec 11 14:50 D
-rw-r--r-- 1 nuucp mail 108 Dec 11 14:50 C.btyA4KAW
-rw-r--r-- 1 nuucp mail 665 Dec 11 14:50 D.btyB4KAV
-rw-r--r-- 1 nuucp uucp 75 Dec 11 08:12 AUDIT
-rw-r--r-- 1 nuucp uucp 1837 Dec 11 05:14 SYSLOG
-rw-rw-r-- 1 nuucp uucp 13168 Dec 10 23:57 Sys-WEEK
-rw-rw-r-- 1 nuucp uucp 53145 Dec 10 23:57 Log-WEEK
-rw-r--r-- 1 nuucp mail 59 Dec 10 21:33 D
-rw-r--r-- 1 nuucp mail 2633 Dec 10 21:33 D.pclesB4K93
-rw-r--r-- 1 nuucp mail 114 Dec 10 21:33 C.pclesA4K94
-rw-r--r-- 1 nuucp mail 114 Dec 10 21:33 C.pclesA4K4O
-rw-r--r-- 1 nuucp mail 59 Dec 10 21:33 D
-rw-r--r-- 1 nuucp mail 1531 Dec 10 21:33 D.pclesB4K4N
$ cat C.remoten4KAd
S /usr/spool/uucppublic/group /usr/spool/uucppublic david \
-dc D.0 644
```

The contents of the workfile tell uucico that the file /usr/spool/uucppublic/group must be sent to the directory /usr/spool/uucppublic, that the originator of the request is david, and that the mode of the file is 644.

Because our system has been set up for delayed calling (as explained earlier in the section "Saving Big Bucks"), this workfile sits around waiting until we poll the system called remote (or they poll us). If all goes well, the file is transferred, and the workfile is removed.

Why do we continually specify the /usr/spool/uucppublic directory for file transfers? On most systems, this is the UUCP "public directory" (PUBDIR in some of the documentation), which can always be assumed to permit file transfers into or out of a UNIX-based computer system. With proper security, this directory is the only one that your system should use as well. Because the name is so long, it can be shortened to a single tilde (~) in UUCP commands, as in this example:

```
$ uucp file.c remote!~
$
```

This saves a great deal of typing. If you are using the C shell, you have to "backslash" the ! character:

```
% uucp file.c remote\!~
%
```

Copying Files from Other Systems

If you can have a UUCP connection to another system with normal security levels, a regular user can ordinarily perform the following tasks:

- Copy files from the PUBDIR area of the local system to the PUBDIR area of the remote system

- Copy files from the PUBDIR area of the remote system to the PUBDIR area of the local system (except on HDB releases)

- Send mail to a user on the remote system

- Queue mail to the remote system for transmission to more distant systems to which the remote is connected

Some UUCP systems have the utilities uuto and uupick, which are easier to use than uucp for sending and receiving files from remote systems.

Electronic Mail and Usenet

Apart from file transfer, you will find UUCP most useful for sending electronic mail to remote computers. Around the world is a network of tens of thousands of UNIX computers. By setting up a UUCP connection to one of these connected sites, you can contact any of the millions of users on these systems. (Actually, many of the connected systems run operating systems other than UNIX. The E-mail connections have been extended to other networks, including CompuServe.)

You may be interested in Usenet—a loose collection of systems that do far more than pass mail back and forth. They send collections of "articles" to each other, organized by "newsgroups" about various subjects. These articles are written and contributed by any of the thousands of people on the net. Usenet is sort of like a daily newspaper with different columns—sports, music, technical discussions, and so on—except that anyone can write for the net. As you might expect, a great variety of material, in both quantity and quality, can be found on Usenet.

The process of setting up and maintaining UUCP mail and Usenet news is a major system administration topic of its own. It's covered in detail in Chapter 14, "Mail and News Systems."

kermit and *xmodem*

kermit is not standard UNIX. It is a communications protocol developed to make file transfer possible among minis, micros, and mainframes. It will go places that cu and UUCP will not. cu will talk to anything, even a toaster, if it has an RS-232 port and an I/O board. cu does not packetize data, however, and is not practical on long or "dirty" lines. kermit will go anywhere as long as there is a kermit program at the other end, and it does packetize data, which greatly increases data reliability. kermit is a public domain program and available from sources such as Columbia University in New York City for the price of the tape and handling, as well as on the Usenet network and BIX. With the exception of Ward Christensen's modem7 program, few communications programs have spread as quickly as kermit.

modem7 is a program written many years ago to enable personal computer users to transmit files to one another with some degree of error checking. While originally written in assembler language for the 8080, modem7 was ported to many different architectures and languages, including C. xmodem is a UNIX implementation of the modem7 protocol, which gets you into the act. xmodem is also available on Usenet and BIX. Most PC communications programs support one or another of these communications protocols.

The use of kermit or xmodem is simplicity itself. You must first determine that the identical program is present on the remote site, and know the device name of your outgoing modem. Once you have made the initial connection (using kermit or even cu), you just type **xmodem s filename** on the sending computer and **xmodem r filename** on the receiving computer. The two programs "sync up" with each other, and the file is transferred. There are several different implementations of both kermit and xmodem (the program you actually run may be called ckermit or umodem), but the general idea is the same for all of them. Some have batch transfer capabilities, so you can type **kermit s *.c** and send all the C programs in a directory. One version of kermit allows you to set up a mail system by using kermit to transfer the files rather than using UUCP.

Transmission without Tears

An important consideration in UUCP file transmission is the use of packet transmission. You've already seen that "noisy" phone lines can make data transmission difficult with cu, a transmission method without packet checking.

Here is a brief review of packet transmission. Data is sent in packets—small bundles of characters put together by the sending system and taken by the remote system. Each packet contains a checksum, a number generated by adding the actual bit patterns of the characters sent. The receiving system uses the same checksum algorithm. If the checksums don't agree, something is wrong; "dirt" has entered the line. The packet is then rejected and re-sent. Watch UUCP working by observing the send and receive lights on your modem. In the first phase, when your system is sending, the send light stays on for a few seconds, and then the receive light flickers. In the second phase, when the system is receiving, the receive light stays on, and the send light flickers. The flicker is the transmission of the checksum from the receiving system.

For short transmissions—such as on a local (direct) line that is shielded and of a reasonably short length, or a local call on a very clean dialup line—cu *may* get your data across in one piece. If it is ASCII text, like a letter or memo, it may be OK. Code or data usually isn't worth risking. Use a packet transmission method like UUCP, xmodem, or kermit.

There is more to the overall UUCP system than uucico. Polling must be taken care of in an orderly manner. Unsent packages and old log files must be swept up and thrown out with the trash. These tasks, as well as how to automate them, are covered next.

The *cron* Files

Two tasks must be handled automatically on a regular basis in order for UUCP to function well. These are polling and cleaning up /usr/spool/uucp. The following is a crontab excerpt from HDB:

```
# root's crontab entry
#
41,11 8-17 * * * /bin/su uucp -c "/usr/lib/uucp/uudemon.poll" \
> /dev/null 2>&1
45,15 * * * * /bin/su uucp -c "/usr/lib/uucp/uudemon.hour" \
> /dev/null 2>&1
50 23 * * * /bin/su uucp -c "/usr/lib/uucp/uudemon.cleanup" \
> /dev/null 2>&1
```

The first entry says, "At 11 and 41 minutes after the hour from 8 AM to 5 PM any day, poll those systems listed in /usr/lib/uucp/Poll." uudemon.hour runs uucico for any systems with outstanding work (including systems set up to be polled by uudemon.poll). The last entry says, "At 10 minutes to midnight (11:50 PM) every day, clean up logs and directories." (This is accomplished within the shell procedure called uudemon.cleanup, which removes any logs and directories more than three days old.) If you have regular file transmissions on Fridays, you may want to use a different schedule.

You can perform many of these tasks manually. uudemon.cleanup cleans up, but you have the option of saying when and how often. uucico and Uutry can be used to force polling.

The shell program uudemon.admin may be run once a day (before uudemon.cleanup) to have daily statistics about UUCP mailed to the administrative login uucp.

One or Two Modems?

In the past, all serious UNIX systems with communications ran on a minimum of two modems: one for incoming calls and one for outgoing calls. Under HDB, the uugetty command makes running with one modem possible because a port can now be bidirectional. With the old UUCP, the ports can be switched programmatically with a script or C program that changes the definition of the port in /etc/ttys and resets the modem for incoming or outgoing calls. Here is a shell script to do that for those old systems:

```
# modem
# adds or removes getty from modem port and
# switches echo on or off
#
if test $# -eq 0
then
 echo " usage: modem -in for incoming data calls"
 echo " modem -out for outgoing data calls"
fi
case $1 in
 -in)
 ed /etc/ttys > /dev/null <<EOF
 1,$s/09tty5/19tty5/
 w
 q
EOF
 echo "ATE0\r" > /dev/tty5
 echo "ATQ1\r" > /dev/tty5
 kill -1 1
 stty 1200 even odd*>/dev/tty5
 chmod 666 /dev/tty5
 chown nuucp /dev/tty5
```

```
;;
-out)
ed /etc/ttys > /dev/null <<EOF
1,\$s/19tty5/09tty5/
w
q
EOF
echo "ATE1\r" > /dev/tty5
echo "ATQ0\r" > /dev/tty5
kill -1 1
sleep 2
stty 1200 even odd -raw cbreak \
-nl -lcase echo -tabs > /dev/tty5
chmod 666 /dev/modem
;;
*)
echo "no $1 option"
exit 1
;;
esac
```

Note that this script is a kludge, not a cure-all. It must be called each time the direction of a modem port has to be changed. Also SCO UNIX and XENIX use `enable` and `disable` to turn the `getty` on and off.

Naturally, if you have System V but not `uugetty`, you can still turn a modem from incoming to outgoing by setting up the appropriate entries in `/etc/inittab` and switching `init` levels. But modem control problems might still preclude this alteration.

Uugoodies

A number of UNIX programs (commands) make life easier for the UUCP user and the system administrator. Many are available as public domain software and are on the Usenet network. They are quite handy, but be forewarned that they may not compile on your system. Many are BSD (Berkeley software) programs and make reference to header files that may not be available on your system. Here are some of the more interesting commands from the standard AT&T UNIX distribution:

uucheck	Check the system for necessary UUCP files
uulog	Print out data from the UUCP log files
uuname	Set or get the system name (node name)

uuto	Similar to uucp but deliberately restricted
uupick	Accept or reject files sent to user
Uutry	Try uucico with debugging messages

Some of the more interesting public domain programs are these:

uuq	Manipulate the UUCP queue
uusub	Monitor the UUCP network
uuhosts	Extract and interpret network maps from the mod.map newsgroup
pathalias	Figure out the optimum path to any system from network maps and build database
msg	Screen-oriented mail program that can automatically send mail using pathalias database

Handy Shell Programs

As for the printer spooler subsystem, you should try to set up your UUCP subsystem so that it requires as little hands-on maintenance as possible. These little shell scripts are handy tools for determining what you need to automate and what may have gone wrong when UUCP isn't behaving.

uul

The uul program quickly shows you the contents of the spool directory, in time order:

```
ls -lt /usr/spool/uucp
```

uufol

uufol is a must when watching UUCP connections. It sits on the log file and shows you every new entry, until it is killed:

```
tail -f /usr/spool/uucp/LOGFILE
```

On HDB, you can use uulog -f system instead.

uutail

uutail is a quick command that lets you see the last few UUCP transactions and file transfers:

```
cd /usr/spool/uucp
tail LOGFILE
tail SYSLOG
```

On HDB, uulog -10 gives the same effect.

uurmst

uurmst is a useful program when things appear stuck. It removes all the old status files that may be preventing your system from dialing out:

```
rm -f /usr/spool/uucp/ST*
```

For HDB users, the equivalent is

```
rm -f /usr/spool/uucp/.status/*
```

poll

poll is an absolute must for testing new connections. It should be used only when no other UUCP activity is in progress (especially outgoing). poll forcibly removes any old lock and status files and polls the system named on the command line. The -x9 flag can be used if you like. Here is the poll program:

```
if $# < 1
then echo usage: $0 system [-x9] ; exit 1
fi
rm -f /usr/spool/uucp/STST.$1 /usr/spool/uucp/LCK*
/usr/lib/uucp/uucico -r1 -s$1 $2
rm -f /usr/spool/uucp/STST.$1
```

On HDB, you can use Uutry -r system instead.

sysname

The marvelous C program in Listing 12.1, by Pat Wood, actually changes the node name compiled into your kernel, so you can set the node name even if your kernel isn't reconfigurable. sysname doesn't actually change the file

/unix, /xenix, or whatever your kernel is called (this should be set in the program on the line that starts with #define UNIX), but instead changes the in-memory copy while the operating system is up and running. Therefore, if you need this program, you should run it whenever the system is rebooted (probably from /etc/rc). Just use the syntax

        # sysname *newname*

where *newname* is the name that you want your system to be known as. Note an example:

        # **sysname kramden**

Listing 12.1. sysname.

```
#include <types.h>
#include <sys/utsname.h>
#include <fcntl.h>

#define KMEM "/dev/kmem" /* kernel memory */

main (argc, argv)
int argc;
char *argv[];
{
 struct utsname uts;
 int memory;
 unsigned long nameloc;
 unsigned long unixname();

 if (argc != 2)
  {
  printf ("%s: needs system name\n", argv[0]);
  exit(1);
  }
 if (strlen (argv[1]) > 8)
  {
  printf ("%s: system name must be <= 8 chars\n", argv[0]);
  exit(1);
  }

 nameloc = unixname ();
```

```
      if (nameloc == 0)
  {
  printf ("%s: cannot get address for utsname\n", argv[0]);
  exit(1);
  }
if ((memory = open(KMEM, O_RDWR)) == -1)
  {
  printf ("%s: cannot open %s\n", argv[0], KMEM);
  exit(1);
  }

 lseek (memory, nameloc, 0);
 read (memory, &uts, sizeof (uts));
 strcpy (uts.sysname, argv[1]);
 strcpy (uts.nodename, argv[1]);
 lseek (memory, nameloc, 0);
 write (memory, &uts, sizeof (uts));
}

/*
** unixname -- look up name in UNIX namelist
** argument is a string to look up in UNIX
** returns address
*/

#define ATTSV /* define if running System V or V.2 */
/* #define BSD /* define if running BSD */
/* #define V7 /* define if running V7 SYS3 or XENIX */

/*
** name of the "utsname" structure changed
** as of System V from _utsname to utsname
*/
#ifdef ATTSV
# define UTSNAME "utsname"
#else
# define UTSNAME "_utsname"
#endif

/*
** define UNIX to be name of unix object file,
** e.g., /unix, /vmunix, /xenix.
```

continued

Listing 12.1—*Continued*

```
*/
#define UNIX "/unix"

#if defined(ATTSV) ¦¦ defined(BSD)
# include <nlist.h>
#else
# include <a.out.h>
#endif

unsigned long unixname ()
{
 struct nlist list[2];
 static char *name = UTSNAME;
 /*
 ** the following #ifdef is necessary due to a change of
 ** the definition of the n_name element from an array
 ** to a pointer
 */
#ifdef ATTSV
 /* set up name list array */
 char array1[10];
 list[0].n_name = name;
 list[1].n_name = "";
#else
 /* set up name list array */
 strcpy (list[0].n_name, name);
 list[1].n_name[0] = 0;
#endif

 /* get name list entry for "name" */
 if (nlist (UNIX, list) == -1)
 return (0L);
 return ((long) list[0].n_value);
}
```

Summary

Sharing files and information between computers is now an essential part of computing. When the systems are far apart, modem connections are often the most cost-efficient way of sharing at this level. The old-fashioned way of sharing was through direct serial connections and UUCP. Long distance connections include modems and phone lines as the media. As you learned in this chapter, UUCP connections are still widely used. But high degrees of sharing are available with the real-time networks—LANs (local area networks) and WANs (wide area networks). These are discussed in the next chapter.

13

Networks

etworks extend the usefulness of computers by increasing the communications and the number of ways in which different resources can be shared. Because UNIX wide area networks (such as ARPANET and INTERNET) provide many of the same facilities as local area networks, non-UUCP networking can be lumped into a single class of operation: real-time networking. Unlike UUCP networks, the real-time network connections can simultaneously connect several systems together. You can extend your local system with real-time networking in three common ways:

- *Remote logins.* Equivalent to cu, the user programs are rlogin, telnet, and windowed terminal emulators such as xterm.

- *Remote file systems mounted on local computers.* These are the facilities offered by NFS (*Network File Services*) and RFS (*Remote File Services*).

- *Distributed computing, in which part of the application resides on one system and the other part on another.* (The other two networking facilities are actually distributed computing applications.) One system (the server) provides some service to another system, the client (the consumer).

Your local system may be the system providing the services to another system or user, in which case your system is a *server*. The services might be the use of disks and tape drives, in which case the system is called a *file server*. The fastest CPU with the most memory could be doing all the heavy computing for the other systems on the network; in that case, the CPU would be a *compute server*. Some top-of-the-line printers can be hooked directly to the network and manage all the spooling and font management; you guessed it, that printer would be a *print server*.

The categories of server and client often overlap. For example, the X Window System program xterm can use the resources of a remote system to do the terminal emulation on that system, and open up a shell on that system so that any applications run in that window. The local system handles only the display of the window and the activities in it. The window display information itself is created on the remote system; only display *instructions* are sent to the system with the fancy display. In this case, the display is the *X server* system, and the system running the application has the *X client* processes.

Using real-time UNIX networks is no more difficult than running the cu command over serial connections. Often the use of this kind of networking is transparent to the user, who can be unaware that the computing or storage resources are on a remote system.

Setting up real-time networks is actually simpler than setting up UUCP connections, even though a great deal of mystery seems to surround real-time networks. But difficulties do arise when the systems are using different kinds of networks, protocols, and even versions of common network software.

The most common UNIX LAN installations use TCP/IP on Ethernet or thin Ethernet. The design of both Ethernet (actually a hardware and low-level software specification) and the TCP/IP operations and utilities is complex, and the subject of many books. You do not need to understand the many layers of design and operations in order to install, administer, and use these elements of UNIX networking. You just need to be able to identify and work with a few simple pieces of hardware and configuration files.

Ethernet

Three common varieties of Ethernet are used with UNIX systems. The popular terms are *thick-wire*, *thin-wire*, and *twisted-pair* Ethernet. (A fourth, very high-speed connection, known as FDDI, is just emerging as of this revision.) The thick-wire version (also known as 10BASE5 cable) is more appropriate for large networks with heavy use. It provides the greatest data transmission loads (10 million bits per second) and the greatest total network distance (500 meters). The thin-wire version (10BASE2 cable) can reach only a total of roughly 185 meters.

Twisted-pair (10BASET) configurations are not strung out from workstation to workstation. The entire network actually resides in a single box (the repeater) with separate cables (a maximum length of 100 meters each) running out to each station. This design is consistent with the office telephone wiring that is commonly used to implement this kind of network. All the lines may meet in a phone wiring closet at the 10BASET repeater.

The cable-naming scheme for Ethernet uses the bandwidth (in millions of bits), the kind of network (BASEband), and the maximum length of a segment (in hundreds of meters). For example, the 10BASE2 cable is 10 million bits per second and roughly 200 meters.

The main advantage of the thin-wire Ethernet is the cost of installation: the wire costs a fraction of that of thick-wire Ethernet; computers can be tapped into the cable at almost any point between .5 meters and the maximum length of cable allowed. Thin-wire Ethernet transceivers (the intelligent devices that link a computer to the network cable) are usually internal to the computer and less expensive than their thick-wire counterparts (MAUs).

Each Ethernet segment must be a simple string of computers; no loops or branches are allowed (see Figure 13.1). Except for making the cables, the physical connection to a thin Ethernet is simple: put a BNC tee connector at each system and connect a cable to another computer on each side of the tee. The beginning and end of the string must have a terminator (50 ohms) connected. This is usually done at the tee at the first and last computers in the network segment.

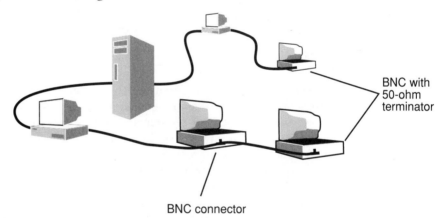

BNC with
50-ohm
terminator

BNC connector

Figure 13.1. *A simple thin-wire Ethernet.*

A thick-wire Ethernet is only slightly more complex to hook into (see Figure 13.2). At specified tap points in the Ethernet cable, you can attach transceivers. One transceiver may have connections for several systems. A cable, vaguely like a serial cable, connects the computer to the Ethernet transceiver. As with the thin Ethernet, a terminator is at either end of the string of systems.

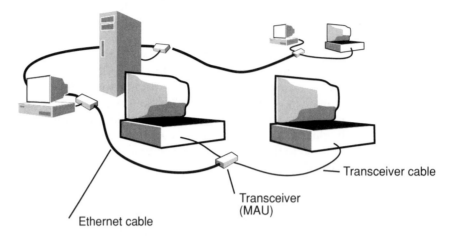

Transceiver cable

Transceiver
(MAU)

Ethernet cable

Figure 13.2. A simple thick-wire Ethernet.

You can create more complex networks by adding bridges and gateways, as well as repeaters.

Repeaters

A *repeater* is the simplest extension to a single string of computers tied together on the same network segment (see Figure 13.3). The repeater allows you to tie several segments together into one simple network. (Internetworking is covered in the next section on bridges.) Because an Ethernet network can have only four repeaters, the maximum total length of any single network is two kilometers. (This discussion is about LANs, not WANs, wide area networks.) Repeaters are little more than data amplifiers. The maximum time delay for data to move from one end of the network to the other is still the limiting factor on total length. Repeaters merely solve the problem of signal loss. But if you have *two* networks tied together, they can operate under separate limitations because the signal synchronization of one network is not dependent on the other. For this configuration, bridges are used. A repeater is cheaper, simpler to install, and easier to manage than a bridge.

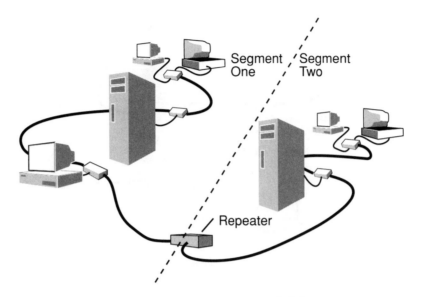

Figure 13.3. A repeater connecting two simple Ethernet segments.

Bridges

A *bridge* is a system (or network device) that exists on more than one network at the same time (see Figure 13.4). The bridge can be a computer or just an expensive dedicated "black box." The purpose of a bridge is to connect different networks together. Each bridge listens to each network and retransmits the data packets on the other networks. Networks joined by a bridge may feature different hardware designs; for example, one network may be an Ethernet 10BASE5 and the other an Ethernet 10BASET. But if the networks use totally different technology (for instance, Token Ring and 10BASE5, or TCP/IP and Netware), the connection requires a gateway. Bridges retransmit; gateways translate and retransmit.

Gateways

Gateways are responsible for translating protocols from one kind of network to another. For example, you would need a gateway between an Ethernet network and a Token Ring network, or even between a 10BASET running Netware 386 (an MS-DOS network) and a 10BASET running TCP/IP.

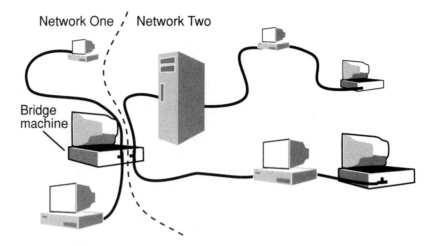

Network One **Network Two**

Bridge
machine

Figure 13.4. A bridge connecting two separate Ethernet networks.

TCP/IP

TCP/IP literally stands for *Transmission Control Protocol/Internet Protocol*. As for UUCP, TCP/IP is the name given to an entire collection of protocols and programs that operate above (and somewhat independently of) the underlying hardware.

When data is moving from system to system in the same data stream as that used for other communications, the data must be broken into pieces (packets); each piece must be identifiable as to where it came from and where it is going, as well as contain other information used to ensure complete and accurate transmission. Sometimes the packets need to be reassembled into larger blocks at the receiving system, but because the order in which the packets are received doesn't represent the order in which they are sent, there must also be information about what order to use when the packets are reassembled. The rules for this are specified by the TCP/IP protocol suite—the underlying structure to many UNIX network operations, often including the mounting of file systems that exist on remote systems with NFS (*Network File Services*).

The programs that make up the TCP/IP suite include (among others) application programs for logging into remote systems (telnet and rlogin), running programs on remote systems (rsh), and moving files from system to system (rcp and ftp). The UUCP equivalents are cu, uuxqt, and uucp. There are also daemons (such as inetd and smtpd) that run in the background, waiting for and processing requests from remote systems. The network daemons are covered later in this chapter.

As system administrator, you will be mostly concerned with maintaining a few important configuration files, such as /etc/hosts. Electronic mail connections become more complex when you have more than one type of mail connection. (Chapter 14 helps with this problem.) Your responsibilities may also include monitoring the network load and quality, and maintaining security over the entire network. These tasks may seem trivial, but they can become onerous when the network is large, complex, or always in a state of change.

Setting Up a Network

Just as with serial communications, networks have a hardware side and a software side. Before you can get the software completely working, you must have the hardware properly connected; thin Ethernet is much easier to use than thick Ethernet (unless, of course, you have someone else do the cable connections).

The Physical Connection

For standard Ethernet (10BASE5), the network cable and location of taps (connection points) must be laid out with care in order to prevent the data signals from interfering with each other. A transceiver (MAU) is connected at the tap on the Ethernet cable. Often a single transceiver will handle more than one device connection. The devices (workstations, servers, repeaters, gateways, and so on) connect to the transceiver with a multilead cable that has a special plug with a locking clip on either end. You do not need to bring the network down each time you connect (or disconnect) a device, but you might want to warn users on the network that their service will be interrupted while the new connection is being made. If the transceiver is already in the line, there is no interruption.

Thin Ethernet (10BASE2) connections are far less complex because the transceiver is built into the device's Ethernet hardware. You can tap into the cable at any point. The only difficulties come from the fact that the coaxial cable must run in *and* out; you cannot connect the device by using a branch from the cable.

The cable that is required for 10BASE2 is 50-ohm coaxial, commonly known as RG-58. The connectors are designed with a barrel shape that locks with a simple twist (BNC). Each device needs a BNC tee connection at it. The devices at either end of the Ethernet segment need a terminating resistor (50 ohms) in place of an outgoing cable. Because the Ethernet cable is actually cut at each device (rather than nondestructively tapped, as is possible with 10BASE5), you need to have BNC connectors on the incoming and outgoing wire. We have found that it is not necessary to use soldered connectors, but noisy networks will come from poorly installed connectors.

The twisted-pair Ethernet (10BASET) wiring is the simplest to connect but requires the most planning because all the devices are connected to a central point. Unlike coaxial Ethernet in which you essentially have a single cable that runs through the building, twisted-pair Ethernet requires a separate line for each device. On the plus side, this can be standard phone wiring that may already be in place in the office. (You cannot run both the phone and the Ethernet on the same pair of wires, however.) There is usually a three-pair (RJ-45) connection between the device and the network outlet at each station. All you need to do is plug the network card to the network jack with a fat phone cord and go to work, very much like installing a telephone in a flexible office plan.

A Simple Software Connection

Assuming that the TCP/IP programs are installed on the local system, the single item that you must pay attention to is the file describing which systems are connected to which network. The file is /etc/hosts, and here is a simple example:

```
# /etc/hosts
# address        system names
#
127.0.0.1        localhost
192.1.1.33       ronin ronin.ronin.UUCP
192.1.1.34       amiga
192.1.1.35       visual
192.1.1.36       mips
```

The structure is simple enough: the address (a number and dot combination) associated with a system name and optional alias names.

There isn't any mystery to the system name; you know about setting your system name from the material on setting up UUCP in Chapter 12. If you don't know what your system's name is, issue the command hostname.

The address field uses what is known as a DARPA Internet (IP) address. Although this can take several forms (classes), the most common (class A) is *net.sub.sub.host*, where each part (separated by dots) is a number from 0 through 255. Some special rules cover the *net* section (the network-

ID): the `localhost` must have this field as 127; the value 0 is reserved for systems whose addresses are known; the value 255 is the address interpreted as all systems (in other words, the broadcast address). Traditionally, systems that are not directly linked to the ARPANET use the network address of 192. The *sub* entries can be used to specify subnetworks and sub-subnetworks. The *host* entry must be unique for each subnetwork and sub-subnetwork. (Subnetworks are individual networks that belong to a larger, collective network. For example, a company may have a single, company-wide network composed of departmental networks.)

For a simple network (such as the one described in the sample `/etc/hosts` file), all you need to do is be sure that all the systems in the network have matching `/etc/hosts` files, and that all the systems are identified with unique host numbers and IDs. You are ready to start using the network—provided that all the TCP/IP programs are installed and the daemons are running.

Checking Your Network Connection

The simplest check for a good network connection is to use the program `ping` (which you must run as superuser). For example, assume that you are logged onto the system `ronin` and you want to check the TCP/IP installation and connections. You can start with testing the "loopback" by `ping`ing `localhost`:

```
# ping localhost
PING localhost: 56 data bytes
64 bytes from 127.0.0.1: icmp_seq=0. time=16. ms
64 bytes from 127.0.0.1: icmp_seq=1. time=0. ms
64 bytes from 127.0.0.1: icmp_seq=2. time=0. ms
64 bytes from 127.0.0.1: icmp_seq=3. time=0. ms
64 bytes from 127.0.0.1: icmp_seq=4. time=0. ms
64 bytes from 127.0.0.1: icmp_seq=5. time=0. ms
^C                                        — Interrupt the program
----localhost PING Statistics----
6 packets transmitted, 6 packets received, 0% packet loss
round-trip (ms)  min/avg/max = 0/1/16
#
```

If you are not successful with this test, something is wrong on the local system. (Some possibilities are considered in the following sections.) If you are successful, go ahead and try a remote system. Note the following example:

```
# ping visual 512 10
PING visual: 512 data bytes
520 bytes from 192.1.1.35: icmp_seq=0. time=0. ms
520 bytes from 192.1.1.35: icmp_seq=1. time=0. ms
520 bytes from 192.1.1.35: icmp_seq=2. time=0. ms
520 bytes from 192.1.1.35: icmp_seq=3. time=0. ms
520 bytes from 192.1.1.35: icmp_seq=4. time=0. ms
520 bytes from 192.1.1.35: icmp_seq=5. time=0. ms
520 bytes from 192.1.1.35: icmp_seq=6. time=16. ms
520 bytes from 192.1.1.35: icmp_seq=7. time=0. ms
520 bytes from 192.1.1.35: icmp_seq=8. time=0. ms
520 bytes from 192.1.1.35: icmp_seq=9. time=0. ms

----visual PING Statistics----
10 packets transmitted, 10 packets received, 0% packet loss
round-trip (ms)   min/avg/max = 0/1/16
#
```

This example specifies a test of the connection to visual, an X terminal (you learn more about X terminals in Chapter 15). The test uses 10 520-byte packets. Once you have established the connection on the network, you are ready to take advantage of the network resources.

Sharing Files and Directories over a Network

The TCP/IP and UUCP utilities allow users of one system to access files on other systems by giving the users such programs as ftp, rcp, and uucp to copy the files from one system to another. But having multiple copies of files spread about on a network is usually not efficient use of disk space and certainly not desirable if the file holds information that changes frequently. With the facilities of BSD's NFS or AT&T's RFS, a single copy of a file can be used on any system in the network.

From the user's point of view, NFS and RFS are virtually the same: files or even entire directory trees appear in the directory tree of a user's local system. Almost all file operations on remote files are done as if they existed on the local system. There are a few additional controls and some small restrictions; otherwise, remote files are indistinguishable from local ones. One of the greatest benefits of sharing file systems comes from the services of a file server, a system specially designed for large-capacity disks and efficient backup devices. By maintaining all of a network's critical files on these systems, file system maintenance for an entire network becomes almost as simple as file system maintenance for a single system.

There are some differences between NFS and RFS. Both are good designs but with different goals. NFS is designed to work in networks of heterogeneous operating systems. As a result, the file operations must meet the requirements of the least common denominator of all operating systems; for example, you cannot mv directory names across NFS remote mounted file systems. RFS, however, works only in a homogeneous UNIX environment and is therefore much faster and more predictable. UNIX programs that use file operations, such as distributed processing, are much easier to port to RFS than to NFS.

Both NFS and RFS are implemented in UNIX System V Release 4 (VR4). It is possible to have both NFS and RFS sharing the operating system at the same time.

The users will hardly be aware of the differences between RFS and NFS, but as system administrator, you will discover that SVR4 has common tables and utilities for managing both NFS and RFS.

To mount files on remote systems, you need to know a few things, including how to specify which directories should be available (exported) to which systems, and how to mount these directories on the other systems.

Bringing Up NFS Servers

On NFS systems before System V.4 (BSD and those derived from Lachman System V NFS), for a directory to be exported (made available to other systems), it must be listed in the control file /etc/exports. Each entry in /etc/exports contains the full path to the head of the directory, and an optional list of which systems can use it. Entries without system names are presumably available to all systems. Note an example:

```
# cat /etc/exports
/usr/catman                                # any system
/usr/mail                                  # any system
/usr/spool/news                            # any system
/usr/lib/news                              # any system
/usr/db byteact elwimpo honker             # limited access
/usr/production bytedit byteprod honker    # limited access
/usr/develop bytepb ronin elwimpo mozart   # limited access
```

Here the online manual (/usr/catman), the mail files, and the Usenet news system reside on this system and can be used on any system in the network. The other directory trees are limited to just the systems listed after the path name. The name (and IP address) of each of the host systems in /etc/exports must be listed in /etc/hosts.

Because UNIX System V Release 4 is designed to run both NFS and RFS, the control structures must be sufficient for both. On these systems is the subdirectory /etc/dfs, in which you will find the control file /etc/dfs/sharetab. Putting a directory name in this table is necessary if you want the catman file tree to be automatically available for export as the system comes up in multiuser network mode (init level 3). If you want to make the file available on a one-time basis, you can invoke the share command to make the directory tree /usr/public available to other systems:

```
# share -F nfs /usr/public
#
```

You can see what is available for export with the command dfshares:

```
# dfshares
RESOURCE                          SERVER ACCESS    TRANSPORT
    amiga:/usr/public               amiga   -          -
#
```

The share program adds an entry to the file /etc/dfs/sharetab. You don't manipulate the SVR4 version of sharetab by hand, but you can inspect it at any time:

```
# cat /etc/dfs/sharetab
/usr/public      -      fs    rw
#
```

If you want to remove a directory from share status, the command is unshare (obviously), and it has the same syntax as the share command:

```
# unshare -F nfs /usr/public
```

All of this sharing and unsharing may seem a little murky when compared to the simplicity of the earlier System V and BSD organization for NFS control with the /etc/exports file, but SVR4's organization is actually a great refinement. First, adding a directory tree with a command is easier than editing a file. Second, you have more control with share because there are more options than with the entries in the /etc/exports file. The entire syntax of share is

```
share [-F nfs¦rfs] [-o options] [-d description] [path]
```

Here are share's options:

-o rw   Read-write for all clients.

-o rw=clients   Read-write for the systems in a list of
                         clients separated by colons, such as
                         ronin:mips:sony.

-o ro	Read-only for all clients.
-o ro=*clients*	Read-only for the systems in a list of *clients*.
-o anon=*userid*	suid to *userid* for unauthenticated users.
-o root=*hosts*	Only root users from the specified *hosts* (format like *clients*) will have root access. Unless specified, *no* host has root access. This is an important security feature.
-o secure	Only authenticated users can access the directory tree. Authentication is provided by the RPC (*r*emote *p*rocedure *c*all) facilities.
-d *description*	A comment (statistical utilities will display it).

The options in the following example make /usr/develop available as an NFS tree, but only for reading:

```
share -F nfs -o ro -d "development files" /usr/develop
```

When the system is booting and network facilities are started, the initialization script will use the /etc/dfs/dfstab file to establish which directories are available for exporting. In a way, this file serves the same purpose as the /etc/exports file in older systems. The format of /etc/dfs/dfstab is simple; it is merely a list of the share commands that should be run, as in this example:

```
# share [-F fstype] [ -o options] [-d "<text>"] <pathname> <resource>
share -F nfs -d "public sources" /usr/local
share -F nfs -oro -d "public information directories" /usr/public
```

The network initialization script calls shareall to run this file. Its counterpart, unshareall, will prevent all directories from being shared across systems.

If RFS, not NFS, is running on your SVR4 system, these same utilities and tables are used. The obvious difference is that the file type for share is rfs rather than nfs:

```
share -F rfs -d "public sources" /usr/local
```

If you want to know which file system types are available on your system, they are described in the file /etc/dfs/:

```
nfs        nfs utilities: version 1.0
rfs        rfs utilities: version 2.0
```

The first type in the list is the default file system type.

NFS on Client Systems

Making the directories available on the server systems is only half the work. The other half is mounting the remote directories on the remote systems (the clients). The procedure is essentially the same as for mounting file systems that are local; the only difference is that you must specify that the files are on remote systems by prefixing the available directory tree with the system from which you are importing it. Be sure to have a mount point (an empty directory) on which to mount the remote tree. On some systems, you must specify also that the file system type is nfs or NFS:

```
# mount -f NFS amiga:/usr/public /amiga/public
```

Here -f NFS specifies that this is an NFS file system. amiga:/usr/ public specifies that you are mounting the directory tree starting at /usr/ public on the system amiga, and that /amiga/public is the mount point on the local system.

Some problems can occur with a simple NFS mount. What if the server is not available, either during the mount or during a remote read/write operation? Things are going to hang. For this reason, you can create what is called a *soft* mount; when the remote operation fails, the network file manager will return an error.

The following mount options are available:

-r	Mount as read-only
-d	Mount as a resource
-c	No local caching (force immediate reads and writes)
-fNFSspecial_options	Described in Table 13.1

Table 13.1. The `special_options` available with NFS mounts.

Option	Description
`soft`	Return error, rather than endless retry, if the server does not respond.
`rsize=n`	Set the read buffer size to *n* bytes. The default size is 8192 bytes.
`wsize=n`	Set the write buffer size to *n* bytes. The default size is 8192 bytes.
`timeo=n`	Set the timeout to *n* tenths of a second. You might want to set the level up a few notches for slow networks and servers.
`retrans=n`	Limit the number of retransmission attempts to *n*.
`port=n`	Set the server IP port number to *n*.
`nosuid`	Ignore `setuid` and `setgid` bits during `exec`.
`bg`	Do this mount in the background, allowing other processes to continue. This option is most valuable when the mount is part of the system startup.

Unless you are mounting remote directories on a one-time basis, you will want to have the process included along with other system startup operations. As explained in Chapter 5, the list of files to be mounted is usually contained in `/etc/fstab`, `/etc/vfstab` (SVR4), or `/etc/default/filesys` (SCO UNIX). To find out which is appropriate for your system, read the man entry for `mountall`.

A sample SVR3 `/etc/fstab` is:

```
# format: mountdev fs [-[rd]] [fstype]
# This file is used by mount, mountall, and rmountall

/dev/dsk/0s3 /usr
elwimpo:/usr/catman /usr/catman -r NFS,rsize=8192,wsize=8192,soft
elwimpo:/usr/ben/bix /usr/ben/bix  NFS,rsize=8192,wsize=8192,soft
```

A sample BSD /etc/fstab is

```
/dev/root                /          ffs rw 0 1
/dev/dsk/sdc0d0s6        /usr1      ffs rw 0 2
/dev/dsk/sdc0d0s7        /usr2      ffs rw 0 2
/dev/usr                 /usr       ffs rw 0 2
```

A sample SVR4 /etc/vfstab is

```
#      file-system-table format:
#
#      column 1: special- block special device or resource name
#      column 2: fsckdev- char special device for fsck
#      column 3: mountp- mount point
#      column 4: fstype- File system type
#      column 5: fsckpass- number if to be checked automatically
#      column 6: automnt-  yes/no for automatic mount
#      column 7: mntopts-  -o specific mount options
#      a '-' in any field is a no-op.

/dev/dsk/c6d0s1     /dev/rdsk/c6d0s1     /      s5   1     no    -
proc        proc             /proc      proc 1    no    -
fd          fd               /dev/fd    fd   1    no    -
```

And the SCO /etc/defaults/filesys looks like this:

```
  #
  bdev=/dev/root cdev=/dev/rroot \
      mountdir=/ mount=no fstyp=AFS \
      fsck=no fsckflags= \
      desc="The root filesystem" \
      rcmount=no rcfsck=no mountflags=
  bdev=amiga:/usr/public mountdir=/usr/public
      fsck=no rcfsck=no rcmount=yes
      mount=no fstyp=NFS nfsopts="soft,rsize=1024,wsize=1024"
```

The Daemons

The network daemons that run in the background are crucial to the operations of TCP/IP. Each daemon is watching for a signal to perform its own sort of activity. When you look at all the processes of a system running at the network level, you see a substantially greater process list than on a single, isolated system:

```
# ps -e
    PID TTY       TIME COMMAND
      0 ?         0:00 sched
      1 ?         0:43 init
      2 ?         0:00 vhand
      3 ?         0:02 bdflush
    342 syscon    0:04 sh
    243 ?         0:00 strerr
    172 ?         0:00 logger
    221 ?         0:01 cron
    235 ?         0:00 cpd
    227 ?         0:01 lpsched
    248 ?         0:01 inetd          — Network superserver
    274 ?         0:00 portmap        — RPC to IP mapping server
    250 ?         0:00 routed         — Network routing daemon
    253 ?         0:05 rwhod          — Network status server
    344 03        0:04 ksh
    258 ?         0:00 deliver— MMDF mail delivery daemon
    276 ?         0:00 mountd         — NFS mount request server
    278 ?         0:00 nfsd                    — NFS server
    282 ?         0:00 biod           — NFS block I/O daemon
    283 ?         0:00 biod
    284 ?         0:00 nfsd
    285 ?         0:00 biod
    286 ?         0:00 nfsd
    287 ?         0:00 biod
    288 ?         0:00 nfsd
    290 ?         0:00 statd              — NFS status monitor
    294 ?         0:01 lockd       — NFS lock for remote requests
    296 ?         0:00 rexd       — RPC remote execution server
    473 02        2:37 word.pr
    345 04        0:03 ksh
    346 05        0:03 ksh
    850 ?         0:01 uugetty
    723 ?         0:00 rshd            — Remote shell server
    348 06        0:01 getty
    725 ?         0:12 xterm
    735 p0        0:05 telnet
    740 ?         0:00 rshd
    742 ?         0:01 xterm
    743 p1        0:01 ksh
    889 03        0:00 ps
#
```

Not all TCP/IP and NFS installations will have all of the following daemons, but you should at least know what each daemon does:

- inetd — Network superserver

  Because many different services can run on TCP/IP, a *superserver* is needed to spawn the service that is requested.

- portmap — RPC to IP mapping server

  This daemon keeps track of which services are connected to which IP ports and directs incoming remote procedure calls appropriately.

- routed — Network routing daemon

  Listening on the appropriate socket for requests to go out over the network, this daemon figures how to get packets where they are supposed to go.

- rwhod — Network status server

  This daemon does more than serve remote requests for the who command. rwhod periodically (generally every five minutes) queries the state of the network and the system and then broadcasts this information. rwhod is also responsible for listening for other rwhod servers' statuses, validating them, and recording them.

- mountd — NFS mount request server

  This daemon answers requests about which file systems are available to which systems and users.

- nfsd — NFS server

  More than one of these little monkeys are usually running. The oldest is the parent; the others are the children. Each nfsd handles client file-system requests on the server.

- biod — NFS block I/O daemon

  biod is a close relative to nfsd, and more than one biod is usually running. These are the client processes that handle the local caching (read-ahead and write-behind) of blocks.

- lockd — NFS lock for remote requests

  Yes, there must be a way to extend the file- and record-locking facilities of UNIX out over the network for NFS file activities. This is the daemon that deals with that.

- `statd` — NFS status monitor

  A close friend of `lockd`, `statd` is responsible for handling crash and recovery services.

- `rexd` — RPC remote execution server

  This daemon handles both interactive (such as `xterm`) and noninteractive operations (such as NFS programs).

- `rshd` — Remote shell server

  This is the network client daemon for programs (such as `rcmd` and `rcp`) that need a noninteractive shell on the remote system.

Some of the preceding daemons are started by the network level `/etc/rc` script, but many are started by parent servers. For example, `rshd` is started by `inetd`.

First take a look at the `rc` script operations that are run by `init`. (The actual `init` level that starts these daemons is system-dependent.) The following is a much simplified version of an `rc` script:

```
#    initialize the nfs server with 4 children
/usr/lib/nfs/nfsd -a 4 > /dev/console 2>&1
#    initialize the biod server with 2 children
/usr/lib/nfs/biod 2 > /dev/console 2>&1
#    initialize the mount daemon for nfs & rfs
/usr/lib/nfs/mountd > /dev/console 2>&1
#    initialize the status daemon
/usr/lib/nfs/statd > /dev/console 2>&1
#    initialize file locking daemon
/usr/lib/nfs/lockd > /dev/console 2>&1
#    read the sharetable (only appropriate on V.4
#    and similar systems)
/usr/sbin/shareall -F nfs
#    mount all nfs partitions
/sbin/mountall -F nfs
```

This script just sets up and starts any file system sharing—a necessary preparation before starting other services, because there may be remote servers for other services. Serious network initialization scripts check the existence of any of the corresponding tables and programs before trying to run them.

Network Administration

The management and maintenance of large networks can be as complex and time-consuming as all the rest of system administration. There are special-purpose computers and software programs for doing some of the work, such as protocol and traffic analysis. Many tools for checking and monitoring the operations of the network are part of most distributions of TCP/IP. The simplest of all these programs is ping (introduced earlier in this chapter):

```
# ping visual 512 10
PING visual: 512 data bytes
521 bytes from 192.1.1.35: icmp_seq=0. time=0. ms
520 bytes from 192.1.1.35: icmp_seq=1. time=0. ms
520 bytes from 192.1.1.35: icmp_seq=2. time=0. ms
520 bytes from 192.1.1.35: icmp_seq=3. time=0. ms
520 bytes from 192.1.1.35: icmp_seq=4. time=0. ms
520 bytes from 192.1.1.35: icmp_seq=5. time=0. ms
520 bytes from 192.1.1.35: icmp_seq=6. time=16. ms
520 bytes from 192.1.1.35: icmp_seq=7. time=0. ms
520 bytes from 192.1.1.35: icmp_seq=8. time=0. ms
520 bytes from 192.1.1.35: icmp_seq=9. time=0. ms

----visual PING Statistics----
10 packets transmitted, 10 packets received, 0% packet loss
round-trip (ms)  min/avg/max = 0/1/16
#
```

In the preceding example, packet number 6 required a longer time because other activity was on the network. Whenever you run ping, check to be sure that all the packets are getting through. Look at those statistics at the end of the report. If you are missing some packets, you may have a break in the cable, a bad transceiver, or a missing terminator. Note that you must have superuser status to run ping.

Network Analysis with *netstat*

A general-purpose tool that is part of most TCP/IP distributions is netstat. In its simplest use, netstat provides a report of all known network connections and each connection's status. Running netstat on system ronin produces the following:

```
# netstat
Active Internet connections
Proto Recv-Q Send-Q  Local Address       Foreign Address       (state)
tcp       0      0   ronin.1592          mips.telnet           ESTABLISHED
tcp       0      0   ronin.1471          visual.6000           ESTABLISHED
tcp       0      0   localhost.1464      localhost.1465        ESTABLISHED
tcp       0      0   localhost.1465      localhost.1464        ESTABLISHED
tcp       0      0   ronin.1021          amiga.1018            ESTABLISHED
tcp       0      0   ronin.shell         amiga.1019            ESTABLISHED
tcp       0      0   ronin.1423          visual.6000           ESTABLISHED
tcp       0      0   localhost.1416      localhost.1417        ESTABLISHED
tcp       0      0   localhost.1417      localhost.1416        ESTABLISHED
tcp       0      0   ronin.1022          amiga.1020            ESTABLISHED
tcp       0      0   ronin.shell         amiga.1021            ESTABLISHED
tcp       0      0   ronin.1414          visual.6000           ESTABLISHED
tcp       0      0   localhost.1407      localhost.1408        ESTABLISHED
tcp       0      0   localhost.1408      localhost.1407        ESTABLISHED
tcp       0      0   ronin.1023          amiga.1022            ESTABLISHED
tcp       0      0   ronin.shell         amiga.1023            ESTABLISHED
```

You can also use netstat as a continuous monitor of network activity, as in this example:

```
# netstat 5
      input   (lo0)      output              input   (Total)     output
packets errs  packets errs  colls packets errs  packets errs  colls
4232    0     4232    0     0     24837   0      25702   0     4
0       0     0       0     0     5       0      5       0     0
1       0     1       0     0     4       0      6       0     0
0       0     0       0     0     5       0      6       0     0
0       0     0       0     0     21      0      18      0     0
```

The first line of data is a running total of each report column since the system was booted. With a command line parameter of 5, a new line is generated every 5 seconds. The display goes on for 20 lines and then repeats the header. The left half of the report is for the most active single connection. The right half is for all connections seen by the reporting site. Within each of these two consecutive reports are columns for the number of incoming and outgoing packets, the number of associated errors, and the number of collisions.

There are many different netstat formats; most of them report on information too detailed for this general text on system administration.

Why Does Network Administration Seem Complex?

When you move from a single-user, single-tasking operating system (like MS-DOS) to UNIX, you may ask, Why is it so complex? The answer lies in the fact that the responsibilities of the multitasking, multiuser operating system are an order of magnitude greater than simple MS-DOS. Networking is another order of magnitude; it is multi-multiuser, multi-multitasking. In other words, there are considerations that require coordinating many tasks across many separate systems.

Network management for a stable and simple network can be very simple, provided that the scripts and tools already exist (or are easily installed) on your system. But a lot is going on in a network, most of it behind the scenes.

Backing Up on a Network

Now that you have had the pleasure of giving network service to everyone else, you might as well take advantage of your best tape drive to back up other systems on the network. The following is a simple version of a backup, using tar format. The technique involves creating the backup format on a remote system and then streaming the result onto the local device:

```
rsh system tar cvf - * ¦ dd of=/dev/tape bs=20k
```

You can build any sort of variation on this theme that you want. Be aware that there are restrictions on root executing remote shells, so you will need a nonroot login on all the systems.

Summary

Local area networks (LANs) are the most efficient and inclusive method of resource sharing. The basics of setting up a simple network are almost trivial, but design and management can get so complex that they require full-time attention. The breadth of network administration tasks is as great as that of the rest of the UNIX system administration tasks put together. The fundamentals presented in this chapter will help you get started and will give you enough understanding (and tools) to be able to solve most simple problems and diagnose many complex problems. Don't be afraid to seek out a specialist in UNIX networks when problems get really tough.

14

Mail and News

Systems

Once you have your system up and running and your users start logging in and using it, they will want to use some of the famous UNIX communications facilities, particularly electronic mail and Usenet news. After getting through the twisty little passages of setting up your UUCP communications (Chapter 12) and establishing your LAN connections and services (Chapter 13), you are probably thinking that getting the electronic mail and news running will be a simple task. On some systems, this assumption holds true, but on many systems, installation and maintenance of these UNIX "benefit" applications can be a nightmare unless you have some good idea of what you are trying to do and what problems lie ahead.

From the users' point of view, mail is simple. You just send a letter, receive a letter, and reply to a letter. The only detail that the users have to worry about is accurate addressing. Now, with the institution of domain addressing (the kind with the @ character, as in ben@bytepb.byte.com), mail addressing is greatly simplified. (In the old days, addresses had to include the names of all intermediate machines, such as eleazar!dartvax!uunet!bytepb!ronin!ben.) But like conventional postal service, delivering mail is far more complex than sending and receiving it. Consider that all the local mail is collected at a local branch post office and sent to a central post office (if it isn't local mail). The central post office doesn't have direct routes to all other post offices in the world. It must decide on a route to the recipient's region. From there, a package is broken out to the local post office where the package is finally sorted for the mail carrier that delivers to the recipient's address.

If you consider that each E-mail site may connect to a dozen other sites, you can see that UNIX E-mail delivery is even more complex than the postal service. There may actually be thousands of different paths that exist between two remote sites. Some connections are over the Internet; others are over dial-up modem connections. Which is the fastest and cheapest path? That is the question.

Mail delivery is generally a one-sender-to-one-receiver matter, whereas Usenet news delivery is a one-to-many distribution problem. The problem now becomes how to send a message to all the machines without sending it more than once to any machine; this is a problem that programmers who develop news systems, as well as developers of standards, must grapple with. Your first task as system administrator is to install the complex software the news system developers have given you. But that's only the first step. Once you have Usenet news feeds running, you have to deal with 5 megabytes of new information a day—5 megabytes of *compressed* data that expands to 10 megabytes. How long can your system accommodate an increase in your storage needs by 10 megabytes a day—10 megabytes of information of questionable value? How do you decide what to throw away, and when? And you'd better not discard anything in such a way that the news system "thinks" you never received it, or you will receive it all over again in the next Usenet connection!

UNIX intersystem mail and Usenet news are *not* trivial system administration problems.

Electronic Mail Systems

Unlike the MS-DOS/PC-LAN world of E-mail, UNIX E-mail standards are well established, at least for the protocol for mail packets. There are some extended headers for interfacing to other mail systems, such as AT&T StarMail, but for the most part, UNIX mail messages can be sent from any kind of UNIX machine and successfully delivered on any other UNIX system. The major differences in UNIX mail systems are found in the user front ends and mail routers.

All UNIX systems have the simple `mail` front end or a somewhat enhanced version of a line-oriented mail posting and reading program, such as `mailx`. Because of the nature of mail routing systems, all UNIX mail systems enable you to post mail to more than one recipient at a time. You can group several people under a single name, and the mail system will properly distribute a copy to each person. You can "alias" an address in order to simplify sending mail to your more common recipients. These features are standard.

The most valuable enhancement on any mail front end is the facility for managing "folders," separate subdirectories or files of correspondence for each user with whom you communicate. With this facility, you can easily follow the separate threads of hundreds of conversations.

The second most valuable enhancement is the addition of an alias manager, a utility for capturing full E-mail addresses of correspondents and giving them a single, simple name with which you can direct E-mail.

The next level of enhancements includes implementations of E-mail that take advantage of the screen or window operations of your terminal or workstation. There is no doubt that fast, well-organized, menu-driven interfaces make any program more enjoyable to use and easier to learn.

An excellent example of an advanced front end for UNIX mail is `elm`, a freely available program written by Dave Taylor (see his chapter in *UNIX Papers for UNIX Developers and Power Users*, SAMS, 1987).

UNIX systems tend to have many kinds of simultaneous communication connections to other systems: asynchronous serial, X.25, and Ethernet, to name a few. Additionally, most systems have more than one user. When you send a postcard or letter at the local post office, you are not concerned with the kind of truck or airplane that carries your mail. In the same vein, when you send electronic mail, you shouldn't have to be concerned about what kind of connection your recipient has to your UNIX system; this is the work of the mail router.

The three most common UNIX mail routers are MMDF, `sendmail`, and `smail`. Although not as widely used as `sendmail`, the MMDF configuration is distributed with SCO UNIX (SCO is a major vendor of UNIX).

UNIX mail systems are built from layers. There is a layer for delivering mail to remote systems (the *transport agent*); there is a layer for handling mail at the local system (the *delivery agent*); and there is the user interface layer, the program with which users send, read, and respond to mail (the *user agent*). As you can see in Figure 14.1, each upper layer depends on those below it for doing that level of work. But the program at each layer can vary from user to user (in the case of the user interface program) or system to system (in the cases of local and remote delivery programs).

The user agent is the program for letter writing and reading. The most common examples of this kind of program are `mail` and `mailx`, the System V and Berkeley mail programs. As a freely available, extensive, screen-oriented mail interface, `elm` is gaining in popularity but is not usually distributed with systems. Sun, HP, and DEC have their own proprietary mail interface programs. (HP's program is actually a later version of `elm`.) The `emacs` editor comes with its own mail interface.

All mail interfaces must comply with the requirements of the underlying mail delivery systems and standard header formats. The two most common delivery agents are `sendmail` and MMDF, and as mail system

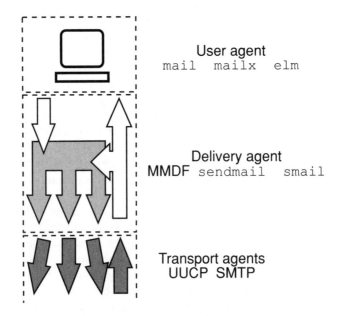

User agent
mail   mailx   elm

Delivery agent
MMDF sendmail   smail

Transport agents
UUCP SMTP

Figure 14.1. The three parts of UNIX mail systems.

administrator, you will be spending most of your time with these agents. As with network administration and news administration, mail administration on large or complex systems can seriously tax your time and emotions.

Even though the sendmail and MMDF systems deliver mail to users on the local machine, they rely on the transport agents to exchange mail with other machines. The transport agents are usually specific to the type of connection between the two machines.

On some systems, all three levels are handled by a single program, but in more common implementations of mail systems, the electronic mail tasks are divided among different agent programs.

MMDF Systems

The popularity of MMDF is due to the weaknesses of sendmail. MMDF provides more security than sendmail and is better designed for directing mail when the remote sites are connected in all kinds of ways. But with flexibility comes complexity. (Have we said that before?)

As you will see, the basic flow of mail through an MMDF system is different from that of other mail delivery systems. New mail is handed to the MMDF system by the submit program. The mail reading programs must be configured to hand off new mail to submit, as must rmail (the UUCP mail interface) and smdf (the local network mail daemon). If you are installing MMDF on a system that does not have the MMDF versions of these programs, you will be unable to make the mail system work. Conversely, if you are trying to install another mail delivery system, such as sendmail, on an MMDF system, you will have to replace mail, rmail, smdf, and any other associated programs.

The submit program is responsible for security, the spooling of incoming messages, and other control operations at the front end of the MMDF mail system. submit is like a postal clerk who checks for the proper postage and addressing method.

submit hands the messages off to the delivery agent, deliver (the name is a giveaway). This program runs in the background as a daemon. deliver is responsible for resolving addresses into the proper domain and channel, and then handing them off to the transport agent, the program that moves the mail down the channel. The deliver daemon uses a "compiled" image of the MMDF configuration tables.

Whenever you change any of the tables that describe MMDF (including mmdftailor, the channel, and the domain tables) you must run the program dbmbuild. The information in these tables is not used in its "raw" state; it must be "compiled" into a form that can be used by the MMDF system.

The *mmdftailor* file

The complexity of MMDF centers on the /usr/mmdf/mmdftailor file. It is best to edit this file only when you absolutely need to. The SCO (Santa Cruz Operation) installation script saves you the trouble of creating mmdftailor. As you can see from Listing 14.1, this file defines what files are used to build the mmdf system tables and the different types of mail delivery channels.

Listing 14.1. A sample mmdftailor file.

```
; mmdftailor

MLDOMAIN UUCP
MLNAME ronin
; MLOCMACHINE systemid
```

continued

Listing 14.1—*Continued*

```
UUname ronin

MSUPPORT ben

MTBL auser,          file="alias.user",   show="User alias"
MTBL lalias,         file="alias.list",   show="List Channel Aliases"
MTBL alias,          file="alias.ali",    show="Local Name Aliases"
MTBL local,          file="local.chn",    show="Local Host Aliases"
MTBL list,           file="list.chn",     show="List Channel"
MTBL uuchn,          file="uucp.chn",     show="UUCP Channel"
MTBL uudom,          file="uucp.dom",     show="UUCP Domain"
MTBL rootdom,        file="root.dom",     show="Root Domain"
MTBL locdom,         file="local.dom",    show="Local Domain"

MTBLDIR "/usr/mmdf/table"

ALIAS    table=alias,   trusted,   nobypass
ALIAS    table=lalias,  trusted,   nobypass
ALIAS    table=auser

MCHN local, show="Local Delivery", que=local, tbl=local, ap=same,
     pgm=local, mod=imm, host="ronin.UUCP"
MCHN list, show="List Processing", que=list, tbl=list, ap=same,
     pgm=list, mod=imm, host="ronin.UUCP", confstr=sender
MCHN uucp, show="UUCP Delivery", que=uucp, tbl=uuchn, ap=same,
     pgm=uucp, mod=imm

MQUEDIR "/usr/spool/mqueue"
MCHNDIR "/usr/mmdf/chans"

MDMN "ronin.UUCP", show="Local domain", table=locdom
MDMN "UUCP", show="UUCP Domain", table=uudom
MDMN "",show="Root Domain", table=rootdom

MMSGLOG    level=FAT,size=20
MCHANLOG   level=FAT,size=20
AUTHLOG    level=FAT,size=20
```

You should check the lines in the `mmdftailor` file that describe your machine name and domain. These lines begin with the keywords MLDOMAIN, MLNAME, and MLOCMACHINE. The sample `mmdftailor` file describes the default (unregistered) domain with these lines:

```
MLDOMAIN UUCP
MLNAME ronin
; MLOCMACHINE          — The ; indicates that this is only a comment
```

If you have a registered domain, your entry should look more like this:

```
MLDOMAIN COM
MLNAME byte
MLOCMACHINE bytepb
```

In the simple version (using `ronin`), it was not necessary to define `MLOCMACHINE`. By defining a `MLOCMACHINE`, you have actually made it possible for all users to trade mail within the domain without specifying which machine is the user's home machine. The added convenience is that no one has to remember who is on which machine. For example, without `MLOCMACHINE` defined, you would have to know that ben has his account on `iris.byte.com`. But with `MLOCMACHINE` defined, you could just address the mail to ben@byte.com. The disadvantage to having `MLOCMACHINE` defined is that all user account names must be unique throughout the entire domain. Therefore, if ben has separate accounts on `iris`, `bytepb`, and `elwimpo`, each has to be a unique account name—a "feature" that makes `rlogin` far less convenient.

Note the address of the user who is in charge of administering the mail system:

```
MSUPPORT ben
```

You could use the name `root` or `mail` (provided that there is an account by that name). In this example, the mail administrator is the user ben.

The next block of definitions, the `MTBL` entries, contains mostly stock items describing the individual delivery channel routing files. The fields after the `MTBL` key field are these:

name=   A name for the table (internal to MMDF)

file=   The file name of the table (the path is defined by the `MTBLDIR` entry)

show=   A descriptive line for use in reports and error messages

For example, the entries

```
MTBL uuchn,          file="uucp.chn",     show="UUCP Channel"
MTBL uudom,          file="uucp.dom",     show="UUCP Domain"
```

define the tables used for the UUCP delivery channel. Later in this discussion, you will see how these tables tie in.

The ALIAS entries describe which tables are used for resolving aliases. In the context of E-mail, an *alias* is a nickname for complex mail delivery paths—for example, a one-to-many relationship where one name (the alias) represents a group of users or even other aliases. You can also define aliases that are mailing lists, log files, and pipes to spoolers and other programs.

The order of the ALIAS entries in the mmdftailor file is important because MMDF searches for aliases in the sequence in which you list them. If you have an alias defined in more than one table, MMDF will use only the first definition it finds.

Each ALIAS entry specifies the table name (from the MTBL list) and an optional list of specifiers:

- trusted

  This specifier allows the table to define delivery to files and pipes. A table without this specifier might describe alias paths for mail that could contain delivery commands which potentially jeopardize the security of your system (for example, the mail messages that were the delivery mechanism of the infamous Internet Worm).

- nobypass

  This specifier prevents alias names prefixed with a tilde (~) from being interpreted literally—that is, without alias expansion. nobypass is another security measure.

  Note the following examples:

  ```
  ALIAS     table=alias,   trusted,  nobypass
  ALIAS     table=auser
  ```

The first entry, the table alias, points at the table of local system-defined aliases. It needs to be a trusted alias table without any loopholes; it is therefore flagged as trusted and nobypass. The second entry, auser, is the user alias table and is allowed to have any kind of entries.

The meat of the mmdftailor definition table is found in the entries that describe channels and domains, the MCHN and MDMN entries. The order of each of these lists is important for the same reason as for the ALIAS list; this is the order in which channels and domains are searched. Logically, the search begins with addresses that are deliverable on the local machine. Next are the mailing list processors because these may generate addresses that are on any machine. The next channels might be the LAN and X.25 channels. The last two entries should be the most costly (slowest) connections: the UUCP channel and the badhosts channel (the channel that figures out what to do with addresses that can't otherwise be resolved). You will want either to log messages with unresolvable addresses (and send an error message back to the sender) or to forward them to a machine that has the capability of resolving the addresses.

The first example of channel definition is the local delivery channel entry:

```
MCHN local, show="Local Delivery", que=local, tbl=local, ap=same,
pgm=local, mod=imm, host="ronin.UUCP"
```

Here reports and error messages will use the string Local Delivery, which is the show parameter. The que parameter is the name of the directory for queueing mail that is to be delivered on this channel. This is not the full path, but only a subdirectory name. The parent directory of que is described by the MQUEDIR (/usr/spool/mqueue in this mmdftailor). The table name in the MTBL list is given by the tbl parameter of the MCHN entry; in this case, it is the local table (you can use the same name for the channel and its table).

The ap parameter specifies the *address parser*, a program that reformats the mail message headers to fit some other standard. If, for example, some mail needed to be directed to an entirely different mail service such as BIX, the addressing method and headers would need to change to meet the requirements of the other system. The parameter specification of ap=same indicates that the headers are not to be altered.

The pgm parameter is the name of the channel program to be used for delivering this channel. The channel programs reside in the subdirectory specified by the MCHNDIR entry in the mmdftailor file. In this example, the local channel delivers using the program /usr/mmdf/chans/local; in other words, this program delivers the local mail.

Now for the mod or mode flags. A delivery channel can have more than one mode, in which case they are cumulative. Most likely, only one is selected. In the example, the mod=imm parameter specifies that this channel works in *immediate* mode; there is no need to spool up the delivery and send it as part of a batch. The delivery programs usually will do any spooling and batching of their own. Here is the entire list of modes:

reg   This is the default mode (regular), which means that this channel program may be explicitly invoked by deliver, a mail delivery program.

bak   This channel program must be invoked by a background deliver daemon.

psv   This channel is passive; some other program will come in and pick up the mail from this channel.

imm	This channel program is immediately invoked.
pick	This channel may pick up mail from the remote host.
send	This channel may send mail to the remote host.

The last parameter in the local channel description is host, the name of the host being used by this channel program. In the example, it is the local host, but in other entries, it might be the name of a system used for relaying mail. This parameter is required for the local, list, badusers, and badhosts entries in the MCHN list.

You can use many other parameters in the MCHN entries. Table 14.1 provides a full list.

Table 14.1. Parameters used in the MCHN entries.

Parameter	Description
name	The channel name
show	A descriptive string for reports and error messages
que	The queue subdirectory name
tbl	The table of hosts associated with this channel
pgm	The channel program name used with this channel
mod	The mode(s) in which this channel works
ap	The address parser for remapping mail headers (if required)
lname	An overriding local host name by which other hosts will recognize this system when connecting through this channel
ldomain	An overriding domain name (similar to lname)
host	The name of the host that is being contacted through this channel (required for local, list, badusers, and badhosts entries)
user	The account name that uses a slave program to pick up from the pobox channel
scr	The name of the dialing script to be used for the phone channel

Parameter	Description
trn	The name of a transcript file
poll	The frequency of polling a remote machine through this channel
insrc	Table name of hosts that control message flow
outsrc	Table name of hosts that control message flow
indest	Table name of hosts that control message flow
outdest	Table name of hosts that control message flow
known	Table name of hosts that are known on this channel (table must have been predefined under the list of tables)
confstr	A configuration and initiation string for another program
auth	Authorization test to be performed on this channel
ttl	"Time to live," a period to wait before retrying failed hosts (default is two hours)
log	Log file (instead of default)
level	Logging level

Most of the parameters listed in Table 14.1 are seldom used.

A domain defines a collection of systems that are somehow related. For example, all the machines connected in the BYTE local area network are in the byte.com domain. The relationship is not necessarily derived from the proximity of the machines, but from the institution to which they belong. There is a world organization responsible for registering domains and ensuring that there are no conflicts in domain names, that mail and internetwork addresses are unique. (The domain .UUCP is a generic domain for unregistered sites.)

Your MMDF mail system is designed to be able to take advantage of domain addressing. Even if you don't belong to a registered domain, you must create some MMDF domain tables for the default domains: the local domain, the root domain, and probably also the UUCP domain. You may also want to have tables for domains that aren't really domains (pseudodomains), such as mailing lists. As with all MMDF tables, the domains are specified in the mmdftailor table—in this case, the specifications MDMN entries. Each has three fields: the domain name, a show string for reports and error messages, and a table name that refers back to the MTBL entries. Here are some sample entries:

```
MDMN "ronin.UUCP", show="Local domain", table=locdom
MDMN "UUCP", show="UUCP Domain", table=uudom
MDMN "LIST", show="List pseudodomain", table=list
MDMN "",show="Root Domain", table=rootdom
```

The domain with no name (""), is the root domain.

The last entries that you see in the sample mmdftailor table are the definitions for MMDF log files:

```
MMSGLOG    /tmp/mmdf.log, level=FAT, size=20
MCHANLOG   level=FAT, size=20
AUTHLOG    level=FAT, size=20
```

Unless specified, the log file name is the predefined default for that specified log type.

The level parameter specifies what kinds of messages are to be sent to the log file. Each higher level of logging includes all the messages of the lower levels. In increasing order, the possible levels are these:

FAT	Send fatal errors only
TMP	Send temporary errors and fatal errors
GEN	Include general diagnostics
BST	Include some basic statistics
FST	Include full statistics
PTR	Include program trace
BTR	Include some better tracing
FTR	Include full tracing—the works

The last two levels, BTR and FTR, are not generally available unless your MMDF system was compiled with debugging flags.

The size parameter of the log files specifies the maximum file size for the logs. The size is in 25-block units, so a value of 20 on a file system that uses 512-byte blocks would mean 250 kilobytes.

There is an optional third parameter to specifications for log files: stat. There can be more than one stat (logging file operation flag).

Generally, you would specify stat=SOME, which means that when the file reaches maximum length, close the file and cycle logging, and wait if the file is busy. Other options are CLOSE (close the file at the end of each entry) and WAIT (if the log is busy, wait for it to free).

Here are the different log files:

MMSGLOG	Logging from the deliver and submit programs
MCHANLOG	Logging from most other MMDF programs
PHLOG	Logging on phone channels
AUTHLOG	Authorization logging

The Channel Tables

Compared to the complex mmdftailor file, the tables that describe the actual connections (the channel and domain tables) are simple. For each MCHN entry in the mmdftailor file, there must be a corresponding channel table. These tables list the host machines to which each channel is connected. For example, all the hosts that are contacted with UUCP connections are listed in the UUCP channel file (usually uucp.chn as defined in mmdftailor):

```
sosco.UUCP        sosco!%s
bytepb.byte.com   bytepb!%s
infopro.UUCP      infopro!%s
p100.UUCP         p100!%s
maxx.UUCP         maxx!%s
```

The left side of the channel table contains the *host.domain* for the connection. The right side contains a string that the channel program requires for contacting that host; in the case of the UUCP channel, the string is the "bang" path for a generic user at that site. The UUCP channel program would see the address tyager@bytepb.byte.com as bytepb!tyager.

Because each channel program has different requirements, the information on the right side may be different. For example, the local channel table (local.chn) looks like this:

```
ronin.UUCP    ronin
ronin         ronin
```

The variant name for the channel is on the left, and its MMDF short name is on the right.

When mail is submitted to the MMDF router, the data compiled from each channel table is checked until the address is resolved. If there is no resolution, the message is sent to the badhosts channel. If the message is totally undeliverable, MMDF returns the message to the sender with an error.

The Domain Tables

The domain entries defined in the mmdftailor file must have corresponding tables. Each entry on the left side of the table has a corresponding, fully qualified domain name on the right. For example, the domains that are associated with the UUCP channel are

```
sosco      sosco.UUCP
bytepb     bytepb.byte.com
byte       bytepb.byte.com
infopro    infopro.UUCP
p100       p100.UUCP
maxx       maxx.UUCP
```

and the domain associated with the local channel is simply

```
ronin:     ronin.UUCP
```

MMDF Utilities

No system this complex would be complete without some utilities to help set it up and administer it. MMDF is not an exception. The SCO distribution of MMDF (a standard part of SCO's UNIX licenses) includes uulist (found on SCO systems in /usr/mmdf/table/tools), which builds the UUCP domain and channel tables for MMDF. Additionally, SCO provides mnlist and mmdfalias for building the tables for Micronet channels and for converting alias files from XENIX and other sendmail systems. There is an undocumented program, /usr/mmdf/bin/setup, which appears to build your mmdftailor file for you (this may not be for human use!).

More important are two utilities found with dbmbuild. These are dbmedit (a general-purpose interface to the compiled MMDF database tables) and dbmtest (a test and evaluation of the paths through the tables). Both of these utilities work directly on the compiled database table, not the textual sources discussed earlier. Any changes that you make with dbmedit will not be reflected by the .chn and .dom files. Neither of these utilities is well-documented, but their output is fairly understandable. Note this example:

```
# dbmedit
dbmedit> ?
help      Print out help text
add       Add an entry
delete    Delete an entry
change    Change an entry
print     Print an entry
quit      Quit the program
dbmedit> p amiga
key "amiga": table "smtpdom": value "amiga.UUCP"
key "amiga": table "smtpchn": value "192.1.1.34"
dbmedit> a mips smtpdom mips.UUCP
dbmedit> a mips smtpchn 192.1.1.36
dbmedit> p mips
key "mips": table "smtpdom": value "mips.UUCP"
key "mips": table "smtpchn": value "192.1.1.36"
dbmedit> q
#
```

You can issue an entire dbmedit command as a parameter when you invoke it:

```
# dbmedit d
Usage: delete key [ table [value] ]
# dbmedit delete mips
# dbmedit p mips
key "mips" not found in database
#
```

The dbmlist program is a simple report of what exists in the compiled database:

```
# dbmlist
bytepb.byte.com:   uuchn bytepb!%s
list-processor :   rootdom list-processor<\034>list
                   list-processor
infopro.uucp   :   uuchn infopro!%s
bytepb.uucp    :   uuchn bytepb!%s
sosco.uucp     :   uuchn sosco!%s
ronin.uucp     :   local ronin
postmaster     :   alias mmdf
amiga.uucp     :   smtpchn 192.1.1.34
maxx.uucp      :   uuchn maxx!%s
infopro        :   uudom infopro.UUCP
bytepb         :   uudom bytepb.byte.com
```

```
sosco            :  uudom sosco.UUCP
ronin            :  locdom ronin.UUCP<\034>rootdom
                    ronin.UUCP<\034>local ronin
amiga            :  smtpdom amiga.UUCP<\034>smtpchn
                    192.1.1.34
mmdf             :  alias mmdf
maxx             :  uudom maxx.UUCP
byte             :  uudom bytepb.byte.com
com              :  rootdom bytepb.byte.com
#
```

In the preceding report, the last entry, com, will probably cause some problems. It implies that a user can address mail as tyager@com and it will go to tyager@bytepb.byte.com. Well, there are many .com domains.

A utility that you should use is checkaddr. This simply tells whether a particular address is acceptable or not, as in this example:

```
# checkaddr bongo
bongo: (USER) Unknown user name in "bongo"
# checkaddr david@bongo
bongo: OK
```

Wait! We know that no user is named "bongo," nor is any system named "bongo." What is okay about that second address? That address is okay because there is a badhosts channel. All sites that are *otherwise* unresolvable are handled by this channel. In other words, the test is not to see if david@bongo is a valid address, but to see if MMDF knows how to handle it.

The last MMDF administration utility, checkque, generates a report that you may want to have sent to you by a crontable entry:

```
# checkque

Sat Feb 16 17:06:  3 queued msgs / 208 byte queue directory
             11 Kbytes in msg dir


    0 msgs    0 Kb (local   ) local   :  Local Delivery
              deliver start            :  Sat Feb 16 16:15
              deliver message          :  Sat Feb 16 16:15
              deliver end              :  Sat Feb 16 16:15 / 0 hours

    0 msgs    0 Kb (smtp    ) smtp    :  SCO SMTP Delivery
              deliver start            :  Mon Dec 10 22:45
              deliver message          :  Mon Dec 10 22:45
```

```
            deliver end                   :  Mon Dec 10 22:45
            pickup start                  :  Fri Jan  4 20:27
            pickup message                :  Fri Jan  4 20:27
*** OVERDUE **  pickup end                :  Fri Jan  4 20:27 / 1028 hours

0 msgs    0 Kb (list    ) list    :  List Processing
            No deliver start
            No deliver message
            No deliver end

0 msgs    0 Kb (micnet  ) micnet  :  Micnet Delivery
            No deliver start
            No deliver message
            No deliver end

3 msgs   10 Kb (uucp    ) uucp    :  UUCP Delivery
            deliver start                 :  Fri Feb 15 05:40
            deliver message               :  Fri Feb 15 05:40
*** OVERDUE **  deliver end               :  Fri Feb 15 05:40 / 35 hours
*** WAITING **  First message             :  Tue Oct 30 20:35

0 msgs    0 Kb (badhosts) badhosts :  Last-Chance Routing
            deliver start                 :  Wed Feb  6 20:01
            No deliver message
            deliver end                   :  Wed Feb  6 20:01 / 237 hours
```

Now, if that doesn't tell all. . . . In fact, there is more to this report than anyone would want to wade through. Nonetheless, a time will come when you'll welcome the level of detail that checkque provides.

Don't Forget

Be sure that the directories exist for the spool and lock files listed in your mmdftailor file. If you add a new channel, you will probably also want to have corresponding spool, log, and lock files set up so that you can easily debug and administrate the new channel separately from the others.

Furthermore, don't forget that every time you make any changes to any MMDF source tables, you must rerun dbmbuild (usually found in the same directory as the MMDF tables), but dbmbuild will overwrite any dbmedit changes you made, because they are not reflected in the source files. The solution is to use either dbmedit or dbmbuild and the source tables, but not both dbmedit and dbmbuild.

MMDF is a mail system for secure sites. It is necessarily complex. Don't give up patience and perseverance!

sendmail and *smail* Systems

Like most UNIX utilities that originated at Berkeley, sendmail started as a student project. As you are aware, such a humble beginning does not imply a simple system or a limited distribution. sendmail is a big, overly flexible address-rewriting system. Its flexibility and complexity lie in the structure of a single configuration file, /usr/lib/sendmail.cnf (it may be located elsewhere). As far as distribution is concerned, sendmail is the most commonly distributed mail handler on UNIX systems!

The smail system is a much simpler mail handler, limited to UUCP connections. Often smail is installed along with sendmail to handle just the UUCP end of things. Like MMDF, sendmail does the mail routing and spooling, but relies on additional programs like smail (and smtp) to deliver the mail. The sendmail term for these programs is *mailer*, which is roughly equivalent to MMDF's *channel*.

Both MMDF and sendmail support aliasing, customized mailers (channels), message spooling and batching, use and error logging, automatic forwarding, and retransmission. But sendmail combines both the MMDF functions submit and deliver into a single program that usually runs as a daemon. MMDF is much more secure than sendmail. Usually, you don't have a choice; you are provided with either MMDF or sendmail.

When a user's mail reader/sender program (or any other sender, such as rmail) submits a message to sendmail, it collects and stores the message in a spool space while it processes the arguments of the submission and the header of the mail message. If all goes well, the message is handed off to the delivery program. If the mailer can't handle the message until later, sendmail queues the message for retransmission to the mailer. If either the mailer or sendmail finds errors in the mail message format or difficulties in delivering the message, the original message is returned to the sender with an error report added at the beginning.

Almost all sendmail configuration information, including its parsing rules, are read at runtime, when the sendmail daemon is first started. For this reason, if you change any of this information, you must restart sendmail. (This is not a concern if you are not running sendmail as a daemon but invoke it only when needed. Daemons require processing and memory resources.)

sendmail.cf—The Configuration File

Most of the configuration and rules are contained in the infamous `sendmail.cf` file. This file was designed more from the point of view of how the `sendmail` program would parse it than from how a human might understand and modify it. A typical `sendfmail.cf` file is 500 lines long (including comments). Hopefully, you will need to modify parts in just the first 30 lines:

```
# Host name and domain name macros.
#     Dw sets $w
#     DD sets $D
#     CD sets $=D
# This configuration file uses the uname default,
# unless otherwise modified.
# $D and $=D list all domains in which this host sits.
# $D goes into outbound addresses, i.e. "user@$w.$D".
# it will be turned into $D.
# HOSTNAME needs to be modified for each site
# (if there is no Ethernet).
Dwbytepb
DDbyte.com
CDLOCAL local uucp
# /etc/hosts.smtp The list of hosts sites using
# smtp (tcp/ip-Ethernet)
FE/etc/hosts.smtp %s
# /usr/lib/uucp/Systems The list of hosts sites
# connected directly via uucp
#FU/usr/lib/uucp/Systems %s


# Mock top-level domain names.  These names designate
# a transport mechanism and appear internally only,
# set in S3, used in S0, and removed in S4 and
# (possibly) the ruleset for the particular mailer.
CTETHER UUX
# Relay host.  Used at the end of S0 as the general
# depository for addresses which didn't resolve locally.
# R is used as the Ethernet relay host, S
DRuunet
#  End Local configuration options
```

As is obvious, the lines that begin with the hash mark (#) are comments. These first lines define the "macros" used elsewhere in the configuration file.

The first character of the noncomment lines specifies an assignment or action. For example, the lines that begin with D are symbol definitions (D for *de*fine). Lines that begin with C define a class from a list, and those that begin with F define a class from a file. A *class* is a logical group of objects—that is, names with some common relationship, like a table or an array. (Many other actions are specified by sendmail.cf, but these are all that you need to be concerned with for now.)

The second character is the symbol that specifies the recipient of the action. The active lines in the sample piece of sendmail.cf can be read like this:

Dwbytepb	Define the symbol w to be bytepb. This will be used later as the host name. In other words, wherever there is a $w, it will expand to bytepb.
DDbyte.com	Define the symbol D to be byte.com. This will be used later as the domain name.
CDLOCAL local uucp	Define the class D to have three members: LOCAL, local, and uucp. The sendmail program will handle these lists with the same mailer.
FE/etc/hosts.smtp %s	Define the class E to have the members that are listed in the file /etc/hosts.smtp. This file contains the list of sites connected through Ethernet (E for *E*thernet) and using smtp.
#FU/usr/lib/uucp/Systems %s	Define the class U to have the members listed in the /usr/lib/uucp/Systems. This file contains the list of all the sites that connect by way of UUCP. This entry has been commented out in this example because smail will be used to handle all of the UUCP connections.

CTETHER UUX	Define the class T to have the two members ETHER and UUX. This is the list of transport mechanisms (T for *t*ransport).
DRuunet	Define the symbol R to be the name uunet. This will be used as the relay host (R for *r*elay), the site that will resolve any unknown addresses (the "smart" mail site). This is equivalent to the MMDF channel for "badhosts."

That isn't so bad. You will notice that the F (class from a file) definitions end with an extra parameter, %s. This specifies how sendmail is to interpret the entries.

To speed up the loading of the parsing information that sendmail uses, you can provide it with a precompiled configuration file, known as the *freeze* file and named /usr/lib/sendmail.fc. You generate this file with the command

sendmail -bz

In fact, you must use this for the sendmail daemon in order to pick up any changes in sendmail.cf.

Although sendmail has many options, most are used by the user agent programs that submit mail to the sendmail system. You do need to know how to start up sendmail after you have killed it. Remember that if it is being run as a daemon, you must kill and restart it in order to use any changes to the aliases or sendmail.cf (sendmail.fc) files. Here is a typical daemon initialization:

sendmail -bd -q15m &

The -bd option specifies that sendmail is to run as a daemon and should listen for mail coming from the SMTP socket. The -q15m option specifies that sendmail should process queued messages every 15 minutes. (You can use s for seconds, m for minutes, h for hours, d for days, and even w for weeks.)

The *paths* File for UUCP Connections

If your system is using smail, either with or without sendmail, it uses a paths file to determine how to reach other sites. If you are using smail, you will need to have a smart site to resolve all the unresolved addresses (the

DR*site* entry in your `sendmail.cf` file). Be sure that at least this machine has an entry in your `paths` file. Most people keep their `paths` file in the same subdirectory as their UUCP Systems file because the two are related—that is, `/usr/lib/uucp/paths`.

The format of `paths` is simple: a site name, a tab character (not spaces—it *must* be a tab), and a bang (!) path to the machine with a `%s` for any user name or other site name that needs to be expanded. The optional third field is the "cost" factor. This number determines whether requests for the site should be queued or delivered immediately. The subject of *cost and queueing threshold* is a technical subject. For simplicity, assume that a value of 0 will prevent queueing and that the omission of a cost factor will cause queueing. The `/usr/lib/uucp/paths` from the site bytepb.byte.com looks like this:

```
.arpa       uunet!%s   0
.byte.com %s    0
.com uunet!%s   0
.dec.com   uunet!%s   0
.edu uunet!%s   0
.org uunet!%s   0
.uu.net     uunet!%s   0
beast       uunet!beast!%s 0
byteme      byteme!%s 0
bytepb      %s    0
bytepb.byte.com      %s    0
bytepb.uucp %s 0
crsfld      crsfld!%s
decvax      uunet!decvax!%s
infopro     infopro!%s      0
maxx maxx!%s    0
maxx.uucp        maxx!%s     0
ronin       ronin!%s 0
smart-host       uunet!%s   0
uunet       uunet!%s   0
uunet.uu.net      uunet!%s   0
```

Notice that the preceding entries are sorted. This is extremely important because `smail` uses a binary search to find entries in the table.

You can see that an explicit path is given to the site beast even though there isn't a direct connection to that machine. You can have as many explicit paths defined as you consider practical. What you don't specify will be resolved by smart-host—in this case, uunet.

The *aliases* File

Another important file, the one that describes who gets what, is the /usr/lib/aliases file. The following aliases is from the site bytepb:

```
##
#  Aliases in this file will NOT be expanded in the header from
#  Mail, but WILL be visible over networks or from /bin/mail.
#
#    >>>>>>>>>>      The program "newaliases" must be run after
#    >> NOTE >>      this file is updated for any changes to
#    >>>>>>>>>>      show through to sendmail.
##


# Alias for mailer daemon
MAILER-DAEMON:root

# Following alias is required by the new mail protocol, RFC 822
postmaster:root
smart-host:uunet
## The regular type aliases
uucp:ben
root:ben
usenet:ben
bensmith:ben
bixpb:bytepb
# Aliases to handle mail to msgs and news
news:ben
msgs:ben
nobody: /dev/null
```

As you might infer, user ben is the system administrator and general do-it-all on this machine; he gets mail for just about any activity involving UUCP and news. The entry bensmith:ben is there to be sure that mail directed to his old login, bensmith, is redirected to his current account, ben. The names bixpb and bytepb are site names. This entry ensures that mail directed to the now-nonexistent site bixpb is redirected to the site bytepb (this site).

Some mailers cannot resolve addresses or account names; the result is nobody addresses. These will just be dumped in the UNIX trash can, /dev/null.

Any additions or changes to the `aliases` file must be hashed and fed to `sendmail`. The process (after changing the textual `aliases` file) is

```
# newaliases
# sendmail -bi
```

And don't forget to restart `sendmail`.

Usenet News

Usenet (User Network) news is not the news that users read when they run the command `news`, which is merely a local bulletin reading program. That `news` is a supported product of most UNIX licenses. Usenet news is *not* a supported product. It is a freely-distributed set of programs for public distribution of messages that run across tens of thousands of computers around the world. Usenet represents millions of users, gigabytes of information (if you can call it that), and an amazing structure for what amounts to electronic messaging anarchy.

However, Usenet news and its organization (or lack thereof) stand as a symbol for all the traditions of UNIX, particularly within the educational environment. The symbol can be codified in the single word *sharing*. This is sharing on a grand scale; it is worldwide sharing of information; it is sharing the costs of data transmission and storage for the news messages. It is also the sharing of responsibility for restraining from spouting off misinformation, unnecessary comments, and the needless resubmitting of text from previous messages. Not enough Usenet users follow these guidelines; the result is that a full news feed can amount to more than 10 megabytes of new (uncompressed) data in a day. This must be transmitted to every site in the net and stored on each machine until the information is "expired," deleted with the assumption that everyone has read it and every site that connects has received it. If the information is retained for 10 days, the storage requirement would be about 100 megabytes!

Because of the load on storage and communications, many system managers consider Usenet news as frivolous. System administrators might agree, but users who have ever used Usenet news will disagree. Their feeling is that it is a *necessity*; in fact, some of these people will claim that the main reason they like UNIX is their ability to get (and give) information through Usenet news. Well, in spite of all, Usenet news can be beneficial to the system administrator. She, like any other user, can use it to get help with her system administration problems. There are special news groups just for this purpose.

Exchanging News

Each user reads the news on his local machine or local network news server. This means that each site with Usenet news must have a copy of all the news messages. The problem of sharing messages without multiple receipts of the same message is not a trivial one. The method uses a message numbering system that uniquely identifies each message, despite the fact that the messages originate at thousands of different sites. Each site has its own counter (`/usr/lib/news/seq`). Each message posted on a system is given an ID that uses the site name along with this sequence number, such as `1190@dms.UUCP`. The message IDs from larger sites may be more complex—for example, `<9102061425.AA01439@lilac.berkeley.edu>`—but are nonetheless unique.

A news feed can take several forms: batch method, NNTP (*network news transfer protocol*), ihave/sendme, and mail.

The batch mode and NNTP collect a list of all incoming news messages destined to be passed on to other sites. When the two sites are communicating, *all* of these messages are passed on to the other site. As the recipient site processes the incoming news messages, it checks the message ID against those it already has. If the messages have already been received from another site, the new copy is throw out. The batch mode is used for UUCP connections.

NNTP is used with real-time network connections such as TCP/IP sites. NNTP can be used also to set up a news server—a single site in a local area network that does all of the Usenet spooling and transmissions. The other sites in the network can use NNTP to run the news reading and posting programs on the server.

The ihave/sendme method makes more efficient use of the communications channel. Before the actual messages are sent, the two sites that have set up the ihave/sendme protocol exchange lists indicating which messages each site has. By comparing these lists, the sites can determine which locally unreceived messages the other site has. Only the necessary messages are exchanged. The trade-off for more efficient communications is the great increase in local processing.

If your site is just a leaf node (you don't forward news to any other sites), you can elect to receive news messages as mail messages. These can be sent to mail lists of your users. The major drawbacks are that each user will have a separate copy of each Usenet message, and your local users cannot post to Usenet.

Usenet Control Files

Even though many control files are used by the Usenet system, you need to be involved with only two: `sys` (the list of connecting sites and the newsgroups they want to receive) and `active` (the list of active newsgroups and currently held messages).

Here is a sample `sys` file:

```
ronin:net,world,comp,news,sci,rec,misc,soc,talk,\
ne,mod,alt,bionet,inet,ddn,na,usa,biz,gnu,to.m2c,\
m2c,pubnet,unix-pc,to.matlab::
#
decvax:net,world,comp,news,sci,rec,misc,soc,talk,\
ne,mod,alt,bionet,inet,ddn,na,usa,biz,gnu,to.m2c,\
m2c,pubnet,unix-pc,to.matlab:L:
#
bytepb:comp,misc,net,world,usa,na,to.bytepb:F:\
/usr/spool/batch/bytepb
```

(If you have a large `sys` entry that isn't behaving properly, be aware that B News quietly restricts each entry to 1024 bytes.)

Each entry in the `sys` file consists of four fields delimited by colons. The first field is the site name (the local site can be abbreviated as ME). The second field is a comma-separated list of the newsgroups that site should receive. You can also list newsgroups that should not be received by preceding the newsgroup name with a bang (!).

The third field describes (among other things) the kind of news processing associated with this entry. The third (and fourth) field may be left empty. The most common values in this field are F, L, and I.

If an F is in the third field, the fourth field should be the full path name of the file used by the batching/transfer program—for example, the name of the file that contains all the articles that are to be batched together for sending to the site.

An L in the third field indicates that only the news messages which are generated on the local site are to be sent to the receiving site. This flag is often used by leaf sites to prevent transmitting news to supplier sites—news the suppliers probably already have.

An I in the third field indicates that the ihave/sendme protocol is used with this site. For this to work, both sites must be set up with this protocol specified in their corresponding `sys` entries. If you are using the ihave/sendme protocol, the fourth field in the `sys` entry must be blank.

If the fourth field is used, it is either a command or a file name that is part of news processing for the `sys` entry.

Here is a much simplified example of sys:

```
ME:world,all::
decvax:world,all::
bytepb:world,all,!rec,!alt::
dragon:world,all:IF:
```

(This list is not equivalent to the first example.)

The other important administrative file is /usr/lib/news/active (the path may vary from site to site). Each entry in this file consists of four space-delimited fields: the newsgroup name; the highest message number posted for that newsgroup; the lowest message number still available for that newsgroup; and either a y or an n, indicating whether posting to that newsgroup is okay. (Messages your system receives that belong to newsgroups you don't want to post will be sent to the junk newsgroup.) The message numbers in the active file are not the same as the number that is part of the message ID (from seq) but are part of a separate sequence for each newsgroup. These numbers are used as the file name (under the corresponding newsgroup directory) for the message. For example, the message 14569 in the group comp.unix.admin will be in the file /usr/spool/news/comp/unix/admin/14569.

An active file may have more than five hundred entries, some of which might be like these:

```
control 20486 19800 y
junk 29889 27001 y
comp.benchmarks 00315 00315 y
comp.doc 00254 00254 m
comp.mail.sendmail 02685 02432 y
comp.sources.bugs 02790 02333 y
comp.sources.games 01073 01000 m
comp.sources.misc 01770 01745 m
comp.sources.sun 00102 00102 m
comp.sources.unix 01501 01501 m
comp.std.c 03773 03750 y
comp.sys.ibm.pc.digest 00420 00401 m
comp.unix.admin 00880 00810 y
comp.unix.aux 03662 03650 y
comp.unix.cray 00345 00343 y
comp.unix.misc 00766 00755 y
comp.unix.programmer 00882 00834 y
comp.unix.shell 01168 01145 y
comp.unix.sysv286 00098 00097 y
comp.unix.sysv386 04161 04031 y
```

```
comp.unix.wizards 00127 00120 y
comp.unix.xenix.misc 00094 00094 y
comp.unix.xenix.sco 01406 01403 y
comp.unix 00673 00672 m
comp.virus 03284 03234 y
misc.forsale 24541 24523 y
misc.headlines 25568 24551 y
misc.invest 12533 12523 y
news.admin 11395 11243 y
news.announce.important 00034 00030 m
news.announce.newusers 00579 00556 m
news.config 01777 01755 y
news.groups 24972 24934 y
news.misc 05711 05687 y
news.newsites 01655 01645 y
news.software.b 06090 06088 y
news.software.nntp 00993 00976 y
news.software.notes 00176 00175 y
news.stargate 00272 00271 y
news.sysadmin 03559 03552 y
rec.humor.funny 02201 02156 m
rec.music.beatles 10374 10100 y
talk.bizarre 66343 65334 y
talk.origins 13442 13412 y
talk.philosophy.misc 04659 04621 y
talk.politics.misc 69532 69432 y
talk.politics.theory 08445 08445 y
talk.religion.misc 36081 36000 y
talk.rumors 05667 05645 y
```

The first two entries (control and junk) are important to the operations. Messages posted in the control newsgroup are run as scripts that remotely manage the news system—for example, creating and deleting news groups. The junk file is the place where all messages that are not otherwise accepted by the local news site are tossed. These would be messages in newsgroups that are not listed in active.

Many other files are important to the running of Usenet news, but these are maintained entirely by the news system. history (or the history.d directory, which contains the history files) is significant because it includes the IDs of messages that have been received by the local site.

The Usenet Programs and Utilities

If it weren't for the `expire` utility, the file system with your Usenet articles would be swamped by the quickly growing disk requirements of the incoming articles. `expire` deletes the old news articles, updating the `active` and `history` files. This utility is usually run from `root`'s (or `news`') `crontab`. The `crontab` entry looks like this:

```
3 3 * * * /bin/su news -c "/usr/lib/news/expire -e5" \
  > /dev/null
```

This version is designed for `root`'s `crontab`. Because the files that `expire` creates and manipulates must be readable by `news`, the `expire` command is run from a `su` shell. The `-e5` option specifies that all articles older than 5 days are to be expired. The default time is 15 days.

You may want to expire some newsgroups faster than others, especially the `junk` newsgroup. For this task, `expire` has the `-n` *newsgroups* option. Similar in syntax to the `sys` list, the *newsgroups* list is delimited by spaces, not commas. The negative name (preceded by a bang, `!`) is valuable for protecting newsgroups you want to archive on your site. Note the following example:

```
expire -e1 -n junk
expire -e5 -n alt rec misc
expire -e15 -n !comp.sources.unix
```

The executable file that posts incoming news is `rnews`. (It must be listed in your `/usr/lib/uucp/L.cmds` or `/usr/lib/uucp/Permissions` file because it is run from `uuxqt` by the site supplying the news feed.) The remote site requests this program (using `uux`) when the site is sending a news feed. When `rnews` runs, it may generate a log file (`/usr/lib/news/log`) of its activity and an error log file (`/usr/lib/news/errlog`). These files must be trimmed from time to time. If your news distribution is complete, you will have a `trimlib` program for this purpose. That program is another candidate as a `crontab` entry.

When you first install Usenet news, pay close attention to the activities of your news system, the disk requirements, and the files. The Usenet system can be a real monster for small systems.

Summary

What appears simple to the user is actually quite complex. Mail systems are basically straightforward but become increasingly complex with the multiplicity of paths used for mail transfer. The Usenet news system, however, is just complex in every way. One of the many problems of administering Usenet news is that it is unsupported by UNIX licenses and vendors. But you aren't on your own with any of your UNIX administration problems when you use these resources yourself. Every UNIX administrator has the same problems, and most are willing to help you through E-mail and the Usenet news groups.

15

Workstations,
X Terminals,
and PCs

The recent move of UNIX systems has been away from large, general-purpose systems with many serial connections for terminals and output devices. The new direction is toward having many smaller systems tied together with networks. Each of the smaller systems is configured to work optimally for a narrow range of special purposes—for example, disk storage, high-speed numerical computing, or graphics display and manipulation. From the growth in this new direction, the personal workstation was born.

The personal workstation is a computer with the technology and complexity of mainframe computers but with the philosophy of the PC (personal computer): "One CPU, one processor." The technology is high performance (at least 6 million 32-bit integer instructions a second), high-resolution graphics (very memory intensive), and high connectivity (usually Ethernet and TCP/IP). All modern UNIX workstations have a graphical user interface (GUI) to the operating system and application programs. The GUI might be based on the NEWS (a PostScript-based graphics system) or an X Window System (a graphics system definition from MIT). Open Windows (from Sun Microsystems) uses both.

The personal workstation typically has some unique system administration problems that are a part of its special niche in the UNIX computer world: this workstation relies on external systems (servers) for many of its operations (some workstations don't have a disk for any files), and requires some care in initializing and customizing its graphical user environment.

There are categories of workstations: the fully loaded workstation, the dataless workstation, and the diskless workstation. A *fully loaded workstation* is a computer that can run completely by itself, with enough mass storage (and other resources) to hold not only the operating system and application programs, but also any data (and text) files the users may generate or require. Of course, there is *never* enough disk space for everything the users might *wish* to have, but that is another problem.

A *dataless workstation* is a computer that is configured with enough mass storage to hold the operating system (from which it can boot), but not necessarily enough to hold data files or most of the application programs. For these services, a dataless workstation must rely on file servers.

A *diskless workstation* does not have any mass storage disk drive. This kind of workstation relies entirely on servers to supply the operating system, application programs, and data storage. What this workstation does have is enough memory and processor power to run both the operating system and the applications. The diskless workstation may also have a small, high-speed disk for swapping memory. (Memory swapping across a network seriously degrades the performance of both the network and the applications.) Permanent memory (ROM and EPROM) holds the basic operations for communicating on the network and seeking the operating system boot from an external file server, as well as the local configuration information.

An *X terminal* is closely related to the diskless workstation but is capable of doing only the work of an X display server (screen, keyboard, and mouse operations). For X terminals, all computing, other than X server facilities and network communications, must be done on more complete computers. An X terminal can work only with graphical environments that rely on the protocols of the X Window System. But a workstation can (at least theoretically) run any number of different graphical environments one at a time, and on some systems, concurrently.

The high-end *personal computer* is often used for running the UNIX operating system. Before the price of RISC-processor-based workstations dropped at the beginning of this decade, the only easily affordable UNIX systems were the Intel 286- and 386-based computers, designed primarily to run MS-DOS. Because of their design, these UNIX systems have some restrictions and special system administration considerations. Still, there are more PC computers running varieties of UNIX than any other type of operating system.

Before you consider the details of X terminals and PCs, you should take a look at some of the resources that are special to the general class of workstations.

The X Window System

Besides the capability of networking, another common attribute of modern workstations is the graphical window system, a feature that distinguishes the workstation from other networked computers. Although other window systems are available, the X Window System dominates as the underlying protocol on general-purpose workstations. To understand the administration of the elements of the X Window System, you need to be familiar with the design and operations of the X Window System.

The design goal of the X Window System was to create a *network-transparent* and *hardware-independent* graphical operating environment for workstations. Central to the X Window System is the X Network Protocol by which *all* X operations must communicate. This protocol can operate both locally, where everything is on the same workstation, and across different systems. There is a natural division between the activities specific to the devices that are responsible for the user input/output and the application programs that take advantage of the I/O facilities. The I/O activities (keyboard, mouse, control knobs, and so on) and video output (a bitmapped, high-resolution screen) are handled by the X server process. The application programs are called X clients.

Unlike Presentation Manager, Microsoft Windows, Apple Finder, and other window systems, the X Window System assumes that the X server and X clients *may* be operating on different systems connected by a network. In the case of workstations, the X display server and X clients often run on the same system; but in the case of X terminals, only the X display server runs on the X terminal, and all X clients run on another system.

The X Window System provides the protocol and functions on top of which both Open Look and OSF/Motif applications are built. For both Open Look and Motif applications to work, the X Window System must already be operating—in other words, there must be an X display server running and available for the application. The application can be running on a system that has no X display server—for example, a mainframe.

The concept of *resources* is fundamental to the operation and customization of X clients and servers. A resource is a configurable attribute of an X application, such as the color of the background of an application's window. Another example is the character font and size used for the text in the title of an application. Many resources are common throughout all X applications. Most applications also have some resources that are unique to the application. The system defaults for applications are usually found in the path `/usr/lib/X11/app-defaults`.

Another common term in the jargon of the X Window System is *widget*. A widget is an abstract element of any X application's input and output. Buttons and scroll bars are widgets, but so is the entire area of a window. The X Window System design follows the paradigm of object-oriented programming. The concept of a widget is that of an object within the structure of an X window. Widgets are grouped into classes. When the user specifies a value for any class resource, the entire class inherits that specification; however, the specification for a specific instance will override the specification for the class.

Widgets are often composed of other widgets or subclasses. A scroll bar, for example, is composed of the slider area and several buttons. Because each widget assumes some input and/or output activity, the entire structure of the widget is completely defined, thereby greatly increasing the program requirements for each new widget. The X11R4 release also defines a *gadget*, which is a reduced version of a widget. A gadget does not, in itself, hold the structure for I/O activity, but may be composed of widgets that do. Again, in the example of the scroll bar, the entire window of the scroll bar may not provide I/O, but the elevator bar and buttons that are part of the gadget do.

The X Window System does not restrict the developer to any set of widgets and gadgets. It just provides the definitions and structure with which they may be created. But collections of widgets and gadgets are available for developers. Soon after the acceptance of the X Window System, the Athena widget set became popular. Now the Motif widget set and the Open Look widget set are important. If an application is developed within the confines of one of these widget sets (and associated toolkits and developer guidelines), the appearance and behavior of the application will be consistent with other applications that use the same style. The underlying structure and protocol are consistent throughout all X applications, so no matter what style an application uses, it can run on any system that supports the X Window System, independent of the style of the window manager: Athena, Open Look, Motif, or any other widget set. Of course, if an application follows one style and the window manager follows another, the user is going to have a rough time. For this reason, it is obviously preferable to have everything with the same style.

Administering the X Window System

The specifics of installing the X Window System are system-dependent, but there are some traditional locations for different files. You should follow tradition unless your X distribution expects other locations for its files.

The standard location for all executables is the subdirectory /usr/bin/X11. The customary locations for character fonts are subdirectories below /usr/lib/X11/fonts. These are the two most important collections, but there are others, most of which are found in other subdirectories of /usr/lib/X11. (UNIX SVR4 often uses the path of /usr/X for all X files. Therefore, you would find the binaries in /usr/X/bin and the libraries under /usr/X/lib.) An X system user needs to have the path to the executables in his PATH environment. You could modify the login scripts for new user accounts or modify the default PATH in the appropriate file (for example, /etc/profile):

```
PATH=$PATH:/usr/bin/X11
```

The X server maintains control of which hosts are allowed to run applications that use the server for user I/O. You can assume that the local host will be part of that list, but you can't necessarily assume that any other system can run clients for the local X server. The key to this limited security is the program xhost. To check which hosts should be allowed to use the local display and keyboard, you can use xhost without any parameters:

```
$ xhost
amiga
```

To add and subtract X client hosts, you precede the host name with a plus or minus sign:

```
# xhost +mips -ronin
```

To open the X server to all hosts (turn off the security), you use the plus sign without any host name:

```
# xhost +
```

Finally, to deny access to all external hosts, you use a solitary minus sign:

```
# xhost -
```

As system administrator, you can set up the file /etc/X*n*.hosts to automatically handle the xhost requirements when the system boots. (The *n* indicates the display number attached to the workstation. The X Window System supports multiple displays. For the most common workstation configuration—one with a single display—the X permissions file is /etc/X0.hosts.) Each line in /etc/X0.hosts contains the name of an acceptable X client host:

```
amiga
mips
ronin
```

In addition to including /etc/X0.hosts, each user's account home directory should also include an .rhosts file if she expects to run the rsh command from remote systems. Because the remote copy command rcp uses rsh, an .rhosts file is necessary.

xdm—The X Display Manager

Workstations that use the X Window System as the default user interface usually bring up the X server from the boot script (one of the rc scripts). When the users log in through an X client rather than through the standard character-based getty and login, they are beginning UNIX from the X display manager, xdm, which runs as a daemon. As with nearly all X client programs, xdm can be customized.

The only time that xdm reads its configuration files is when it is first started, and, if no other file is specified, the configuration is taken from the xdm-config file, if it exists. This file describes which files are part of the configuration and where they can be found. (The file may contain a few other configuration values as well.) On most systems, the xdm configuration and control files are found in the subdirectory /usr/lib/X11/xdm, although another common path is /usr/X11/etc/xdm.

A sample xdm-config file looks like this:

```
DisplayManager.servers:        /usr/lib/X11/xdm/Xservers
DisplayManager.errorLogFile:   /usr/lib/X11/xdm/xdm-errors
DisplayManager*resources:      /usr/lib/X11/xdm/Xresources
DisplayManager*startup:        /usr/lib/X11/xdm/Xstartup
DisplayManager*reset:          /usr/lib/X11/xdm/Xreset
DisplayManager*session:        /usr/lib/X11/Xsession
```

The X11 Release 4 configuration may also include the following:

```
DisplayManager.pidFile:        /usr/lib/X11/xdm-pid
DisplayManager._0.authorize:   true
DisplayManager.*authorize:     false
```

Here is a complete list of xdm-related files:

xdm-config	The configuration (more information is provided on this later)
Xservers	A list of the hosts that are permissible X servers
xdm-errors	The log file for xdm errors
Xresources	The list of resources loaded by xdm
Xsession	The default login session
Xstartup	The xdm startup script
Xreset	The xdm reset script

The Xstartup and Xreset files are scripts that run immediately after the user is verified and immediately after the user logs off. Both files are run as root and therefore should be carefully written. They are not really necessary for simple xdm installations.

The Xservers file is a short list of displays that the display manager is responsible for managing. A single workstation can support more than one display—hence, a display number is appended to any host number. The first display on any host is always :0. Note an example of an Xservers file:

```
:0 local /usr/bin/X11/X
visual:0 foreign Ben's X terminal
ncd:0 foreign JRS's X terminal
```

The display manager may manage a single, local server, in which case only the first entry is required.

As just indicated, xdm reads its configuration and control files only when it starts up. Therefore, if you make additions or changes to these files, you must restart xdm to apply the changes. By its default nature, xdm will restart automatically if you kill it by sending the parent xdm a SIGHUP signal, as in kill -15.

The last of the xdm files to be mentioned is the resources file. Here is the distributed Xresources file:

```
xlogin*login.translations: #override\
    <Key>F1: set-session-argument(failsafe) finish-field()\n\
    <Key>Return: set-session-argument() finish-field()
xlogin*borderWidth: 3
#ifdef COLOR
xlogin*greetColor: #f63
xlogin*failColor: red
xlogin*Foreground: black
```

```
xlogin*Background: #fdc
#else
xlogin*Foreground: black
xlogin*Background: white
#endif
xterm*Foreground: black
xterm*Background: white
```

The most important resources that you should describe in /Xresources are for the login window and its behavior. Notice that an action is specified for the F1 function key: run a failsafe xterm window. Also notice that the resources for an xterm are specified. This is the session xterm. Session messages are displayed in this window. When the user kills this xterm process, the session ends.

Resources

Resources are the aspects of an application's look and behavior that the user or system can change. Most application programs (X clients) have enough defaults defined within the program that they will run without any specification on the command line or in a defaults/resources file. For example, you can usually launch a clock window with the command

$ xclock &

provided that the X server is already running. There doesn't need to be any resource file. You will see a clock on the root (background) screen of your X display. But this doesn't mean that xclock has no resources. It has many. For example, a resource declaration for xclock might be this:

```
xclock*update:          1
xclock*hands:           red
xclock*highlight:       yellow
xclock*analog:          True
xclock*chime:           False
xclock*padding:         4
xclock*width:           50
xclock*height:          50
xclock*background:      black
xclock*foreground:      red
xclock*font:            9x15
xclock*reverseVideo:    False
```

Note the following explanations for the preceding resources:

update (class Interval)	The update time in seconds (special)
hands (class Foreground)	The color of the solid part of the clock hands (special)
highlight (class Foreground)	The color of the edges of the hands (special)
analog (class Boolean)	True for a clock with hands and False for a digital clock (special)
chime (class Boolean)	True for bell on the hour and the half hour (special)
padding (class Margin)	The number of pixels to pad between the outside of the clock and the window frame (special)
width (class Width)	The width of the clock, in pixels (core)
height (class Height)	The height of the clock, in pixels (core)
background (class Background)	The color for the background of the window (core)
foreground (class Foreground)	The color of the text for a digital clock, or tick marks and stroke marks for an analog clock (core)
font (class Font)	The character style for the numbers in a digital clock (core)
reverseVideo (class ReverseVideo)	The foreground and background colors are swapped if True (core)

You will notice that some of the preceding explanations are annotated as *special* and others as *core*. The special resources are particular to the client application. The core resources are common to most X applications and can be defined globally by defining the resource without any object. Note an example:

```
*font:   9x16
```

The *class* labels need some explanation. By setting the attribute of a resource class, you are setting the resources for all the members of that class. Notice that each class name starts with an uppercase letter. Therefore, if you make the declaration

```
xclock*Foreground:   red
```

it would be equivalent to these three statements:

```
xclock*hands:        red
xclock*highlight:    red
xclock*foreground:   red
```

If you follow the class resource declaration with the declaration of a specific member, that member maintains its unique resource. Thus

```
xclock*Foreground:   red
xclock*highlight:    yellow
```

is perfectly valid and would be equivalent to these statements:

```
xclock*hands:        red
xclock*foreground:   red
xclock*highlight:    yellow
```

Many of an X client program's resources can be specified as options on the command line. For example, the line

```
$ xclock -update 1 -hd red -fg yellow -hl yellow &
```

means to display the update every second, using red hands with yellow highlights and a yellow foreground.

The concept of *class* derives from the object-oriented design of the X Window System. The resources fall into *class hierarchies*, a concept remotely like the UNIX directory tree. In the case of the class structure, the children inherit the characteristics of the parent. The hierarchical structure reaches beyond the resources of a single application. You can, for example, define the default foreground for all applications by omitting the client program name:

```
*foreground:         white
```

Or you can omit the entire Foreground class:

```
*Foreground:         yellow
```

The asterisk (*) "binds" the resource *attribute* to the client program, an *object*. As you delve deeper into resource specifications, you will find that some resource names are quite complex. A client program may have objects, some of which may have subobjects, sub-subobjects, and so on. For each of these, you can specify a resource value. For instance, to set the background to blue for just the Motif window manager's root menu (the one that appears when your pointer is on the background), you could declare

```
Mwm*menu*RootMenu*background: blue
```

Or you could declare that all Motif window manager's menus have blue backgrounds:

```
Mwm*menu*background: blue
```

(The section "OSF/Motif Configuration" provides details about Motif resources and menus.)

There are two kinds of bindings: loose and tight. You specify loose bindings by linking the levels of objects together with the asterisk (*), as previous examples illustrate. A loose binding means that you are being arbitrary about the levels of binding involved. The `Mwm*menu*background` specification is a fine example of loose binding. Some specifications may need to be explicit; the binding between a parent and only its immediate child must be specified. Tight bindings are specified with a dot (.), as in

```
xterm.vt100.scrollBar:    True
```

The preceding example specifies that there should be a scroll bar on the side of all `xterm` windows in the emulation of a DEC vt100 terminal. You can also mix loose bindings with tight bindings:

```
Mwm*vt100.scrollBar:    True
```

Usually, the `man` pages on an X client don't specify the entire list of the resource hierarchy. You must be familiar with the internal design of the application in order to find out these relationships. It helps to know what widget set was used to create the application. The three most popular widget sets are Athena, Motif, and Open Look. The client application for passing text between windows, known as `xclipboard`, is an example of the Athena widgets. An `xclipboard` resource specification might look like this:

```
XClipboard.shell.quit.top: ChainTop
XClipboard.shell.quit.bottom: ChainTop
XClipboard.shell.quit.left: ChainLeft
XClipboard.shell.erase.fromHoriz: quit
XClipboard.shell.erase.top: ChainTop
XClipboard.shell.erase.bottom: ChainTop
XClipboard.shell.erase.right: ChainRight
XClipboard.shell.text.fromVert: quit
XClipboard.shell.text.top: ChainTop
```

```
XClipboard.shell.text.bottom: ChainBottom
XClipboard.shell.text.left: ChainLeft
XClipboard.shell.text.right: ChainRight
```

To understand these resources, you need to go to the documentation for Athena widgets, where you will find a description of shell subobjects. Under a description of new resources for the Athena widget set, you can find bottom, top, left, and right—all of the class Edge. This class specifies how an object repositions itself when its parent changes in size; the five possible values are ChainTop, ChainBottom, ChainLeft, ChainRight, and Rubber.

Even though most X programs have enough default resources defined internally to run without external resource declarations, some programs need to have some of their resources defined before being launched. The xclipboard resources in the preceding example *need* to be defined.

Resource Specification Files

Each user has the facility to specify his own default X client resources. The best way is to use the .Xdefaults file in the home directory. Because .Xdefaults files are too technical for the newcomer to the X Window System, it is a good idea to give X users a copy of some vanilla .Xdefaults when their accounts are created (although this isn't necessary in order for users to be able to run X). Listing 15.1 is an example from a system that uses Open Look on a monochrome display—for example, an Amiga 3000UX with a Monoterm. (Open Look is discussed in the section "Open Look Configuration.")

Listing 15.1. .Xdefaults for a monochrome display.

```
# Monochrome Xdefaults for Open Look
# Amiga 300UX
*TextPane.background:    white
*TextPane.fontColor:     black
*adjustBtn:              <Button2>
*autoFocus:              true
*background:             white
*beep:                   always
*borderColor:            black
*cancelKey:              <Escape>
*constrainBtn:           Mod1<selectBtn>
*copyKey:                Ctrl<c>
*cutKey:                 Ctrl<x>
```

```
*duplicateBtn:          Mod1<selectBtn>
*fontColor:             black
*foreground:            black
*helpKey:               <F12>
*iconBorder:            true
*iconGravity:           south
*inputFocusColor:       black
*menuBtn:               <Button3>
*menuDefaultBtn:        Ctrl<menuBtn>
*nextFieldKey:          <Tab>
*panBtn:                Mod1<selectBtn>
*pasteKey:              Ctrl<v>
*prevFieldKey:          Shift<Tab>
*propertiesKey:         Ctrl<p>
*selectBtn:             <Button1>
*selectDoesPreview:     false
*stopKey:               Ctrl<s>
*undoKey:               Ctrl<u>
*windowLayering:        true
olwm*windowFrameColor:  black
olwsm.menuPinned:       false
olwsm.workspace:        white
xclock*background:      black
xclock*foreground:      white
xclock*geometry:        -10+10
xclock*hands:           white
xclock*hd:              white
xclock*update:          1
xronin*background:      black
xronin*boldFont:        8x13bold
xronin*cursorColor:     white
xronin*font:            8x13
xronin*foreground:      black
xronin*save_lines:      500
xronin*scrollBar:       True
xterm*background:       white
xterm*boldFont:         8x13bold
xterm*cursorColor:      black
xterm*font:             8x13
xterm*foreground:       black
xterm*save_lines:       500
xterm*scrollBar:        True
```

Notice that comment lines have the same syntax as in shell scripts; each comment line begins with a hash sign (#). The .Xdefaults file is consulted every time an X client is started from a shell.

Each client program may also have a system default resource specified in a file found in the path /usr/lib/X11/app-defaults (this may vary from system to system). By convention, the associate file is the application name with a leading uppercase letter. For example, the system defaults for xterm are specified in /usr/lib/X11/app-defaults/Xterm.

The file /usr/lib/X11/Xresources (this path may also vary from system to system) serves the same purpose as the .Xdefaults file, but for the system defaults and also for X clients over which users have no control. Systems that have the X login front end, xdm, use Xresources. Listing 15.2 is an example of an Xresources file from a MIPS workstation that uses xdm.

Listing 15.2. Xresources (from a color system that uses xdm.)

```
/*
 * Resources for xdm's xlogin window and default xterms.
 */
*BorderWidth:                   3
*BorderColor:                   White

xlogin*login.translations:      #override\
    <Key>F1:  set-session-argument(failsafe) finish-field()\n\
    <Key>Return:  set-session-argument()     finish-field()

xlogin*borderWidth:             5
xlogin*greeting:                Welcome to RISCwindows
xlogin.Login.y:                 20

#ifdef COLOR /* { */

    xlogin*greetColor:          SpringGreen
    xlogin*failColor:           Magenta
    xlogin*Foreground:          Cyan
    xlogin*Background:          NavyBlue

#else    /* } COLOR { */

    xlogin*Foreground:          Black
    xlogin*Background:          White

#endif    /* } COLOR */
```

```
XTerm*font:                    9x15
XTerm*boldFont:                9x15
XTerm*TtyModes:                erase ^H kill ^U
```

Notice that comments follow the syntax of C language programs and that the compiler preprocessor instructions of #ifdef, #else, and #endif are valid (among others). The Xresources file is processed only when a new xrdb session begins. It is run through M4, the C preprocessor, before its declarations are instituted.

OSF/Motif Configuration

Configuring for OSF/Motif means defining (or modifying) the default window manager menus, mouse actions, and keyboard function-key operations, as well as defining Motif resources. As with each of the popular widget sets (including Open Look and Athena), the Motif widgets have their own resources, all of which are available to all Motif applications, whether or not the resources are used. The most important Motif application is the window manager, mwm. Before examining the mwm resources, take a look at the menus and key bindings.

When the mouse pointer is on the root (background) of the display, it can have one behavior; when it is within the different regions of a window, it can have other behaviors. Each user can define these behaviors in his private copy of $HOME/.mwmrc. But the system-wide defaults are defined in system.mwmrc (usually located in /usr/lib/X11 or /usr/lib/X11/mwm). Listing 15.3 is an example from a common distribution of Motif.

Listing 15.3. system.mwmrc from a common distribution of Motif.

```
#     @(#) system.mwmrc 1.2 89/04/04
#   DEFAULT mwm RESOURCE DESCRIPTION FILE (system.mwmrc)
#
#
# menu pane descriptions
#
Menu DefaultWindowMenu MwmWindowMenu
{
    Restore        _R   Alt<key>5 f.normalize
    Move           _M   Alt<key>7 f.move
    Size           _S   Alt<key>8 f.resize
    Minimize       _n   Alt<key>9 f.minimize
    Maximize       _x   Alt<key>0 f.maximize
```

continued

Listing 15.3—*Continued*

```
    Lower              _L    Alt<key>minus   f.lower
    no-label                             f.separator
    Close              _C    Alt<key>4 f.kill
}

Menu RootMenu
{
    "Root Menu"                  f.title
    "Clients"          _C    f.menu ClientsMenu
    "New Window"       _N    f.exec "xterm -sb  &"
    "Shuffle Up"       _U    f.circle_up
    "Shuffle Down"     _D    f.circle_down
    "Refresh"          _R    f.refresh
    no-label                 f.separator
    "Restart"                f.restart
    no-label                 f.separator
    "Quit"                   f.quit_mwm
}

Menu ClientsMenu
{
    "xclock"                 f.exec "xclock &"
    "xload"                  f.exec "xload &"
    "xcalc"                  f.exec "xcalc &"
    "xbiff"                  f.exec "xbiff &"
    "xmag"                   f.exec "xmag &"
    "bitmap"                 f.exec "bitmap $HOME/tmp_bitmap &"
    "xeyes"                  f.exec "xeyes &"
    "ico"              f.exec "ico &"
}
#
# key binding descriptions
#
Keys DefaultKeyBindings
{
    Shift<Key>Escape            icon¦window      f.post_wmenu
    Meta<Key>space          icon¦window      f.post_wmenu
    Meta<Key>Escape         root¦icon¦window f.next_key
    Meta Shift<Key>Escape       root¦icon¦window f.prev_key
    Meta<Key>Tab            root¦icon¦window f.next_key
    Meta Shift<Key>Tab          root¦icon¦window f.prev_key
```

```
        Meta Ctrl Shift<Key>exclam   root¦icon¦window
    f.set_behaviour
    }


    #
    # button binding descriptions
    #

    Buttons DefaultButtonBindings
    {
        <Btn1Down>          root        f.menu      RootMenu
        <Btn3Down>          root        f.menu      RootMenu
        <Btn1Down>          frame               f.raise
        <Btn2Down>          frame¦icon          f.post_wmenu
        <Btn3Down>          frame¦icon          f.post_wmenu
        Meta<Btn1Down>      icon¦window         f.raise_lower
        Meta<Btn3Down>      icon¦window         f.move
    }
    #
    #   END OF mwm RESOURCE DESCRIPTION FILE
    #
```

Listing 15.4 shows the default resource file from the same system.

Listing 15.4. A system resources file for a system that runs a common distribution of Motif.

```
#
#  System defaults / app-defaults   RESOURCE SPECIFICATIONS FOR MWM
#
#
# general appearance resources that apply to Mwm (all parts)
#
*font:                  fixed.snf
*backgroundTile:        background
*activeForeground:      Black
*activeBackground:      Cyan
*activeTopShadowColor:  LightCyan
*activeBottomShadowColor: Black
*makeActiveColors:      false
*foreground:            Black
*background:            Gray
*topShadowColor:        White
```

continued

Listing 15.4—*Continued*

```
*bottomShadowColor:        Black
*makeColors:               false
*buttonBindings:           DefaultButtonBindings
*keyBindings:              DefaultKeyBindings
*rootMenu:                 RootMenu
*windowMenu:               DefaultWindowMenu
*useIconBox:               true
*showFeedback:             restart
#
# general appearance resources that apply to specific parts of Mwm
#
*menu*background:          Gray
*menu*topShadowColor:      White
*menu*bottomShadowColor:   Black
*menu*makeColors:          false
#
# Mwm - specific appearance and behavior resources
#
*positionOnScreen:         false     # prevents xterm downsizing on
ega
*xGranularity:             8    # VGA/EGA Optimization
*transientDecoration:      title  # no resize frame for popup windows
*execShell:                /bin/sh # f.exec shell
#
#  END OF RESOURCE SPECIFICATIONS
#
```

Open Look Configuration

Unlike Motif, Open Look currently (as of this book's revision) does not rely on system default definitions down in the /usr/lib/X11 path. Open Look *requires* that each user have his own array of definition and startup files in his home directory. The administrator should run the oladduser script for an existing user account in order to create the necessary files and modify the user's startup script. The path on a System VR4 is /usr/X/adm/oladduser. As a matter of fact, most of the X-related files—including binaries, libraries, and fonts—are found under /usr/X rather than /usr/lib/X11 and /usr/bin/X11. (Open Look is the standard graphical user interface for System VR4.) The source copy for user files is also found in /usr/X/adm. Here are the user's files specific to X and Open Look:

- .olsetup

  A short script that starts up your Open Look session on login if you want it to. It is not recommended that you edit this file, but you may find that some of the environment variables defined here are not correct unless you edit the source copy. Listing 15.5 is an example of .olsetup.

- .olinitrc

  The Open Look equivalent to .xinitrc, .olinitrc starts the window manager, file manager, and any other appropriate programs such as an xterm. Listing 15.6 is an example of .olinitrc.

- .olprograms

  A list of applications that appear in Open Look's Programs submenu. Although this list should be modified by an Open Look application, you can make the changes by hand, particularly to the source copy. Listing 15.7 is an example of .olprograms.

- .olinitout

  A log of system messages from commands executed from the workspace manager.

- .oliniterr

  A log of system messages from the process of starting up and running an Open Look session.

Listing 15.5. .olsetup, the script that starts up Open Look on login.

```
#ident      "@(#)olpkg.oam:adm/.olsetup   1.1"

DISPLAY=unix:0 export DISPLAY #!@ Do not edit this line !@
OLINVOKE=no export OLINVOKE   #!@ Do not edit this line !@
XNETACCESS=on             #!@ Do not edit this line !@
PATH=$PATH:/usr/X/bin export PATH#!@ Do not edit this line !@

if [ "$OLINVOKE" = "yes" -a -r /usr/X/bin/olinit -a -x /usr/X/bin/olinit -a -r
/usr/X/bin/olwsm -a -x /usr/X/bin/olwsm ]
then
     /usr/X/bin/olinit /usr/X/bin/olwsm ---xnetaccess $XNETACCESS
fi
```

Listing 15.6. `.olinitrc`, the file that starts the window manager, file manager, and any other clients.

```
#ident      "@(#)olpkg.oam:adm/.olinitrc  1.1"

olwm&
olfm&
```

Listing 15.7. `.olprograms`, the file that defines a personal applications menu.

```
Amiga:         exec Amiga.sh
Mips telnet:   exec xterm -e "telnet mips"
Ronin:         exec Ronin.sh
Clock:         exec xclock
Phoon:         exec /usr/X/bin/xphoon
Ico:           exec ico -r
kill Icos:     exec killicos.sh
Wizard:        exec /home/ben/bin/wizard.sh
Goofy:         exec xsetroot   -bitmap /home/ben/bitmaps/goofy
Xcalc:         exec xcalc
```

Other, related user files are `.profile`, `.Xdefaults`, `.xinitrc`, `.xinitout`, and `.xinitrc`. A corresponding script, `olremuser`, is available for removing Open Look from a user account. The `oladduser` program edits the `.profile` and makes copies of the `.Xdefaults` and `.xinitrc` files to `/usr/X/adm`.

Diskless Workstations

A diskless workstation has all of the computer processing and memory necessary to run the application programs the user needs, but this workstation relies on another system, the file server, for storing all of its files, whether they are data, text, or programs. The advantages of a diskless workstation are that a disk drive (a major expense) is not required for each workstation, and the file management (backup and cleanup) can be done at one central system. The disadvantages, though, may outweigh the advantages. If, for example, the application programs exceed the memory of the diskless workstation, it may try to swap memory across the network.

You can avoid this problem by having a relatively small and fast swap disk on the "diskless" system. Another danger is the heavy network load from disk-intensive application programs, such as a database whose database server software resides on the diskless system, and CADD (*Computer Aided Design and Drafting*) systems. It is foolish to run these kinds of programs on a diskless system and still expect good network performance.

Each computer manufacturer/OEM has a different file system organization. Sun Microsystems, for instance, puts the files in /export on the server. Each kernel resides in /export/root. For the example, the kernel for a system named pong would be the file /export/root/pong on the server. Other, more generic executables are found in the path bearing the model (or series) name of the systems for which they are intended (for example, /export/exec/sun4/sys/sun4/).

X Terminals

The only programs that X terminals run are the X server and network communications programs. X terminals put less of a load on the network but a heavy load on the CPU that serves them. Although X terminals usually contain more than one font internally, they require that fonts be stored on the server. Most servers must have all the necessary font files if they are running the X Window System for their own use. However, a decent CPU not running its own X server may make good sense: the X Window System puts heavy demands on memory, and X terminals are designed to handle these requirements on their own.

Some distinct advantages of X terminals are that they seldom require fan cooling (and are therefore quiet) and that they are easy to install and move. Although the high-resolution color X terminals cost as much as the low-end diskless workstations, low-end, monochrome X terminals are not much more expensive than serial terminals and are ideal for text and data processing.

You usually configure X terminals with pop-up menus that reside on ROMs in the terminal. The most important tasks are declaring the name and IP network address for the X terminal, specifying the font server and the paths to the fonts, and specifying the hosts (and their addresses) that are going to connect (equivalent to editing the /etc/hosts file on a full system). Don't forget that the names and addresses of the X terminals must also reside on those systems. And don't forget to share the font path or include it in the font server /etc/exports file.

PCs Running UNIX

The hardware requirements of a single-user, single-tasking operating system, such as MS-DOS, are different from those of UNIX, a multiuser and multitasking operating system. The original Intel 8088 and 8086 processors that are in the low-end PCs are far from ideal for UNIX. Nevertheless, early Altos UNIX systems did use the 8086. Despite some very clever engineering, there were some unsurmountable dangers in protecting the system from being crashed by a user process. With the introduction of the Intel 80286-based PC/AT computer, it became feasible to run a small and still somewhat restricted version of UNIX, known as XENIX. Because XENIX systems were relatively inexpensive compared to the full-blown UNIX minicomputers and workstations of the day, and because they could easily support several simultaneous users through intelligent multiport asynchronous communication cards, XENIX proliferated. The trend of putting UNIX on an Intel-based computer was established.

When COMPAQ and other manufacturers took the basic design of the IBM PC/AT and enhanced it by replacing the 80286 CPU with the i386 and adding true and full 32-bit memory, the PC/AT became capable of running true UNIX rather than XENIX. Furthermore, a feature of the i386 that allows emulations of the 8088 to be run concurrently meant that users could run MS-DOS programs at the same time that UNIX was running.

Hardware Considerations of PCs

Despite the fact that this high-end PC design can be used by a serious multiuser, multitasking system with dozens of users, there are still problems that hamper the installation of the sophisticated controller and peripheral boards in the standard bus of the PC/AT design. The problems lie with the design of the bus and the way in which the devices plugged into it communicate their needs with the CPU and other devices. The requests from each board are carried on its own communication line, an *interrupt request* (IRQ) line. In addition, a separate area of memory is set aside for data communication to and from the device. The original PC design used only 8 interrupt lines. The PC/AT design expanded the number to 16. This may sound like enough lines for any devices you might want to add in order to make a serious computer. In fact, these lines might easily be enough except that many of them are reserved for special purposes and many of the boards are designed for the older bus with only 8 interrupts. Table 15.1 lists the common and reserved IRQ lines.

Table 15.1. Common and reserved IRQ lines.

Line	Description
IRQ0	Clock (reserved)
IRQ1	Console—screen (reserved)
IRQ2	Networks, tapes, and so on
IRQ3	Serial COM2
IRQ4	Serial COM1
IRQ5	Alternate parallel port (lp2)
IRQ6	Floppy disk (reserved)
IRQ7	Main parallel port (lp0 or lp1)
IRQ8	Real-time clock*
IRQ9	Redirected to IRQ2*
IRQ10	Reserved only with IRQ2*
IRQ11*	Reserved only with IRQ2*
IRQ12*	Reserved only with IRQ2*
IRQ13	Never available (math coprocessor uses this to communicate with the CPU)
IRQ14	Fixed disk controller*
IRQ15	Reserved only with IRQ2*

*These interrupt request lines may be used along with IRQ2 for the special purposes indicated. *Without* IRQ2 signaling at the same time, these lines are available for any purpose.

When installing devices in the bus, you must also consider the memory addresses that the devices use for communications. Some devices need much larger blocks of memory than others. Your main concern should be conflicts in addresses. Keep a record (on paper) of the jumper settings of each of the boards you have in your 386 systems. Tape the record to the inside cover of the computer so that you won't have to redo the accounting when you add or change equipment. Also keep all those little hardware installation manuals together and in a safe place. They may be written in a strange mixture of technical language and a foreign grammar, hand-printed, and nearly unreadable, but they are your only clue to the uses of the switches and jumpers on each board.

Typically, a 386-based PC UNIX system will have two floppy disk drives (one 5 1/4-inch and one 3 1/2-inch), an SCSI disk drive controller, a VGA (or better) display, a standard asynchronous port for the modem connection, an intelligent multiport asynchronous board, and a thin Ethernet transceiver board. The tape drive may not be an SCSI drive and therefore require its own controller. Table 15.2 shows a typical configuration.

Table 15.2. A typical interrupt and memory configuration for a PC/AT class system running UNIX.

| Device | IRQ | I/O Address | |
		From	To
bus mouse	3	23c	23f
serial port	4	220	227
network card	5	240	25f
parallel port	7	378	37f
tape drive			

You should follow these steps when adding a new device:

1. Make a note of existing device drivers, their addresses, and interrupt request lines. You can do this with the command line provided just after these steps.

2. Shut down the system. Never work on a powered-up system! Ground yourself and the system to drain off any potential static charge before you handle any of the electronic boards. Some of the chips are easily destroyed by even a small static shock.

3. Set the jumpers or switches on the device or its controller board so that it has a unique (and appropriate) interrupt request line (IRQ). This may require that you redo some of the existing boards.

4. Set the jumpers or switches to specify the I/O memory address for the device so that they don't overlap the memory used by another device. Common conflicts are found between intelligent multiport boards and some VGA display boards.

5. Physically install the board in a bus slot when the computer is off. Leave the cover off the computer but reconnect the monitor and keyboard when you power up and test your physical connection. Stick around while you bring the operating system back up. Smoke or sparks are obviously not a good sign (but can occur). In case of fire, don't use one of those baking soda extinguishers; they will do more damage than good. A pure carbon dioxide extinguisher is good for electrical fires; it doesn't conduct electricity and doesn't hurt delicate disk drives or the environment.

6. Install the device driver if it isn't already part of your system kernel. Even though device drivers often come with peripheral boards, there may not be a device driver for the specific flavor of PC UNIX you are running. Before purchasing a peripheral board, look in your UNIX Release notes to see which devices are supported by your UNIX. If the board is listed, drivers may exist as part of your UNIX distribution. In either case, check to see whether the board manufacturer/OEM supplies drivers for your UNIX.

7. Reset the addresses and interrupt request lines to avoid conflicts you have encountered. Hopefully, you won't have to do this step, but it's a good idea to leave the cover off the system until everything is working, *just in case*.

The command for checking device drivers on ISC (Interactive Systems Corp.) 386 UNIX systems is

```
cat /etc/conf/sdevice.d/* ¦ \
  awk '$0~/^[*]/ {next;} $2 == "Y" && $6 > 0 { print0; }'¦ \
  sort -n +5
```

The installation of a device driver may not be as simple as advertised. The installation script may make some assumptions about how you have configured the board, and you will end up with conflicts between the driver and the board or between the driver and other drivers, or even both. The installation often requires configuring and building a new kernel. The configuration will fail when there are potential conflicts between device drivers. On 386 UNIX systems, the information about device interrupt request lines and addresses is maintained in a collection of files in /etc/ conf/sdevice.d. Each little file contains the information for a potential device. Here is some actual sdevice.d information from an SCO UNIX system:

cn	Y	1	1	2	1	0	0	0	0
sio	Y	1	7	1	4	3f8	3ff	0	0
wdn0	Y	32	5	1	5	240	25f	d0000	d1fff
fd	Y	1	5	2	6	3f0	3f7	0	0
pa	Y	1	2	1	7	378	37f	0	0
ad	Y	1	5	1	11	330	332	0	0
fp	Y	1	1	1	13	0	0	0	0
hd	Y	1	5	1	14	0	0	0	0
wd1	Y	2	5	1	15	170	177	0	0

And here is some information from an Interactive UNIX system:

kd	Y	1	6	2	1	64	64	0	0
logi	Y	1	6	1	3	23c	23f	0	0
ct	Y	1	5	1	4	220	227	0	0
wd	Y	32	5	3	5	240	25f	d4000	d5fff
fd	Y	1	4	2	6	3f0	3f7	0	0
lp	Y	1	3	1	7	378	37f	0	0
rtc	Y	1	5	1	8	0	0	0	0
gendev	Y	4	5	1	11	0	0	0	0
fp	Y	1	1	1	13	0	0	0	0

The fields of an sdevice.d file are these:

1. Device driver name

2. Inclusion of the driver in the kernel (Y or N)

3. Subunit number (0 for devices with only one minor number)

4. Interrupt priority level (0 for drivers that don't use interrupts)

5. Device driver type (0—doesn't use interrupts; 1—uses an interrupt for each controller; 2—controllers can share an interrupt; 3—controllers can share an interrupt, and multiple device drivers can share the sample interrupt priority level)

6. Interrupt request line (vector)

7. Bottom of I/O address

8. Top of I/O address

9. Bottom of controller address

10. Top of controller address

Figuring out which file belongs to which device requires some guesswork because there is no file-naming standard. A parallel port driver may be named pa on one system and lp on another. A serial port driver may be named sio on one system and ct on another. Be sure that the file for the device you are installing has the correct values. Then scan the list to see what conflicts might exist, both in interrupt request lines and I/O addressing.

Sometimes you can resolve problems by removing an unneeded driver; you simply change Y to N in the second field in its file. More likely, though, you will have to change some interrupt request lines and addresses and reconfigure the boards themselves.

After you have resolved any differences, you must try again to configure and relink the kernel. You accomplish this through the command `idbuild`, which calls `idconfig` and `idmkunix`. Once the new kernel is built, it will be installed as the default kernel the next time the system is booted. Most driver installation scripts call `idinstall` (an editor/checker for the `sdevice.d` files) and `idbuild` to do their work, but if they fail, you will have to do some of the work by hand. All of these programs belong to the Driver Software Package (DSP).

Concurrent MS-DOS

One of the advantages of running UNIX on an i386 (Intel) processor is that there are optional packages to let you run MS-DOS concurrently with UNIX. The two packages for doing this are Merge (developed by Locus) and VP/ix (developed by Interactive Systems Corporation). Now, however, there are also PC DOS software emulators for SPARC systems, Hewlett-Packard PA (Precision Architecture RISC) systems, and IBM RISC System/6000 systems.

All of these DOS-under-UNIX packages let you have DOS files under a UNIX file system. There are countless advantages to letting a UNIX system serve DOS applications, but there is an inherent danger that goes with it: because DOS doesn't have the same levels of permissions as UNIX, DOS file operations can cause havoc. Furthermore, the users can easily become confused about where they are in the UNIX file system when the directory and file names are greater than the DOS maximum of eight characters and a three-character extension.

If you are planning to run DOS sessions on a 386 UNIX system, be sure to provide a megabyte of extra memory for each concurrent DOS session. When a DOS session starts, it immediately grabs the maximum unextended memory for its use.

Regardless of all the problems, most UNIX systems today are on PC/AT-style computers, with Intel processors and ISA buses. Despite the competitive RISC systems, the PC has such a strong development and distribution network that it will be a long time before the simplicity of running UNIX on systems specifically designed for it is accepted by the mass market.

Summary

Workstations, X terminals, and PCs running UNIX all have their special attributes and problems. The single-user workstation requires some administrative skills from the user. The X terminal requires little from the user but

more resources from the network and server machines (and their administrators). PCs require tinkering with the hardware and kernel. Remember
that UNIX runs best on systems that were designed to run it. Saving money
on hardware means other expenses, usually decreasing performance and
increasing administrative time.

A

Shell

Programming

hell scripts are your helpers for solving UNIX system administration problems. Your facility with writing scripts that use the UNIX utilities is your greatest strength.

Introduction to the Bourne Shell

A comprehensive Bourne shell tutorial is beyond the scope of this book. (*UNIX Step-by-Step*, listed in the Bibliography, is a good book to start with.) However, because Bourne shell scripts are such a vital part of commercial UNIX system administration, this appendix first covers some Bourne shell basics. Then the discussion jumps right into some system administration shell scripts and examines how they work, why they work, and when you should use them.

At this writing, the Bourne shell is still considered the official UNIX system shell interpreter. The C shell (BSD) is also a shell interpreter, and it's very popular. The syntax is C-like, much more elegant in appearance than the Bourne shell. But don't let appearances fool you. The Bourne shell runs 4 to 20 times faster than the C shell, and the C shell passes scripts to the Bourne shell unless deliberately told to do otherwise. The Bourne shell is a bit clunky to use interactively and is also rather difficult to learn because of its somewhat clumsy syntax. But it is extremely powerful, and once you get the hang of it, you can move programmatic mountains. Even if you prefer the C shell, we recommend that you save the C shell for interactive use and rely on the Bourne shell for official system administration use. This gives you the additional advantage of ensuring the portability of your system administration scripts from machine to machine.

The Korn shell is now becoming widely distributed. It has many features beyond those of the C shell and the Bourne shell, the most important being a combination of speed and internal arithmetic processing. One attractive feature of the Korn shell is that its syntax is nearly identical to the Bourne shell. Again, the least common denominator is still the Bourne shell.

The Bourne shell is a command interpreter language. There are Bourne shell compilers (for example, CCsh from Comeau Computing) that will greatly improve the performance of long or iterative Bourne shell scripts by reducing them to the C programming language, which can then be compiled on down to your system's machine language.

But most users use only a few operating system commands during the course of the day, and they think of them as isolated messages to the operating system. In contrast, system administrators must not only communicate with the operating system but manipulate it as well. That's where command interpreter languages enter the picture. The Bourne shell is a sophisticated interpreter language, an excellent vehicle for UNIX system administrators.

Command interpreters are not new, nor are they exclusive to UNIX. IBM has EXECs and REX. CP/M has SUBMIT. Minis such as those from Data General have macros (not to be confused with the programming term *macro*). They all serve the same purpose: they take in command names and arguments and then act on them. However, the Bourne shell comes close to being a fully developed programming language. Not only that, all UNIX commands and utilities are at its disposal. Thus, any feature the Bourne shell lacks can be picked from one of the outstanding UNIX utilities, such as awk, grep, and sed.

Levels of Shell Programming

Shell programs vary in complexity. They can be a simple series of standard UNIX commands entered into a file by an editor, or they can be complex with nested programs and loops. All the major programming constructs are at your disposal as a shell programmer. There are ifs, if-then-elses, and elifs (else-ifs). There are both for and while loops and an elegant case structure. The shell is extremely powerful, and it's a tremendous timesaver. A complex, two-page shell script could require almost a thousand lines of

C code to duplicate it. It is not absolutely necessary to know C in order to run a UNIX system, but it *is* necessary to be able to program with shell scripts.

The *for* Loop

Programs of any kind are most often written to perform repetitive tasks, and looping is the ideal construct for this. The most common loop forms are for loops and while loops. The for loop works as long as an argument list exists. The loop exits once the argument list is exhausted.

Here is a simple shell program that writes a list of names to the screen (all shell scripts must be made executable with chmod, such as chmod +x simple, before they can be used as a command):

```
$ cat simple
for name in root bruce karen david susan
do
 echo $name
done
$ simple
root
bruce
karen
david
susan
$
```

When the preceding program executes, it takes the list following in (line 2) and assigns each word in turn to the variable *name*, executing the echo once for each word. The $name is replaced by the string (in this case, a name) stored in the variable *name*.

Notice the structure of the for loop:

```
for variable  in list
do
   command(s)
done
```

The commands are executed once for each word in the *list*, with the shell variable *variable* assigned to a different word each time.

The Bourne shell commands (and scripts) are not as free-form as one might think. The line breaks in the preceding for statement are required as shown. The indentation, however, is just for clarity.

Getting Mileage out of the *for* Loop

The argument list in the preceding program does not need to be built into the program. The list also can be passed to the program from the command line or generated by other means. Consider the following script:

```
$ cat for_demo
for arg
do
  echo $arg
done
```

The shell gets just a bit tricky here. No argument list is explicitly specified to the for loop. The list of command-line arguments is used instead. Notice the arguments (1 2 3 4 5 6 7 8):

```
$ for.demo 1 2 3 4 5 6 7 8
1
2
3
4
5
6
7
8
$
```

The for loop takes the argument list (here the numbers 1 through 8) and assigns them in turn to the variable arg.

Positional Parameters

Positional parameters is a fancy term for the items in an argument list. The shell maintains 10 special variables, 0 through 9, each of which is assigned an argument from the command line. Note the following example:

```
$ cat echo.prog
echo $0
echo $1
echo $2
echo $3
$
```

The preceding program runs like this:

```
$ echo.prog one two three
echo.prog
one
two
three
$
```

The positional parameters are 0, 1, 2, and 3. Thus, $1 is replaced by the first argument, $2 is replaced by the second argument, and so on. The argument $0 is special and refers to the actual name of the executing program. Some other special shell variables are $#, the number of arguments, and $$, the process ID (*pid*) number of the shell itself. These variables are shown later.

The *while* Loop

The while loop is similar to the for loop except that while uses the exit status of a command to determine when to quit looping. The while loop also lacks the for loop's connotation of being incremented. while is usually used with the test command and has this form:

```
while test expression
do
 command(s)
done
```

while looks like this in use:

```
$ cat printall
while test $# != 0
do
 echo printing $1
 lp $1
 shift
done
$ printall file1.c file2.c file3.c
printing file1.c
request-id is laser-1442 (1 file)
printing file2.c
```

```
request-id is laser-1443 (1 file)
printing file3.c
request-id is laser-1444 (1 file)
$
```

Here test is testing the variable $# (the number of arguments). As long as it isn't zero, there are still arguments to process, and this script sends $1 to the printer. Note the word shift. This is a shell programming device that shifts the positional arguments down: $3 becomes $2, $2 becomes $1, and $1 goes away. $# is also decremented by one. When the argument list is exhausted, the while loop finishes because $# will be zero.

Another Look at *test*

Don't expect the shell to perform like a high-powered programming language such as C or PL/I. The shell has most of the programming constructs of any language but has two failings. First, the shell is exceptionally picky about syntax and whitespace. Second, it needs some hand-holding.

The shell needs the help of test or some other program or command that returns a valid exit status:

```
while test $# != 0
while test $1 != temp1
while grep "UNIX" $1
```

The use of test might offend some programmers. Fortunately, you can change the first two lines in the preceding code to

```
while [ $# != 0 ]
while [ $1 != temp1 ]
```

The left bracket ([) means test, and the right bracket (]) balances the statement. This is one of the nonintuitive places for spaces: before and after the brackets. These characters are actually just commands like any other (they are linked to test) and therefore must be separated by whitespace.

Table A.1 provides a partial list of useful test options.

Table A.1. Some `test` options.

Option	Description
-r *filename*	True if the file *filename* exists and is readable
-w *filename*	True if the file *filename* exists and is writable
-f *filename*	True if the file *filename* exists and is a regular file
-d *filename*	True if the file *filename* exists and is a directory
-s *filename*	True if the file *filename* exists and is greater than zero length
-z *s1*	True if the length of string *s1* is zero
-n *s1*	True if the length of string *s1* is nonzero
s1 = *s2*	True if the strings *s1* and *s2* are identical
s1 != *s2*	True if the strings *s1* and *s2* are not identical
s1	True if *s1* is not a null string
n1 -eq *n2*	True if the integers *n1* and *n2* are algebraically equal
n1 -ne *n2*	True if the integers *n1* and *n2* are algebraically *not* equal
n1 -gt *n2*	True if the integer *n1* is algebraically *greater than* n2
n1 -ge *n2*	True if the integer *n1* is algebraically *greater than or equal to* n2
n1 -lt *n2*	True if the integer *n1* is algebraically *less than* n2
n1 -le *n2*	True if the integer *n1* is algebraically *less than or equal to* n2
-a	Logical AND operator
-o	Logical OR operator
(*expr*)	Parentheses for grouping

Note: -a has higher precedence than -o.

The *if-then-else* Construct

The shell has a fully developed if-then-else construct as well as an elif (else-if) construct. Note several variations.

IF THEN:

```
if test expression
 then
 command(s)
 fi
```

IF THEN ELSE:

```
if test expression
 then
 command(s)
 else
 command(s)
 fi
```

IF THEN ELSE IF:

```
if test expression
 then
 command(s)
 elif test expression
 command(s)
 else                                        — Optional
 command(s)
 fi
```

Here is a simple example of the use of if:

```
$ cat if.test
if [ "$1" = "yes" ]
then
 echo You typed in yes
else
 echo You did not type in yes
fi
$ if.test yes
You typed in yes
$ if.test no
You did not type in yes
$ if.test
You did not type in yes
$
```

You can combine `if` with other constructs, like `while`:

```
while test $# != 0
do
 if test -s "$1"
 then
 echo printing $1
 lp $1
 fi
 shift
done
```

The preceding shell script is just like `printall` except that this script tests to see whether the specified file(s) exist and contain data (`-s` option to `test`) before printing them.

As with the `while` statement, you don't have to use `test`; you can use any command that returns a valid exit status:

```
$ cat if1.test
if grep UNIX "$1" > /dev/null
then
 echo "$1 contains UNIX"
else
 echo "$1 doesn't contain UNIX"
fi
$ if1.test intro
intro contains UNIX
$ if1.test junk
junk doesn't contain UNIX
$
```

The *case* Statement

The `case` construct, a multiple branch, goes all the way back to FORTRAN. Many programmers prefer to use `case` rather than an `if-else` construct because `case` is more straightforward. The `case` construct is particularly useful when you are doing multiple branching on a string. Its form is

```
case word in
 pattern1 )
   command(s) ;;
 pattern2 )
   command(s) ;;
```

```
    ...

patternN )
  command(s) ;;
esac
```

If *pattern1* matches *word*, command list 1 is executed; if *pattern2* matches *word*, command list 2 is executed; and so on. A *pattern* is any string and may include shell file-name expansion characters (*, ?, and [ ]). A pattern may be a composite of other patterns separated by the vertical bar (the pipe symbol, ¦), which implies a logical ORing of the patterns.

Here is a simple example of the case construct. It displays different messages depending on what you type:

```
$ cat case.test
case "$1" in
 bh)
 echo "Hi Bruce! How are ya?";;
 kh)
 echo "Hi Karen! How are ya?";;
 df)
 echo "Hi Dave! How are ya?";;
 sf)
 echo "Hi Susan! How are ya?";;
 *)
 echo "Who are you?";;
esac
$ case.test bh
Hi Bruce! How are ya?
$ case.test sf
Hi Susan! How are ya?
$ case.test pw
Who are you?
$
```

$1 is used as the string to match against the patterns in the case. The $1 argument variable is quoted (more on this later) to make sure that it doesn't get misinterpreted if it contains a blank or is empty. Notice the use of * as a pattern, which is like saying, "If nothing else matches, I will."

Quoting

An executing shell program reads (parses) each character and token and interprets them. Some characters have special meaning to the shell. These include the following:

```
# * ? \ [ ] { } ( ) < > " ' ` ¦ ^ & ; $
```

One of the first shell script tricks you learn is to keep these characters from being misinterpreted. You do this by *quoting*, and there are four different ways to quote. Deciding which method to use is one of the most confusing shell programming techniques. At first, it seems like a cross between art and alchemy. But it gets easier after you use the methods for a while.

This section presents some shell quoting specifics. It does not go into quoting complete-to-the-last-detail but covers only what is necessary for you to learn the basics. Here are the quoting devices themselves:

" "	Double quotes	Prevents all the shell's special characters from being interpreted except for $, `, and (in certain cases) \.
' '	Single quotes	Prevents all the shell's special characters from being interpreted.
\	Backslash	Prevents the character following it from being interpreted. This device works the same as putting the character inside single quotes.
` `	Grave accents	Replaced by the result of any command(s) trapped within them.

To get a feel for quoting, now try the following experiments.

EXPERIMENT #1:

```
$ echo hi there
hi there
$ echo "hi there"
hi there
```

The double quotes removed the special meaning associated with the space character (word separation).

EXPERIMENT #2:

```
$ echo "$PATH"
/bin:/usr/bin:/usr/local:.
```

The double quotes allowed the shell to interpret $PATH as the contents of a variable.

EXPERIMENT #3:

```
$ echo '$PATH'
$PATH
```

The single quotes *prevented* the shell from interpreting $PATH as the contents of a variable.

EXPERIMENT #4:

```
$ echo pwd
pwd
```

This is straightforward. But look at the next experiment.

EXPERIMENT #5:

```
$ echo `pwd`
/us/bruce/work
```

The expression `pwd` allowed pwd to execute as a command and pass its results back to echo.

EXPERIMENT #6:

```
$ echo $PATH
/bin:/usr/bin:/usr/local:.
$ echo \$PATH
$PATH
```

Here the \ removed the special meaning of the $.

A good example illustrating the difficulties encountered with shell quoting is the following line from a script called rml+f (for "remove lost and found"):

```
if [ "lost+found" != `basename \`pwd\` ` ]
```

The script has to compare the basename of the current directory with the string lost+found. (basename is a command that returns the last portion of a qualified file name—that is, the name to the right of the last /

in the full path. The `basename` of `/usr/spool/crontab/cron` is `cron`.)
Trapping a command between grave accents returns the output of the
command. But what happens when you need to execute a command within
a command, such as `pwd` executed within `basename`, and all of that within
a shell script? You must prevent the inner `` `pwd` `` from being interpreted too
early. So that the command is preserved, the grave accents are quoted with
backslashes.

expr

`expr` is a useful command you can use inside grave accents to perform
integer arithmetic with the shell. The arguments given to `expr` are dealt with
as an expression in `expr`'s own peculiar way. There is a great deal of escaping
with the backslash character, because `expr` uses some of the shell's special
characters as operators (such as `*` for multiplication). Here are brief
descriptions of the most useful operators and keywords for `expr`:

expr relop expr	*relop* stands for one of the following: =, >, <, <=, >=, or !=. The action yields 1 if the indicated comparison is true, or 0 if the comparison is false. The comparison is numeric if both *expr*s are integers; otherwise, the comparison is lexicographic.
expr + expr *expr - expr*	The + and - operators perform addition or subtraction of the arguments.
*expr * expr* *expr / expr* *expr % expr*	The multiplication, division, or remainder (modulo) operators are as straightforward as the addition and subtraction operators, performing the operation with the arguments.
(expr)	Parentheses may be used for grouping.

A few examples of *expr* should show you how it works:

```
$ expr 5 + 21
26
$ expr 17 - 2
```

```
15
$ expr 23 \* 22
506
$ expr \( 23 + 22 \) \* 2
90
```

In the last two examples, the *, (, and) operators are quoted with a backslash to keep the shell from interpreting them.

Here is a simple shell program that increments a variable inside a while loop:

```
$ cat expr.test
j=1
while test $j -le 10
do
 echo $j
 j=`expr $j + 1`
done
$ expr.test
1
2
3
4
5
6
7
8
9
10
$
```

Putting *basename* to Work

The system administrator has the unending task of removing files from the system where they tend to accumulate unnoticed. An active system that crashes from time to time quickly fills the many lost+found directories attached to each mounted file system. Those that fill the fastest are /usr/spool and the root because of the many invisible tmp files created. These files never show unless the processes are interrupted. The rml+f program (shown next) was written to remove all the tmp files (after restoring those that are found to be necessary to the users). This program has one argument:

the date. Today's date is normally used unless the crash occurred yesterday and the night operator didn't clean up the mess. (Operators are not always system programmers and should not be expected to clean up the system; they just do their best to keep it alive and inform you of problems.)

Notice that this script is bulletproof. You have to be in lost+found to execute it, or it will exit. This keeps you from firing it up in any other directory where it would clobber the contents and send you back to last night's backup:

```
# rml+f
# removes file from lost + found
# bhh 8/2/85
# modified by phw
#
if [ "lost+found" != `basename \`pwd\`` ]
then
 echo "you must be in lost+found"
 exit
fi
if [ $# -ne 1 ]
then
 echo "usage: rml+f date"
 echo "as in rml+f \"Jul 24\" "
 echo "used to remove all lost+found"
 echo "files except those dated Jul 24"
 exit
fi

echo "files found: \c"
ls ¦ wc -l

rm -f `ls -l ¦ grep -v "$1" ¦ cut -c55-`

echo "files left: \c"
ls ¦ wc -l
```

Notice the heavy use of quoting. pwd is executed within basename, as mentioned earlier. The grave accents must be quoted, as in

```
`basename \`pwd\``
```

Notice also that quotes are required around $1 in the grep; otherwise, the shell will interpret a date such as Jul 24 as two arguments, and grep will go looking for the string Jul in the file 24.

Special *sh* Commands for Programming

Some shell programming commands don't fit exactly into any specific category, but they are too important to ignore, even in this brief treatment of the shell. These commands are break, continue, and exec.

break and *continue*

break and continue are right out of the C language. Both are used in for and while loops. The break command causes an immediate exit from a loop. The continue command causes the program execution to continue on the next iteration of a loop. In pseudocode, these commands look like this:

```
for names in name_list
do
 if name = "Uncle Harry"
 then
 continue
 fi
 if evaluate money_left = 0
 then
 break
 fi
 print invitation
done
```

Here the user is looping through a list of names and printing invitations. If the name of the infamous, unpopular *Uncle Harry* comes up, the program execution goes back to the for loop without sending him an invitation. If the amount of money left for the party drops to 0, the break command causes the program to abort the for loop altogether.

Both break and continue take an optional integer argument:

```
break 3
continue 2
```

Use these arguments in nested loops to tell continue or break how many nested loop structures it must deal with.

exec

exec causes the command used as its argument to be executed in place of the current shell, instead of spawning a new shell. In a shell script, an exec to another script is equivalent to a GOTO; there is no return. But unlike an exit, the exec can take you anywhere, not just end the current script or shell.

File System Manipulation

You use find to search a directory hierarchy and perform some action on the various files and directories found. find's syntax is

```
find dir(s) options/actions
```

where dir(s) is one or more directories to search, and options/actions is a list of options telling find what it should do with each file found.

Most often, find is used simply to list *every* file in a directory and all its subdirectories. This action is performed with the -print option:

```
# find / -print
/
/unix
/dev
/dev/console
/dev/syscon
 ...
#
```

Here every file on the system will be listed.

With the -type option, find's search can be limited to certain types of files. -type is followed by a single character that specifies what type of file is to be found. Valid characters are these:

f Regular file

d Directory

p FIFO (named pipe)

c Character-special (device file)

b Block-special (device file)

Thus, if you want to list the names of all the directories on your system, you use find with the -type d option:

```
# find / -type d -print
/
/dev
/dev/dsk
/dev/rdsk
```

389

```
/dev/mt
/dev/rmt
/etc
/bin
/tmp
/bck
/lib
/lost+found
/usr
/usr/bin
   ...
```

Note that -print *is* still required if you want to list the file names and that it comes *after* -type d. This order is used because of the way find works internally: it combines the various options from left to right. Therefore, -type is used before -print to filter out all nondirectories before requesting to print them. Reversing the order of these options will cause a file to be listed before it is tested to see whether it's a directory. Table A.2 lists the find options that are most often used.

Table A.2. The find options used most often.

Option	Description
-print	Print the found file's name.
-type *char*	Find files of type *char*.
-name *name*	Find files named *name*.
-atime *num* -mtime *num* -ctime *num*	Find files accessed or modified, or whose inodes were changed in *num* days. +*num* means more than *num* days, and -*num* means less than *num* days.
-size *num*	Find files *num* blocks in size. *num* may be preceded by a + or -, as in the preceding time options.
-user *name*	Find files owned by the user *name*.
-group *name*	Find files owned by the group *name*.
-exec *command*	Execute *command* for each file found. Whenever the string {} is encountered in *command*, it is replaced by the found file's name. The command must be terminated

Option	Description
	with a semicolon (;). Because the shell interprets ; in its own way, the semicolon should be quoted.
-cpio *device*	Write out all found files to *device* in cpioformat.

The find options can be grouped together inside parentheses (()), preceded by a ! to get the logical negation of an option, and combined with -o to logically OR options.

Here are a few examples of find.

List all files in the current directory structure that are larger than 10 blocks:

```
find . -size +10 -print
```

List all directories on the system owned by root:

```
find / -type d -user root -print
```

Remove all files owned by the user jim:

```
find / -user jim -exec rm -f {} \;
```

cpio all files owned by root, bin, and adm to tape drive zero:

```
find / -user root -o -user bin -o -user adm -cpio /dev/rmt/0m
```

Remove all core and dead.letter files older than one day:

```
find / \( -name core -o -name dead.letter \) -mtime +1\
 -exec rm -f {} \;
```

The *xargs* Command

You can combine find with the xargs command to reduce the number of times a command is executed on found files. For instance, the two finds that use rm in the preceding examples run it once for each found file; that could be a lot of invocations. xargs takes a list of arguments on its *standard* input and constructs a command based on these and its own command-line arguments. For example, the line

```
ls | xargs rm -f
```

removes all the files in the current directory. It takes the output of ls and runs rm -f on it. The difference between this and

```
rm -f `ls`
rm -f *
```

is that after the shell performs all of its expansions on * or `ls`, the size of the command line may cause an error. xargs generates command lines (from standard input) of manageable size, running the specified command as few times as possible without overflowing the maximum command-line size. So the two finds just mentioned can be rewritten as

```
find / -user jim -print ¦ xargs rm -f
find / \( -name core -o -name dead.letter \) -mtime +1\
 -print ¦ xargs rm -f
```

and xargs will run rm as few times as possible on the found files.

fs—File Search

If you have been working on a UNIX system for a couple of years, you have accumulated many programs, scripts, and files. Scores of directories and hundreds of files attest to the fact that you have been on the system long enough to make a permanent mark. So one of these days you are bound to need a file that you created a few years ago but now can't find. The fs script was written not only to find elusive files but also to tell you what sort of files they are, once found.

Here is the fs script:

```
#
# fs -- find file(s) on system
# fs file ...
#
if [ $# -eq 0 ]
then
 echo "Usage: fs f1 ... fn"
else
 names="( -name $1"
 shift
 for flist
 do
 names="$names -o -name $flist"
 done
 names="$names )"
 file `find / $names -print 2> /dev/null` ¦
 pr -t -e25
fi
```

The code first tests to see if there are any arguments:

```
if test $# -eq 0
then
 echo "Usage: fs f1 ... fn"
```

If there are no arguments, the script gives some instruction.

Notice that the program is built around the UNIX find and file commands. find finds the files, and file tells what they are. When you write a script that builds on commands with other commands, you are using the traditional UNIX building-block principle.

A couple of lines in the preceding script bear further explanation. The code builds up a find argument that looks for several files at the same time. The form of the find argument is

```
( -name file1 -o -name file2 -o ... )
```

so the command

```
find / \( -name fred -o -name john \) -print
```

looks for any files named fred or john on the system and prints their full path names.

The code

```
for flist
do
 names="$names -o -name $flist"
done
```

builds up an argument consisting of an arbitrary number of file names to look for, and

```
find / $names -print 2> /dev/null
```

looks for all the specified files, disregarding errors.

The pr -t -e25 part of the script formats the output with tab stops every 25 columns instead of every 8. Because file uses tabs in its output, the fields are aligned in columns 1 and 26:

```
$ fs tt up
/us/Script/tt           ascii text
/us/Script/up           ascii text
/us/Sysad/Bourne/up     ascii text
$
```

ds—Directory Block-Usage Reporter

Major UNIX file systems are organized as trees. /usr is an example of a tree. Subtrees are anything less than a tree but larger than a directory. ds is written to give a block-usage report of each directory in a tree, subtree, or directory. The standard UNIX df command does somewhat the same thing, but for trees (mounted file systems) only. When it comes time to clean out your system to gain back some disk space, this program is invaluable. Now for the code:

```
# ds
# prints block usage by directory within a tree
# Robert E. Singer 11/06/84
# modified by phw 2/23/86

if [ $# -ne 1 ]
then
 echo "usage: ds directory_name"
 echo "for best results use a fully qualified path name"
 exit 1
fi

echo "Blocks Directory"
echo "------ --------"
du$1 ¦ sort +1 ¦ sed "s/<TAB>.*\//<TAB>/"
```

The sort +1 sorts the output of du on the second field (fields in sort start at zero), which is the full path name. The sed simply strips the leading path from the file name. You may want to remove sed, because seeing the full path name can be useful from time to time. (*<TAB>* is a Ctrl-I or *tab* character).

Here is some typical ds output:

```
$ ds /us
Blocks Directory
------ --------
3975 us
34 AT+T
8 admin
24 Amdahl
1 cmd
```

```
187 C
1 Cbook
237 Cj
72 Doc
36 HCR
198 Bourne
135 Uts
145 bruce
4 3B
18 bin
1 misc
4 src
2 cmd
1 include
1 tmp
19 uucp
$
```

ts—Tree Search

The `ts` script searches a mounted file system (tree), subtree, or directory; separates out each directory; notes its name and qualified path; and then presents its contents through a long listing. Note the following example:

```
# ts the tree search
# singer/wood

if test $# -gt 1
then
 echo "Usage: ts [dir]"
 exit
fi
if test $# -eq 1
then
 pwdir=$1
else
 pwdir=`pwd`
fi

echo
```

```
for dir in `find $pwdir -type d -print`
do
 echo
 echo "$dir"
 ls -lsi $dir
 echo
done
```

System Administration Scripts

System administration scripts aid the system administrator in her day-to-day chores. Such scripts may be created out of necessity or convenience, but many of them end up being an integral part of a working UNIX system.

monitor—For System Diagnoses and Statistics

Systems running at less than 60 percent CPU capacity are in little danger of displaying the infamous symptoms of the "fully loaded" syndrome. But over 60 percent, it's panic city. An operating system must take a percentage of its available CPU time for itself. UNIX spends its time in the kernel just trying to keep the system's sanity and handle the workload. The more the system is used, the more the overhead. Kernel time goes up exponentially at the expense of user time.

When a system becomes overloaded, all sorts of nasty bugs come crawling out of the woodwork. A system that never crashed before crashes daily in the midst of prime time. Memory swapping becomes so rapid that nothing seems to be accomplished. Trivial response (the time it takes to get the screen to react) goes from milliseconds to seconds. Disk usage gets so high that the read/write heads don't settle. They lag behind I/O requests and create "contention."

Even before you start to remedy the overloading, you have to diagnose precisely where your problems are. Many UNIX system diagnostics are available, but which one should you use and how often? The following script, called `monitor`, calls most of the system diagnostic commands. The results are written to a special directory created for holding system statistics. `monitor` is called from `cron` (`/user/spool/cron/crontabs/root`). It is fired every 10 minutes, 5 days a week, during prime working hours. Its output is then analyzed for trouble areas, such as commands taking too much CPU time, excessive contention, high page rates, abnormal user activity, and other nasty side effects. Here is the `monitor` script:

```
# monitor
# a program to monitor
# number of users and response time
# bhh 05/13/856
# added active processes 06/05/85
# tmp 06/24/85 - modified for UTSA
#
FILE="/sys/monitor/dat/mon`date +%m%d%y`"
echo "********************************">>$FILE
echo>>$FILE
date >> $FILE
users=`who ¦ wc -l`
echo "$users users">>$FILE
processes=`ps -a ¦ wc -l`
echo "$processes active user processes">>$FILE
time mkdir /tmp/mon.$$ 2>>$FILE
time ls /tmp/mon.$$ >/dev/null 2>>$FILE
time rmdir /tmp/mon.$$ 2>>$FILE
smart d dasd %cnt ¦ grep UTS>>$FILE # these lines
iostats>>$FILE # are specific
stats >>$FILE # to UTS
ind >>$FILE #
sar>>$FILE
ps -af >>$FILE
```

This script is straightforward. There are no decision-making or branching constructs, only a straight run from top to bottom.

Notice how the file name is created from the date command with the %m%d%y notation:

```
FILE="/sys/monitor/dat/mon`date +%m%d%y`"
```

The constant FILE is used throughout the code to cut down on code density.

When you try to diagnose the problems causing an overloaded system, one of the main items to watch is response time (trivial response). Three trivial responses are recorded: the time required to create a directory, the time required to ls that directory, and the time required to remove the directory. Note the following example:

```
time mkdir /tmp/mon.$$ 2>>$FILE
time ls /tmp/mon.$$ >/dev/null 2>>$FILE
time rmdir /tmp/mon.$$ 2>>$FILE
```

Here the standard error (file descriptor 2) is being written to $FILE because time writes the execution time of the specified command to standard error. On a happy system, the time required to create, remove, or `ls` an empty directory is less than the `time` command's unit of granularity (1/10 of a second). Thus, any measurable time is trivial response, the delay caused by the system's inability to respond. Look at the response time for a few commands so that you can get enough samples to avoid any random fluctuations in response time.

Cleaning Up the Script

The original `monitor` script just presented was born of necessity and created on the fly as a quick and dirty program. Because it turned out to be a valuable tool, it was kept as a permanent part of the system. But the continuous writes to $FILE make the program run much slower than necessary. The script was cleverly modified to make just one major write, thus maximizing efficiency:

```
# monitor a program to monitor number of users
# and response time
# bhh 05/13/85
# added active processes 06/05/85
# tmp 06/24/85 - modified for UTSA
# made pretty 8/20/85 Lou & Bob

FILE="/sys/monitor/dat/mon`date +%m%d%y`"

(
echo
echo "*****************************************"
echo
date
users=`who ¦ wc -l`
echo "$users users"
processes=`ps -a ¦ grep " 6.. " ¦ wc -l`
echo "$processes active user processes"
time mkdir /tmp/mon.$$
time ls /tmp/mon.$$ > /dev/null
time rmdir /tmp/mon.$$
smart d dasd %cnt ¦ grep %CNT
smart d dasd %cnt ¦ grep UTS
ind
stats
iostats
sar
ps -af
) >>$FILE 2>&1
```

Notice the ingenious use of parentheses to trap all of the executable commands into a single shell:

```
(command;command;command,...command)>>$FILE
```

The output from the script goes to the file in one fell swoop.

The `time` command, used to measure trivial response time, sends its output to standard error. Unless something is done to capture standard error, the results of the time will be lost. The notation

```
2>&1
```

takes the standard error (file descriptor 2) and joins it to the standard output (file descriptor 1).

pwdchk

The following shell script, `pwdchk`, looks up entries in the password and group files:

```
# pwdchk
# test tentative login data for previous entries
# bhh 7/29/85
# phw 2/23/86
#
if [ $# -eq 0 ]
then
 echo \
"usage: $0 [login] [-l login] [-u UID] [-g GID]
use -l to specify login name (default)
use -u to specify UID number
use -g to specify GID number"
 exit
fi

flag=login
for data in $*
do
 case $data in
 -l) flag=login;;
 -u) flag=uid;;
 -g) flag=gid;;
 -*) echo "$0: $data is not a valid option";;
 *) echo "$flag = $data:"
 case $flag in
 login) grep "^$data:" /etc/passwd
```

```
                    grep "^[^:]*:[^:]*:[^:]*.*[:,]$data" /etc/group;;
                    uid) grep "^[^:]*:[^:]*:$data:" /etc/passwd;;
                    gid) grep "^[^:]*:[^:]*:$data:" /etc/group
                    grep "^[^:]*:[^:]*:[^:]*:$data:" /etc/passwd;;
                    esac;;
                    esac
                done
                $ pwdchk root
                login = root:
                root:JV3Oxc30vuylA:0:0:The Super User:/:/bin/ksh
                root:x:0:root
                $ pwdchk -g 51
                gid = 51:
                dave::51:dave,bruce,les
                dave:EWFFochOFmBdI:201:51:davef:/us/dave:
                bruce:GZbLL4w26mFTQ:202:51:bhh:/us/bruce:
```

This script can be a valuable aid to maintaining good security.

die

You use the die program to kill a user's processes quickly, without consulting ps or who. die sends a HANGUP signal (number 1) to the specified user's processes, waits five seconds, and then sends a KILL signal. This program makes use of the fact that when kill is given a process number of -1, kill sends the given signal to all the processes owned by the calling user. su is first used to change identity to the specified user, and kill is then called with the appropriate arguments. die also has an "immediate" mode (-k option) in which a KILL signal is sent posthaste. Here is the die program:

```
# die [-k] user
# kills all processes owned by specified user
# sends HUP signal first to allow programs
# like vi to attempt to preserve files and exit
# lists processes after the first kill and sends
# a KILL signal (can't be caught) five seconds later
# (the su command is killed as well)
# The -k option may be used to immediately send a
# KILL signal to that user's processes.
# Note that any user may run this command, but only
# root will NOT be prompted for the user's password
```

```
# pat wood
# 02/20/86

if [ $# -eq 0 ]
then
 echo "Usage: $0 username"
fi

if [ "x$1" != "x-k" ]
then
 echo "Sending hangup to $1's processes"
 su $1 -c "kill -1 -1"
 ps -fu $1
 echo "Sending kill to $1's processes,"
 echo "DEL to abort (5 seconds)"
 sleep 5
else
 shift
fi

su $1 -c "kill -9 -1"
```

Summary

Although you have taken a brief look at the Bourne shell, there is much more to be considered. Most UNIX system administration programming is done in the Bourne shell, but be aware that the Korn shell is often used to translate permanent shell scripts into faster and more flexible programs. C code is substantially longer, but it runs 10 times as fast. Exploring the extensive realm of C programming is beyond the scope of this book, but there are programs, such as CCsh from Comeau Computing, that translate Bourne shell scripts into C so that you can achieve the speed (and security) of running compiled programs for your system administration tasks.

B

The RS-232

Blues

When you need to add a peripheral to your machine—such as a terminal, printer, plotter, or modem—you have to find a hardware technician to cable the device to the machine, or do it yourself. Cable connections are expensive to have made, and they can be very frustrating to create yourself. Either way, you're looking at some aggravation. We remember one shocking news story about a new computer owner who asked the manager of the computer store to cable a device to the new computer because the customer couldn't do the job himself. The bill was over $100.00. He was so angry that he shot and killed the store manager! Most of us will never become that frustrated over a cable connection, but we may come close.

Naturally, everything you need to know about the RS-232 specification cannot be included in one appendix, but some vital concepts are covered. You may want to supplement what you learn here with further reading.

Basic Definitions

You first need to know a few basic definitions. It's difficult to talk about the RS-232 specification without mentioning handshaking. Loosely defined, *handshaking* is a condition in which two pieces of equipment tell each other that both are ready to move data.

All electrical devices that transmit information work around a ground reference. That ground is said to be at 0 potential (voltage). A pin is said to be *asserted* when it has a positive or negative voltage on it. These voltages run approximately +12 V (high) or –12 V (low). A positive voltage "asserts the pin high." A negative voltage "asserts the pin low."

When you *pull up* a pin, you take the positive voltage from another pin already asserted high and use it to pull up the voltage on the unasserted pin.

A *breakout box* helps you do all the tricky work needed to make a cable connection. This box is somewhat similar to an old-fashioned telephone switchboard that allows connections to be made by wires plugged in from here to there. Whenever you attach peripheral equipment to your UNIX system, unless you want to pay someone to make the cable, you will probably need a breakout box to do the job.

The RS-232 Specification

The RS-232 specification was created primarily for modem-type communications. It has turned into a fits-all-do-all concept, and like so many other universal solutions, it doesn't fit everything perfectly. Still, this specification is good enough to become an industry standard.

The first important RS-232 terms to learn are DTE and DCE. DTE stands for *data terminal equipment*, and DCE stands for *data communications equipment*. Unfortunately, DTE was intended for terminals, and DCE was intended for modems, so problems crop up because they now also have to apply to printers, plotters, and computers. Bear in mind that now DTE means something like "it looks a little like a terminal because data goes out on pin 2," and DCE means "it looks a little like a modem because data goes out on pin 3."

DB-25 Pin Connector

RS-232 connections make use of the DB-25 pin connector. Twenty-five pins translate into 50 potential problems (25 at each end), but sometimes connections can be made with as few as 3 pins. Of the 25, you need to be concerned with only 9, and when you break these pins down into groups, some of the mystery is removed. Here are the DB-25 pins, with their abbreviations and descriptions:

Pin 1	FG	Frame Ground
Pin 2	TD	Transmit Data
Pin 3	RD	Receive Data

Pin 4	RTS	Request To Send
Pin 5	CTS	Clear To Send
Pin 6	DSR	Data Set Ready
Pin 7	SG	Signal Ground (common)
Pin 8	CD	Carrier Detect
Pin 20	DTR	Data Terminal Ready
Pin 22	RI	Ring Indicator (rarely used)

Pin 22 is listed here for consistency with the DB-9 pins discussed later.

Ground Pins

The first group includes the ground pins:

| Pin 1 | FG | Frame Ground (optional) |
| Pin 7 | SG | Signal Ground |

The frame ground pin allows both devices to have their chassis at the same potential (voltage). The signal ground pin guarantees a ground reference for the remaining seven critical pins.

Data Pins

The next pins transmit and receive data:

| Pin 2 | TD | Transmit Data |
| Pin 3 | RD | Receive Data |

Pin 2 sends data, and pin 3 receives data. But there's a catch. The send/receive relationship is established by the data terminal equipment (DTE) device standard. Most terminals are DTEs. Most modems are DCEs, so that takes care of modems and terminals, but what about computers? There is no standard. Some are DTEs, and others are DCEs. You are going to have to "sex" the computers to find out whether they are DTEs or DCEs. Consider DTEs males and DCEs females.

Pins That Send Condition Signals

Of the nine pins used for most connections, five deal with signals that are neither data nor ground pins. There are no hard-and-fast rules determining which pins send signals and which pins receive signals. In practice, pins that send signals are found to be asserted. Pins that receive signals are normally not asserted. Be aware that this generalization does not hold true in all cases.

Two pins are supposed to tell how the equipment is doing. They tell you if the device is ready to go to work:

Pin 4	RTS	Request To Send
Pin 20	DTR	Data Terminal Ready

When pin 20 goes high (+), it signals to whatever it's connected to that the DTE is ready to go to work. (The DTE always controls DTR, and the DCE listens for DTE.) Pin 4 (RTS) was intentionally set to signal the DCE—most often a modem—that the device is ready to transmit. In practice, pin 4 can signal that any device is ready, such as emitting a signal from the computer to show that it is alive.

Pins That Receive Signals

On DCEs, pins 5 and 6 are mostly used to take signals from other pins, such as pins 4, 8, or 20. Pins 5 and 6 cause the piece of equipment to which they are attached either to receive data or to transmit it:

Pin 5	CTS	Clear To Send
Pin 6	DSR	Data Set Ready

In the IEEE RS-232 specifications, all pins are treated as functional, but in practice, this is seldom true. For example, the clear-to-send pin is defined as a terminal pin (DTE) which, when pulled up, tells the terminal that it's okay to go about its business. However, in practice, terminals rarely need pin 5 high. Only some computers, such as the AT&T 3B2, will not work unless pin 5 is high. Pin 6 (data set ready) has a similar function, but it was originally intended to show that the modem was connected to a communications device and not in test mode. No matter what the original intentions were, the signal send/receive pins 4, 5, 6, 8, and 20 rarely do what they were originally designed to do. Remember that the IEEE RS-232 specifications are for terminal-to-modem connections and are seldom followed completely on small machines. The most common connections are terminal-to-computer, modem-to-computer, and computer-to-printer.

DB-9 Pin Connectors

On some computers, particularly PC/ATs, the serial ports use DB-9 connectors. Here are the pins for these ports:

Pin 1	CD	Data Carrier Detect
Pin 2	RD	Receive Data
Pin 3	TD	Transmit Data

Pin 4	DTR	Data Terminal Ready
Pin 5	SG	Signal Ground
Pin 6	DSR	Data Set Ready
Pin 7	RTS	Request To Send
Pin 8	CTS	Clear To Send
Pin 9	RI	Ring Indicator (rarely used)

From Theory to Practice

You are now ready to take a "walk" through a typical cabling session. RS-232 theory is not enough. You need to know what is involved in a real-world situation.

The Breakout Box and Hunter's $1.98 Pin Tester

A breakout box deals dynamically with the connection between the two devices. This box has switches, sockets, and jumpers, and is laid out like an RS-232 worksheet. The breakout box is cabled between the two pieces of equipment to be attached, usually the computer and a peripheral, and various combinations are tried until data can be successfully transmitted.

Breakout boxes come in many flavors. Inexpensive breakout boxes (about $100) have *l*ight-*e*mitting *d*iodes (LEDs) on only a few pins. On the DTE side, the LEDs are on TD, RTS, and DTR (as a minimum). On the DCE side, there are diagnostic LEDs on RD, CTS, DSR, and CD. This arrangement is hardly ideal, but an inexpensive box will do the job. The best breakout boxes ($250 and up) have LEDs on most pins and use tri-states rather than red LEDs. These breakout boxes glow red when a pin is high and green when the pin is held low, making it easier to envision what's going on. They also have bisexual connectors (handling both male and female connectors). There are 24 switches capable of closing the circuits of each pin, and 50 pins can be wire-jumpered to one another.

Good breakout boxes are not cheap, but a single, custom-installed cable can cost you as much or more than a good box. Serious interfacing work cannot be done without a good breakout box. However, in order to start your connections, you need to test each pin individually. You can do this with an inexpensive breakout box, but it's a minor hassle. Only expensive, tri-state breakout boxes instantly tell you the condition of every pin. If you have an inexpensive breakout box, Hunter's $1.98 pin tester can save a great deal of time (see Figure B.1). For a couple of dollars, you can construct this handy-dandy pin tester, which is ideal for the initial pin-testing work. It is a simple device that uses a tri-state, light-emitting diode (LED), a 470-ohm resistor, and a couple of RS-232 pins.

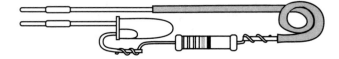

Figure B.1. *Hunter's $1.98 pin tester.*

Be sure to attach the wire to the side of the LED with a flat. The opposite pin should be directly soldered or crimped to an RS-232 pin. Two of these $1.98 pin testers are even more useful, one with male pins and one with female pins. The male version is used more often, but some equipment, such as a DEC VT100 terminal, has male pins and requires female testers.

The First Step

Test pins 2, 3, 4, 5, 6, 8, and 20 to see whether they are asserted (is there a voltage on the pin?). Plug the negative lead (the pin without a wire) into pin socket 7, the signal ground. Then walk the wired end from pin to pin. Active pins cause the LED to light up. Pins that are low (–) cause the LED to glow green. Pins that are high (+) cause the LED to glow red. Test the pins on either side (DTE and DCE) and write the results on a worksheet. Then analyze the data. Note the following sample RS-232 worksheet:

```
    DTE           DCE

    TD  ¦¦ -> ¦¦  2

    RD  ¦¦ <- ¦¦  3

    RTS ¦¦ -> ¦¦  4

    CTS ¦¦ <- ¦¦  5

    DSR ¦¦ <- ¦¦  6

    CD  ¦¦ <- ¦¦  8

    DTR ¦¦ -> ¦¦  20
```

Sexing A Device

Sexing the equipment is like turning a puppy over to find out whether it's Max or Maxine. When RD (pin 3) or TD (pin 2) is active, it is low (–). If pin 2 glows green when tested, the device is a DTE. If pin 3 causes the LED to glow green, the device is a DCE. This step is just that simple. Write the information on the worksheet. If both are green, either you have two DTEs or two DCEs butting their heads together, or the port isn't even an RS-232 port. No lights? Probably no power is getting to the port.

Testing the Remaining Pins

Once you have tested pins 2 and 3, continue with pins 4, 5, 6, 8, and 20. Test each one and note the results on the worksheet. These pins are the signal pins (2 and 3 are data pins, and 1 and 7 are ground pins). Knowing their condition is critical to making the final working connection. The pins that are high (+) are going to assert other pins. The pins that are low (–) may have to be asserted high or go high to signal ready. For example, on the AT&T 3B2/300, when you pull up pins 5 and 6, pin 20 goes from low to high.

First-Pass Jumpering

If you haven't already connected the breakout box to the two devices, do that next. You are going to need feedback from the breakout box and your computer to verify the connection. Wiring pin 1 to pin 1 (chassis ground) and pin 7 to pin 7 (signal ground) is standard operational procedure. Many people ignore pin 1, but this is not a good practice, as it can permit excess voltage to build up between the equipment. Even so, many manufacturers connect pin 1 to pin 7 internally, so the minimum connection still uses pins 2, 3, and 7.

Now refer to your worksheet. Terminal-type equipment (DTE) sends data on pin 2 and receives it on pin 3. Modem-type equipment (DCE) takes data on pin 2 and sends it on pin 3. The simplest connection has one piece of equipment (like a terminal) that is clearly a DTE with pin 2 asserted negative. The other piece of equipment (the computer) is clearly a DCE with pin 3 asserted negative. If the terminal is dumb and the computer isn't fussy about signal pins, an off-the-shelf ribbon cable with all pins in makes a good connection. Even a cable with pins 2, 3, and 7 straight-wired will do the job. However, if both devices are the same type—DTE to DTE, or DCE to DCE— a *null-modem* connection is required.

In some rare instances, this simple connection is enough to get data moving. (Some OEMs ship their computers with the I/O board jumpered so that CTS is internally true. As a result, CTS does not respond to external signals. The good news is that you can wire terminals quickly with either straight cables or three-wire cables. The bad news is that hardware handshaking is impossible without rejumpering the I/O board.) However, if you want any sort of handshaking, you will need at least a fourth wire. The cu command allows you to talk directly to the port, but some machines such as the AT&T 3B2/300 allow only a few seconds for a port to show a connection before they give it up. (If you have the new HDB uucp, be sure to enter the port in /usr/lib/uucp/Devices as a direct device, even if the port is also listed as an ACU to debug your cable connection.) Redirecting data to the port is simpler. Note this example:

```
$ ls / > /dev/tty5
```

The computer now buffers the data until the connection can be made.

The Next Stage

Now the scenario is set. With data buffered, your breakout box in place, and the ground and data lines connected, it is time to start the pin guessing game. At the computer end, pins 5 (CTS) and/or 6 (DSR) frequently have to be asserted to get data flowing. Take the voltage from any convenient pin (refer to your worksheet). Pins 4 and 20 are frequently asserted positive, so one of them may be available for this purpose. On modem connections, you need to pull up pin 8 as well.

At the other end, the nature of the device determines (to some extent) the pins to pull up. Printers want to turn off when their buffers are filled. They will frequently need to have pin 4 or 5 (RTS or CTS) asserted to make them work. Modems are wire-intensive devices. You must wire pin 8 (CD) to gain reasonable control of the device.

The Dart Board Game

Taking voltage from any reasonable source, apply it sequentially to pin 5, pin 6, and (in the case of modems) pin 8. Try this on both sides until data starts to flow. When the screen of the sending terminal redisplays the prompt, you know that you're in business.

Common-Sense Rewiring

Once data has successfully moved, write down the asserted pins on the worksheet and start thinking about better places from which to channel the asserting voltage. If, for example, you have used pin 4 to pull up pin 6 on the same side of the connection, you may want to consider taking pin 20 (data terminal ready) from the opposite side to pull it up. The reason for this is to have DTR (data terminal ready) on the one side signal DSR (data set ready) on the other side when DTR is ready. If the sending device fails or gets disconnected, the receiving end shuts down with this combination.

Many wiring combinations are possible. Experience is your best teacher. You work with 9 pins on each side for a possible 18, but only 2 pins, RTS and DTR, are normally asserted to signal a device to be ready. At most, 3 pins have to be asserted when the other end is ready: CTS, DSR, and CD.

Making the Cable

Once the breakout box connection works, you already know a simple way to wire the cable. At that point, if you think there is a better way to wire the cable to get the same results, look for it. You saw in the preceding example that if you used pin 4 on one device (one side of the breakout box) to pull up pin 6 on the same device, it's a good idea to get the source of the asserting voltage from the other device (the other side of the breakout box). If you take the voltage from the other side, should that piece of equipment fail, it causes a break in transmission, instead of allowing the device to sit there telling itself (with its own line) that everything is okay.

Installing a peripheral device to your UNIX system involves more than merely establishing a cable connection between the system and the device. You still need to take care of the software end. In other words, UNIX needs to know not only that the device is there, but also some specifics about the device. For this information, refer to the text.

Other Possibilities

Also available is a diagnostic device that you can place between any two RS-232 connectors, with LEDs on the most important pins to show their status. Such a device generally costs about $40 and is a good compromise.

Another possibility is a so-called "intelligent cable." It consists of a small plastic box with a few lights and switches, and RS-232 connectors on both ends. For about $90, you simply follow the directions and plug the cable into whatever you want to connect; the cable figures out how to detour the signals all by itself. This method will save you a great deal of time and may be the best idea in the long run for some people.

C

Using the -X9
Option

hen you initially set up uucp, you can benefit from watching the action of the phone dialing as well as the strings being passed back and forth for logins. Using the poll shell program presented in Chapter 12 on modems, along with the -x9 option to uucico, you can see a great deal of information. Although some of it is of interest only to those working with the innermost secrets of the program, using the maximum debugging information available is recommended the first few times you run uucp. After you feel more comfortable with the program, you can use -x4 or -x1 for less data, and finally you can turn off debugging completely.

An annotated log is generated by executing

```
$ poll attunix -x9
```

which is the equivalent of executing

```
$ /usr/lib/uucp/uucico -r1 -sattunix -x9
```

directly. One mail message (consisting of two files) has been queued up to be sent to attunix. The system (InfoPro Systems' Cadmus) is connected to a Hayes Smartmodem 1200, and the trick (outlined in Chapter 12) for dialing directly from the L.sys file is used. Here is the entry in L.sys for this machine:

```
attunix Any tty23 1200 tty23 ATDT12015226805\r \
?login:-\r-?login:-\r-?login: attunix\r
```

This particular machine has an L.sys format that is slightly different from the usual format. Here a carriage return (denoted by \r) is sent if the login: string is not received within the timeout period. The messages you get from your machine, of course, may be different, but they should be recognizably similar. Any mismatch of strings, or failure to log in, will become immediately apparent with this level of debugging.

Here is the log itself:

```
finds called
getto called
call: no. tty23 for sys attunix login called
send them <ATDT12015226805\r>
expect <login:>
```

uucico has found the L.sys entry, uucico has sent the dialing command string to the modem, and it is waiting for the login: message:

```
ATDT12015226805___CONNECT__got ?
send them <\r>
expect <login:>
```

The modem echoes the command string and then reports a CONNECT. Because a string has been received that did not correspond to the expected string, a newline is sent:

```
___login:got that
send them <attunix\r>
```

The login: string has been received, and the actual login name is sent to the remote machine:

```
enter us_sst, status is : 11
Enter us_open, file: /usr/lib/uucp/L_stat
normal return from us_open.c
s.sysname : hunter
s.sysname : whuxcc
s.sysname : bty
s.sysname : topaz
s.sysname : clyde
s.sysname : harpo
s.sysname : tmmnet
s.sysname : pcles
s.sysname : attunix
enter ub_sst, status is : 0
Rmtname: attunix
Enter us_open, file: /usr/lib/uucp/L_sub
normal return from us_open.c
```

On the `infopro` machine, the status files are opened to keep track of the connection. The software searches through past records until it finds the correct one for the machine being polled:

```
imsg >\341tt\365\356ix\215\12UN\311\330\240S\371\363te\355
\240V\240\322ele\341\363e\240\262.0.\264\2403B\262\240
Ver\363io\356\240\262\215\12\341tt\365\356ix\215\12\3030
\366e\344\215\12\20< Shere=attunix\ 0 imsg >\ 20 <
```

You get the login message from the remote machine. The message is garbled with numbers and backslashes because some bytes have their parity bit set, but a few strings are readable. Sometimes you will see a long /etc/motd message here. When control is passed to the /usr/lib/uucp/uucico program on the *remote* machine (analogous to getting into your shell), the Shere=attunix message appears. Once the uucico on the calling machine sees this Shere, the connection has officially started up. Some machines just echo the Shere without their actual node name.

The log continues with the following:

```
ROK\ 0 msg-ROK
Rmtname attunix, Role MASTER, Ifn - 4, Loginuser - root
rmesg - 'P' imsg >\ 20 <
Pg\ 0 got Pg
wmesg 'U'g
send 73
rec h->cntl 73
send 61
state - 1
rec h->cntl 61
send 53
state - 3
rec h->cntl 53
state - 10
Proto started g
protocol g
```

In the preceding sequence, the remote computer has been identified as attunix, and the g protocol has been selected. (Actually, this is the only protocol in use.)

Next is a scan through /usr/lib/uucp/L_stat until attunix is found:

```
enter us_sst, status is : 09
Enter us_open, file: /usr/lib/uucp/L_stat
normal return from us_open.c
```

```
s.sysname : hunter
s.sysname : whuxcc
s.sysname : bty
s.sysname : topaz
s.sysname : clyde
s.sysname : harpo
s.sysname : tmmnet
s.sysname : pcles
s.sysname : attunix
```

Now that a protocol has been established and the participants in the transmission have been verified, it is time to see what work needs to be done:

```
*** TOP *** - role=1, wrktype - S
wmesg 'S' D.attunixB4M4F D.attunix
send 210
rmesg - 'S'
rec h->cntl 41
state - 10
rec h->cntl 211
send 41
got SY PROCESS: msg - SY
```

In the preceding sequence, uucico determined that it's time to send the first queued-up file. So send it:

```
SNDFILE:
send 221
send 331
send 341
sent data 117 bytes 0 secs
rmesg - 'C' rec h->cntl 42
state - 10
rec h->cntl 43
state - 10
rec h->cntl 44
state - 10
rec h->cntl 224
send 42
got CY
PROCESS: msg - CY
```

The file has been sent and acknowledged. The CY received from the remote means that all went well with the transfer.

Now for the second file:

```
RQSTCMPT:
*** TOP *** - role=1, wrktype - S
wmesg 'S' D
send 252
rmesg - 'S'
rec h->cntl 45
state - 10
rec h->cntl 235
send 43
got SY
PROCESS: msg - SY
SNDFILE:
send 263
send 373
send 303
sent data 72 bytes 0 secs
rmesg - 'C' rec h->cntl 46
state - 10
rec h->cntl 47
state - 10
rec h->cntl 40
state - 10
rec h->cntl 240
rec h- >cntl 240
send 24
got CY
PROCESS: msg - CY
```

The second file has been accepted by the remote. Next are some administrative operations:

```
RQSTCMPT:
*** TOP *** - role=1,
enter us_rrs, cfile: C.attunixA4M4G request status: 3000
Enter us_open, file: /usr/lib/uucp/R_stat
normal return from us_open.c
```

The transfer of both files has been logged in the R_stat file. The work is done, and here are some closing remarks:

```
jobn : 4
wmesg 'H'
```

```
send 214
rmesg - 'H' rec h->cntl 40
send 44
state - 10
rec h->cntl 41
state - 10
rec h->cntl 251
send 45
got HY
PROCESS: msg - HY
```

No more work is available, so the machines prepare to hang up:

```
HUP:
wmesg 'H'Y
send 225
send 10
send 10
cntrl - 0
enter us_sst, status is : 00
Enter us_open, file: /usr/lib/uucp/L_stat
normal return from us_open.c
s.sysname : hunter
s.sysname : whuxcc
s.sysname : bty
s.sysname : topaz
s.sysname : clyde
s.sysname : harpo
s.sysname : tmmnet
s.sysname : pcles
s.sysname : attunix
send 00 0,imsg >\ 20 <
```

In the preceding sequence, the log file is closed, and the hangup message is transferred. Notice the final sequence:

```
\11 \210 \252 "\11 \20 \2 \25 \250 \262 \15 HY\0 imsg ><\200
\201 \1 2\0 \0 \37 \12 \0 \0 \0 \0 \0 \0 \0 \0 \0
\0 \0 \0 \0 \0 \0 \360 \200 \210 \205 \264 \300 \2
\22 x\300 \2 \22 \210 @\0 \2 \210 \300 \2 \22 h\300
\11 \242 \252 \10 \11 \20 \11 \242 \252
\10 \11 \20 000000\ 0 imsg >\20 <
000000\ 0 exit code 0
```

The connection has been broken, but initially only by logging off from attunix. Once the `exit code 0` message is printed, the RS-232 line DTR pulled down to a low-voltage state ("dropped") to force the outgoing modem to hang up.

Bibliography

AT&T Bell Laboratories Technical Journal, 63, no. 8, part 2 (special issue, October 1984).

Comer, D. *Operating Systems Design*: The Xinu Approach. Englewood Cliffs, NJ: Prentice-Hall, 1984.

Kernighan, Brian W., and Rob Pike. *The UNIX Programming Environment*. Englewood Cliffs, NJ: Prentice-Hall, 1984.

Kochan, Stephen G., and Patrick H. Wood. *UNIX Shell Programming*. Carmel, IN: Hayden Book Co., 1985.

Smith, Ben. *UNIX Step-by-Step*. Carmel, IN: SAMS, 1990.

Sobell, Mark G. *A Practical Guide to UNIX System V*. Menlo Park, CA: The Benjamin/Cummings Publishing Co., 1985.

Strang, John. *Reading and Writing Termcap Entries*. Newton, MA: O'Reilly and Associates, Inc., 1985.

Todino, Grace, and Tim O'Reilly. *Managing UUCP and Usenet*. Newton, MA: O'Reilly and Associates, Inc., 1986.

Wood, Patrick H., and Stephen G. Kochan. *UNIX System Security*. Carmel, IN: Hayden Book Co., 1985.

Index

qualified, 144
restoring data, 152-153
schedules, 147
scripts, 169-173
  tar command, 156
small system, 147-148
tar command, 154-156
  restoring, 156-157
unqualified, 145
volcopy command, 166-169
walking, 145
write protection, 151-152
baud rate, 206
  serial printers, 211
best-fit algorithms, 145
/bin directory, 62-63
biod TCP/IP daemon, 308
block device drivers, 64-65
blocks, 25-26
  checking with fsck command, 40-44
  free block list, 47-48
  superblock, 37
booting, 16-17
  automating startup, 21-22
  checking file system, 20
  multiuser mode, 20
  single-user mode, 19
  system time and date, 18-19
  warm start, 39
Bourne shell, 2, 374
brc scripts, 89
break statements, 388
breakout boxes (RS-232), 404, 407-408
bridges, 295-296
buffers, 75-77

C

C programming language (relationship to
    UNIX), 4-5
C shell, 3
cancel command, 224
cartridge disks, 150

cartridge tapes, 151
  DAT tapes, 151
case statements, 381-382
CD (modem control), 251-252
channel tables, 327-328
character device drivers, 64-65
checkaddr MMDF utility, 330
checking file system, 20
  clri command, 30
  dcheck command, 30
  fsck command, 27-28, 39-40
    blocks and sizes, 40-44
    checking connectivity, 45-46
    checking free block list, 47-48
    checking path names, 44-45
    checking reference counts, 46-47
  icheck command, 30
  lost files, 30-31
  ncheck command, 29
checkque MMDF utility, 330-331
checksecure shell program, 198
chgrp command, 177-178
chmod command, 178-179, 185-186
  symbolic modes, 178-179
chown command, 136, 177
classes of printers, 223
classes of resources (X Window
    System), 354
client systems
  NFS, 304-306
coding (encrypting) data, 194-195
command path (/bin directory), 62-63
commands
  accept, 231
  cancel, 224
  chgrp, 177-178
  chmod, 178-179, 185-186
  chown, 136, 177
  clri, 30
  cpio, 161-165
  crontab, 70-74
  crypt, 194-195
  ct, 246
  cu, 245-246
  date, 18-19
  dcheck, 30

cu command, 245-246
  HDB, 261-264
  null modem connections, 255-259
  sending files, 255
  testing, 254
cylinders (hard disks), 109-110

D

daemons, 210-211
  inetd, 90
  lpsched, 211
  TCP/IP networks, 306-309
  ttymon, 90
DARPA Internet addresses, 298-299
DAT tapes, 151
data encryption, 194-195
data packets, 296
dataless workstations, 346
date command, 18-19
DB 25-pin connectors, 404-405
  data pins, 405
  ground pins, 405
  receptor pins, 406
  send condition pins, 405-406
DB 9-pin connectors, 406-407
dbmedit MMDF utilty, 328-329
dbmlist MMDF utilty, 329-330
dbmtest MMDF utility, 328
DCE, 404
dd command, 159-161
deliver program (MMDF mail router), 319
delivery agents (E-Mail), 317-318
/dev directory, 63-66
  security, 196
device drivers, 63-66
  block special files, 64-65
  character special files, 64-65
  communications, 258-261
  connecting parallel printers, 214
  connecting serial printers, 212-214
  stty, 217-218
devices
  adding to PCs, 367-371
  hung, 125-126

  killing processes, 125
  vs. printers, 223-224
df command, 104
die shell program, 400-401
directories
  /bin, 62-63
  client systems (NFS), 304-306
  /dev, 63-66, 196
  /etc, 77-89
  execute permission, 179
  home, 133, 136
  lost+found, 30-35
  permission bits, 179-180
  read permission, 179
  sharing on networks, 300
    NFS, 300-304
    RFS, 300-301
  source code, 74
  /usr, 67
  /usr/bin, 67
  /usr/lib, 68-69
  /usr/lib/crontab, 70-74
  /usr/local, 68
  /usr/spool, 75-77
  /usr/src, 74
  write permission, 179
dirty telephone lines, 248
disable command, 232
diskless workstations, 346-365
disks/disk drives
  cartridge disks, 150
  cylinders, 109-110
  disk packs, 150
  disk partitions
    backing up, 161
    creating file systems, 104-107
  floppy, 150
  interleaving, 108-110
display management (X Windows System), 350-352
distributed networks, See networks
domain tables, 328
dospell shell program, 95-96
ds shell program, 394-395
DTE, 404
DTR (modem control), 251

device drivers
   stty, 217-218
handshaking, 218-219
interface programs, 233-243
parallel, 214
serial, 211-214
spooler, 210
   daemon, 210-211
   lp, 222-229
   lpr, 219-222
   testing, 219
troubleshooting, 215
   double-spaced output, 215
   garbage output, 216
   lp spooler, 230-232
   missing output, 216
vs. devices, 223-224
processes
   hung, 123-124
   killing, 123-124
   killing device processes, 125
   niceness, 122
   owners, 120
   ps command, 120-123
   size, 122-123
   sleeping, 122
   zombie, 121-122
PROM (Programmable Read Only
   Memory), 16
protection bits, 176-179
protocols
   kermit, 279-280
   xmodem, 279-280
ps command, 120-123
pwdchk shell program, 399-400

Q

qualified backups, 144
quoting in shell programs, 383-385

R

rc scripts, 83-88
read permissions, 176
real-time networks, *See* networks
reel-to-reel tapes, 149-150
reference counts, 46-47
reject command, 231
removable disk packs, 150
removing users, 137-139
renaming files, 25
repairing file system, 50-56
repairing superblock, 50-56
repeaters, 294-295
resources (X Window System), 352-356
   classes, 354
   resource specification files, 356-359
restoring backed-up data, 152-153
   cpio command, 164-165
   tar command, 156-157
restricted shells, 191-193
rexd TCP/IP daemon, 309
RFS, 300-301
rm command, 138-139
rnews Usenet utility, 343
root permissions, 22-23
routed TCP/IP daemon, 308
routing E-mail, 317
RS-232
   asserted pins, 404
   breakout boxes, 404, 407-408
   DB 25-pin connectors, 404-405
     data pins, 405
     ground pins, 405
     receptor pins, 406
     send condition pins, 405-406
   DB 9-pin connectors, 406-407
   DCE, 404
   DTE, 404
   handshaking, 403
rshd TCP/IP daemon, 309
rwhod TCP/IP daemon, 308

S

T

1952-22
22-06